UNDRESSED TORONTO

UNDRESSED TORONTO

From the Swimming Hole to Sunnyside, How a City Learned to Love the Beach, 1850–1935

DALE BARBOUR

UNIVERSITY OF MANITOBA PRESS

Undressed Toronto: From the Swimming Hole to Sunnyside, How a City Learned to Love the Beach, 1850–1935

25 24 23 22 21 1 2 3 4 5

University of Manitoba Press
Winnipeg, Manitoba, Canada
Treaty 1 Territory
uofmpress.ca

Cataloguing data available from Library and Archives Canada
ISBN 978-0-88755-947-1 (PAPER)
ISBN 978-0-88755-951-8 (PDF)
ISBN 978-0-88755-949-5 (EPUB)
ISBN 978-0-88755-953-2 (BOUND)

Cover image: "Bathers, Sunnyside," City of Toronto Archives, William James family Fonds 1244, Item 225, 1911.
Cover design by David Drummond
Interior design by Jess Koroscil

Printed in Canada

This book has been published with the help of a grant from the Federation for the Humanities and Social Sciences, through the Awards to Scholarly Publications Program, using funds provided by the Social Sciences and Humanities Research Council of Canada.

The University of Manitoba Press acknowledges the financial support for its publication program provided by the Government of Canada through the Canada Book Fund, the Canada Council for the Arts, the Manitoba Department of Sport, Culture, and Heritage, the Manitoba Arts Council, and the Manitoba Book Publishing Tax Credit.

Funded by the Government of Canada | Canada

CONTENTS

Acknowledgements

I need to thank Albert, Dupree, Joy, George, and countless others who left traces of their encounters with Toronto's rivers and waterfront. Their moments of joy and tragedy brought Toronto to life for me in a way I never imagined possible. And I need to thank the Don River, a space of refuge while I was writing this book. I never knew I could love a river until I met the Don.

My research was conducted at the University of Toronto with the help of the Ontario Graduate Scholarship Program, including the Arthur Child, Rene Efrain Memorial, and Thomas and Beverley Simpson scholarships, and the Jeanne Armour Scholarship. St. John's College's Visiting Researcher in Western Canadian Studies Fellowship and the University of Winnipeg's Sanford Riley Postdoctoral Fellowship have supported me during the publication process. An earlier version of Chapter 4: "The Don River and the Bathing Boy" appeared in *Urban History Review* in 2019 and I appreciate their permission to use the material here.

I owe a debt of gratitude to Steve Penfold, Ian Radforth, Mariana Valverde, Sean Kheraj, Ruth Sandwell, and Sean Mills for guiding my research.

Thank you to John Huzil, Lawrence Lee, and Sharon Anderson at the City of Toronto Archives, PortsToronto archivist Jeff Hubbell, and to the Toronto Public Library system, Archives of Ontario, and Library and Archives Canada.

Friends, colleagues, and inspirations: Ben Bradley, Bret Edwards, Peter Mersereau, Ryan Masters, Jonathan McQuarrie, Jennifer Evans, Lindsay Sidders, Vanessa McCarthy, Steven McClellan, Julia Rady-Shaw, Beth Jewett, Sharon Wall, Adele Perry, Veronique Church-Duplessis, Casper, Rembrandt, and Roxie. Brandon University kept my head above water while I was completing my manuscript: it was a pleasure to wander by and visit David Winter, James Naylor, Patricia Harms, Rhonda L. Hinther, and Lynn MacKay.

At the University of Manitoba Press, David Carr has always had my back. Thank you to the entire team.

And, of course, my mom and dad, Flo and John Barbour. You taught me how to read, Mom. I couldn't have done this without you.

UNDRESSED TORONTO

INTRODUCTION

As the end of summer neared in 1925, a *Globe* writer mused about the relationship between Toronto's boys and the city's natural environment in an editorial entitled "A Summer Idyll Urbanized":

> *If one visits certain secluded sections of the Don or Humber, set aside by the city fathers for the benefit of the city's youngest sons, and well protected against feminine intrusion, one realizes that boys seek water as inevitably as water seeks its own level. There is a natural affinity between a boy and a "swimmin' hole," just as marked as the natural antipathy between a boy and a washbowl. . . . These happy little urchins skipping about in frolic zestfulness, or basking in peaceful indolence upon the sand, all clad in nothing but coats of tan that vary in shade from the mere pink of newcomers to the deep walnuts stain or café-au-lait of habitués, make it seem that the Age of Innocence has come again.*[1]

Such spaces were "reservoirs of civic health" that could protect and rejuvenate the city and they needed to be maintained and expanded, the *Globe* writer argued, because "there is no wiser or cheaper investment for future citizenship than merely utilizing natural advantages in order to prevent the diseases or deformities due to overcrowded and undernourished tenement district life." The seasonal rite of boys "frisking about in all the charming freedom of native innocence, their lithe little forms radiating health and joy and the unstudied grace of vigorous statues flushed with eager young life" spoke to the rejuvenation of society itself. But as it faced the growing threat of pollution the swimming hole was a precarious space in 1925. The *Globe* argued it would be "an exceedingly regrettable invasion of the pastoral by the urban [if] any of the more private swimming places, where bathing suits are unnecessary, should have to be closed on account of preventable defects in sanitation."[2]

The "swimmin' hole" is a lucrative space for examining how Torontonians used the bathing boy as an icon to soften the transition into modernity. Within these "Gardens of Eden" bathers played without sin or shame. They created a community with its own rules, hierarchy, and even shared systems of knowledge: it was expected that those with a deeper tan would school the untanned newcomers in the ways of the swimming hole. The price of admission was stripping down and becoming one of the boys. Yet for all the swimming hole's seeming seclusion, the bathers were often in plain view, portrayed as statues that captured the energy of youth. Toronto was caught between staring at its youthful urchins and averting its eyes to ensure their purity.

While the *Globe* mused that similar spaces should be set aside for girls to bathe, it was careful to add that they should be under the watchful eye of police matrons. Girls were an afterthought. The goal of the swimming hole was the production of vigorous masculinity. And like Peter Pan in Neverland, the sanctity of the swimming hole depended on the boys never growing up but instead remaining chaste figures within an all-male homosocial space.[3]

Undressed Toronto is a history of public bathing in Toronto in the period between 1850 and 1935. It begins with the "swimming hole," the unregulated spaces where boys and men skinny-dipped in Toronto's harbour and rivers, and ends with the construction of the Sunnyside Beach and Amusement Park on the city's western waterfront. Sunnyside epitomizes "the beach" and demonstrates how public bathing had evolved by the beginning of the twentieth century from an unregulated homosocial activity into an activity with its own distinct set of rules for dress and behaviour that enabled men and women to bathe together and its own distinct spaces, carefully designed in the case of Sunnyside, for that purpose. The bathing suit became the required uniform for going to the beach with a steadily evolving set of conventions over how it should appear and how much of the body it should cover.

The swimming hole and the practices and social life within it represent a distinct system of bathing that I call "vernacular bathing": this bathing was homosocial and unregulated, bathers were naked or wore swimming trunks, which were popular but illegal up until the 1930s, and relied on each other for help.[4] "Vernacular" is a familiar term. It refers to people, products, or language of low culture produced within the local environment. Vernacular bathers found bathing space within the semi-industrial or marginal portions of Toronto's waterfront and rivers and relied on a shared knowledge of the environment to provide for their own safety. As "A Summer Idyll Urbanized" suggests, vernacular bathers were not entirely isolated; they swam within the heart of the city and could call on passersby for help when they ran into trouble.

Vernacular bathing spaces in Toronto were defined as working-class spaces. But the middle class helped maintain them: middle-class men had bathed in some of the very same swimming holes in their youth and saw it as a male privilege and rite of passage. The nostalgic gaze of the middle class valorized the boys as anti-modern folk figures and helped enable the survival of nude male bathing in the Don River well into the twentieth century.

"Bathing" seems like a charmingly archaic term today. But I am using it deliberately because it was the preferred term in the late nineteenth century and describes an activity that combined swimming and hygiene: you bathed for pleasure, to clean yourself, and as a social activity with others.[5] Bathing could be justified as a hygienic necessity and yet be dismissed as an indulgence.[6] Civic officials wrestled with those contrary meanings as they debated whether they should police and contain it in a suitable setting, or look the other way.

The beach is discussed here not as a physical environment but as a new intervention into the bathing debate. As cultural historian John Fiske suggests, the beach is a set of rules, practices, and social expectations that guide how men and women behave when bathing in public together.[7] It is a distinct system developed in the nineteenth century to manage bathing and solve the challenges that vernacular bathing and the social setting of the swimming hole could not. The "beach" was created in Europe and was consciously imported to and implemented in Toronto after 1880. Its implementation included setting aside distinct spaces of shoreline for bathing and dictating dress and behaviour within those spaces. The beach's appearance was also scripted, with a gentle slope of sand intended to be aesthetically pleasing and to ensure that people could enter the water safely. In Toronto, the city stepped in, adjusting nature to ensure that its beaches met those requirements. Lifeguards were added for security and to maintain propriety. Finally, while the swimming hole was canonized a masculine space, the beach was built to be a space where men and women could mingle. There was no profit in the swimming hole but the beach became part of Toronto's new commercial entertainment infrastructure.

Gender matters in this story. Torontonians valorized the bathing boy as a symbol of virility at a time when they feared industrialization and urbanization were sapping the strength of Toronto's men. The swimming hole was a reservoir of masculinity that fortified working-class youth and comforted their middle-class admirers. The nostalgic admiration of the swimming hole ensured its survival even as the environment around it and water quality within it changed. But using the bathing boy as a nostalgic gloss required that the swimming hole remain a space of perpetual boyhood. It took a degree of labour to successfully maintain the illusion that Toronto's Don River, for example, was a purely boyhood space, and not a more complicated environment that contained men, girls, and women. In contrast, men bathing in Toronto's harbour and in the Humber River punctured that illusion of an innocent boyhood space: their presence created a public spectacle that drew the eyes of police and led to more rigorous city bylaws.

Finally, this is a history of Toronto and its environment. Toronto is defined by its relationship with Lake Ontario, the most easterly of the Great Lakes, bordering Ontario and New York State. The city sits on the north shore of Toronto Bay, with Toronto Island framing the bay's southern boundary. The city was dubbed "York," or less flatteringly "Muddy York" thanks to its lake-side location, when it was founded in 1793. In its early years bathers waded into the shallow bay from a gravelly shoreline. The island was little more than a sandbar. The colonial community had an intimate relationship with the lake with a string of docks pushing out towards deeper water to support a mercantile export economy.

As "Muddy York" grew and was incorporated as the city of Toronto in 1834, its leaders imagined a public walkway, an esplanade, along the bay. But when the esplanade project was launched in the 1850s a quite different space emerged. The project filled in the shallow bay and pushed the front of the city southward, but rather than becoming an open public walkway the Esplanade was turned into a railway corridor.[8] The railway transformed Toronto from a sleepy seasonal mercantile port into an industrial all-season

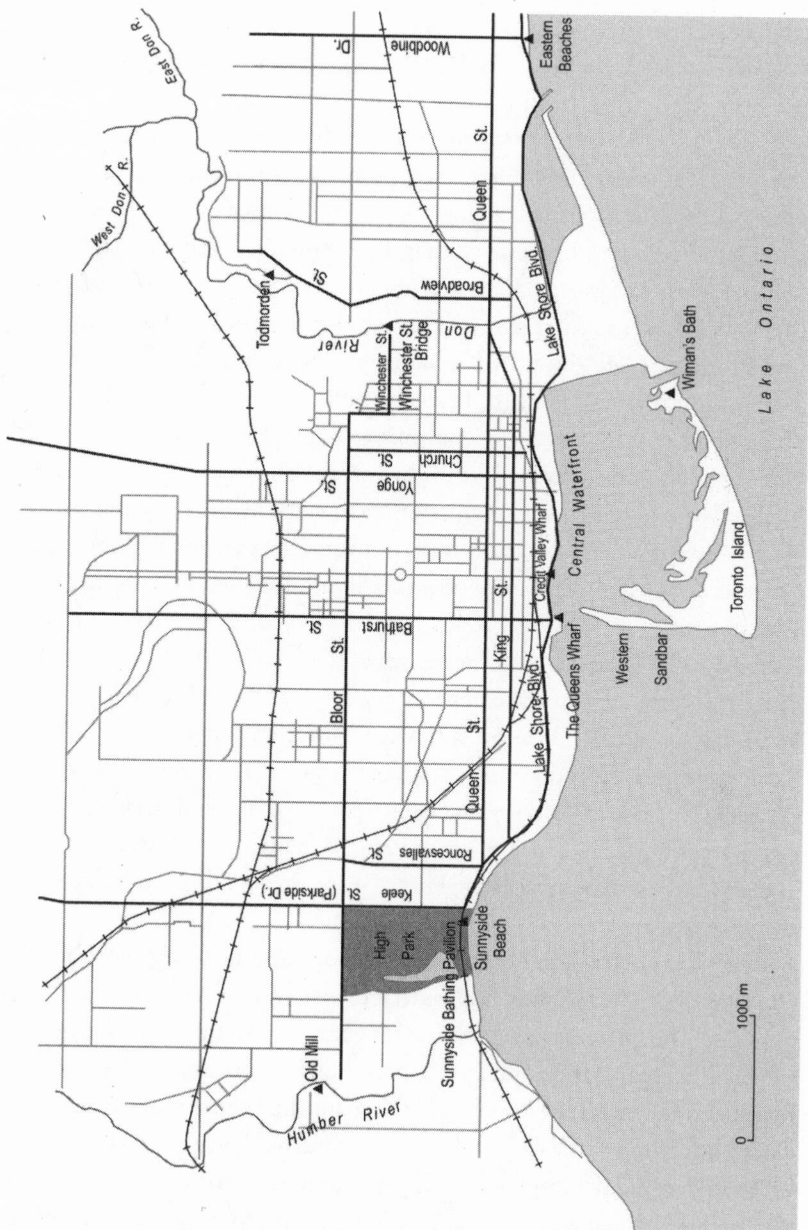

Figure 0.1. Map of the city of Toronto in 1908, showing the Don River in the east, the Humber River in the west, and Toronto harbour and Toronto Island to the south. The Western Sandbar, the home of today's Hanlan's Point Beach, can be seen on the edge of the island.

city. The construction of the Esplanade and the industrialization that followed has traditionally been described by Toronto historians as severing the city's relationship with Lake Ontario. People hoping to bathe, boat, or walk along the waterfront had to cross a dangerous thicket of rail lines to reach the waterline and industrialization polluted the once pristine waters of Lake Ontario.[9] I am challenging that declensionist narrative. Rather than a model of industrial efficiency that Torontonians liked to imagine, the Esplanade project was a haphazard intervention into Toronto's waterfront that took decades to complete. Uneven development ensured sections of the waterfront were left untouched or were only semi-developed.[10] Rather than extinguishing bathing along the harbour, industrialization and the Esplanade project *enabled* it by creating or sustaining marginal spaces where vernacular bathers could wade into the lake or dive off the docks.

The Toronto Harbour Commission was created in 1911 to guide the next great intervention into Toronto's waterfront and the practice of bathing along it. The harbour commission reworked the ramshackle central waterfront into a commercial port, driving out any bathers who still lingered there, turned Ashbridge's Bay, the marsh at the mouth of the Don River, into an industrial district, and transformed the popular but scruffy-looking Sunnyside Beach on the city's western side into a landscaped beach and amusement park. The harbour commission did more than just reshape Toronto's waterfront, it expanded the city's lifesaving and police patrol to monitor and control the new waterfront. The harbour commission remains with us today, as Ports Toronto, with authority over the Port of Toronto and Toronto Island's Billy Bishop Airport.

The Humber River in the west and the Don River in the east are Toronto's bookends; both feature deep valleys that carry them through the urban environment. The valleys create a natural topography that cannot be easily overridden. But colonization and industrialization have treated the Don and the Humber differently. The lower Don was channelled and industrialized in the nineteenth century. The river's middle and upper reaches, sitting within a deep valley, saw mixed development with paper mills and brick factories hugging the river while rail lines threaded their way through the valley. Toronto historian Jennifer Bonnell argues that by the last half of the nineteenth century industrial development and pollution led Toronto to view the Don River as a marginal space. I think the Don's story is more complicated; just as uneven development preserved vernacular bathing in Toronto's harbour, so too did it protect bathing in the middle and upper portions of the Don, creating spaces where "the boys" could be looked upon with such nostalgia by the *Globe* in 1925.[11] The Humber River framed the western boundary of Toronto's civic imagination. It was never industrialized like the Don River and instead turned into a popular recreation space. The Humber's popularity for "acceptable recreation" such as excursions or canoeing meant nude bathers in the river were viewed with suspicion rather than valorized.

Bathing in History

The history of bathing usually starts after the adoption of the bathing suit, but here I include what I refer to as "vernacular bathing." Other historians have used different terms to describe this type of bathing. Alain Corbin uses the term "vulgar" bathing to describe people bathing together in the nude in Europe and suggests men and women of different social classes shared bathing spaces in Britain and France up to the eighteenth century.[12] John Travis uses the term "folk tradition" to describe early vernacular bathing in Britain and argues that folk bathing spaces were used for centuries before being co-opted, transformed, and legitimated by the aristocracy in the eighteenth and nineteenth centuries.[13] By the nineteenth century women were being driven out of these shared nude bathing spaces in France and Britain and restrictions against male nude bathing were increasing.[14] Early efforts to control public bathing in Britain were left to municipal governments to manage as a question of time and space so that where you could bathe and when varied from town to town.[15] Nude bathing was increasingly confined to dusk, or nightfall, or spaces that were out of sight. It was policed, but also indulged by a society that had no issue with and even expected men to bathe in the nude, provided they did so discreetly.[16] That nineteenth-century logic followed British immigrants as they settled in Toronto.

Bathing usually falls under histories of the Reform Era in Canada (or the Progressive Era, as it is known in the United States), which lasted from about 1890 to 1920. During the Reform Era business people, church leaders, journalists, women's rights activists, labour organizers, and medical professionals joined forces in an effort to govern the urban environment and the people within it.[17] Reformers considered the city to be, as historian Paul Rutherford describes it, "a poorly-functioning mechanism [that needed] to be streamlined and regulated."[18] Toronto was dubbed "Toronto the Good" in the nineteenth century for the zeal with which its city leaders attempted to use legislation and moral suasion to create a better community.

Reformers were driven by new anxieties around race, class, and gender. Rapid industrial growth in nineteenth-century Canada created a large working-class population while immigration created a growing level of ethnic diversity within urban centres. While 90 percent of Toronto's population was of Anglo-Saxon origin at the start of the twentieth century, growing numbers of Jewish, Eastern European, and Asian immigrants were changing the city's social and demographic character.[19] A growing female workforce and the drive for women's emancipation also transformed the urban landscape. Collectively the changes left Toronto's Anglo-Saxon middle-class male elite scrambling to re-establish a clear hierarchy that ensured they remained on top.[20]

We can see Reform Era logic at work in efforts to manage bathing. Civic officials attempted to drive working-class nude bathers off the waterfront as part of this broader effort to control and define urban space.[21] Reformers also valorized the hygienic role of bathing and pushed bathers towards public bath houses where it was hoped they could be scrubbed and transformed into efficient healthy liberal subjects.[22] As Andrea Renner suggests in her study of bathing in the United States, reformers aimed to bring about a "humanity without smell": it was a utopian vision in which everyone shared white, Protestant ideals.[23] But when it comes to bathing, reformers were less zealous than we might think. Parsimony kept cities in Canada from expanding services for bathers. As Robert S. Kossuth demonstrates, the financial cost of providing swimming baths in late nineteenth-century London, Ontario, trumped concerns about public morals, public nudity, or the physical safety of people bathing in hazardous environments. And there are moments when Toronto did not want to police its bathers or, as with the "Summer Idyll," looked the other way.

I want to get beyond the fixation of looking at bathing simply as a moral issue and look at it instead as an activity that needed to be managed. When we do that we can see that vernacular bathing and the beach were both adaptations to the urban environment. As Michel Foucault suggests, nineteenth-century liberal democracies attempted to influence the "conduct of conducts" in such a way that certain actions became possible while others were closed off.[24] The regime of rules, technologies, and practices focused on bathing was just one thread within a growing tapestry of governance that shaped how people experienced and saw each other.[25] People were taught where to walk and how to move in the urban environment.[26] The tools driving this process included laws and surveys that dictated land use, maps, and photographs that set expectations for what activities were acceptable and when in particular spaces.[27] This system of governance is fundamental to creating a liberal subjectivity by setting the parameters within which a person, as an individual, defines themselves.[28] And the state does not sit above this system of governance as some sort of silent guiding hand but rather it is just one more part of it, confined by its own rules and expectations.[29]

Mitchell Dean lays out a useful tool kit for using Foucault's approach to look at how an activity, in this case bathing, is governed.[30] First, we need to think about how bathing and the people doing it are "rendered visible" so that they can be governed.[31] We will need to think about how bathers in Toronto were seen or, as the "Summer Idyll" suggests, sometimes not fully seen, which allowed them to slip out of the city's control. Second, we need to think about the tactics, technologies, and vocabularies required for governing an activity and their limitations. The tools for managing bathing ranged from bylaws to dress codes; these were intended to keep bathers out of sight and to manage how they appeared when they were in sight. Third, we need to look at how different types of knowledge and rationales for governing dictate how an activity is managed. As I suggest below, bathers created their own vernacular body of knowledge to secure their safety in the swimming hole: they shared knowledge of potential dangers and pollution sources. That embodied knowledge and experience is superseded by germ theory and new biomedical discourses in the twentieth century. By the 1920s, city officials used medical expertise to define a healthy bathing environment. Securing bathing spaces became a civic, not a personal, responsibility with doctors defining water quality and lifeguards defining environmental risks. Once popular spaces were now deemed insecure or too polluted and closed down. Finally, as Dean suggests, identities form at the intersection between efforts to govern people and resistance to those efforts. When we look at bathing we will see how identities coalesced around bathing and bathing spaces.

Entering the Vernacular Bathing World

Bathing in a swimming hole depended on a relationship with the physical environment.[32] As historian Joy Parr has noted, people attune their material body to the physical world around them to create an intimate relationship with place.[33] It is a relationship we take for granted when we move through familiar terrain, knowing what to expect from every footfall and understanding the message and meaning of the scents and sounds around us. We can look at this embodied relationship with the environment as an example of what historians such as Tina Loo refer to as "local knowledge": knowledge generated within distinct environments or workplaces through the process of watching or doing.[34] Within the swimming hole, creating this local knowledge relied on using the body as a tool to understand and relate to the environment. Bathers needed to understand the physical performance of the rivers and lakes they swam in and the hybrid—industrial and natural—riparian environment that surrounded them.[35] Tactile senses warned them of dangers in murky waters and shifts in temperature and currents. The soundscape flagged the threat of passing trains, police enforcing often-flouted bathing bylaws, or the potential assistance of nearby work crews.[36] Smell and taste helped bathers navigate the sewage and pollution of Toronto's rivers and waterfront to find the safest places to bathe. People bathed in a world that echoed, stank, and tasted of the nineteenth century and they shared their experiences to create a collective knowledge of the spaces they were bathing in.[37] That collective knowledge was the only way to create security in an unregulated environment. It was a language of place that was shared, taken up, and clung onto in a way that helped some bathing spaces survive for generations. Within the vernacular bathing environment, nudity, or use of the ubiquitous but still illegal bathing trunks, was a mark of belonging and identity formation. There was a recognition even in the nineteenth century that bathing nude was an act of resistance against the normal confines of society.

To understand how people were still skinny-dipping in the heart of Toronto in 1925 we need to consider how vernacular bathing slipped through the fingers of regulation or, in the case of the *Globe*'s "Summer Idyll," was even canonized. The first reason is that bathing was a confusing activity to govern. The second is that the bathing boy became an anti-modernist symbol for Torontonians troubled by the industrial transformation of their urban environment.

Toronto's city leaders had a hard time defining the bathing body. Governing the city required establishing legal, social, and economic boundaries between "the public" and "the private" but, as a boundary-crossing activity, bathing confounded that effort. It was a private, hygienic necessity that required public space to do in a period where private bathing facilities were limited. Toronto's city leaders hesitated to police a healthy activity.[38]

Torontonians also struggled to envisage the swimming holes scattered throughout the city. As Dean has suggested, governing the urban landscape depended on making it visible to the people enforcing the rules. But when Torontonians drew maps of their city, took pictures, or created planning documents, they portrayed an orderly world.[39] Bird's-eye-view maps even modelled what people should be doing in the urban environment by displaying them walking and riding horses or vehicles on the streets.[40] Photographers snapped pictures of acceptable settings or activities.[41] Because nude bathing breached the orderly vision of the city it was left off the map and out of the pictures. And yet by choosing not to see or record these bathing moments, Torontonians created blind spots that enabled nude bathing to continue.

The most popular vernacular bathing spaces in Toronto were in the Don River and along Toronto's waterfront precisely because they fell into the city's blind spot. The economic marginality of these spaces enabled working-class people to repurpose docks and wharves and carve out "transient and fluid" spaces of their own.[42] These were hybrid spaces that blended industry and the natural environment, and they confounded turn-of-the-century efforts to define them. Caught in the tension between industry and nature, these bathing spaces became, as Rob Shields describes them, marginal places "'left behind' in the modern race for progress" and capable of evoking nostalgia and fascination."[43] That nostalgia was promoted by photographers such as William James, who snapped pictures of Toronto's boys skinny-dipping in the Don River. James helped turned the Don River into an oasis against modernity.[44] But rather than revealing vernacular bathing by capturing the motley groups of men and boys who actually used the river, these pictures distilled it into an innocent boyhood activity, just as the *Globe* did in 1925 when it waxed eloquent about the "Summer Idyll."[45] Some of these bathing spaces were used over the course of generations and, while they were defined as working-class spaces by the end of the nineteenth century, they were remembered with nostalgic affection by middle-class men who had swum in them as youths.[46]

Those middle-class memories of bathing suggest the role that gender played in canonizing the bathing boy. Concern about threatened masculinity drove anxiety during the reform period. White middle-class men saw their dominant position, their very identity, within society as threatened. Industrial change disrupted their relationship with the natural environment.[47] White-collar work was emasculating. The increasing presence of women as workers, consumers, and political actors threatened male control of the urban environment. Social Darwinist attitudes pushed white men to see immigration as both a threat to their sexual dominance within society and a threat to the strength of the white race itself. What was a turn-of-the-century man to do when the modern world seemed to be dismantling the very ingredients that defined him as a man? Embrace his masculinity, shuck off the withering urban environment, and immerse himself in nature. U.S. President Theodore Roosevelt demonstrated this attitude with his full-throated call for the strenuous life and promotion of national parks as rejuvenating spaces. The end of the nineteenth century witnessed the growth of Wild West shows, sports clubs, swimming, and bodybuilding, and, above all, colonial expansion, with conquest providing an opportunity for a white male elite to prove their superiority against other races around the world.[48]

The bathing boy served as an anti-modernist symbol for our unsettled male population. As Jackson Lears suggests, anti-moderns both loved and detested modernity, and to balance that polarized view they attempted to cloak the progress around them in a "pastoral haze."[49] Masculine angst created a longing for the charming simplicity of boys gathered around a swimming hole and the symbolic moment of "real life" that they represented.[50] The bathing boy was part of the "pastoral haze" in Toronto, or, with a nod to Ian McKay, a folk figure to counter modernity and the threat of lost masculinity that it represented.[51] The timeless purity of male youth even acted as a soothing balm to cleanse the semi-industrial spaces and make the swimming hole a place of nature rather than industry.[52] The presence and symbolic use of the boys enabled bathing to continue in spaces such as the Don River under the approving eye of city writers.[53] McKay argues that in Nova Scotia middle-class anti-modernists imagined farmers and fishing crews as timeless "folk" with cultural links to the pre-industrial past and repositories of ancient cultural wisdom, songs, and stories.[54] Vernacular bathers played the role of folk in Toronto, but instead of coming from outside the urban setting, they were in the very heart of it—ensconced in bathing spaces along Toronto's rivers and waterfront—and instead of cultural wisdom offered through song or story it was their physicality that provided an embodied link to a pre-industrial environment.[55] Vernacular bathing was imagined as an authentic experience in contrast to the inauthentic, homogenized experience of strolling the boardwalk.[56] The link between bather and land even took on a nationalist tone in Canada because forging a relationship with the environment was seen as fundamental to becoming Canadian.[57]

Ian McKay suggests the "folk" never really existed as a "self-defined group" but instead were defined by an urban elite imagining a pastoral purity.[58] But in Toronto the mythology of the bathing boy was not simply imposed from above; working-class people were active participants in its creation.[59] In the most practical sense, they were showing agency and making use of the available swimming spaces within the city.[60] They headed out from the Toronto Brickworks at lunch, for example, to go for a swim in the Don River. But a dip in the Don could also be a conscious rebuttal of the formal clothed bathing offered at Toronto's beaches. The working class used the bathing boy to symbolize independence, character, and resistance.[61] Vernacular bathers, in other words, were not simply discursive symbols to be observed and meditated upon, but people who could, and did, look back.

Only some bodies fit the vision of the swimming hole: those that represented Anglo-Saxon ethnic and cultural unity.[62] The "Summer Idyll" imagined a white European unity even if, when we investigate the Don River or Toronto's waterfront, we find a more ethnically diverse population rubbing shoulders. Women were excluded from the swimming hole, but they did make their own spaces and, at times, young girls slipped the restrictions of gender and joined in the experience. "Men" were excluded as well: while the bathing boy served as a repository for budding masculinity, the bathing man was either erased from these bathing environments or seen as a moral threat.

The Beach

Our modern idea of the beach has its roots in Europe. Ancient Greeks and early Christians viewed the ocean as a dangerous amorphous space: the home of monsters and gods.[63] But Europeans began to embrace the beach in the eighteenth century, envisioning it as a space that could fortify them against a modern lifestyle that seemed increasingly outside of the rhythms of nature.[64] It is no surprise that the beach emerged when it did. The same attitude towards natural spaces drove nineteenth-century Romantics and was the wellspring behind Frederick Law Olmsted's vision of Central Park in New York City and the parks movement in North America.[65] There is a debate over whether the beach emerged from vernacular spaces that were taken up and monetized by the European aristocracy, or whether it was the aristocracy that led the way to the coast, to be followed by the middling classes. In either event, creating the beach as a public space required transforming it into a place where men and women clothed themselves for propriety, swam together, and even indulged in a culture of display.[66]

The beach shifted in the nineteenth century from a space to encounter nature to a space where one socialized, flirted, and promenaded. Its evolution reflected changing attitudes towards gender and courtship, which saw courtship shift from something done in private within the home or discrete ethnic or religious social groups to a public activity in a growing collection of commercial establishments.[67] Industrialization helped the beach, the boardwalk, and the seaside amusement park emerge by spurring a consumer society and encouraging the presence of women in public spaces.[68] The historiography around the beach, both in Toronto and internationally, has focused on its role as a space where the boundaries between men and women could be challenged.[69] Robert Thomas Allen captures that feeling in the foreword to Mike Filey's *I Remember Sunnyside* when he describes sitting on the merry-go-round at the resort and being "lulled by music and the faint breeze, with your worries flung gently outward by centrifugal force, sometimes falling in love with some girl who was waiting her turn, who floated past you rhythmically like someone in a lovely séance."[70] And in *Boardwalk Memories*, Barbaranne Boyer describes how "young ladies and their beaus strolled hand in hand" through the gardens along the eastern beaches.[71] Even the titles of the books capture the sense that the beach is an escape, with Filey referring to the "Magical Era" of Sunnyside and Bill Freeman calling Toronto Island "A Magical Place."[72]

While Sunnyside and Toronto Island's beaches seem timeless, I want to denaturalize Toronto's relationship with its beaches and consider the ideological and physical spadework that was needed to create them. As a heterosocial cultural space, the beach did not emerge in Toronto until the 1880s when the bathing suit was made a requirement for daytime bathing. My work will demonstrate how the beach as a system of governance was laid over Toronto's physical and social environment; land was reshaped to create a safe, aesthetically pleasing entry into the lake, the bathing suit was instituted to ensure the moral security of men and women, and lifeguards were hired to patrol the shore and rescue people in danger.[73] The beach solved security problems that vernacular bathing never could.[74] Vernacular bathers, tucked in unregulated marginal spaces, had looked after their own security, often with tragic results. The beach answered that problem by placing bathers within a surveillance system, which included watchtowers, binoculars, speedboats, and trained lifeguards.[75] The bathing suit wrapped and regulated the body to provide the moral security needed for men and women to bathe together.[76] More profoundly, the beach provided a discrete space where bathers turned their gaze upon each other, and their collective appraisal and judgment helped lock in new codes of behaviour.[77] The beach, as John Fiske usefully describes it, "is desire institutionalized" and is built to numb and contain the experience of bathing rather than enliven it.[78]

Today, we take the rules and expectations that come with a day at the beach as a given. Its victory seems inevitable. But in the nineteenth century new cultural codes and expectations could not simply be imposed, Torontonians had to learn how to use the beach.[79] Even those who had toured seaside resorts before had to decide how the experience should work in their own community. Men had to be convinced to give up the privilege of nude bathing and both men and women had to be convinced to display themselves in front of each other. The bathing suit could not simply be slid over a docile body; people had to be taught how to perform, look, and be looked at within it. Sometimes nude bathers held on tenaciously to their old spaces. On the western side of Toronto Island, nude bathing continued just north of one of the city's new bathhouses in the 1890s. The "boys" refused to budge and the city, casting a nostalgic gaze on their activities, refused to make them go. If anything, as going to the beach and wearing a bathing suit became the expected norm in Toronto, the nostalgia of the swimming hole increased and nude bathing became an act of resistance for a working class that portrayed a dip in the swimming hole with the boys as more authentic than suiting up for a day at the beach.

The beach also helped make ethnic communities visible in Toronto. As a new public space, it created boundary points where people of different ethnicities, races, and sexualities could mix and where boundaries between groups could be crossed.[80] Academic interest in which boundaries were being crossed at the beach traditionally reflects national social, ethnic, and racial dynamics. British writers focus on class boundaries, Australians on the beach's role as a space of colonial performance, while American writers point to the beach as a space where whiteness was produced.[81] In Canada, the beach and the boardwalk are both a space of colonial performance and a boundary point where people of different ethnicities interact.[82] Jewish people, as a large urban immigrant population in Canada at the dawn of the twentieth century, were often singled out as the face of this ethnic encounter in cities such as Winnipeg and Toronto.[83] We will see how Jewish people carved out spaces for themselves along the boardwalk and amusement park spaces of Sunnyside.

I have built my chapters around a series of contact points between the bathing body and Toronto's physical environment. In each of these physical spaces we are also going to see how an intervention into the physical or social environment helps drive change within that space or makes the social expectations around bathing visible.

My first two chapters look at Toronto's central waterfront and how Toronto's settlers began their bathing relationship with Lake Ontario. The presence of Indigenous people ensured Toronto's rivers and waterfront remained contested into the nineteenth century, even as the land around Toronto was developed for agriculture. Colonial-era rules dictated when and where people could bathe and laid out a human geography over the waterfront that reflected the Town of York's earliest boundaries and the natural environment by easing restrictions in areas where the curve of the shoreline allowed people to bathe out of sight. This human geography survived the intervention of the Esplanade project in the 1850s, a project which extended the shoreline outwards and created a corridor of railway lines between the city and Toronto Bay. Popular vernacular bathing spaces remained entrenched within Toronto's civic imagination even as pictures and maps of the new waterfront imagined an industrial environment. Traditional histories look at how new bylaws, police enforcement, and environmental change drove people off the waterfront, but I want to demonstrate how this effort to govern the waterfront was ignored or circumvented, abetted by a middle-class male elite that viewed bathing through a pastoral haze. Even as the city worked to move the bathers off the waterfront at the end of the nineteenth century, that pastoral haze ensured nude bathing remained a foundational part of the experience.

Toronto turned to Toronto Island in the 1880s to reinvent bathing as something men and women could do together. It is here, at the Wiman Baths on the eastern side of the island, where we will see the bathing suit and the beach formally introduced. The baths provide a unique window into the process of containing and dressing Toronto's bathers and the effort needed to create an acceptable heterosocial bathing environment. Toronto imported the bathing suit and the bathhouse from Europe and the United States, but those innovations still had to be negotiated and redeployed to fit a self-conscious Toronto environment where middle-class men chafed at giving up the privilege of bathing in the nude and women wrestled with bathing under the gaze of men. We will also see how the western side of the island, today's Hanlan's Point, emerged as a popular nude bathing space in the nineteenth century.

The Don River demonstrates both the idealization of vernacular bathing and its practical experience. Industrialization and the Don Improvement Project, which straightened the lower reaches of the river in the 1880s, closed the river off as a space for elite recreation, and yet that seal of industry ensured that the vibrant male bathing culture of the middle Don—a hybrid space of industry and nature—did not compete with middle-class users. Vernacular bathing survived in the middle Don well into the twentieth century and its history has been embellished and romanticized in Toronto as a formative experience for working-class youth.

The Humber River tells a different story. It was a popular space for vernacular bathing but it was also an excursion point in the nineteenth century, and its scenic, lightly industrialized valley became an aquatic promenade for canoeists as courtship moved into the public realm. The competition for space rendered bathers all too visible: rather than boys to be indulged, the bathers in the Humber were viewed as men engaged in aberrant behaviour and a group that needed to be driven out of the river. When Toronto debated building the Humber River Boulevard through the river valley in 1911, its ability to bring moral order to the river among bathers and courting couples alike was held up as a key selling point.

Sunnyside Beach, which sits in the Humber Bay on Toronto's western side, demonstrates the work needed to create a beach in the early twentieth century. The Toronto Harbour Commission's 1912 waterfront plan sought to end the hybrid use of the city's waterfront and to create an ordered division between commercial, industrial, and recreational uses. The new Sunnyside Beach, boardwalk, and amusement park valorized and monetized the mixed-gender experience of bathing. The harbour commission hoped the new architecture of the beach would inspire and uplift people bathing in its waters, while an expanded surveillance system would keep them safe. This was a system of commercialization and control that the *Globe*, in its "Summer Idyll," imagined the bathing boy and the swimming hole as being quite outside of.

In the epilogue we will see how the memory of bathing in the Don River, which hung on so tenaciously throughout the twentieth century, is now starting to fade in Toronto's civic imagination. We will also see how Hanlan's Point re-emerged as an official clothing optional beach in the twentieth century.

A Word on Sources

This project relies on a variety of sources. I have used Toronto's city council and committee minutes extensively. The Toronto Harbour Commission Archives provide a record of what the harbour commission planned to do to Toronto's waterfront, and the letters and exchanges between harbour commissioners, staff, and engineers offer a window into how each group thought about the waterfront. The harbour commission also has life-saving and police patrol records that detail its efforts to extend a net of surveillance over the waterfront and the challenges it faced in doing so. Photographs and artwork have also played a critical role in demonstrating how Torontonians looked at their city and what they wanted to see. I look at photographs as being proscriptive as much as they are descriptive; in other words, sometimes what photographs do not show us is more important than what they do.

Much of my evidence is drawn from Toronto's newspaper archives. Newspapers were the foot soldiers of middle-class regulation in Toronto but their ability to sway opinion was limited.[84] While they were part of the effort to change bathing habits, they also capture the ambivalence around vernacular bathing and rarely spoke with one voice; opinions could shift within the same newspaper—even on the same page—from demanding enforcement to berating the city for targeting boys bathing off the docks or in the rivers.[85] Canadian historian Joy Parr suggests electronic media, such as sound, videos, and so forth, might help us break out of a history that has privileged the written word and led us to a more sensuous history.[86] But I believe the sensuous can be found within print media. Toronto's newspapers look deeply into vernacular bathing worlds and create rich narratives on the physical environment, the behaviour of the lake or stream, the industrial elements around it, the role of the weather, and the behaviour of the groups of people bathing within these spaces. Journalists understood vernacular bathing and the ingredients required to secure safety within that world. They described this world because, without a formal life-saving apparatus to interpret what went wrong, it was left to them to explain and narrate deaths or near drownings. Through their efforts to make sense of the moment when something went wrong, Toronto's newspapers detail the social life of the swimming hole and give us a window into the lives of the people who bathed within it.

1

CENTRAL WATERFRONT

Testing the Waters

Toronto's early waterfront seemed crafted for bathing. The city fronted on a shoreline that included "a shingly beach" wide enough for a carriage to ride along and water shallow enough to wade into.[1] The city's early nineteenth-century wharves stretched out into the shallow bay to reach water deep enough for ships to anchor and were ideal spaces for bathers to dive from. The shoreline at the mouth of the Don River on the eastern side of the bay approached the lake at a gentle slope but rose into a high ridge of land, called the Ontario Terrace, which towered thirty or forty feet above the shoreline, as you moved west.[2] The Ontario Terrace was high enough that in the 1830s a soldier, who had been out drinking and was found passed out in the Freeland Soap Factory, was able to skulk unseen along the shoreline and reach the Fort York military garrison.[3] If the soldier had not been trying to keep out of sight, he could have taken a gravel path along the top of the terrace. According to Toronto historian Henry Scadding, the path, with wood-hewn bridges to cross the ravines along the waterfront, was maintained by the garrison.[4] "From its agreeableness," Scadding adds, "overlooking as it did, through its whole length the Harbour and Lake, this walk gave birth to the idea, which became a fixed one in the minds of the early people of the place, that there was to be in perpetuity, in front of the whole town, a pleasant promenade, on which the burghers and their families should take the air and disport themselves generally." [5]

Toronto was never supposed to be Ontario's capital. After Britain used the Constitutional Act to split Quebec into two new colonies in 1791, Upper Canada (Ontario), for United Empire Loyalists who had left the United States after the American Revolution, and Lower Canada (Quebec), for French Canada, Governor General Guy Carlton favoured Kingston for Upper Canada's capital, thanks to its location at the head of St. Lawrence River, which was the lifeblood of the British North American colonies.[6] Upper Canada's new Lieutenant Governor, John Graves Simcoe, preferred a site along the Deshkan Ziibi River, which he quickly renamed the Thames River, because he imagined its location in the heart of the colony would help with administration and defence. But Toronto also drew Simcoe's eye. Bolstered by Joseph Bouchette's survey of the bay in 1792, Simcoe envisioned Toronto Island serving as a defensive perimeter for a new garrison town that would manage Upper Canada until a new capital was settled upon.[7] Simcoe arrived in Toronto in 1793, gave it the new British name "York," and set about building up the colony. Toronto reclaimed its original name when it was incorporated as a city in 1834 and became the colony's, and eventually the province's, permanent capital by default.

We are going to look at the environment that Simcoe, and the settlers that followed him, found when they arrived in Toronto. This was still a contested terrain at the start of the nineteenth century, with Indigenous people working to keep access to the territory's rivers and lakes, and settlers who went for a swim fully expected that they might encounter Indigenous people along the waterline. The practical and metaphorical presence of Indigenous people influenced how these early European bathers thought about their new bathing spaces. We will see how Toronto's early lawmakers worked with the city's physical environment and how that affected attempts to police people bathing openly on the central waterfront. Finally, I will look at the construction of the Esplanade in the 1850s: a project intended to create a public walkway and a rail corridor on the Toronto waterfront. The Esplanade has been blamed for breaking Toronto's relationship with its waterfront. But when it comes to bathing the Esplanade did something more complex; it created a patchwork waterfront where some areas were developed and industrialized while others were left incomplete and could be co-opted by vernacular bathers. Haphazard development enabled activities such as nude bathing to survive even as the social restrictions against nude bathing solidified in Toronto.

The island that drew Simcoe's eye was little more than a "spit of sand" in 1793.[8] Still tethered to the mainland as a peninsula, the territory "was a waste of sand, with here and there clumps of willows and stunted poplars," to quote newspaper editor and historian John Ross Robertson.[9] The name Toronto itself, or Tkaronto, in its original Mohawk form, has been interpreted as "Trees Rising out of the Water" and erroneously attributed to the island. But even in the nineteenth century that idea was being debunked by Scadding. He argued the name referred to the Lake Simcoe region but was used as a shorthand for the island and Toronto region because they were a turning point for people heading north to Lake Simcoe along the Carrying-Place Trail, an Indigenous portage route that ran along the Humber River valley.[10] Even today the origin of Toronto's name is still debated.[11]

C. Pelham Mulvany refers to the Don and the Humber Rivers as the "Cyphissus and Ilyssus of Toronto" in his 1884 history of the city, taking the names from Greek river gods to suggest how the rivers guarded the boundaries of Toronto.[12] Elizabeth Simcoe and Scadding describe the natural beauty of the Don River at length. The Don was charming enough that the Simcoes built Castle Frank, a summer cottage named after their son, on the high ground overlooking the Don Valley. The Don was adopted by settlers as a bathing space almost immediately; in 1802 the *Oracle*, Upper Canada's first newspaper, noted that Scottish settler Peter McGreg had drowned in the river while bathing near one of York's earliest bridges.[13]

It was the Humber River that drew Europeans to Toronto. Teiaiagon, located just a few kilometres up the Humber from Lake Ontario, was a substantial Haudenosaunee community in the seventeenth century.[14] The Carrying-Place Trail ensured that Toronto was a critical trade conduit for Indigenous groups—the Wendat and later the Mississauga—that were heading north from Lake Ontario or east or west after having reached the lake from the north. Toronto Island, just a short distance away, provided a sheltered space for travellers on the lake. The French established a post at Toronto by 1720 to tap this lucrative trading conduit; their claims were passed on to the British after the Seven Years' War in 1763.

The American War of Independence was decisive for Toronto's fate: the 1783 Treaty of Paris drew the boundary between British territory and the new United States of America through the Great Lakes and turned Toronto into a border region. United Empire Loyalists who were pushed out during the war or who left willingly after it moved into the land around Lake Ontario.[15] Land surrender agreements with Indigenous groups followed. Brokered in 1787, the Toronto purchase was an agreement between the Mississauga and the British government, intended to transfer ownership of a wedge of land about 28 miles (45 km) deep and 14 miles (22.5 km) wide, which ran from the Etobicoke Creek in the west to a point just east of the Don River, in exchange for £1,700 in cash and goods.[16]

The Toronto Purchase was challenged immediately: the Wendat argued the Mississauga had no right to sell the land and the Mississauga disputed what had been included in the agreement.[17] Even the colonial government recognized the dubious authenticity of the Toronto Purchase and held a second meeting with the Mississauga in 1805 to "confirm" what was included in the agreement. As Toronto historian Victoria Freeman has argued, the 1805 revision took advantage of the Mississauga, who had negotiated the Toronto Purchase.[18] The colonial government used the 1805 revision to expand the territory included in the Toronto Purchase, and added Toronto Island, which had been excluded from the original agreement. The 1805 revision offered a pittance of ten shillings, or about two dollars, in return as compensation for the expansion. The underhanded negotiations led to a land claim that was finally settled in favour of the Mississauga in 2010 with compensation of $145 million.[19]

It is clear when we look at the Toronto Purchase and the 1805 revision that the Mississauga wanted to retain their relationship with the water and riparian resources. The Toronto Purchase included provisions intended to hold on to the fisheries in the Etobicoke Creek, "which they, the said chiefs, warriors and people, expressly reserve for the sole use of themselves and the Mississaugue Nation."[20] During the 1805 revision, the use of Lake Ontario and the rivers was once again a key point of contention; for Indigenous people these areas were a resource, a trade route, and a conduit through settler-occupied land. The Mississauga argued that promises of a new relationship with settlers made during the Toronto Purchase negotiations had not been kept. They had been told "the farmers would help us, but instead of doing so when we encamp on the shore they drive us off and shoot our dogs, and never give us any assistance, as was promised to our old chiefs."[21] As Freeman notes, to the British, agreements over the continued use of waterways and hunting grounds were "fundamentally instrumental—to be observed until circumstances changed and compliance was no longer in their interest."[22] The Mississauga were tactical in their requests asking for allotments at the mouths of Twelve Mile (Bronte) Creek, Sixteen Mile (Oakville) Creek, and the Credit River, along with their cornfields and huts "along the flats and bottoms" of the creeks: it was land that was a critical resource to the Mississauga but was located in areas not easily surveyed and divided for settler development. In the end, the Mississauga were left only with land along the Credit River, and even their right to that land continued to be challenged. Finally, in 1847, the Mississauga, now known as the Mississauga of the Credit First Nation, relocated to land near Brantford offered by the Six Nations Confederacy; a quid pro quo for the land and help that the Credit First Nation had given the Six Nations in the eighteenth century.[23]

The Toronto Purchase represented a critical dividing line for European settlers. After depriving local Indigenous communities of their land, Toronto underwent what Freeman refers to as a deliberate process of "forgetting" in the nineteenth century, with the new colonial city and Indigenous people seen as antonyms, "at opposite ends of a national past and imagined future."[24] Prior to the agreement Indigenous people were part of the region; after it they were consigned to the past and portrayed as an impediment to future development.[25] This process of exclusion thickened across Canada as treaties were signed in Northern Ontario in the mid-nineteenth century and the Numbered Treaties and reserve system that followed them were established in Western Canada after confederation. The treaties, the Indian Act, and the newly empowered Indian agents helped enforce the boundaries between settler Canadians and Indigenous peoples.[26] But the experience of the Mississauga of the Credit First Nation in Toronto suggests how Indigenous people remained even after settlement was well under way. While Toronto's nineteenth-century historians and artists do the trenchwork of consigning Toronto's Indigenous population to the past, they also demonstrate the uneven geography of this process, with Indigenous people remaining a presence along the shoreline and rivers. William Henry Bartlett's painting of the 1841 fish market along

Toronto's waterfront, for example, is deliberately picturesque and plays a role in assigning Indigenous people to a nostalgic past, but it also captures the expectation that Indigenous people would be trading along the waterfront in the 1840s.[27]

The presence of Indigenous people along the waterline ensured that the first generation of European bathers in Toronto were aware they were dipping into what had been Indigenous terrain and it gave bathing a transgressive element that remained part of the experience well into the twentieth century. Henry Scadding's work is seeded with references to how the waterfront and rivers were a contact zone between Indigenous people and settlers. Born in Great Britain in 1813, Scadding moved to "York" with his family in 1821. This was a return trip for his father, John Scadding, who had worked as a government clerk with Simcoe and been granted land in Upper Canada before returning to England in 1896.[28] That personal history ensured that Henry Scadding understood he was ranging about in a colonial community in his youth and coloured his encounters with the world around him. Scadding's recollections of Indigenous encampments on Toronto Island lock in Indigenous people as a fading presence in the region. He describes how, "Here, in comfortless wigwams, we have seen Dr. Lee, a medical man attached to the Indian department, administering from an ordinary tin cup, nauseous but salutary draughts to sick and convalescent squaws."[29] But when we push through Scadding's language the encampments and the encounters remain. John Ross Robertson details similar stories of encampments on Toronto Island in the years between 1834 and 1840 and a collegial relationship between the Indigenous people and Toronto Island lighthouse keeper George Durnan. Robertson demonstrates how the potential presence of Indigenous people rendered the island an exotic space for early Torontonians by noting that when Durnan's mother was told her son was going to be lighthouse keeper she immediately fretted, "Are there Indians on the Island and do the people who live there wear clothes?"[30]

Indigenous people also represented alternative possibilities for Scadding. Looking back at his youth, Scadding wrote "the sons of even the most respectable families were brought into contact with semi-barbarous characters. A sporting ramble through the woods, a fishing excursion on the waters, could not be undertaken without communications with Indians and half-breeds and bad specimens of the French voyageur."[31] Scadding argues these moments of contact offered a window into an alternative life. The youthful members of Toronto's elite could "run away to the Nor'-west," a land that Scadding writes they envisioned as "a sort of savage 'land of Cockaigne,' a region of perfect freedom among the Indians."[32]

Unlike their European counterparts, when settlers headed to the shore or the rivers to bathe in their new colonial community they did so knowing another group of people, Indigenous people, might well be there. Historian Cameron White has described how Australia's nineteenth-century middle-class elite turned picnics along the seashore into "a staged, commercial, nostalgic rendition of the victory of the white presence over the bush frontier."[33] Bathing in Canada was not a victory but it was an immersion, a moment of contact, with indigeneity: a settler moment when it could be imagined that a bather becomes Indigenous and linked to nature.[34] The story of bathing in Toronto is one in which Indigenous people are not dismissed but rather used to add meaning to the bathing experience.

Taking to the Water

Public bathing was a cross-class male experience in the early nineteenth century. The waterfront was shallow enough that bathers could wade into the bay and pre-industrial development was intimate enough that work, play, and home life commingled.[35] A social geography of bathing quickly emerged in the new community, with numerous popular bathing spaces, including a "much frequented bathing-place" at the foot of Peter Street.[36] Social and physical geography combined to create the bathing space at Peter Street. The street sat on the edge of the old Town of York, which had encouraged bathers to seek a bathing space just outside the town limits, and the shore was sheltered by the Ontario Terrace, which allowed bathers to enter the water out of sight from people walking above. This "splendid beach" remained a popular bathing space to the end of the nineteenth century, even as the waterfront around it became industrialized and transformed.[37]

Early bathers had access to a mix of commercial and unofficial infrastructure, including the privately owned Royal Floating Baths in the 1830s. As the name implies, the enclosed structure floated on the lake and gave bathers access to ten cool and ten warm baths, along with vapour and steam baths.

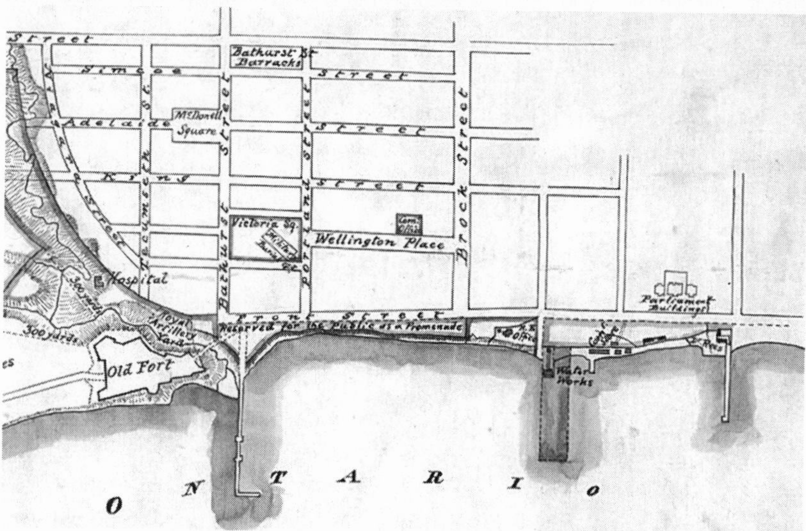

Figure 1.1. This drawing shows the foot of Peter Street, where a popular bathing area existed. Maps from the period depict a muddy and marshy Toronto waterfront so it is likely the drawing was presenting a cleaned-up version of the waterfront. Image courtesy of Toronto Public Library.

Figure 1.2. Rees's Pier, a popular bathing space, is on the right side of this 1850 map of Toronto. Peter Street is to the left of the Upper Canada Parliament Buildings.

Women and men entered via separate doorways and used separate pools inside. The baths were elegant enough that, after bathing, "customers relaxed in reading rooms where attendants sold tea, coffee, soda water, ginger beer and lemonade and a variety of desserts."[38] The floating baths served a wealthier clientele; however, they went out of business by 1843, setting off what would be an ongoing struggle in Toronto to find viable, and enclosed, commercial replacements for the more well-to-do. Over the next forty years a variety of commercial enterprises would operate in the city offering everything from bathtubs to gender-divided pools for people of means.[39]

Longer lasting was Rees's Pier, which was built by Dr. William Rees in 1837 as an investment property and public bathing area for immigrants. The pier continued to be used for decades and it's clear that in its earliest years it was a community bathing space for rich and poor, men and boys.[40] Conyngham Crawford Taylor describes how: "Here on a fine summer's morning, many of the leading merchants and clerks from King Street might be seen indulging in the healthy exercise."[41] According to John Ross Robertson, "It was the favourite pier for early morning swimmers, and frequently fifteen or twenty citizens with their sons might be seen diving and swimming off the pier-head before the sun was well up in the morning."[42] Taylor and Robertson's efforts to mythologize these bathing experiences cloak how they would have been a mundane and expected part of the early nineteenth-century urban life. On a summer morning in 1850, for example, three strangers bathing in the lake came under the watchful eye of a police officer who, fearing they were pausing between petty thefts, stripped down and went in bathing down the shoreline to keep a better eye on them. People strolled past indifferently as the men bathed.[43]

Legal Tools and Their Limits

European settlers brought their attitudes, practices, and an evolving legal framework towards bathing with them when they came to Canada. Men and women had bathed together throughout Northern Europe along rivers and shorelines, but by 1800 women were being pushed out of public spaces. Britain passed new laws to ensure that bathing did not take place within sight of an occupied house, although enforcement remained lax and usually involved a warning rather than a fine.[44]

Still, these thickening restrictions meant that when Toronto's city charter was established in 1834 it followed Britain's lead and took certain attitudes towards public bathing for granted. The Upper Canadian government left the authority to regulate and police bathing in the hands of local governments; this downloading of authority ensured an idiosyncratic attention to local physical and social geography.[45] These early bathing laws were focused on concerns about time and space rather than morality, and that logic lingered to the end of the nineteenth century.[46] Toronto's first restrictions on bathing were included in Bylaw No. 4, an "Act concerning nuisances and the good government of the city," which blended the moral, managing individual behaviour, and the mundane, managing activities that impacted the urban environment; some entries were concerned with policing card games and billiards while others targeted urban activities such as driving horses, moving sand, or getting rid of dung. The bylaw noted, "any person bathing or swimming along or near the piers, wharves, or shores of the said city, at any time between the hour of six in the morning and the hour of eight in the evening shall forfeit ten shillings for every such offense."[47] People could bathe by twilight or night but not by day. But Toronto's bylaw also allowed bathers in the area immediately west of Peter Street, which would have been the original town limits and already established as a popular bathing space, an extra hour in the morning—there you could bathe until 7:00 a.m.—suggesting how geography and long-standing bathing practices influenced the legal framework. (Daylight saving time was not widely adopted in Canada until the First World War, which means Toronto was operating on standard time during the period under consideration. As a result, dusk would have come earlier in the evenings and dawn earlier in the mornings than we are used to today. For example, under daylight saving time, sunset on 21 June in Toronto falls at just after 9:00 p.m. but in the nineteenth century the sun would have set at just after 8:00 p.m.)

The bathing body was under the jurisdiction of local officials six days a week, but after the Lord's Day Act was passed in 1845 it fell under control of the colonial government on the seventh day. The Lord's Day Act was intended to ensure Sunday was "duly observed and kept holy." It made bathing on Sunday illegal "in any exposed situation in any water within the limits of any incorporated City or Town, or within view of any place of Public Worship, or private residence."[48] The act trumped local bylaws and became a new tool for the middle class to police working-class leisure activities.[49] At least in theory. In practice, judges hesitated to charge bathers engaged in what they viewed as a hygienic necessity.[50]

The ambiguity over whether bathing was a moral concern or merely a nuisance remained in the Upper Canadian statutes in 1859. Bathing near a public highway in a county, city, or town fell under the category of "Public Morals," which had provisions that addressed vice, vagrancy, and indecent exposure.[51] But regulation of bathing within or near a city or town came under the category "Nuisance," and was managed alongside such matters as the construction of privy vaults or restrictions on the ringing of bells.[52]

None of the early and mid-nineteenth-century bylaws included a provision for bathing suits, or, as they were called then, "bathing dresses." It was assumed that people bathing in public were doing so in the nude and that they were male; the bylaws focused on eliminating or limiting public nudity.

Toronto had little legal infrastructure to police violations of the bathing bylaw. When Conyngham Crawford Taylor stripped down to bathe at the Commissariat Depot along the waterfront, in front of the Parliament Buildings near the foot of Peter Street, it fell to a watchman to issue a warning.[53] Toronto created its police force in 1835 but the informally structured force launched with just eight officers. It was not until 1858–59 that a board of police commissioners was set up with the power to appoint a chief constable, recruit a larger force, and weigh in on public order offences.[54] Toronto's efforts mirrored the expansion of police forces across the North Atlantic and a new focus on managing citizens within the urban environment. Bathing drew more attention from the 1860s on and in the next chapter we will see how a distinct geography of enforcement emerges for policing the activity.[55] But while newspaper reports of people being charged or threatened with charges suggest police were keeping an eye on bathers, there is little indication they saw it as a high priority. Annual reports from police chiefs to council between 1870 and 1930 do not cite the public exposure of bathers as a concern.[56] It was not until 1896 that bathing even warranted a mention: "A boat was built during the [previous] summer to be used for the suppression of illegal fishing, shooting, bathing, etc."[57] Toronto's police stepped in more aggressively after 1900 to police nude bathing in what they considered inappropriate areas. However, it is worth noting how late this change comes. In contrast, the police chief actively called for public urinals in 1879, 1880, and 1881 to stem the number of men relieving, and thus revealing, themselves in public.[58] We can track the number of people charged with indecent exposure through city council reports, but those numbers include people exposing themselves within the city, including men caught urinating, rather than people bathing specifically: throughout the 1870s there were never more than two or three people charged with indecent exposure, and in the early 1890s the figure was still little more than a dozen.[59] In practice being caught for nude bathing resulted in the perpetrator's name being taken and the issuing of a summons to court, where first-time offenders, as was tradition, were let off with a warning.[60]

Esplanade Constable George Williams represented the face of regulation along the waterfront between 1863 and 1896; he also demonstrated its ambivalence.[61] Born at Petty Harbour, Newfoundland, in 1831, Williams moved to Toronto with his parents as a youth and his career included running a trading schooner and owning a hotel. *The History of Toronto and County of York Ontario* noted Williams's "urbanity and general kindliness of disposition earns the respect of all who know him."[62] The Esplanade constable's duties, outlined in his own words when he appeared before city council to request a raise in 1889, included ensuring "that all the railway companies comply with the By-laws regulating the use of the Esplanade, and that all steamers and other craft observe the law in occupying the slips at the foot of the streets; to take care of the morgue and to drag for the bodies of persons drowned in the Lake, Toronto and Ashbridge's Bay and the river Don."[63] There was no expectation that he would act in a lifesaving capacity and no expectation, as Williams saw it, that he should police bathers either, although the media did see that as part of his job and complained that he was not enforcing the bylaw.[64]

The Esplanade: Reimagining the Waterfront

When Conyngham Crawford Taylor and others talked about bathing along the waterfront they situated their recollections to a time "before the Esplanade," thus establishing the project, which began in 1853, as the end point of an organic cross-class bathing experience.[65] The Esplanade project and the railroad and industrial development that followed it have been described as severing Toronto's relationship with its waterfront.

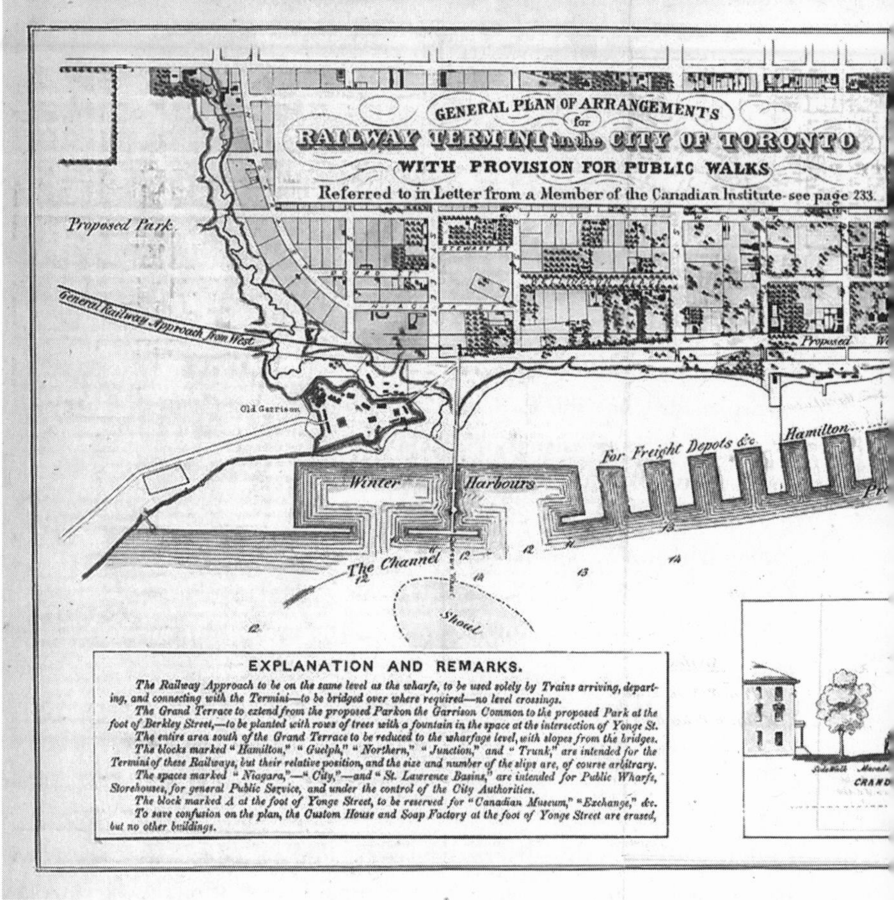

Ken Greenberg argues the insertion of the Esplanade meant "for almost a hundred years the relationship between the city centre and Toronto Bay was interrupted by a port/industrial district. There was little reason for the general public to enter the waterfront area, except to use certain services such as the public ferry docks which provided access to the Toronto Islands, a popular place for recreation."[66] Peter G. Goheen tweaks the timing slightly:

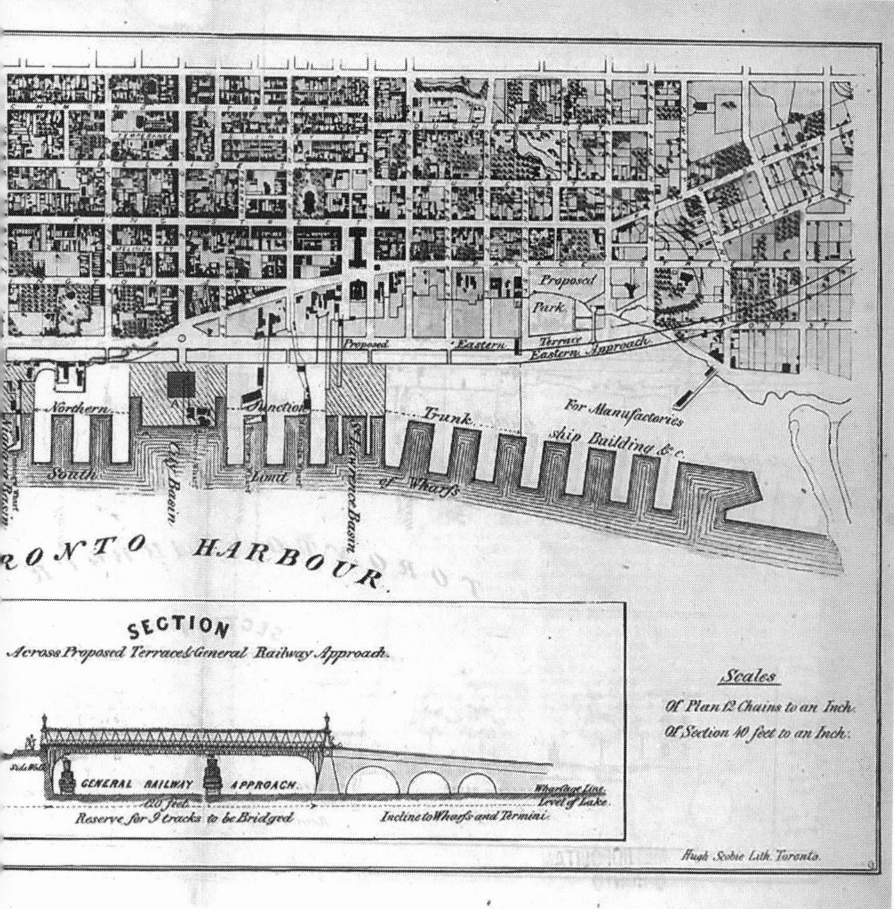

Figure 1.3. Fred Cumberland's plan for Toronto's waterfront envisioned sinking the railway corridor so that people could more easily see and reach the waterline. This 1853 image, attributed to lithographer Hugh Scobie, was produced to demonstrate Cumberland's plans. Image courtesy of Toronto Public Library.

the waterfront remained a mixed space in 1860s, but after that Toronto orientated away from the lake, leading to "the death of the waterfront as an amenity."[67] However, the death of the waterfront has been overstated. While the Esplanade was *intended* to stamp a new industrial order on the waterfront, the parsimony of civic and private actors limited what the project was able to accomplish and the decades of haphazard development

Figure 1.4. This 1876 bird's-eye view of Toronto portrays a seamless link between watercraft, rail, and roads. Image courtesy of Library and Archives Canada.

Figure 1.5. The Barclay, Clark & Co. 1893 bird's-eye view of Toronto included people, allowing it to demonstrate how the city was supposed to work. Image courtesy of Toronto Public Library.

that followed ensured the survival of a hybrid environment and a vibrant bathing culture.

Toronto had dreamed of an Esplanade since 1818, with proponents imagining an open walkway along the lakefront.[68] But it was demand for a railway corridor that pushed the project ahead and led the city to call for proposals in the 1850s. Kivas Tully, an architect and former city council member, and Fred Cumberland, who represented the Northern Railway, both pitched plans that retained open public space along the waterfront. Tully called for the erection of bridges to span the rail lines, while Cumberland suggested constructing a walkway along the front of the city and then sinking the rail corridor so that it could be crossed at grade.[69] Contemporary supporters argued Cumberland's walkway would have commanded "a view of the beautiful bay and, free from the dust and noise of the streets, it would be a delightful place of recreation for the people."[70] Tully and Cumberland both envisioned keeping a link between the city and the lake; had either of their plans been built, that openness, and the potential surveillance of the waterfront that came with it, would likely have driven nude bathing from the harbour. The people bathing would have been too exposed to allow the practice to continue. But instead a quite different vision carried the day.

The winning plan by C.S. Gzowski and Company dismissed the public walkway as needlessly expensive. The company's proposal reduced the width of the Esplanade to sixty feet and laid plans for a row of warehouses on the north side of the road and railway tracks on the south. The Grand Trunk Railway pushed for Gzowski's plan because it was the cheapest option and the one that best served the industrial players. Toronto city council members were complicit. At best, they gave up the waterfront to attract the rail companies and ensure the industrial future of the city; at worst, they supported the Esplanade project in hopes of lining their own pockets from land development—many of them held land along the waterfront or positions with the rail companies.[71] The project went ahead in 1853, and the Grand Trunk Railway and its competitors were entrusted with doing the work. The project extended Toronto's shoreline and created a rail corridor. The goal was also to harden the shoreline and create a waterfront that sat a consistent one metre above the waterline.[72]

As an intellectual intervention, the Esplanade successfully laid a vision of industry and order over the waterfront. That vision was demonstrated through contemporary reviews of the project, maps, and pictures that purported to show the transformation of the waterfront. However, as a practical intervention, the Esplanade was incomplete and perpetually evolving. *Both* aspects were critical for preserving bathing: the first by cloaking the waterfront in an air of respectability and modernity within which vernacular bathing could hide and the second by preserving or creating physical spaces that could be used for bathing.

The Esplanade was portrayed by contemporaries as a space of order. At a public meeting in 1855, Alderman J.B. Robinson argued, "the Esplanade would add greatly to the beauty of the city, and impress strangers with the conviction that Toronto held no mean position among the cities of Upper Canada."[73] Summing up the project in 1873, Henry Scadding wrote, "While the archaeologist must regret the many old landmarks which were ruthlessly shorn away in the construction of the modern Esplanade, he must, nevertheless, contemplate with never-ceasing admiration that great and laudable work."[74] Maps and bird's-eye-view illustrations portrayed the Esplanade and waterfront as an orderly and vibrant contact point between land and water transportation. The illustrations also portrayed what people were expected to do on the waterfront, with images of people riding, walking, boating, and even fishing. Public bathing was not included among the images of things that people should be doing on the waterfront.[75] As Patrick Joyce notes, "the map represented the city as a place of standardized entities through which common identities could be realized."[76] In other words, these colourful maps tutored citizens in how they should behave within the urban environment but did not necessarily show how they actually did behave.

Photographs and artwork of the Gooderham and Worts distillery allow us to trace a shift on the waterfront from the pastoral to the industrial. Artwork prior to the 1860s envisioned a natural shoreline and pastoral settings, but that portrayal shifts after 1860 to display a clean and orderly establishment with hard edges on the waterfront.[77] The picture of the stone distillery from 1863, shown in Figure 1.6, captures a blend of the industrial and the pastoral, while the 1896 image, shown in Figure 1.7, portrays an industrial waterfront.[78] Postcards at the turn of the century took up the theme sufficiently well that when a sightseer named Martha sent her mother one on 9 July 1901, the front image, filled with an orderly flotilla of steamers, became reality for her. She wrote, "Just look at these pictures and you will see just what we saw today. We took a ride in that steamer you see coming from the bay. Toronto is lovely"[79] (see Figure 1.8.). Thanks to changes

DISTILLERY OF MESSRS. GOODERHAM & WORTS, TORONTO: FRONT VIEW.—[See Supplement.]

GOODERHAM & WORTS, LTD.
TORONTO, CANADA.
CANADIAN RYE WHISKY

Figure 1.6. The Gooderham and Worts stone distillery, displayed in the 25 April 1863, *Canadian Illustrated News* still carried a hint of the pastoral.

Figure 1.7. The Gooderham and Worts distillery is in full industrial glory in this 1896 image. Courtesy of Toronto Public Library.

Figure 1.8. Toronto harbour postcard, 1901. Toronto's waterfront distilled into a postcard image. Image courtesy of City of Toronto Archives.

in printing and photography technology, postcards became ubiquitous in the last years of the nineteenth century and created a well-ordered schema, with nature "reduced to vistas seen on vacation, witnessed by solitary figures" and a man-made world that was "not only grand but balanced, graceful, and harmonious" and populated by docile and well-managed crowds.[80]

This intellectual ordering of the waterfront and cityscape reflects what Leo Marx calls the technological sublime. Marx argues that nineteenth-century Americans came to see the mingling of technology and the environment not simply as practical or necessary but as a thing of beauty. The industrial became the sublime.[81] Technology became linked to progress. "To look at a steamboat," as Marx phrased it, "is to *see* the sublime progress of the race."[82] In so doing Americans reconciled the machine "as a symbol of progress and freer of man from want, with their notion of a garden, and a middle ground relationship between man and nature."[83] The effort to see beauty and order on the waterfront created a discursive coherence that hid bathers and the hybrid world that continued to exist.[84] The visual culture that emerged from this ideology erases public bathing by portraying a world too busy, too industrial, and too ordered to have hosted bathing.

The practical experience of the Esplanade during construction and afterwards was a waterfront perpetually in the process of being remade, and that disorder opened space for bathing. The Esplanade project tore the Ontario Terrace—the prominent rise that had overlooked the shoreline—away and used the material as landfill to extend the shoreline.[85] But there was neither enough material nor fiscal inclination from the rail companies to complete the project. While the waterfront was supposed to be finished in 1859, portions remained unfilled until 1880 and were perpetually under construction thereafter.[86] Goad's fire insurance maps demonstrate how the waterfront remained in a constant state of flux from the 1860s on, as some wharves expanded and others sat vacant or were covered with bulk materials.[87] The railroad transformed Toronto into an industrial city with year-round rather than seasonal shipping. But divided ownership and competition among the railways worked against an orderly waterfront, and the wide swath of tracks—there were more than a dozen rail lines in some places—created a moat between the city and the lake, resulting in isolated pockets of accessible waterfront.[88] The pre-Esplanade waterfront had been used for freighting, storage, and small-scale manufacturing. But industrial development brought new industries and an even greater demand for raw materials, with wharves repurposed to serve as storage depots for coal, grain, and timber.[89] Non-industrial use lingered with the passenger trade, recreational users, and boathouses, leaving the area subject to middle-class scrutiny.[90]

Private industry's dominant role in the Esplanade ensured uneven development. As Jason Gilliland argues, capitalists were happy to build up their own businesses but had little interest in investing in "the urban vascular system to make it more efficient and effective."[91] Faced with limited direct returns, Toronto's railway companies and businesses improved their own infrastructure, but ignored the rest of the waterfront and squabbled with the city over repairs to the Esplanade. This uneven development justified the intervention of the Toronto Harbour Commission in 1912, but in the nineteenth century it created an opening that vernacular bathers could wade into.

The creation of the Esplanade is a pivotal moment in the history of Toronto's waterfront, but when it comes to bathing it did not create the transformation that its proponents or even critics might have imagined. Instead of putting an end to bathing, the Esplanade project enabled it. However, bathing ceased to be a cross-class experience after the 1860s. Middle-class bathers decamped to commercial establishments or headed to Toronto Island, where they demanded access to bathing facilities that men and women might be able to enjoy together. Meanwhile, on the central waterfront the working class carved out new bathing spaces or clung to traditional bathing spaces, now hidden within the uneven development around them.

2

CENTRAL WATERFRONT

Vernacular Spaces

It was hot. "Scorching": that is how a *Globe* reporter described the weather after he ventured down to the city's waterfront in early August 1887.[1] It had been hot all summer. Daily highs averaged 28.6°C in July and the heat lingered into August.[2] Caught in a sweltering urban environment that generated its own heat island, Torontonians turned to nature for relief. Men had it easier; they slept in the parks without fear of danger or sanction, or stripped down and dove into Toronto's rivers or Lake Ontario without shame to escape the heat.[3] It was bathers along the waterfront that the *Globe* reporter was seeking.

They were not supposed to be there, not in a state of undress anyway. By 1887, Toronto had revised its bathing bylaw to allow people to bathe during the daylight hours provided they wore a neck-to-knees bathing dress. Nudity during the day, however, remained officially forbidden. But the reporter knew the human geography of the industrial waterfront: "A great rallying place for bathers is at The Credit Valley Wharf. This structure stretches well out into the water, and as the freight shed, which stands on the shore, is not used, the place from the land is somewhat secluded. It is, however, in most conspicuous view of the ferries as they pass and repass to Hanlan's Point," an amusement park on Toronto Island.[4]

And what might people on a ferryboat see?

> *On fine warm days this wharf, from end to end, forms a gallery of living statuary of all sizes. The urchins paddle naked in the warm, dirty water near the shore, which the scum floating on the surface renders perfectly opaque, while a little further out are to be found those who are better swimmers, and have ambitions towards the end of the dock. This later point is the stamping grounds for a number of young men almost full-grown, with a certain following of boys who, boylike, are over anxious to follow in the footsteps of their leaders no matter into what danger it may lead them. All of them, of course, are guiltless of attire, and when not diving into the deep water stand in rows upon the end of the wharf waiting until they feel like another plunge.*[5]

The naked masculinity of Toronto's working-class bathers displayed itself for the *Globe* reporter and the city's elite as they cruised upon the bay. And yet, for all that he flagged the environmental and safety risks of bathing off the waterfront, the reporter did not call for an end to it. Rather his debate was over what to do with the public presentation of the naked male body: "That for the sake of public decency the bylaw should be enforced goes without saying, but it may be asked would it not be well to allow bathers to use such places as the Credit Valley wharf if clad in trunks, without requiring bathing dresses to be used? . . . One thing is certain: the young men and boy offenders will never wear the more cumbersome dresses."[6]

The *Globe*'s story earned a rebuttal letter from A. Johnson: "Your young man does not seem to have much to do these warm days, so it seems that he is exerting himself to discover some place where the boys may be indulging in a bath in the bay. His keen eye has spied the boys enjoying themselves, without bathing dresses, screened by the Credit Valley Railway Storehouse on the Esplanade. And why should not the boys 'go in swimming' naked as they came into the world? A bathing dress takes away the luxury of a bath. The human body in a healthy state is a beautiful object to behold."[7]

The *Globe* described the bathers as being on display for passing ferries and highlighted the mingling of men and boys. But Johnson portrayed them as screened and hidden by the industrial infrastructure: if people saw them it was because they consciously chose to look. Johnson also infantilized the

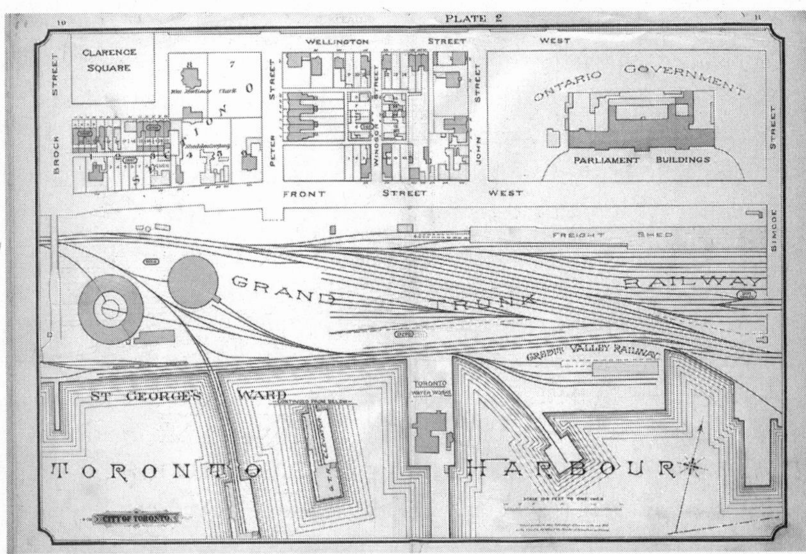

Figure 2.1. Toronto Fire Insurance maps show the Credit Valley Wharf on the waterfront in 1889. The railroad yards discouraged passersby from accessing the waterfront at the wharf.

Figure 2.2. The Credit Valley Wharf, Toronto waterfront, 1901. Image courtesy of City of Toronto Archives.

bathers, turning them all into boys, to maintain their innocence. "Poor boys," he concluded, "just let them bathe where your young man saw them. No person is obliged to go and look at them. Evil be to him who evil thinks."[8]

By the 1880s Toronto's waterfront was supposed to be too industrial and too polluted to be used for bathing.[9] The Esplanade project was supposed to have severed Toronto's relationship with the lake after the 1850s. Yet the bathers were there in 1887 and, as we will see throughout this chapter, the central waterfront remained a popular vernacular bathing space throughout the nineteenth century. Rather than ending bathing, the Esplanade project enabled it. The haphazard nature of the project allowed pockets of undeveloped or underdeveloped space to be claimed or retained by bathers.[10] The Credit Valley Wharf, for example, used new infrastructure but was metres away from the end of Peter Street, where people had bathed since the early nineteenth century. Claiming and keeping bathing spaces depended on the very act of using and reusing spaces: bathers had entrenched themselves in that area of the waterfront and they retained their position there even as the built environment around the bathing space changed.[11]

Tools for controlling bathing in the nineteenth century included the bathing bylaw, which treated the activity as a territorial issue rather than a moral one, the police, and judges. We think of the late nineteenth century as being the high tide of the Reform Era and efforts to create an organized and moral landscape in Canada but, as we will see in this chapter, Toronto's middle class hesitated to control the urban environment.[12] The bathing bylaw was often ignored and middle-class men reveal themselves as sympathetic to bathers and nostalgic for what they saw as a lost moment of their own youth.[13] Rather than pushing to end nude bathing, they called on people to ignore it and look the other way. And when they did look, they often chose to see boys rather than men in an act of discursive slippage that gave the bathers a gloss of innocence and cast them in the role of a timeless folk, thus preserving an embodied relationship with the environment.[14] Where one could bathe nude in Toronto evolved as a spatial dialectic between working-class agency and resistance, the regulatory impulse of bylaws, and active middle-class indulgence.[15]

Ultimately, changes to this vernacular system of bathing emerged through two challenges that the system could not answer on its own. The first challenge was the need to find a way for men and women to bathe legally, publicly, and morally during the day, and the second was the need to create a safer bathing environment. The bathing suit answered the first question and the beach answered the second. We will see in the next chapter how Toronto set about implementing a new system of bathing on Toronto Island and quarrelled over how bathing suits should look and how men and women should interact in the new shared bathing spaces. But in this chapter, we will see how working-class males continued to reject the bathing suit and how that resistance, combined with the ambivalence among the city's elite, ensured that when the city actively attempted to move bathers off the waterfront in 1897, its new free bathing program had no room for girls and women and continued to allow "the boys" the privilege of bathing in the nude.

Finally, heat matters; a summer day with soaring temperatures could shake up the careful balance between bathing, visibility, and regulation.[16] Rather than a steady march towards increasing governance, policing of the waterfront was often impacted by contingent factors such as weather.[17] As we will see, hot weather sent more men into the lake for relief, leading to tighter policing of bathing. A tragic drowning during a week of hot weather pushed the city to create its new free bathing system for children in 1897. While Toronto was following international trends in pushing nude bathers off its waterfront during the nineteenth century, local decisions still turned on a hot summer day.

A Spatial Dialectic between Industry, Pollution, and Visibility

Toronto grew rapidly in the period between the 1860s and 1900: its population soared from 45,000 to just over 200,000.[18] The construction of the Esplanade allowed a string of railroads to be laid across the waterfront and tethered the growing city to the rest of Ontario and Canada. The railroad, as J.M.S. Careless has argued, turned Toronto into Ontario's metropole, at the expense of competing cities in the province, and extended its commercial and industrial reach into Western Canada.[19] Population growth brought diversity to Toronto with German, Italian, Dutch, and Jewish populations starting to lay a bigger footprint on the urban environment; nevertheless in 1901 Toronto's population remained nearly 92 percent British. St. John's Ward, the working-class neighbourhood tucked between Queen, College, and Yonge Streets and University Avenue, included a mix of British, Irish, and African American residents in the nineteenth century. As Toronto's Jewish population grew in the early twentieth century, St. John's Ward, simply called the Ward, became a Jewish neighbourhood and, as we will see when we look at Sunnyside Beach in Chapter 6, the visual presence of Jewish immigrants along the waterfront unsettled the British population. However, these ethnic communities were not being flagged when the Toronto establishment looked at bathing spaces along the central waterfront, whether through newspapers or city council reports; what it saw were working-class "boys."

The Esplanade's railroad corridor, and the industrialization that followed, laid a new geography over the waterfront and created differences between the eastern and western sides. We can use York Street as a boundary between the two sides. East of York Street the rail corridor narrowed and was surrounded by a mix of small-scale industrial development and wharves that were primarily used for bulk storage. The eastern waterfront included boathouses tucked within the industrial wharves and the ferry terminal at the end of Yonge Street; just a block north, businesses, offices, and hotels lined Front Street.

As one headed west of York Street, however, the waterfront changed. Union Station served as a gateway for travellers heading west; beyond it the Grand Trunk Railway and the Northern Railway yards acted as a wide moat between Toronto and its waterfront. Even the original Ontario Legislature building, built in 1832 and in use intermittently until 1893, was severed from the lake and looked out at a railway shed instead. Piers linked the railyards with waterborne traffic, but between the piers the waterfront was a mix of semi-filled or undeveloped spaces that served as bulk storage areas for lumber rafts and, critically for our interests, bathing spaces. North of the railyards was a growing working-class neighbourhood filled with tightly packed housing. The middle-class denizens that had lived along the western waterfront were moving northwards to the edge of the city by the 1880s.[20]

The human and physical geography of the waterfront shapes what transpired. On the eastern side the mixture of uses opened opportunities for bathing, but the visibility of that bathing also pushed the city to step in more aggressively to police the presence of naked bodies and push bathing out by the 1880s. On the western side, the thicket of railyards allowed the practice of bathing, fed by the adjacent working-class neighbourhoods, to continue. There were only mild complaints about the bathers until the end of the nineteenth century, when the hazards, combined with the visibility, of swimming in an industrial waterfront finally pushed the city to consider new solutions.

In the East

Men and boys bathed at numerous locations along the eastern waterfront. We can find evidence in Toronto's newspapers of them diving in at the foot of West Market Street,[21] York Street,[22] and the foot of Bay Street.[23] Nairn's Wharf, at the end of Church Street, where the "bathing bylaw is being openly violated day after day, Sunday included," was particularly popular and provides a useful example of the experience.[24] Bathers jumped in from the wharf, secure in the knowledge that the piles of coal stored there would cloak their presence as they entered the water. But once in the water it was a different matter. In 1877, the *Globe* groused, "A number of men and boys were bathing in the Bay off Nairn's coal wharf" in the late afternoon and "in order to show their utter contempt for the law two of the bathers swam up within a few yards of the Yonge-Street wharf, on which were a number of ladies and gentlemen."[25] The grit and dirt of Nairn's Wharf, and the bathers who made use of it, sat mere feet away from the crowds of people using the Yonge Street Wharf to catch a ferry. The proximity destined that the nude bodies could not be ignored.[26]

So why bathe in a place where they could be spotted? It may have been a tactical decision by bathers seeking cleaner water. The eastern waterfront faced the heaviest sewage outflows and bathers need to navigate around the pollution.[27] The city was discharging 18,700 cubic metres of sewage into the bay each day by 1891, with conditions at their worst between Yonge and Sherbourne Streets. The sewage, rather than being swept away, sank where it entered the bay and needed to be removed with dredges.[28] But the Church Street bathing space may have been sheltered. While there were sewage outflows at Yonge and Jarvis Streets, both outflows were next to wharves that could contain or direct the sewage away from Nairn's Wharf.[29] While the threat of pollution drove bathers out of other spaces on the waterfront, it is not cited as a concern at this location.[30] There's little doubt the lake water was dirty by today's standards, but we cannot judge the experience of

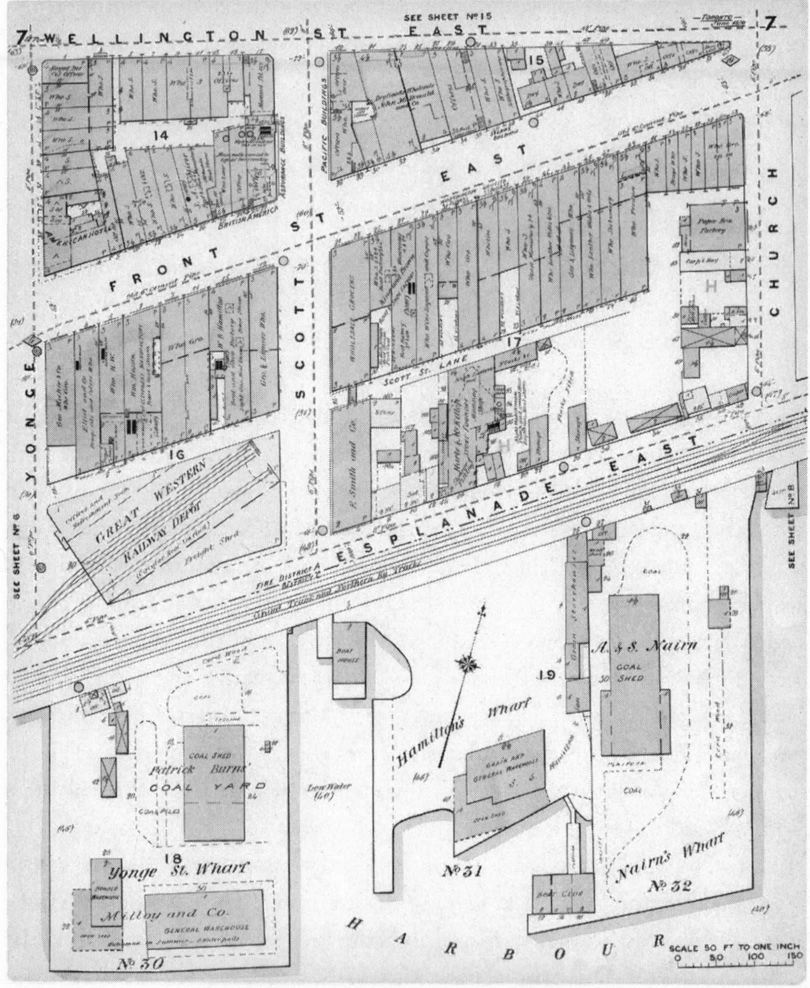

***Figure* 2.3.** Nairn's Wharf, *Atlas of the City of Toronto and Vicinity*, 1880. Fire insurance maps indicate that Nairn's Wharf was used for coal storage, which discouraged pedestrian traffic and opened space for bathing.

nineteenth-century bathing through the hygienic and aesthetic sensitivities of the twenty-first century.[31] We need to consider how the people in that historical period navigated their environment.

By the end of the 1870s there was a clear effort to drive nude bathers out of the busier portions of the eastern waterfront. John Morgan, twenty-seven,

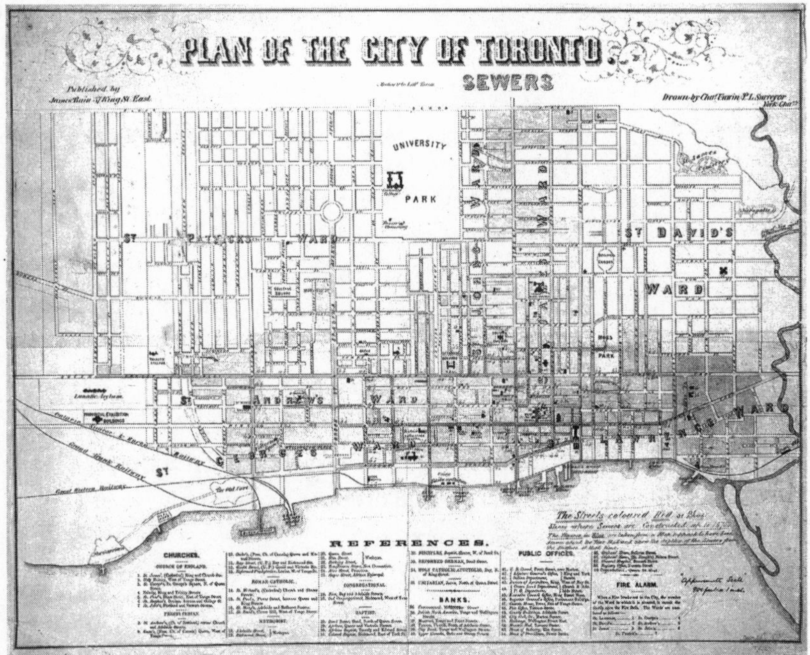

Figure 2.4. Drawn in 1858, this map shows sewage network updates to 1875. Nairn's Wharf was located where Maitland's Wharf appears in this map and falls between the sewage outlets. Image courtesy of Toronto Public Library.

for example, was charged with exposing himself on Nairn's Wharf on a Friday evening, 3 August 1877, and faced a fine of five dollars and costs or thirty days in jail. Morgan's fine was exceptional in a period when bathers were given a warning and then a one-dollar fine. The next season entrepreneurs stepped in and tried to solve the bathing problem by fencing in a space next to the wharf: for a modest fee people could bathe within what they called a "bathing box."[32] But the ability to uphold propriety through a fence only worked if people stayed within the fence. On a warm afternoon in July the passenger ship *Maxwell* was passing the wharf when a couple of men clutched onto swings within the enclosure "and notwithstanding that they were quite naked, they made their bodies rise above the wooden fence right in the faces of those who were on the steamer. This is not the first occasion on which reference has been made to the disgraceful conduct of those who go to this bathing box."[33] We do not hear about the bathing box after 1878, which suggests it was short-lived.

The city finally revised its bathing bylaw in 1880: the revisions opened new space for bathing by allowing people to bathe during daylight hours provided they wore a bathing dress. Nude bathing continued to be allowed in most spaces after dark. However, the revisions specifically attempted to drive it out of the busiest spaces of the harbour, where ferry ships docked, by restricting all bathing between "York Street on the West and Jarvis Street on the East."[34] The new laws coupled with public pressure cut down the number of people bathing on the eastern waterfront. We can still find examples of people being charged for bathing at the foot of Yonge and Church into the 1880s, suggesting the activity had not been entirely snuffed out. But we do not find outraged editorials in the newspapers targeting the practice suggesting that the number of people doing it had dropped or, as we will see in the next chapter, had turned towards new options.[35]

Bathing in the West

Bathing in the western side of the harbour held out longer: the traditional bathing space at the end of Peter Street survived and a new space next to the Queen's Wharf emerged. The promontory that had sheltered bathers at Peter Street had been "eaten away by the ruthless tooth of the steam excavator" during the construction of the Esplanade, but the bathers remained, and, as we have already seen, claimed the nearby Credit Valley Wharf as their own.[36] The tenacity of this space demonstrates how behaviours, as Rob Shields suggests, become intellectually sedimented into the landscape, resisting environmental change and efforts to dislodge them.[37]

A series of editorials in the *Globe* demonstrated the popularity of the Peter Street bathing space. An editorial published on 19 June 1876 stated, "During the week, and more especially on Sunday, large numbers of young men and boys are in the habit of resorting to that part of the Bay opposite the Grand Trunk engine houses for the purposes of bathing and it is no unusual thing to see a dozen persons in the water at a time."[38] The *Globe* called the bathing an affront to working-class families who wanted to stroll along the bay and enjoy the "cool breeze off the water," and argued that alternative bathing facilities should be created.[39] Just over a week later the *Globe* again complained, arguing that women were "being shocked by the unseemly exhibition which at present takes place."[40] "Where are the police," it asked, calling out Esplanade Constable George Williams by name, "that they cannot act in the matter; or do they wink at the contravention of the city by-laws?"[41]

The Credit Valley Wharf was a late addition to the waterfront and owed its role as a bathing space to the cutthroat competition between the rail companies. The Credit Valley Railroad had built the wharf in the 1880s but reaching it required crossing a labyrinth of twenty-three active Grand Trunk railway tracks.[42] The Grand Trunk, seeing a vulnerable competitor, did nothing to ensure those tracks were open. The wharf became a white elephant: it was underutilized and left derelict, which made it a perfect space for bathers.[43]

Further down the waterfront was the Queen's Wharf. It had been leased by the Northern Railway in the 1850s; it expanded to serve the grain trade but was also a popular space for recreational boaters and pedestrians.[44] Next to the Queen's Wharf was a 1.5-hectare storage basin that remained unfilled throughout the construction of the Esplanade.[45] Envisioned by the city as a winter harbour, the space was claimed by the Northern Railway and, with the addition of a pier across its eastern side and a boom across its front, the railway used it for storing timber.[46] The basin was free of sewage and the Queen's Wharf helped direct the polluted water of Garrison Creek away from it.[47]

Pictures of the basin from the 1870s show a space cluttered with timber and seemingly hostile to bathing (see Figures 2.6 and 2.7). Yet it was isolated by the railroad yards, accessible, relatively unpolluted, and contained, which helped moderate the temperature.[48] The rafts and timber provided infrastructure that bathers could clamber on or use to evade police; in 1881, for example, a group managed to get dressed by the time the police reached them, thereby avoiding a charge.[49] This was, in other words, an ideal swimming hole. As early as 1865 it was noted that the "rafts at the Queen's Wharf and some of the wharves at the East End of the city seem to be favourite places for all the ragged urchins in the city to bathe on Sunday. The Esplanade policeman would do well to have an eye on them."[50]

Tragedy struck on 8 July 1876. It was a Saturday afternoon, with the temperature hitting a high of nearly 34°C, when William Calder called on his friend Hugh Jackson and asked him to go for a sail. But the two decided

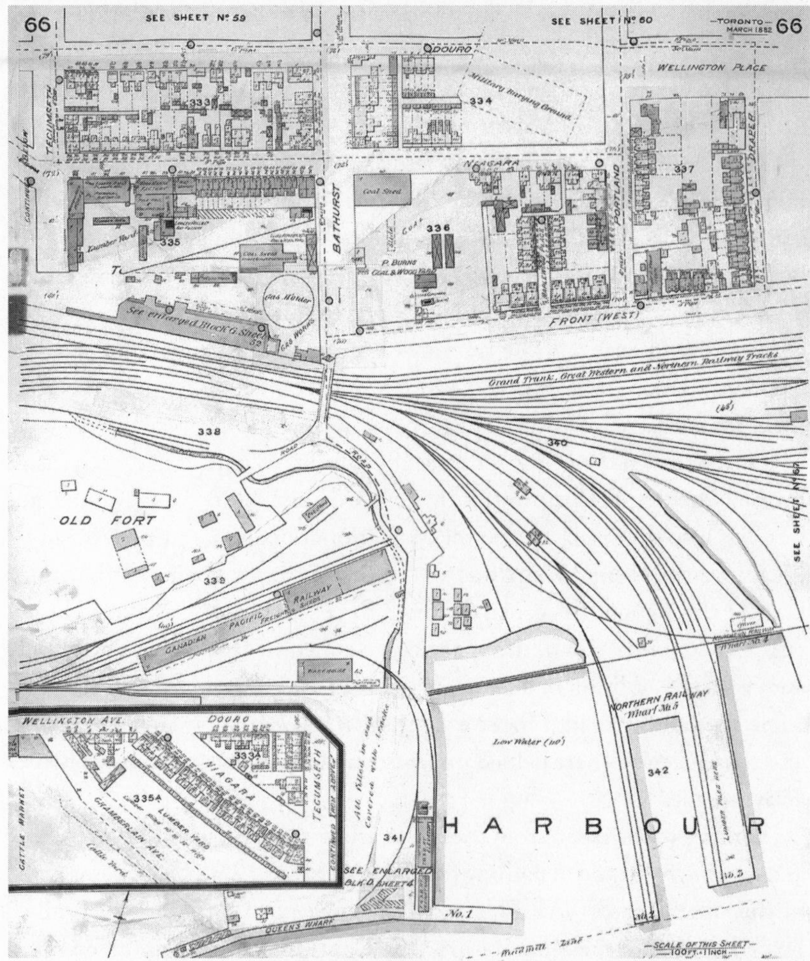

Figure 2.5. The Queen's Wharf is shown on the left-hand side of this map: the open basin in the centre was a popular bathing space.

to go for a swim first and headed "down to the rafts above the Queen's Wharf for that purpose."[51] They joined a group at the wharf and headed into the water but Jackson chose to go in on his own from a different wharf. The choice proved fatal. Jackson was soon missed by his friends, who spotted his clothes lying on a raft. They searched desperately for him, diving and using a

Figure 2.6. The view from the Northern Railway Elevator, at the foot of Spadina Avenue, looking west. The scene includes the lumber-filled basin next to the Queen's Wharf, where people bathed.

Figure 2.7. View from the Northern Railway Elevator, looking east past the Grand Trunk Railway wharf and elevator, 1870. Image courtesy of Toronto Public Library.

pike pole, before finally borrowing a set of grappling irons from the harbour master and dragging them along the lake bed to recover the body.[52]

The inquest into Jackson's death reveals how the city managed bathing without safety measures such as lifeguards or the contained space of a public beach. The city was not concerned that the bathers had been breaking the bathing bylaw by swimming during the day. It did not fault them for bathing in the Queen's Wharf basin. Rather the inquest focused on Jackson's skills as a swimmer and whether his friends had done everything they could to help him.[53] Evidence indicated that Jackson's struggles had been witnessed and that rescuers had tried to reach him with a boat, but they had been stymied by the presence of a lumber boom.[54] The inquest jury considered whether Jackson had been alone—he had gone with friends who "were not absent from him more than ten minutes"—and whether he was sober—he was—and a good swimmer—and, again, it was stated that he was.[55]

The inquest demonstrates how there was no legal expectation in 1876 that the city workers should have saved or helped recover Jackson, or that the city was responsible for the physical environment in which the drowning took place. Deputy Harbour Master Archibald Taylor was on hand when one of the boys came over to borrow the grappling irons, but made no effort to manage the recovery himself and was not chastised in the report for not getting involved.[56] The inquest did not call for an end to bathing or for more policing; it merely reported the death as accidental and suggested that Jackson, based on comments he had made to his friends before the incident, had gone into the water in an overheated condition and been "seized with apoplexy." Safety was an issue of personal responsibility first, the collective responsibility of fellow bathers second, and the city not at all.

The *Globe*, in contrast, called for community accountability and for increased policing of the space. After the drowning it lamented that "Last night bathing continued at the spot as usual, but the police made no effort to prevent it."[57] A letter from L.K. defended the right of bathers to use the space. Like those leading the inquest, L.K. blamed Jackson's death on the vicissitudes of bathing while overheated. He argued, "Are we on this account to be hunted out from bathing where the bathing does not offend public decency?" He went on to say that bathers could not be expected to wait until the city provided baths and repeated, "How can the police interfere when the bathing is done at a spot to offend no one?"[58] It begs the question:

what did constitute an offensive location? Jackson and his group were using a busy part of the waterfront, busy enough that several people were called as witnesses. The harbour master was on the scene and noted a dozen bathers had been in the water at the time, a situation that he had not objected to or attempted to police.[59] No women were quoted or signed off as witnesses, which suggests that the wharf was an all-male environment or that women's presence on that part of the waterfront was dismissed. It is clear that for L.K. the long-standing use of the space for bathing, its industrial nature, the hot weather, and the indifference of the people around the space should insulate bathers from critique.

Policing and Preserving the Vernacular Moment

When we turn from looking at spaces on Toronto's waterfront to looking at how the bathing bylaw was applied it is tempting to argue that Toronto was simply following international trends towards tighter restrictions on bathing. We can see a tightening noose of regulation as the enforcement zone expanded and the hours in which people could bathe were restricted.[60] But looking at how the law was deployed in Toronto reveals something more complex: the changes were also a contingent effort to adapt and *prolong* nude bathing privileges within a growing urban environment.

When we look at events during the summer of 1868 we can see it was the tension between bathing, visibility, and temperature that created a push for tighter rules. Tension along the waterfront kicked off at the end of June, with a daytime high on Saturday, June 27, hitting close to 28°C. The warm weather pushed bathers to the waterfront and middle-class ferry patrons to the bay, ensuring that an activity usually ignored stood out in high relief. A number of "young lads"—their ages were not provided—were brought before the courts for swimming off the wharves over the weekend; while Wm. Richardson, Fred Littleton, and George Todd were discharged with warnings, John McCann, likely a repeat offender, was fined one dollar and given a lecture.[61] The judge complained about "the number of bathers, who, during the crowded state of the Island upon Saturday and other afternoons, sought the more exposed positions to recreate themselves, regardless of the proprieties of decency."[62] Breaking the law to bathe during the day was expected; the issue was with those who displayed themselves doing it. Indeed, the judge griped, bathers

were seeking positions that guaranteed exposure when the waterfront was busy with excursionists. Henceforth, he intoned, police officers would be stationed and watching.[63] But temperatures remained hot throughout July, with an average daily high of 29.7°C and a mean temperature of 24.4°C, setting the city up for a summer of debate over bathing in an urban setting and a round of changes to the bylaw in the fall.[64]

The 1868 revisions shifted the time period in which bathing was restricted: bathing, which had been forbidden between 6:00 a.m. and 8:00 p.m. was now forbidden between 7:00 a.m. and 9:00 p.m.[65] As the city debated how to manage bathing in 1868, the *Globe* acknowledged that "decency" required "public bathing along our wharves and within city limits" must be restricted; but, it argued, "At the same time is it not dutiful in those who prohibit the lieges from using the bay for bathing purposes in exposed situations, to provide some place or places handy and large enough for all bathers to enjoy themselves in a quiet and becoming manner, without being subjected to the

Figure 2.8. An artist's conception of Toronto, c. 1876, looking northeast from Northern Railway Elevator cleans up the flotsam that would have been sitting in the waterfront and portrays a busy industrial setting. Image courtesy of Toronto Public Library.

inconvenience of a long journey, or the expense of a trip to the island, to say nothing of the risks to be met with there?"[66] Toronto Island fell outside the bathing bylaw in 1868, although people on the island still had to manage where they bathed. But getting to the island required access to a canoe or boat or paying for a five-cent ferry ride. People who bathed—a habit *The Globe* considered "a prime necessity both for health and comfort, for all ages and for both sexes"[67]—were being forced into an inconvenient situation, danger, or indecency. Toronto historian Tony Joyce argues the new restrictions in 1868 denied working-class people "the closest and most convenient location to swim" and, mirroring the *Globe*'s critiques, pushed those without the means to reach the island to the edges of the city or into the Don River, where bathing continued to remain unrestricted.[68] The 1868 bylaw, in other words, destroyed the public commons that bathing off the waterfront had represented. And yet, we should not overstate the impact of the bylaw change in 1868: it was merely a tweak to the existing way of managing bathing. The overall time allowed for bathing did not change, people were allowed more time in the morning and less at night, and the geographical space covered by the bylaw remained focused on the central waterfront. Finally, the changes did not attract much attention after 1868: when the *Globe* was quizzed two years later about bathing restrictions it still quoted the prior hours of between 6:00 a.m. and 8:00 p.m.[69]

Toronto introduced significant revisions to its bathing bylaw in 1880 that would change how bathing operated in the city. Previously the bylaw had ignored Toronto Island and the Don River; bathing in those spaces had been unrestricted. But the amendments in 1880 stretched the civic gaze across the entire waterfront.[70] New time limits, prohibiting bathing between 6:00 a.m. and 10:00 p.m., entrenched it as a nocturnal activity.[71] According to Esplanade constable George Williams the changes followed complaints from "parties who are in the habit of boating, and also by keepers of boat-houses," suggesting how this was a victory for the heterosocial use of the waterfront and the genteel middle class.[72] "Bather," a letter writer in 1880, called the changes "an injustice to all the workingmen of the city" and an effort to drive bathers off the waterfront.[73] While some city council members suggested the city needed to step up and provide new sheltered bathing spaces, others were sanguine, suggesting that if bathing in the bay was forbidden the private sector would step forward to provide new bathing structures.[74] Up until 1880, Toronto had managed public bathing under the assumption that it was predominantly a male activity, that people were bathing in the nude, and that they should be doing so out of sight. Now the city finally wrestled with a new question: how to create a public space for an activity that was supposed to be unseen.[75]

The *Globe* and its respondents defended vernacular bathing as the debate unwound in 1880. The newspaper argued the city needed to recognize that there were distinct social spaces on the waterfront: bathing in high-profile areas needed to be restricted but the rules should be relaxed in out-of-the-way spaces. The new bylaw treated the waterfront, the island, and riparian spaces such as the Don River as one coherent space to which the same rules should apply. But that treatment made no sense to the *Globe*; it argued that "what was wanted was a restriction of the area in which bathing in daytime should be prohibited. If bathing were prohibited between 9:00 a.m. and 9:00 p.m. all along the lake front, and not allowed at all during day light within one hundred yards of the passenger steamboat wharves, a compromise would be reached which would be acceptable to everybody."[76] A letter from "Bather" agreed, "The law before was stringent enough, and the *only fault to find with it was the fact that it was not carried out*."[77]

The bathing suit, or bathing dress as it was originally called, solved the bathing conundrum: it shifted regulation, once focused on time and place, onto bodies, while opening the door to mixed-gender bathing. We can think of it as a new technology for managing bathers who presented themselves in public. Following the introduction of tighter bathing restrictions in 1880, Alderman Taylor proposed a second bylaw almost immediately to allow "bathers in proper costumes to bathe along any part of the waterfront of the city or Island."[78] Proper costume was defined as a bathing dress from "from neck to knee."[79] Taylor's bylaw legalized daytime bathing in Toronto by making it contingent on clothing. Previously there had been no provision for clothed bathing; if you bathed, it was assumed you did so naked, and the law was predicated on the fiction that people would bathe in darkness to cloak their nudity. Taylor and supporters of the bylaw hoped commercial bathing houses would emerge to provide bathers with a place to change, and called on hoteliers on Toronto Island to step forward.[80] The bathing suit would eventually alter the geography of bathing in Toronto. It would pave the way for public beaches on the city's eastern and western sides and on Toronto Island. As we will see in the next chapter, Erastus Wiman, a former Toronto alderman turned New York businessman, stepped forward to build a bathhouse on Toronto Island where men and women, properly dressed in a bathing suit, could bathe together in public.[81]

However, as we have already seen at the Credit Valley Wharf, vernacular bathing and the homosocial male culture that underpinned it proved difficult to unseat on the city's western waterfront; nude male bathing, abetted by male advocates on city council, continued much as it always had despite the tighter restrictions.[82] For example, former alderman James H. Morris, strolling along the western waterfront on a Sunday morning in 1881, spotted men bathing among the lumber rafts at the foot of Brock Street, in front of the Grand Trunk Railway yard, and then witnessed the group being challenged by a police constable for contravening the bathing bylaw. Morris reported the incident to city council and said he had walked the length of the Esplanade without meeting a single woman. Nor did he expect to, given "there was no reason why [women] should be there before that hour, as their domestic duties should keep them at home."[83] Morris recommended relaxing the deadline for bathing to 10:00 a.m. on Sundays, except between Bay and Church Streets. Council considered the recommendation before deciding the change would have contravened the provincial statute which restricted all bathing on Sunday in an exposed location.[84]

But the city remained committed to preserving vernacular bathing spaces. In 1893, council loosened restrictions so that "any person without such bathing dress may bathe in the waters of the lake between Bathurst Street on the east and a point six hundred yards east of Dufferin Street on the west; and between Waverly Street on the east and a point six hundred yards east of the breakwater between Toronto Bay and the Marsh on the west, from the hour of five o'clock in the evening to nine o'clock in the morning."[85] The act included a provision for signage to show precisely where people could bathe without clothing.[86] The boundaries were tweaked following complaints from Kew Gardens, a popular east end resort, but the spaces remained and the city entrenched a similar space on the island in 1894.[87] Establishing the nude bathing spaces was said to have "struck a responsive chord in the hearts of all the aldermen who had once been boys."[88] It also garnered supportive headlines from papers such as the *Empire*, which wrote, "Ald. Crawford and the Boys—His bylaw gives them permission to take an old-time plunge."[89] Though, Alderman George McMurrich did raise concerns about bathing near the Queen's Wharf or the Dufferin Wharf, where excursionists "might be shocked" by the sight of nude bathers.[90] Women and girls were, as Alderman George Verral clarified, left out.

The city's decision to allow nude bathing between 5:00 p.m. and 9:00 a.m. was met with amusement in the media. As the *Globe* pointed out, "The prohibition remains during the intervening hours of the day doubtless as a protection against sunstroke. Or did the aldermen get their 5's and 9's p.m.'s and a.m.'s somewhat mixed?"[91] The commentary suggests how expectations around bathing were changing. The city's bylaw eased restrictions but followed the traditional logic of trying to prevent bathing from happening during the day. But by the 1890s, with the bathing suit, the beach, and the expectation of daylight bathing becoming normalized, the idea that people, even naked people, should not bathe during the hottest period of the day was held up as an oddity. When complaints were raised the next year about nude bathing along Lake Shore Road, council's views on the issue were split, with Aldermen Jollife and Hubbard against the bathers; Alderman Crawford, the proponent of nude bathing spaces on the lakeshore, called back, "O, give the boys a chance to swim."[92]

Winking at Authority

The phrase "Give the boys a chance to swim" carried the day more often than we might expect. While it is tempting to view the middle class as the tongue-clucking voice—and aggressive hand—of regulation, it was dominated by men who identified with the people bathing along the waterfront. In the mid-nineteenth century, rich and poor men had bathed together in a brotherhood of the bathing space.[93] When middle-class people paddled into the bay or to the island for a swim, they bathed in homosocial groups little different than those on the waterfront: the only difference was the location.[94] The fact that nude bathing was still popular with middle-class men, or at least fondly remembered, explains its perseverance. In 1882, for example, a group of male excursionists slipped away from the crowd at Grimsby Park to go skinny-dipping down by the beach: their adventure came to an amusing end when a group of women passing by on the embankment above stepped in to break up the activity, pelting the group and their pile of clothes with mud.[95] The moment was portrayed as a harmless case of grown-up boys misbehaving.

John Ross Robertson captures the romanticization of the bathing experience and describes the ultimate hybrid space in a description of children bathing around the West Market Elevator. The elevator burned down in 1909, but before that "it used to be a great playground for the youngsters who managed to slip away from home or school for a ramble around the docks."[96] The cribwork around the elevator "had rotted away at the north end, allowing the bank to fall in and form a little beach," suggesting how bathing spaces opened in the midst of industrial ruins and flotsam. A sunken stonehooker served as a diving board: "the youngsters used to swing away out over the slip at the ends of her loosened top mast rigging, letting go with shrieks, and splashes at the end of the stroke." And from there, Robertson mythologizes the experience: "Plump! They would go into the water, and come up, pink and shining, and puffing like young grampuses as they struck out, dog fashion, for the shore. Bathing suits? Not what you would notice. Those were the days when the bay was fairly clean, when policemen were scarce."[97]

Sympathetic judges and officials who had shared the vernacular bathing experience enabled bathing on the waterfront. One of these was Lieutenant-Colonel George Taylor Denison III, who served as a police magistrate in Toronto from 1877 to 1921. While he was tough on striking workers, Irishmen, and Blacks, he could also assume a paternal interest in members of the working class that entered his courtroom.[98] In the handful of cases where his commentary was noted, Denison treated nude bathing as a minor offence: the accused were let off with a warning or asked to pay a one- or two-dollar fine in the 1870s and 1880s.[99] (Fines could reach fifty dollars, but in Toronto the highest I have encountered was five dollars for bathing at the foot of Church Street.)[100] In most cases, the verbose Denison let the verdict, and a comment or two about class or circumstance as a mediating factor, speak for him. But in at least one case he made his familiarity with the waterfront clear by stating, "seeing that I used to bathe there myself when I was a boy, I have an idea of the place."[101]

William Cook, a night watchman at the Bertram Shipyards, was brought before Denison in 1902 for blocking a police officer who "tried to get the names of a number of men who were bathing in a nude state from one of the piers of the Bertram shipyards."[102] While the *Globe*'s reporter referred to the bathers as men, the *Star*'s turned them into boys, writing that, "Cook smiled on the innocent amusement of the boys swimming off the dock at the foot of Bathurst Street, and when Policeman Weston took objection to the nature's garb and wanted to get their names, Cook interfered."[103] The bathers, meanwhile, scattered "without the formality of putting on their clothes."[104] It was an elegant example of how workers enabled bathing on the waterfront. Predictably it had been yachtsmen looking back from the lake that had drawn the police to the scene.[105] Denison gave Cook a lecture for his behaviour, but after the tongue-lashing was complete, Cook, "being a man of character," was handed a nominal one-dollar fine. Denison made precisely no statements on the bathers who, as the *Star* noted, "escaped."[106]

Christopher St. George Clark, the Toronto journalist/muckraker who penned *Of Toronto the Good: A Social Study: The Queen City of Canada as It Is* in 1898, is famed for ferreting out vice and sexual behaviour, real or imagined, in Toronto. He describes men bringing women to their boathouses to despoil them, and couples cavorting in the bushes on Toronto Island. In a backhanded way, Clark shows us the growth of heterosocial space—of a dating culture—in Toronto.[107] Historians have found Clark a useful lens into the Reform Era. Carolyn Strange uses Clark to detail the moral discourse that surrounded single working women and which linked "their pleasure to immorality and their independence to danger."[108] Steven Maynard has noted Clark appraised the sexual behaviour of working-class boys and fretted they were being led into same-sex encounters or relationships by older middle-class men.[109]

But Clark's only critique of male nudity and bathing was reserved for those who looked upon it. He wrote, "It is currently reported that some stately lady used to sit at the hotel window and survey the boys in bathing through an opera or field glass, until she made a complaint with the result that bathing without trunks was prohibited by the police. Like all such prohibitive legislation, however, it is to be remarked that it was regularly and systematically set at defiance."[110] Clark's story of a stately lady and her opera glass may well have been lifted directly from an 1894 *Globe* article that described just that approach to spotting bathers.[111] (Clark is clearly getting his details wrong here because bathing in "trunks" without covering the chest and stomach remained illegal until the 1930s in Toronto, despite the fact trunks were widely available in stores from the nineteenth century on.) Clark's story puts the blame for prohibition entirely on the reproving eyes of a female watcher. We get no sense from him that nude bathers were a sexual threat. Instead, he viewed their ability to take a swim and enjoy the warm weather as a positive.[112] Indeed, Clark critiqued girls as shameful for not allowing their dresses to be lengthened but held up nude male bathers as a modest contrast: "let any man go where there are boys in bathing, naked, and almost every one of them will try to hide his nakedness."[113] For Clark, fixated on the growing presence of women in public space or on aberrant masculine behaviour, the pastoral image of boys chastely bathing was comforting.

Canada's early swimming promoters also weighed in on nude bathing. Captain W.D. Andrews, author of *Swimming and Life-Saving*, and captain and secretary of the Dolphin Swimming Club, which formed in 1875, suggested a practical bathing suit for females: no sleeves and a skirt that can be removed in the water. But when it came to the boys, Andrews romanticizes how they can strip off their clothes and step into a stream "In purest naturalibus."[114] Andrews naturalizes the nudity. He argues, "until the public swimming baths become more numerous, boys should be permitted to bathe in our lakes and rivers without molestation."[115] "Molestation," in this case, is the imposition of a bathing suit or the policing of those who are bathing without one. Andrews rejects surveillance, writing that "Society, of course, ought to be protected, but, on the other hand, the boys ought to swim. It is their nature to do so. It is odd that it never occurs to society to 'look the other way' when the boys are about to swim."[116] Andrews uses a spyglass story of his own to suggest how nude bathing becomes inappropriate only when watched, and finishes by saying, "Let the boys get health and fun in the water, and let society focus its spy-glass in some other direction."[117]

Andrews's book was published in 1889 and fits in the middle of three Canadian books that capture shifting attitudes on bathing: Montreal resident Ebenezer Martin's 1876 *Treatise on the Theory of Swimming Made So Easy That It Can Be Reduced to Practice at Once* and Toronto resident T.W. Sheffield's 1909 *Swimming*. Martin, the earliest writer, assumes men will be bathing in the nude when he describes them diving into a river.[118] Andrews defends the practice as under siege in 1889. Sheffield takes the bathing suit as a given in 1909.[119] But even Sheffield includes an artistic image of two nude boys playfully tussling with each other next to a body of water captioned with the line, "You First."[120] Sheffield's book defines bathing as part of a structured athletic and hygienic world of swim clubs and bathhouses, but even he can not resist the artistic trope of the bathing boy.

Free Bathing

The death of a ten-year-old boy on a sweaty day in July 1897 set in motion a definitive effort to remove bathing from the central waterfront yet preserve the nude bathing experience for boys. Daytime highs climbed above 30ºC on 4 July and stayed there until 9 July.[121] On Wednesday, 7 July, amid the heat wave, a group of cash and message boys employed by T. Eaton's & Co. raced down to Peter Street, stripped down, and went in swimming. A police officer was quickly on scene, but in the tumble of fleeing boys, ten-year-old Dupree Fenton, of 69 Gerrard Street, got into deep water and went under.[122] Albert Spice, age nineteen, dove in to rescue Fenton but it was a fatally long eight minutes before his efforts brought the boy to the surface.[123]

Fenton's death could have been dismissed as one more unfortunate drowning. The *Globe*, a morning paper, only briefly mentioned the story and noted in the same edition that the mayor had been fielding complaints about bathing on the waterfront from Mr. Stewart of Osgoode Hall, a detail that suggests the police patrol had not been random.[124] The city was equally indifferent, and while an inquest was called it was quickly withdrawn.[125] But the *Star* turned the boy's death into a cause célèbre. "Slain by a by-law," it contended on the front page of its 8 July evening edition: "A lad, fearing arrest for bathing without a suit, ran from a policeman last night, jumped into the water and was drowned. He was bathing at a retired part of the waterfront and was doing no injury. He was a young Torontonian, a young Canadian, and his life has been sacrificed to a prudish by-law. That fool by-law killed him."[126]

The *Star*'s defence of vernacular bathing laid bare the human geography of the waterfront and targeted a morality that shamed public male nudity and a middle class that insisted upon looking. The newspaper chastised those who bathed comfortably at home and then went out boating "in places where they ought not to go, and where they would never think of going if they had the slightest consideration for the perspiring and the great unwashed."[127] Nearly two decades after clothed bathing had been established in Toronto, the *Star* called for the establishment of two nude bathing spaces on the central waterfront: one near where the drowning had taken place and another in the east end. Both spaces would be for the "exclusive use of men and boys desirous of going in for a swim at any hour of the day, without the encumbrance of a bathing suit." And, the *Star* suggested, "A high broad fence to set at naught the keen vision of the prudes might also be a necessity."[128] The *Star* argued the industrial nature of the waterfront at the foot of John Street, directly adjacent to the familiar Peter Street bathing space, protected the area: "Few pedestrians ever wander there, and there could not be the slightest objections to nude bathing. If a certain place were fixed upon in this way, the large number of swimmers, men and boys, constantly there would preclude the possibility of fatal drowning accidents."[129] The *Star* turned the bathing boy into a folk hero as it argued, "in spite of vexatious bylaws, nature will assert herself, and wherever there is open water and the typical small boy, which means boys of all ages and sizes, there will be bathing. If not with the consent of the law, then in defiance of it."[130] The link between boyhood and nature transcended time or cultural interference; while the small boy epitomized that link, the *Star* was clear that it should apply to men as well.

The *Star* and its supporters challenged the masculinity of those who objected to nude bathing. A "mother of boys" wrote in to argue bathing during this "terrible weather" is a necessity: "No one is obliged to look at boys or men when in the water. Can't these Levites turn their heads the other way? How can any humane person grudge these poor or rich boys a bath, nude or anyway? It would never do to send these 'male prudes' as missionaries to Africa."[131] The latter statement was an almost-too-obvious encapsulation of the turn-of-the-century imperialist belief that Africa was primitive and its people undressed and yet a space of intuitive masculinity; it was also a call for a domesticated European society to recapture its own masculinity.[132] The *Star* argued that those who object to nude bathing were "a parcel of prudes and womanly gentlemen."[133]

The call for protected nude bathing spaces was also framed as a fight against the commercialization of bathing, with the bathing suit critiqued as a physical imposition and financial burden. "A Father who was once a boy" noted that the working class had no choice but to seek their baths in public rather than in the private luxury of their own tub.[134] The *Star* argued, "very few boys of the masses are able to scrape enough coppers together to go over to the sandbar at the Island, to say nothing of procuring bathing suits. Even if they could amass the necessary coin, by hook or crook, it is only a greedy cormorant of a city where they should be [pushed] into paying for a swim."[135] The requirement of a suit was putting a financial cost on what had been—and could still be—a free activity.

Women—and bathing spaces for girls—were left out of the conversation. But "One who wants to Learn," a female writer, interceded, "I would like to call attention through your paper to the fact that there is scarcely any opportunity for a girl to learn to swim in Toronto . . . Turner's Baths [located on Toronto Island] are overrun with boys, and if a girl does take advantage of a dip in the lake over there, she is stared out by a throng of boys and men who throng the pier. If any public baths are to be erected in Toronto, separate structures should be built for the girls."[136] I will return to Turner's Baths in the next chapter, but the letter writer was arguing for bathing based on the same logic as that of the *Star* and its male supporters. She wanted a homosocial environment where women might bathe together. "One who wants to Learn" was also flagging how the emerging public beach system was based on women displaying their bodies for men, something that she wanted no part of.[137]

Other newspapers joined the cause, but they were not willing to go as far as the *Star* in demanding that space for men, as well as boys, be included. The *World* called for more public swimming baths and hoped a public benefactor would come forward to foot the bill.[138] A couple of days later, the *Globe* penned its own editorial, pointing out the role of the bylaw in leading to the drowning.[139] But the *Globe* focused on the need to teach boys how to swim; while it agreed the bay offered the warmest and most accessible option, there was no mention of men or the need for spaces where men could swim nude.[140]

The *Star* had picked up on a real safety concern: twenty-nine people drowned in Toronto in 1897, a substantially higher number than the eleven and twelve drownings recorded in 1895 and 1896.[141] The city had only begun recording drowning deaths in 1895; this practice can be seen as part of a growing interest in governing the safety of people within the urban environment. Taking a direct role in governing the bathing body was a logical next step, and the city moved quickly to lay out the basis for a new bathing regime, though not quite the one the *Star* had hoped for.[142] At a special meeting on 13 July 1897, less than a week after Fenton's drowning, city council called for dedicated space on Toronto Island, as well as for hiring a ferry to get the boys there, and a free bathing space in the Don River. The bathing sites would be staffed from 2:00 p.m. until 9:00 p.m.[143] Subsequent discussions added another space at Fisherman's Island, near today's Cherry Beach.[144] The city was not legitimizing nude bathing on the waterfront but instead attempting to remove the activity from the industrial areas of the city entirely and into new zones of civic control. These spaces were predicated on the ability to ensure a safe and controlled physical environment, although with the Don River the city acknowledged it could never completely control the unpredictable river environment.[145] The traditional bathing points were used as collection points for the ferry—initially just a tugboat pulling a scow—which stopped near Peter Street and again at the Queen's Wharf before heading to the sandbar.[146]

While the *Star* had called for bathing spaces for men and boys, the city's free bathing spaces left the men out, specifying that "every boy under sixteen years of age will be given free passage."[147] The bathing spaces on the waterfront had allowed the division between men and boys to blur, but the city's intervention imagined a boundary between men and boys even if, in practice, some men did slip into the new free bathing spaces.[148]

However, nudity, as the *Star* had demanded, *was* made a critical selling point of the new spaces. The *Globe* flagged it in an article entitled "The Happy Small Boy: He will get free transportation to bathing places—and he may bathe in the nude when he gets there." The ability to circumvent the bylaw legally was a critical draw for the spaces, and the city's own advertisements noted boys could swim with or without bathing suits.[149] Nudity was considered a key part of the experience when the *Star* toured the new space on the island: "the crowd of swimmers who came out to meet us, as naked as those savages of the Fiji Islands who first met and surrounded Captain Cook. In our case, the savages were found to be perfectly friendly."[150] The white children could fortify themselves in this primitive space. Describing a communal bathing world, the *Star* continued, "Those who have been in the past so prudish in this matter of open-air bathing could not do better than go right amongst the youngsters, and get rid of their false modesty. There were very few bathing suits to be seen. The absolute freedom and abandon with which the bathers gave themselves up to the enjoyment of dashing about in the water, and running races on the warm sand, precluded the thought that there could possibly be anything wrong in giving the youth of Toronto that freedom from which they have been so unjustly deprived."[151] Indeed, the *Star* argued that by casting away their clothes the boys were able to cast away the class differences between themselves and "all for the time being are on one common level."[152]

Photographers rarely, if ever, turned their cameras on vernacular bathing on the waterfront. That erasure reflected the limits of technology in the nineteenth century and the proscription against looking at nude bathers. But when the *Globe* toured the new free bathing spaces it sent a photographer to capture the experience, giving us rare—and grainy—images of the nude bathers cavorting in the water.[153] The photos endorsed and canonized the non-industrial setting of the island as a proper space for bathing.[154] The *Globe* opined, "A bathing suit is to a boy too much like Sunday clothes are to a workingman—a restraint on liberty of motion."[155]

It is tempting to link Toronto's free bathing program with the Reform Era's supervised playground movement, which created Toronto's St. Andrew's Square Playground in 1909 and the *Star*'s Fresh Air Fund, which launched in 1901 and focused on taking kids out of the urban setting into parks or rural areas.[156] There are similarities. All the programs attempted to create a secure environment for children and wrap governance and surveillance around youthful working-class bodies.[157] But there are also significant differences. The free bathing program was not under the control of the parks department—with its expertise and interest in guiding and shaping behaviour—but rather the property department. The latter focused on where bodies went, not on moral behaviour. Lifeguards made a rudimentary effort to watch over children and teach the boys how to swim but there was little effort to organize their activities.[158] And while the parks movement in Canada rallied middle-class advocates, the free bathing attracted little attention after its creation and remained a city program contingent on renewed funding every year into the 1930s.[159] The *Star*'s effort to promote the Fresh Air Fund in 1901 was driven by editor/moral reformer Joe Atkinson and his wife and columnist Elmina Elliot Atkinson (Madge Merton), who both imagined that nature could uplift the city's young citizens.[160] But Atkinson had yet to join the *Star* in 1897 when it searched for a new bathing solution for men and boys.

In the sweaty days of a late nineteenth-century summer, the goal of the free bathing program was simple: it was a contingent answer to the dangers of bathing in an overheated environment.[161] The embrace of the nude body was practical, an incentive to draw the boys to the new space and mitigate the challenges for those who could not afford a bathing suit. But the promotion of the nude boy by the city's newspapers and the public suggests how it had the discursive ability to encapsulate a summer and a physical experience. The free bathing spaces, as they were originally conceived, were as much about capturing the "Summer Idyll" and preserving it in a secure setting as they were about removing people from the dangers of an industrializing waterfront.

3

TORONTO ISLAND

Implementing a Beach

As the Wiman Baths were under construction, John J. Withrow, the local point man on the project, took a party of the city's leading citizens to the eastern end of Toronto Island for a tour. The *Globe* noted, "Many persons had asked him where the baths were," imagining that the bathing area must be contained within a building, to which Withrow replied, "the bath would be all around them. The scheme contemplated the lake being utilized for the purpose."[1] Rather than tucking bathing out of sight under the cover of darkness, behind a fence, or in a building that put men and women in separate pools, the Wiman Baths would turn it into a public spectacle that allowed people to police each other.

The construction of the Wiman Baths in 1882 created a new public bathing system that depended on the bathing suit, bathhouse, and the presence of women to impose a new moral architecture on the waterfront, one that was capable of overwriting the male-dominated vernacular bathing system and establishing a space where men and women could bathe together.[2] But to make the system work Toronto's unruly bodies and physical environment would need to conform to a new set of rules and expectations. Norbert Elias suggests that as a society evolves it internalizes its constraints, pushing "more animalistic human activities" behind the scenes and investing them with feelings of shame.[3] On Toronto Island we see the *effort* needed to impose shame on nude bathing. Creating a public beach required that men and women be trained in how to behave and display themselves within the new heterosocial environment. Proprietors and customers at the Wiman Baths dickered over what cut and fit made a morally acceptable bathing suit in Toronto. Finally, while the middle class is usually portrayed as the face of regulation, at the Wiman Baths its members were the ones being regulated: men chafed under the new regulations and longed for the old ways. Perhaps it is not surprising then that even as clothed bathing was being entrenched on the east end of the island, nude bathers were tenaciously hanging on to a traditional bathing space on the island's eastern end and were even being coddled and encouraged to stay there by Toronto's city council.[4]

Australian cultural theorist John Fiske suggests that, "like all texts, the beach has an author—not admittedly, a named individual, but a historically determined set of community practices that have produced material objects or signs."[5] The Wiman Baths represent a moment when we can see the beach being written in Toronto. Europeans turned the simple encounter between land and water into a deeper encounter between culture and nature, and developed a commercial/social infrastructure to bridge it. The rules and expectations for allowing men and women to use a beach together were written in nineteenth-century England and were then exported to North America.[6] But what a beach should be, how it should work, and how men and women should interact upon it was still a matter of debate in 1882. As a text, the beach lacked the cultural strength to simply be imposed in Toronto; its implementation was negotiated, challenged, and resisted.[7]

The Wiman Baths capture Torontonians struggle to accept the spectacle of display that came with the public beach. The bathing body, as Douglas Booth suggests, constitutes "an historical site of struggle between pleasure and discipline."[8] The bathing suit was meant to bridge that gap. It was a tool that could contain the body and make it morally acceptable for public viewing.[9] But by turning the body into an object of display the bathing suit also eroticized it and forced people to manage their appearance and behaviour accordingly.[10] Women were expected to display themselves at the baths, but were chastised if they attempted to draw the male gaze, and men were chastised for looking.[11]

Men had to give up the formative male privilege of nude bathing and learn how to conduct themselves in a bathing suit.

The isolated location of the Wiman Baths on the eastern end of the island—the area we refer to today as Ward's Island—reflected Toronto's ambivalence to the new system. Advocates wanted bathers to be displayed, but hoped isolation would ensure that only the right people were looking. In the end, the isolation doomed the Wiman Baths: if the beach was going to be built upon a culture of display, then it needed to be in a place where people would go to see and be seen. Instead, bathing took off at the more accessible Hanlan's Point beach on the western side of the island, while the Wiman Baths fell into disuse a dozen years after opening.

Toronto photographer William James solidified Hanlan's Point as the place to be with a series of beach pictures after 1900.[12] Timing matters; news photography did not take off until the late 1890s in Toronto, which meant bathers at the Wiman Baths never had to worry about the prying lens of the camera as they wrestled with how the bathing body should look.[13] James's work suggests how photographs can impose meaning on a space: as we will see in the next chapter, James took many photos of boys bathing in the nude in the Don River. He could have done the same thing at Hanlan's Point where a nude bathing space hung on tenaciously. But instead James focused on the swimsuit-clad crowds at the beach and in so doing helped erase the memory of the nude space. Today, of course, Hanlan's Point is renowned, along with Vancouver's Wreck Beach, as one of only two legal clothing optional beaches in Canada but, as I discuss in the epilogue, that use would only begin to re-emerge in the mid-twentieth century.

Setting

Is it Toronto Island or Toronto Islands? The two names are used interchangeably in Toronto and, in a way, both are accurate; while there is clearly more than one island, the "islands" were carved by currents from the original peninsula that stretched across the front of Toronto Harbour or were deliberately created by the Toronto Harbour Commission after 1912. Even when it was still a peninsula in the early nineteenth century, contemporaries referred to it as an island, a name that reflected the fact that most people used a boat to reach it.[14] A storm clarified the confusion by tearing through the

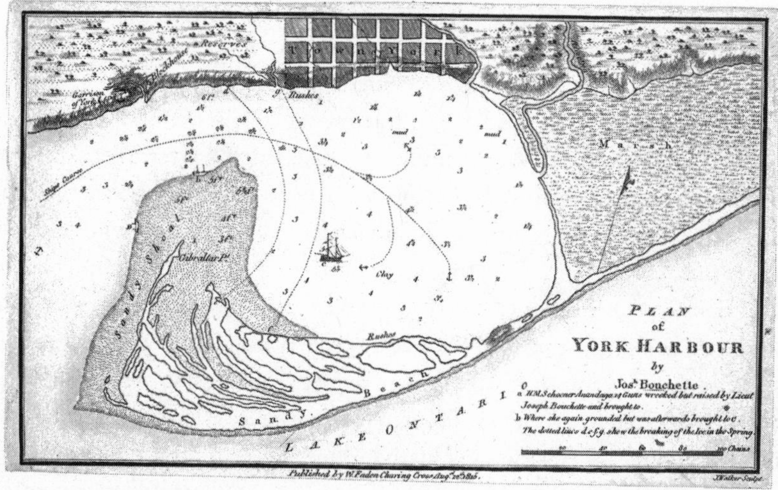

Figure 3.1. This early plan of York harbour by Joseph Bouchette, published in 1815, portrays a marshy Toronto Island still attached to the mainland. Image courtesy of Toronto Public Library.

peninsula's thin neck in 1858 and turning it officially into an island.[15] I will be using the term Toronto Island because I consider it one distinct space.

Sir Richard Bonnycastle described the peninsula in 1835 as a ridge left behind by the retreat of the glaciers thousands of years ago. However, surveyor Sandford Fleming's investigation in the 1850s revealed a more fluid origin: the island is an extended delta of the Don River, pushed westward by prevailing lake currents, and fed by sand from the Scarborough Bluffs.[16] This fluidity left the island in a state of constant change in the nineteenth century, with hydrological forces pushing it across the front of the bay and even threatening to close the western entrance to the harbour.[17]

When we try to imagine the nineteenth-century island we need to resist taking contemporary images of a well-treed island and projecting them backwards. While much of the island had been thickly wooded in the eighteenth century, voracious harvesting by European settlers and flooding in the low-lying eastern end left much of it denuded by the mid-nineteenth century.[18] With the westward flow of sand the island's western side was less thickly covered, even before European axes took their toll.[19] The island's landscape was reforested by the city and private leaseholders in the late nineteenth century and throughout the twentieth.[20] We need to keep that reforestation in mind when we consider stories of nude bathing in the nineteenth century; people were far more visible than we might assume.

The City of Toronto used a legal framework to give the island a stability that its fluid physical environment lacked. The federal government granted the city a licence of occupation for the island in 1847. Dreams of developing it quickly followed, with surveyor John George Howard, who would become famous decades later for donating High Park to the city, laying out a plan in 1850 that envisioned overwriting the topography of the island with residential development and fronting it with a roadway, the Trafalgar Marine Parade, and a beach.[21] Nothing came of Howard's plan. But when possession of the island was finally transferred to the city in 1867, applications to lease land rolled in and the city's Committee on Wharves and Harbours hired Charles Unwin to survey the island and divide the then 400-acre space into five-acre lots.[22] Unwin ignored the natural environment; lots contained a mix of land, marsh, and lagoon, with some entirely underwater. He argued a system of subdivision was necessary, regardless of whether the territory was under water or not, to prevent disputes over land. The legal grid was intended to impose a new system of governance and had to be complete and coherent even if the physical environment upon which it rested was not.[23] But the porous landscape ensured that even if the grid was abided by on paper, it was not in practice, as leaseholders tumbled out of their allotted spaces and trespassed through others' to reach their own.[24] And yet the fiction of the map became increasingly real as leaseholders filled in their lots and began transforming the island. Toronto Island's division into private leaseholds also opened the door for the growth of a vibrant residential community on the island that competed for space with day trippers and bathers.

Toronto Island was treated as an escape from civilization. Historian Patricia Jasen describes how settlers "played Indian" in the nineteenth century when they entered a wilderness setting.[25] Indigenous people were used as racial others to help create that sense of escape on the island, a process that included ham-fisted attempts to dub it "The Island of Hiawatha," a tag that even the 1894 *Toronto Island Guide* dismissed as both an "anachronism and etymologically wrong."[26] But private cottage owners were engaged in the same sort of labour. The *Island Guide* described, "A quaint fancy in naming the cottages is notable, many melodious Indian names being thus perpetuated."[27] As for "Hiawatha," it would pop up again as a street name in the twentieth century.

On Toronto Island, Torontonians imagined themselves briefly indulging in a "primitive lifestyle" before returning to the industrial bustle of Toronto.[28]

When Unwin was laying down his legal framework he deliberately left out the eastern and western ends of the island. The western sandbar, only beginning to form in 1868, and the eastern edge of the island, described as a "low sandy beach," were both considered too insubstantial and waterlogged for development.[29] Foreshadowing the Toronto Harbour Commission's twentieth-century work, Unwin envisioned the northern flank of the island being filled in and extended into the bay to allow for more development.[30] Unwin did not include space for a park; people could promenade on the lakefront, and hotels would take up space within the leaseholds, but it was not until 1880 that Toronto established Island Park.[31] On the lakefront, Unwin included a broad roadway, which could be used for "a promenade, bathing purposes, &c," but he did not say how bathing was expected to work.[32]

Vernacular bathing was already well established on the island by the middle of the nineteenth century. These early nude bathers oriented themselves around the edges of the island that Unwin had left off his map; Moore Higgins of the executive council office and his brother, O.J. Higgins, bathed with a group of men and boys of different classes in 1859, and nearly twenty years later William Griffin and John W. Hamilton rowed over to "Gunsel's Island," aka Fisherman's Island, where they joined men bathing in the eastern gap.[33] On the western side, Upper Canada College boys paddled to Hanlan's Point to camp and bathe.[34] And when William Sisson and Thomas McLoughlin were charged with bathing behind the city's old gashouse on the city's eastern waterfront in 1857, Alderman R.P. Crooks, who served as magistrate for the case, suggested taking a steamer to the island instead, though he readily acknowledged the financial challenges of doing so meant it "was not convenient" for everyone.[35]

Toronto formalized the growing western sandbar as a "ridge of sand from which good bathing can be obtained" in 1876 by building a bridge from Hanlan's Point across the lagoon to the sandbar.[36] But it was taken for granted that bathing on the western sandbar would be done in the nude, so the people who flocked to the sandbar "by the hundreds" during the hot summer in 1876 would have all been male.[37] While people could swim nude from the eastern or western ends of the island, there was no commercial ferry available to reach either end of the island, as the Toronto Swimming Club discovered in 1877

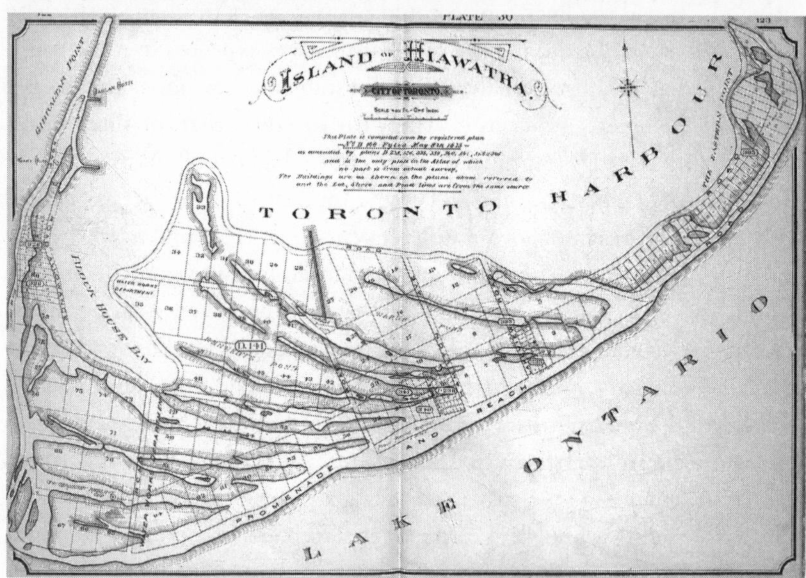

Figure 3.2. Toronto Island in the early nineteenth century, c. 1816. Toronto Island appeared much less forested in the early nineteenth century. Looking north from the Lighthouse, Centre Island, to Fort York, on the left, to the foot of Trinity Street, on the right. William Armstrong, after a painting by Robert Irvine. Image courtesy of Toronto Public Library.

Figure 3.3. Charles Unwin's 1875 survey was used to build this 1884 fire insurance map of the island. Note that the western sandbar is still excluded from the map in 1884. Image courtesy of Toronto Public Library.

when it was attempting to find a practice space.[38] Bathing remained outside the island's commercial infrastructure. In contrast, ferries were bringing male and female excursionists to the centre of the island and Hanlan's Point, which meant that early visitors needed to navigate a recreational environment that included a mixture of dressed and undressed bodies.[39]

The Search for Structure

Toronto was looking to European and American beaches by the 1860s and debating how public bathing might operate locally.[40] Initial suggestions focused on keeping men and women apart: men would bathe at one end of the island and women at the other, with distance ensuring propriety.[41] The bathing machine, a carriage that could be pulled into the water and provide privacy for bathers, was popular in England and was proposed for use in Toronto as early as 1868.[42] The *Globe* argued bathing machines alone would not be enough, but rather certain portions of the beach should be set aside for ladies during "certain periods of the day." The editorial went on to note, "this would imply that the island was placed under strict police regulations, not merely in name but in fact."[43] Bathing, it would seem, required a policed moral terrain to be acceptable.

Toronto's women pushed for access to local bathing spaces. Middle-class women who had experienced bathing in Europe and the United States demanded similar opportunities at home. "Bather" called for individual change rooms, "bathing boxes" that would sit along the shoreline, and pointed to their successful use in the "old country." (Note that "bathing boxes" is being used differently here than it was when it referred to a fenced-in bathing area on the central waterfront.) She argued, "many ladies in Toronto have their pretty bathing costumes used in happier places" and that while men and children were able to bathe where they please "we, because of our age and sex are excluded."[44] Young girls could mingle with the boys, but as they got older they lost the privilege of bathing in public.

Toronto had managed bathing by containing the experience in a commercial bathhouse or behind a fence and keeping men and women separate. Canada had no federal equivalent to England's Bathhouses Act of 1846, which directed federal funding towards local bathhouses, and its cities were loath to use municipal funds to build bathing structures.[45] While they often debated the matter

Figure 3.4. Toronto Island, 1890. The island's lagoons were popular bathing spaces going back to the 1870s. As noted, the name "Island of Hiawatha," used by *Goad's Atlas of the City of Toronto* (1890), did not stick.

in the 1870s, Toronto's city council was never prepared to invest in building bathing facilities and hoped that private citizens would step up instead.[46]

What emerged on the island were temporary structures, fences, and change rooms that preserved nude bathing for men and did little to open space for women. For example, the city built a fence on the island's shore in 1875 for people to bathe behind.[47] But building physical infrastructure to hide bathers was a precarious investment because the beach was not a fixed space. During high-water years the bathing fences washed out and had to be repaired or replaced.[48] Low water levels in 1877 left change rooms a dozen yards back from the water, which meant they were "almost useless for the purpose for which they were put up."[49] The challenge for Toronto was that even if someone were wearing a bathing dress, they were never meant to be seen in it outside of the water. The chief of police also complained in 1877 about "the inefficiency of the bathing fence on the island," which had been left high and dry by the low water levels.[50]

Despite efforts to hide the bathing body, men continued to bathe where they pleased on the island during hot days in the 1870s and felt little shame in doing so.[51] Bathers competed for space with leaseholders and the city fielded concerns that "no one could be expected to build on a lot" that stood opposite a bathing place.[52] The porous landscape meant a designated beach was only a social fiction; people could dip into the water anywhere.[53] With lagoons scattered throughout the "land" of the island there was little incentive to head to the chillier temperatures of the lake. An island leaseholder framed the problem in a 15 July 1878 letter to the *Globe*: "On Saturday last, the shore and ponds in front of houses were covered with bathers many of whom were drunk and using filthy language." He went on to demand more policing of both drinking and bathing on the island, arguing, "There is a good bathing place on the spit [the western sandbar], and there is no excuse for the indecency practiced lately to the great annoyance of the residents."[54] Hot weather, as always, helped inflame the discussion in 1878; highs over the weekend in question ranged between 27°C and 30°C, and lows above 20°C on Saturday created the ideal conditions for both excursions to the island and bathing.[55] The social prohibition against nudity had yet to take hold and unless people bathed on a Sunday, which fell under provincial legislation, nude bathers were not breaking any laws because, prior to 1880, the city's bathing bylaw did not include the island.

A New Bathing System

But something new was on the horizon. Toronto Island was set to be pulled into a new system of public space. New York's Central Park led the way in 1857: public parks were established in other cities with the park-building effort reaching its peak between 1880 and 1900.[56] Toronto's High Park, created on land donated by John George Howard, opened in 1876, and Riverdale Park was created in the early 1880s.[57] City council voted on 1 November 1 1880 to create Island Park, although the park would not officially open until 1888.[58] Kew Gardens and Victoria Beach opened in 1878 on Toronto's eastern waterfront as pleasure gardens for families and courting couples, and eventually popular beaches, and on the western end of Toronto Island Hanlan's Point was emerging as a popular amusement park by the mid-1880s.[59]

The expansion of public space, combined with the presence of people bathing nude on the city's waterfront, created a demand for a system of bathing that could be done in public sight and that men and women could do together.[60] As I noted in the last chapter, the city answered that call with the introduction of bathing suit requirements in 1880. Traditionally bathing had been pushed into the evening or twilight hours to keep bathers out of sight. Some people were already suiting up and bathing during the day prior to 1880, but there was no legal provision for doing so: the city's bylaws assumed bathing would be done in the nude. Toronto's new bylaw in 1880 turned that logic on its head by allowing any person wearing a bathing dress from the neck to the knees to bathe at any time. The new bylaw also extended the city's reach to include all spaces within the bay, Lake Ontario, and the Don River: an extension that meant the island was now included under the bathing bylaw. Nude bathing continued to be allowed between 10:00 p.m. and 6:00 a.m.[61] The bylaw revisions meant clothed bathing was instituted hand in hand with restrictions against nude bathing on the island.[62]

The bathing suit enabled the creation of public heterosocial beaches by pressing regulation directly onto the body itself: once clothed, men and women could bathe together.[63] The change also commercialized bathing; you needed to buy a suit or rent one and you needed a bathhouse to change in. The new regulations would allow the city's beaches to become fully heterosocial middle-class spaces.[64] Alderman Taylor, who tabled the amendment legalizing bathing dresses, specifically had the island in mind and hoped hoteliers would step up to build bathing facilities.[65]

Erastus Wiman, Hygiene, and the Lure of the Bathing Boy

In the end it was New York businessperson Erastus Wiman who stepped up. As Toronto wrestled with the question of who would pay for public bathing facilities, Wiman approached the city and offered to donate money to build a set of bathing structures along the waterfront. But Wiman's initial pitch was not directed at establishing a beach or a new form of public space; rather he spoke the language of the bathing boy and cast it as an effort to preserve the same vernacular bathing experience that he had grown up with. An article in the *Globe*, based on an interview with Wiman, relates his experience: "when a boy in this city it had afforded him extreme delight to go down to one of the wharves, strip, and take a 'header' into the bay, but now the proprieties of refinement, and the decencies of civilization, and perhaps the presence of an unsympathetic peeler, forbade such a ready means of cleansing. When he had thought about those old times he thought how fine it would be if they could drop their cares and revert to some of their primitive pastimes."[66] Terms such as "primitive pastimes" captured the fear that industrialization and modernity were stripping the white race of vitality and masculinity, and Wiman looked to the bathing boy to recapture that lost connection with nature. Within a bathing structure, Wiman said, the boys could "enjoy their dip in the water, and throw aside their cares with their clothes."[67] To that end, Wiman offered the city a donation of $6,000—it would eventually reach $10,000—to construct two enclosed swimming baths for the city's waterfront targeted at working-class patrons.[68]

Wiman was a local boy who had gone on to success in New York City. Born in 1834, he worked as a newsboy, launched a printing company with his cousin William McDougall, and served as an alderman for Toronto's St. Andrew's Ward in 1859. He was hired by the Toronto financial office of R.G. Dun and Company in 1860 and by 1866 was a partner in the firm's New York City head office. Once in New York, Wiman's business interests grew to include investments in the ferry and rail industries and an amusement park on Staten Island. But he also kept a hand in Canadian enterprise as president of the Great North Western Telegraph Company of Canada and as benefactor for numerous projects. Wiman was a strong supporter of commercial union with the United States, and transferring ideas from New York to Toronto came naturally to him.[69]

This was not just an attempt to preserve male privilege and bolster young masculinity. Wiman was also tapping into the reform movement in North America and, with sympathetic statements for "factory girls and women," envisioned females using the baths.[70] Wiman argued bathing was a hygienic and healthy activity that benefited individuals and the community.[71] Reformers linked cleansed working-class bodies with moral propriety and economic success.[72] Wiman created a local trusteeship composed of Torontonians to manage his baths and a committee of middle-class women to encourage and guide the participation of working-class women. The committee's "prominent women" included Elizabeth Jennet McMaster, a notable Toronto philanthropist, administrator, and nurse, who had spearheaded the creation of the Hospital for Sick Children in 1875 and would establish the Lakeside Home for Little Children on the west side of the island in 1883.[73] A bathing space to promote health and hygiene was a perfect fit for McMaster's interests.

Wiman drew on New York's experience. The U.S. city built twenty-five free-floating baths for the East and Hudson Rivers between 1870 and 1888 to provide the poor with a place to swim in the summer.[74] Toronto's floating bath was modelled on the New York model with dressing rooms, a gallery, and a 4.5-foot-deep bathing tank that was perforated to allow lake water to flow through. The bathing area was enclosed but had no roof, leaving it open to the elements.[75] The concept was familiar to Torontonians: the Royal Floating Baths, though more elaborate, had used a similar structure in the 1830s, and Toronto had toyed with building floating baths in the 1870s.[76] The New York model was tailored to a working-class clientele.[77]

Wiman sponsored the construction of two baths in Toronto, but only one of them was a New York–style floating bath. The second, built on Toronto Island, would be quite different. The floating model was nicknamed the Frederick Street Baths, after its first location, as it was tethered to a pier at the end of Frederick Street, but as a floating bath it was moved around the bay in an effort to avoid sewage outfalls.

True to his word, Wiman made a conscious effort to draw working-class women to the Frederick Street Baths. The women's committee ensured new bathing suits were made for women and issued "circulars to factories where girls are employed announcing the opening of the bath, certain days for girls, and that dresses are available [to rent] at five cents each."[78] There was no provision for boys' bathing suits; they would swim naked within the structure. Reflecting traditional rules, males and females did not mix in the facility; the baths were open for women from 5:00 a.m. to 9:00 p.m. Monday, Wednesday, and Friday; men and boys had the other four days. The early opening time allowed clients to bathe at the start of their workday.[79] In a letter to the *Globe*, Miss J. McEwan, the secretary of the ladies' commission of the Wiman Baths, wrote that "one or two of the ladies committee" had committed to swimming at the waterfront baths to ensure "that they are fit for any one's use," and, she added, "I hope that we women of Toronto will show our appreciation of this generous gift to us by using it ourselves and inducing as many others as possible to do so."[80]

The Frederick Street Baths never appealed to women and did little to change the male dominance of Toronto's industrial waterfront. By the end of the first season the allotment for women had been reduced to two days a week and it was lamented that "No girls are taking advantage of the days set apart for them at the Frederick Street Wiman Bath."[81] Tony Joyce argues the Frederick Street Baths went into rapid decline because they lacked a middle-class clientele and revenue to fund improvements, and received indifferent support from the city because working-class users that did go lacked political power.[82] But more specifically, the baths failed to draw working-class women, who had been one of their primary targets. In the end, the only market the Frederick Street Baths really managed to serve were the young boys who were using the waterfront anyway. The floating baths continued to serve that market well into the 1890s, though with little attention, or respect, from the city's middle class.[83]

The Wiman Baths: A New Bathing System

The Wiman Baths on the island brought the beach to Toronto. The island had not been part of Wiman's original plan but he was convinced, "on the suggestion of some citizens," to build there.[84] The unnamed citizens who swayed Wiman towards the island co-opted his donation to suit their own needs for a middle-class bathing space. The Frederick Street Baths were based on a logic of containing the bathing that had existed for decades in Toronto. But while the hygienic role lingered in the name "The Wiman Baths," the island facility was inspired by seaside resorts in the United States. It inverted how Torontonians thought about bathing; rather than attempting to hide bathing within a structure the new baths turned it into a public display. As John J. Withrow suggested while directing a tour of the site, "the bath would be all around them."[85]

The east end of the island was chosen for the Wiman Baths precisely because of its isolation.[86] Already popular with male vernacular bathers, it had been earmarked for the Dolphin Swimming Club before the city changed course and offered it to the Wiman trusteeship for a modest one-dollar annual fee over a twenty-one-year lease. As he led his tour through the site, Withrow said he regretted the isolated location and mused that a space within the emerging Island Park would have been more accessible.[87] There was no ferry service to the east end and the only way to reach the baths was to hire a small boat, though trustees planned to arrange regular ferry service.[88]

The site was environmentally volatile; winter storms in 1882 washed out the proposed location and forced the built infrastructure further inland.[89] Withrow's comment about isolation would prove prophetic as the baths struggled to attract a clientele in the 1890s.

But in the early days, as promoters established the baths and the new system of bathing they represented, the location was celebrated as "detached from the Island proper," quiet, and "one of the best sites on the island for the bath."[90] By the end of the first summer, even Withrow had changed his tune; he claimed that the isolated location, away from hotels, ensured the baths did not draw "rough characters" and that the people who did visit were "eminently respectable and include[d] leading families of the city."[91] The city set a maximum price for renting a bathing dress and towels to ensure the site did not simply cater to an elite.[92] But the location played gatekeeper, preventing the less "respectable" easy access to the baths.[93]

The Wiman bathhouse also included meeting rooms and a 200-seat parlour for hosting middle-class community, religious, and corporate groups. The building was two storeys tall with a tower and steep mansard roof.[94] It originally included change rooms for ninety males and sixty females but was quickly expanded to accommodate an extra 100 men and women.[95] The placement of the bathhouse reflected the porous nature of Toronto Island; situated in the middle of the eastern point it gave bathers the ability to choose whether they wanted to swim in the bay, the lake, or an adjacent pond, which was organically claimed by women and children.[96]

Wiman's trustees debated how to handle the mingling of sexes. Typically, British resorts separated men and women in the water, while American resorts allowed them to bathe together, or at least in close proximity.[97] The women's committee suggested a Lady's Day when women would have the entire facility to themselves.[98] But the trusteeship vetoed the idea and instead, drawing on American examples, suggested using ropes to separate men and women in the water.[99] William Gooderham, of the Gooderham and Worts distillery family, kicked in money to help create the setting; piles were sunk into the water about 200 feet from the shoreline, with the expectation that ropes would be strung between them to create three bathing compartments: men on one side, women on the other, with the middle reserved for "promiscuous use by boys and girls and pairs who may wish to bathe together."[100] (The word "promiscuous" was used in the nineteenth century to indicate the haphazard mixing of men and women and did not necessarily have sexual connotations.) But on the opening day the ropes were not in place, which meant "the sexes are promiscuously mixed up in one grand party while bathing."[101] The ropes appeared later in the summer, but only on the bay side; Withrow noted, "the open lake, where promiscuous bathing can be enjoyed, is the most popular."[102] The ropes were already down again by the middle of the next season as the baths accommodated a greater number of bathers.[103] There is no indication they ever came back: men and women were now in the water together. It would be up to the bathing suit to do the heavy lifting to maintain propriety.

Toronto quickly embraced the mixed-gender environment of the baths as emblematic of a modern city. Nineteenth-century author C. Pelham Mulvany credited the baths with taming the island and creating a wholesome meeting place for Toronto's young men and women.[104] Once a haunt for "the lowest class of roughs"—not a place where a lady could venture—the island had become a respectable middle-class space.[105] Mulvany spelled out how men and women were expected to behave together, with the "athletic youth" taking dives, while "in lovely and close fitting array, more becoming than any ball dress, the maids of our city disport in the shallows, and under the careful guidance venture in the rudiments of swimming." After having their bath, the women settle on the sand or grass, reading, or perhaps chatting to girlfriends or a "boy comrade as they sun their wave-tossed hair."[106] A resort space emerged around the new beach when entrepreneur William Ward opened a temperance hotel with a four-storey tower from which people could watch the bathers.[107]

The effort to establish the Wiman Baths fell within a broader effort to impose order on the island. The city's property committee pushed police to arrest people for nude bathing.[108] Island liquor licences were suspended in 1883.[109] But neither the city nor the Wiman Baths trusteeship could completely control space on the island. Ward lobbied for the right to sell liquor (and was caught with it on his premises), raising fears that there would be drunken patrons sitting next to the bathhouse. A healthy under-the-table business persisted elsewhere on the island. And nude bathers resisted efforts to drive them out. The *Globe* lamented, at the end of July 1882, that a group of men and boys had "enjoyed a 'dip' near the Island bath yesterday without the required dress," but pulled away in boats of their own when a constable rowed up to stop them.[110]

Figure 3.5. The Wiman Baths building, 1954, long after it been converted to apartments. Image courtesy of Toronto Public Library.

The Bathing Suit: Learning to Be Looked at

The bathing suit and the opportunity for bathers to see and appraise each other was key to the experience at the Wiman Baths. This was new. Vernacular bathing depended upon a conscious effort not to see the bathers; a system that broke down when cheeky bathers called attention to themselves and their nudity. The traditional bathing structure, such as the Frederick Street Baths, depended on walls or fences to preserve the space within it from onlookers. For male bathers, who still swam in the nude, that turned the interior into an oasis of freedom against the increasing regulation around them. Within the protected space men could, as Wiman had intended, strip off their clothes and "throw away their cares."[111] Women had no such luxury, even in the homosocial space of the Frederick Street Baths they were required to wear a bathing suit. But at the Wiman Baths everyone would be displayed.

The baths and the new beach experience they represented perform an almost-too-perfect illustration of Michel Foucault's concept of disciplinary power and the panopticon. At the beach, the conventional rules of

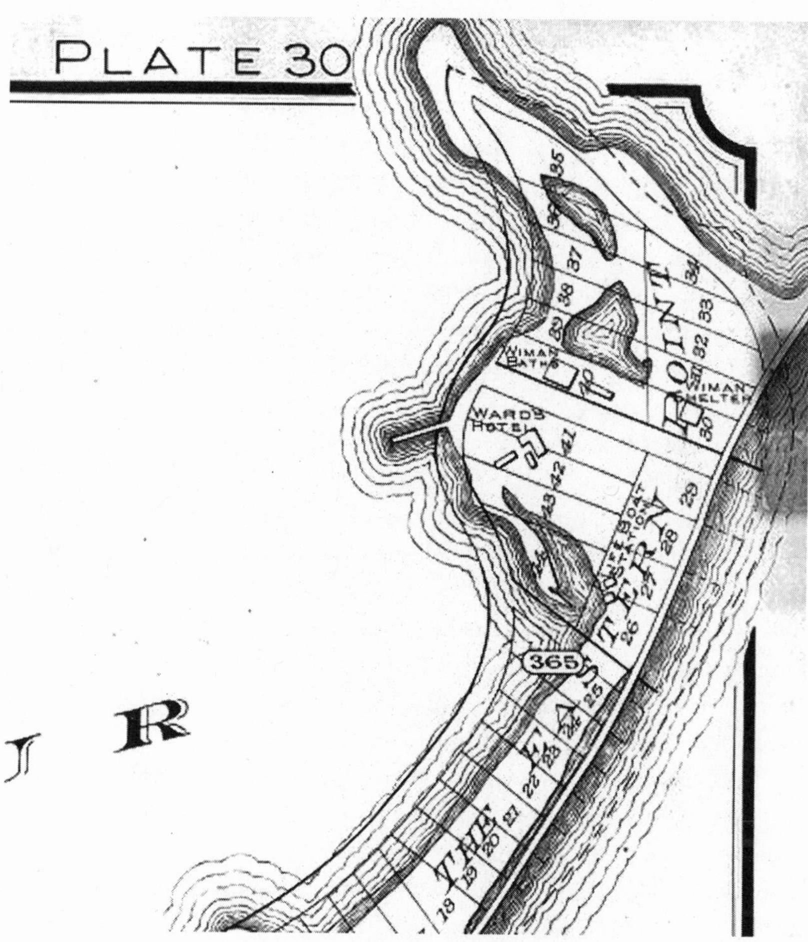

Figure 3.6. Wiman Baths location, 1890. Charles E. Goad, *Atlas of the City of Toronto and Vicinity*, 2nd ed. (Toronto: 1890).

the bathhouse are flipped, with the bathers exposed rather than enclosed. And yet, inverting the regulatory structure strengthened it by turning every spectator and every person who swam in the baths into a regulatory vector.[112] "Visibility," Foucault suggests, "is a trap" that allows each individual to be examined and governed.[113] More than simply people caught in a web of surveillance, the patrons of the baths were active participants in creating that web.[114] The bathing suit attached governance onto the very skin of individual bathers, and allowed them to appraise each other.[115] The beach and the bathing suit allowed new subjectivities to be created: people needed to perform their masculinity and femininity differently in the new mixed-gender setting.[116]

Finally, the increasing expectation that bathing was a public and clothed activity helped confine nude bathing to the margins of acceptable behaviour.[117] Henceforth people were either wearing a bathing suit or they were, as Rob Shields suggests, "forced into wilderness or barren spaces 'outside' of the civilized realm" or into "their own dichotomous spaces."[118] It is precisely this expulsion, as Norbert Elias has suggested, that produces shame.[119] But turning nude bathing into a marginal activity could also turn it into a nostalgic pastime in need of protection; as we will see, a distinct space for nude bathing held out on the western end of the island.

The *Globe* captured the tension around public bathing when it portrayed an exchange between a mother and her three daughters at a meeting intended to promote the baths. The daughters complained that bathing would become a public spectacle, stating, "Oh! I would not bathe at that horrid place where everybody could see me . . . those ugly bathing costumes make one look so absurd" and "Everybody would be sure to look at us."[120] The mother, playing the role of enlightened modernist, argued, "Well, I'm sure they would see a very pretty sight. If all the young ladies would consent to bathe there the place would soon become so famous as Coney Island or Manhattan Beach, and only think how good it would be for your health."[121] The *Globe*'s narrative seems too well-crafted to be real, but the point is clear: if women could be convinced to put themselves on display, Toronto would have a world-class resort.[122]

The bathing suit was not entirely novel for Torontonians by 1880. Middle-class women and men who could afford to travel were used to wearing bathing costumes at European or North American coastal resorts.[123] Toronto's media carried written descriptions of European bathing dresses as early as the 1860s, and small text advertisements for ready-made or made-to-order bathing dresses were running by 1880.[124] Change rooms had already started to appear on the island. Unofficial bathing clothes such as bathing drawers were advertised in 1879 and a bathhouse for men on the island offered to rent "trunks" to bathers.[125] Trunks would not be legal in Toronto until the 1930s, but they appear often enough in newspaper advertisements to suggest their popularity away from the formal setting of the beach.[126]

But there was no agreed-upon language or image in the 1880s for what a bathing suit should look like or how it should be worn. The circulation of mass culture around bathing suits, particularly for men, was not powerful enough to set expectations for appearance. The city's new bylaw simply said the bathing dress should cover the body from "neck to knees."[127] It said nothing about how well and how tightly the suit might hug the male frame: that was something that had to be worked out in practice on the sands of the island. There were no pictures of bathing suits in Toronto's newspapers in the early 1880s to serve as a model. Canada's retail culture was still emerging and while department stores such as Eaton's and Simpson's would be able to define and market products such as bathing suits by 1900, in the 1880s they lacked that cultural heft.[128] By 1900, pictures, comics, and display advertisements would give Torontonians a clear model of what a bathing suit should look like.[129] But in 1883 Torontonians had to settle upon their own expectations of propriety.[130]

The Wiman Baths provide a unique window into the moment when bathing suits were adopted and the visual presentation of the bathing body was debated in Toronto. For men, used to bathing nude, the bathing suit meant reworking how they appeared in public space. They chafed at having to put on bathing suits and having their anatomy and bodily comportment appraised by spectators. Their critics argued that respectable masculinity now meant knowing how to appear in a bathing suit. John Young summed up the issue in a letter to the editor dated 14 July 1883: "The very proper rule against bathers promenading on the landing wharf is openly violated without regard to decency. A thin, wet, clinging bathing dress is a very small remove from entire nudity, and some great hulking fellows, evidently with set purpose to display their physical attractions to the crowd of men, women, and children who are constantly passing to and fro as the ferry-boats arrive and depart, were on exhibition nearly all the time." Young went on to warn,

"Unless the rule is enforced no woman with any regard for modesty would visit the place a second time."[131] Travelling out to "witness" the setting and the scene of the baths at the end of July, the *Globe* suggests how clothing men for the beach remained a novelty and challenge. The "tall, manly young fellow between twenty and thirty" appeared "rather ridiculous" to most observers "clothed from throat to knees, according to rule."[132] And it noted that "some few men, preferring to observe the full dress ordinance less in the spirit than the letter, wear a thin, tight, flesh-coloured jersey from shoulder to knee, that makes them appear at a little distance as though they had nothing on at all."[133] The flesh-coloured jersey was a cheeky way for men to get an experience as close as possible to the nude bathing privilege. The men appeared "rather ridiculous" because wearing a suit was so new in Toronto; it was still assumed the masculine performance of bathing would be done in the nude.[134]

The bathing suit turned the male body into an erotic symbol in a way it had not been before.[135] Vernacular bathing asked people to turn their eyes away from the naked body; the beach, however, centred the gaze on the clothed body. After taking a laissez-faire approach during its first summer, the trusteeship set new guidelines in 1883, insisting that only "stout flannel or serge bathing dresses will be permitted to either sex."[136] It set off a debate over the virtues of cotton versus wool; was the tight fit of cotton more vulgar than the way a sodden woollen suit clung to the male body? Letter-writer "Decency and Morality" argued that any benefits gained from cotton suits, which were considered lighter and better for wearing while swimming, were trumped by the moral risks that came with wearing them. While the Wiman's Baths had made an effort to provide a space where "ladies" might learn to swim, he argued the trustees needed to "insist on the observance of their regulations regarding bathing costumes" because "if there is any doubt as to the insisting upon decency they will cease to come."[137] "Decency and Morality" argued he used the baths to teach his daughters to swim but would pull them out "if costumes were allowed which some men would have the effrontery to wear."[138] But critics countered that the trusteeship's official suits were no better because their loose design guaranteed that when wet, "they cling tenaciously to the body."[139] We need not be coy: the concern was over how well the bathing suits clung to the male frame and male sexual anatomy.[140]

Men were angry about being contained within the bathing suit and ambivalent about having their bodies appraised in new ways. Critics of the trusteeship's bathing suits argued the suits encumbered the bathing experience. Countering "Decency and Morality," writers called "Common Sense" and "A Disappointed Swimmer" argued the "Loose Regulation Dress" endorsed by the baths was "sufficiently cumbrous, ill-made, and uncomfortable to drive any swimmer to despair. It is assumed to have been devised for purposes of decency, whereas the only result is a hideous deformation of the human appearance."[141] It was hard to imagine the statuesque male of the "Summer Idyll," which the *Globe* waxed nostalgic about in 1925, wrapped in a soggy bathing suit.

The problem, according to male critics, was not how men appeared in bathing suits but rather the new culture of spectatorship that was turning its eyes upon them. The solution? Do not look. "Common Sense" complained in a letter to the *Daily Mail*: "[The Wiman Baths] was intended for the benefit of the city in bathing and swimming, for cleanliness, exercise, and lifesaving: it is being mismanaged for the amusement of a crowd of spectators." He suggested tickets to the baths be sold on the mainland and that "no one be allowed to approach the Wiman island without such a ticket, as an earnest *bona fide* intention to use the baths."[142] He railed against the use of opera glasses or telescopes, a familiar trope, to view the bathers. "These," he went on to write, "not the actual bathers and swimmers (who are too much occupied with more wholesome employment), are the ones to be punished." "Common Sense" ended his letter with the familiar phrase that was used to defend nude bathing: "Honi soit qui mal y pense" (Evil be to him who evil thinks).[143] Supporters argued against the effort to attach shame to appearances both in and out of bathing suits. The problem, once again, was in the eye of the beholder. The camera was not included as a threat to decency because it was not expected to be on the beach in 1883.[144]

The saggy bathing suit represented a loss of male privilege and a challenge to middle-class masculinity. A "Disappointed Swimmer" complained that "prior to the erection of the 'Baths' the strip of land on which they stand was about the only place in the vicinity of Toronto where perspiring humanity could take a cooling plunge during the dog days, without a great expenditure of time and labour."[145] "Swimmer" was speaking from a position of privilege: the perspiring humanity would certainly have been male, and reaching the east end of the island prior to the construction of the baths required a boat or a stroll over from ferry docks in the centre of the island. But since the construction of the baths, he argued, "a constant reforming (?) process has been in operation. Every new regulation has been against swimmers and in favour of mere idlers and spectators."[146] Even "Decency and Morality," the writer who demanded secure space for women bathers, had sympathy for the loss of male bathing space: "I could enjoy equally with your correspondent a good plunge in the olden style off the point," but such a plunge, he added, would have to be behind a fence and did not change the debate over how one might dress at the mixed-gender Wiman Baths.[147]

Pushing vernacular bathing off the waterfront had impacted working-class people, but on the island it was predominantly middle-class voices that wept at the loss of privilege and argued for the preservation of a "genuine 'country swim.'" The Wiman Baths formalized changes that had begun in the 1870s. As a *Globe* column argued, "Liberty is given to go into the water from the Island beach, within certain limits, but even that liberty is being narrowed day by day. The Island is becoming more than ever a place of resort, so that now there is hardly any quarter of it where the privacy of the bather or swimmer is respected. Even on the lake side a man cannot doff his clothes at any reasonable hour of the day for the half dozen or more literary females who make this a place of resort to read the latest novel."[148] Do not feel too sorry for the men. For all the complaints, the male propensity to promenade along the docks in bathing suits and occupy space unfettered at the baths suggests how male privilege remained intact.

Women at the Beach

The bathing suit was not a new imposition for women: they had lost the ability to bathe nude in public settings in the eighteenth century.[149] Instead women and men debated whether their new bathing suits were modest enough and how women should be appraised at the beach. The three daughters described in the *Globe* article fretted about being seen in bathing suits. There were complaints that the women's suits at the baths were ugly and that the designs might be acceptable to European or American eyes, but would not be accepted by Toronto ladies, who were still adjusting to public bathing.[150] Women's bathing dresses in 1883 contained the body from neck to ankle but in the water women were not always as clothed as we might think. Captain W.D. Andrews taught women how to swim and recommended that a woman's legs and arms be as unencumbered as possible. But he acknowledged that in the social setting of the baths, women had to wear dresses about their legs and then remove them while they were in the water.[151] During lessons that is precisely how it was handled, with students stripping down in the water. During casual bathing the dresses stayed on.

The Wiman Baths demonstrate the challenge women faced using a nineteenth-century beach. They were subjected to a relentless male gaze that pushed them, or at least was expected to push them, into the water or the change room. Putting on a bathing suit and lingering on the beach was considered inappropriate. Even Mulvany's description of men and women chatting at the baths assumed they were doing so after getting changed out of their bathing suits.[152] The *Mail* described the discomfort of a "timid girl" bathing near the bathhouse and looking up to discover she had an audience who, as she slipped into deeper water to avoid their gaze, "formed a line from the steps to the dressing room door in order to get a good view of her as she passed in."[153] The girl stayed in the water and began to shiver and cry before "slowly it dawned upon some of the cloudy male intellects that there might be in the world a young lady who would object to being made a panorama or a variety show of, and several slunk away." Eventually, the rest followed, and the girl was able to leave the water. "This is said to be rule at the baths," the *Mail* lamented. "Men may bathe without attracting notice, but no sooner do the girls take to the water than the seats and sidewalks are filled with men who vulgarly stare at them . . . to be stared at by a crowd, and to run the gauntlet of hundreds of male eyes coming from and going to the dressing rooms, is an ordeal which few women have the courage to undergo."[154]

Age mattered. The *Globe* took its own gaze to the beach and wrote approvingly of young women playing in the water and disapprovingly of a "forty or thereabouts" woman who, in the newspaper's estimate, was inappropriately drawing attention to herself. The critique suggests a hierarchy of who might justly draw the gaze of men. But even the *Globe* expressed sympathy for women who had to "make the awful rush which *must* be made" to the change room at the end of the bath.[155]

The trusteeship fielded calls to roll back the culture of display by adding physical infrastructure to hide women as they entered the water. But given that the letters were coming from men, the suggestions seem proscriptive for women being seen and for the men looking at them. A letter writer in

1883, offering a description that seems more suitable for managing livestock, suggested the walkway from the bathhouse to the nearby pond be fenced in, "making as it were a partial shoot from the building, and thereby protecting ladies from the public view until they were in the water."[156] The same idea was still being pitched two years later. A writer in 1885 complained, "The lady who does not wish to be seen in her bathing costume, or to see men in the scant garments which are supposed to be quite proper for the bath, should have her modesty, prejudice, or whatever you choose to call it, respected."[157]

The bathing suit eroticized men and women: turning them both into objects to be appraised and scrutinized. The script we are handed by these male-dominated sources suggests women were expected to cower under scrutiny. It is likely not all of them did. We can read the behaviour of the *Globe*'s "forty or thereabouts" woman as an act of resistance: perhaps she was trying to draw attention or perhaps she was simply enjoying herself and ignoring the effort to impose shame on her. Patriarchy ensured men had easier access to and control over the public space of the beach.[158] And yet, complaints from men, used to bathing in the nude, suggest how even they bristled at the appraisal and the need to take on a new system of performance when they were at the baths.

For all the excitement generated by the Wiman Baths, their popularity was short-lived. The isolation and vulnerable environment on the eastern end of the island worked against their survival. In 1883, at the height of the baths' popularity, the federal government stepped in to fortify the island's southeastern shoreline with a 2,000-metre-long breakwater intended to keep storms from breaching the island. The new breakwater was six feet high and forty feet deep with a double wall of sheet piling along the shoreline, backed by brush and rock. Wiman Baths customers could still swim in the bay, but the breakwater created a hard edge along the southeastern side of the island and effectively ended swimming in the lake.[159] The island's industrial role of protecting the integrity of the bay trumped its recreational role.

And Withrow's first view had also been correct; the baths needed to be in a busy location because a bathing system predicated on display needed to draw a crowd to create the experience. Hanlan's Point amusement park was already drawing people away from the Wiman Baths by the mid-1880s, and by the turn of the century the integration of amusement park, beach, and ferry links had made the western end of the island the far more popular space.[160]

Figure 3.7. Turner's Baths, complete with a slide and docks, at Hanlan's Point, c. 1909. Image courtesy of City of Toronto Archives.

The *Island Guide* still flagged the Wiman Baths as an option in 1894 but lamented that they were not in a "more frequented location" and referred to the eastern point as a space where "melancholy souls" might lounge on the breakwater.[161] The baths had shut down by 1902 and were turned over to the city. The main structure survived as apartments into the 1950s, but the change room expansion had already fallen into disrepair.[162]

The "Summer Idyll" Lingers

Middle-class indulgence coupled with environmental contingencies ensured the juxtaposition of nude and clothed bathing on the western side of the island into the twentieth century. Unwin had not bothered to survey the western sandbar—the location of today's Hanlan's Point beach—in 1868. The sandbar had been too insubstantial to bother with. But whereas lake currents chewed away at the eastern side of the island, on the western side the same currents deposited sand on the western sandbar and turned what had been a marginal space into a substantial part of the island.[163] When the city finally discussed dividing the western sandbar into private leaseholds in 1883 its role as a vernacular bathing space was so ingrained that the decision was made to lease the space for bathing instead.[164] It was a decision that took into account the establishment of Island Park and the view that the sandbar should be reserved for public use.[165] In the spring of 1884 Peter McIntyre, a steamboat agent, leased 500 feet of lakefront to build a bath house on the sandbar.[166] The baths would shortly be taken over by Mr. and Mrs. John Turner and become known as Turner's Baths. In practice it was Mrs. Turner who handled the day-to-day operations of the baths; she continued after the death of her husband, and the name stuck even after she left the business in 1907.[167]

Turner's Baths' proximity to Hanlan's Point and good ferry links guaranteed their steady clientele.[168] But unlike the proprietors of the Wiman Baths, Mrs. Turner had little influence over the social tone on the western end of the island.[169] There was no prominent financial backer, trusteeship of men, or committee of women driving the baths' performance. They were not a novelty; by the mid-1880s men and women were bathing publicly in the lagoon at Centre Island, bathing stations had opened at other beaches within the city, and a legal structure for dealing with bathhouses had emerged.[170] The lack of novelty meant that when Turner complained about activities around her establishment her complaints were greeted with a shrug. Turner could only control bathing in the fenced-in area around her bath house.[171]

The challenge Turner faced was that nude bathing was long established and sedimented into the social landscape of the western sandbar.[172] She lacked the financial and social clout to drive it out. Male Torontonians and their city council advocates were not ready to let the privilege of nude bathing disappear. So the baths and a nude—or at least semi-nude because some of the bathers may have been wearing trunks—beach existed in awkward tandem on the western sandbar. Turner argued, nearly every summer, against "men and boys bathing in near proximities of the bathers without proper bathing suits, thereby preventing ladies from using the baths and thus injuring her business."[173] In 1896, she went even further to argue that "her former customers are leaving owing to the increasing habit of nude bathing."[174] This challenge was not unique to Turner or Toronto; in Australia bath operators made similar complaints about nude bathers who were bathing for free outside their commercial operations.[175] The obvious concern was that the impropriety of nude bathing was driving customers away. But nude bathing was also cheaper: no need to buy or rent a bathing suit and pay for a locker at a bathhouse when you could simply strip down and dive in. And, as Turner suggested, nude bathing may have been increasing in popularity next to her establishment as the sandbar crystallized as a space where nude bathing could still be practised. In other words, the western sandbar drew people looking to *consciously* step out of the commercial and regulatory framework of clothed bathing. In that sense, the sandbar really was a forebear of today's clothing-optional Hanlan's Point. However, we cannot draw a direct line between the modern beach and its nineteenth-century ancestor: nude bathing would be driven from the space and not return until the mid-twentieth century.

At the beginning of the twentieth century, however, the city was content to leave the boys alone. The city ignored Turner or tried to mitigate her concerns in a way that allowed vernacular bathing to continue. In the summer of 1890 the city fenced off "a portion of the sandbar at Hanlan's Point, about 500 feet from Turner's baths, for bathing purposes."[176] In 1891, facing more complaints, the property committee again put up a fence and announced "the public could bathe from the shore on the north side, but anyone so doing on the south side without suitable bathing suits would be prosecuted."[177] The ambivalence towards policing nude bathers on the island went hand in hand with the decision to loosen restrictions on bathing without "a bathing dress" in defined spaces on the eastern and western sides of the city.[178] The vernacular bathing space was enshrined in the city's bylaws in 1894 to specifically include a 200-foot stretch of beach, to be fenced in, 1,500 feet north of Turner's Baths.[179]

The media played the role of indulgent father throughout the discussion about nude bathing next to Turner's. The *Globe* announced the protected bathing space with the headline "Where Bathers May Enjoy Themselves Without Molestations."[180] It was a description that continued the masculine view that wearing a bathing suit was a "molestation" of the bathing experience. The *Toronto Island Guide* pointed out in 1894 that "proper bathing dressing covering the body from the neck to the knees" was required for bathing in the city's waters, but noted areas on the eastern and western side of the city could still be used for bathing without dress and that "a part of the

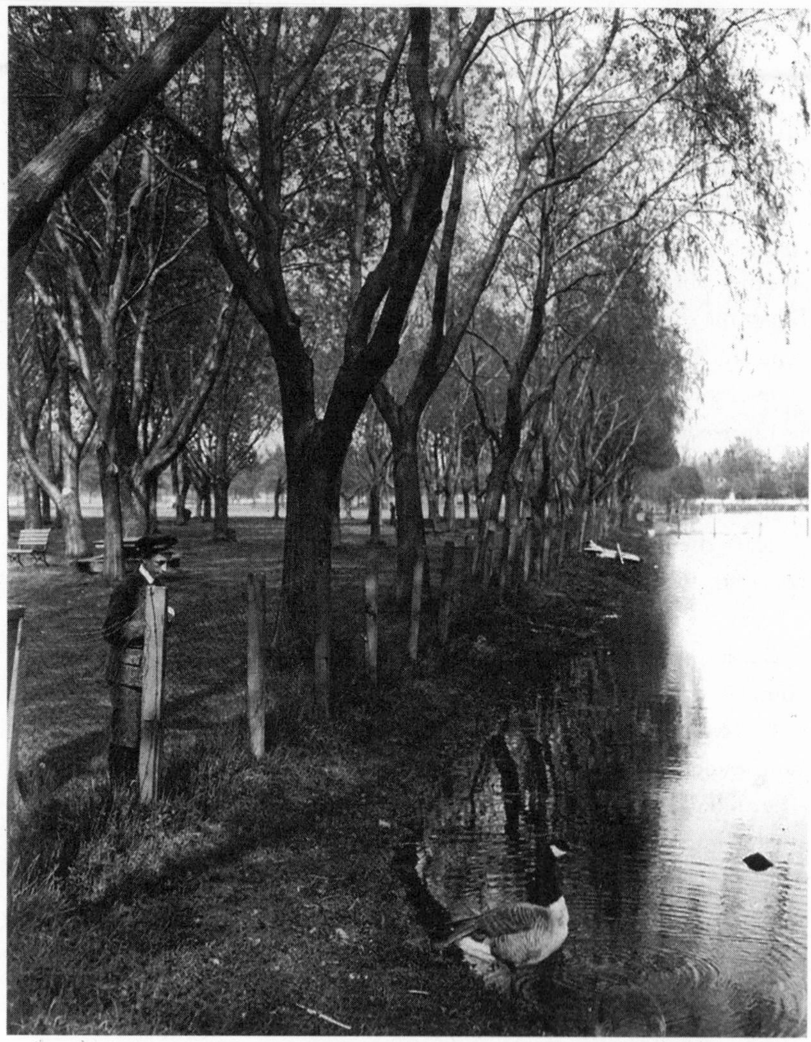

Figure 3.8. Fence along Long Pond, 1907. Fences helped keep people from crossing the once porous boundary between land and water on Toronto Island. Image courtesy of City of Toronto Archives.

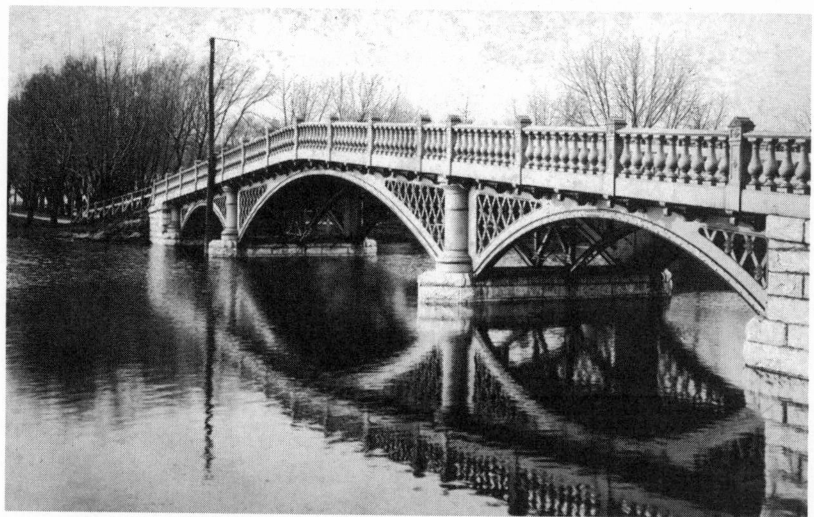

Figure 3.9. Long Pond Bridge, 1907. Long Pond became a space for sightseeing or boating, but was no longer available for bathing. Image courtesy of City of Toronto Archives.

sandbar is being railed off for boys."[181] The vernacular bathing experience was being consciously preserved within the urban environment. And in 1896, the *Evening Star* supported unrestricted bathing, arguing there is "no more suitable or out-of-the-way place than on the narrow spit of land on which is located Turner's Baths."[182] The arrival of the free bathing station on the north end of the sandbar in 1897 formalized that space as a nude bathing enclave; though officially only for boys.[183] While men were not supposed to be part of the free bathing spaces, some younger men did attend and others continued to bathe nearby.

Erasing the Margin

The mixture of bathing systems on the island shifted definitively in 1906 when police swept through in the middle of July and fined twenty-six people for bathing without a swimsuit on the western sandbar.[184] A growing population, and the growing expectation that the beach and the bathing suit were the social norm, made increased policing of nude bathing inevitable, but that the shift happened when it did was related to three factors: the weather, the shifting environment of the western sandbar, and the ongoing effort to impose structure on the porous island. Tensions heated up with the weather: in 1906 the temperature soared in July and stayed warm throughout August. Torontonians were heading to the lake to escape the heat.[185] Meanwhile, Lake Ontario's currents continued to dump sand on the western sandbar and by 1906 created a new sandbar to the west of the island.[186] For bathers it meant "the water has become so shallow that swimming is impossible unless one were to wade a great distance out."[187] The new sandbar was transient and disappeared the next year, but in 1906 its presence ensured that people bathing on the western sandbar were exposed as they made their way into the water. The city also complained men were "taking sun baths" on the sandbar and board of control vice-chairman William Peyton Hubbard, in the face of a letter from a defensive bather, William C. Fox, groused that bathing should be removed entirely from the sandbar because "They carry on disgracefully there."[188] Sunbathing was still a novel activity at the beginning of the twentieth century and bathers were being called out for lingering on the beach in their bathing suits at Kew Beach that same summer. [189] It would not be until the 1920s and 1930s that getting a suntan started to become part of an acceptable beach experience.[190] But in 1906 lingering on the beach and doing so in the nude would certainly have raised eyebrows. The fact that there had been a legal space for nude bathing on the sandbar was not discussed in 1906, but the nude spaces on the mainland were tightened up that summer as well, with nude bathing, in a throwback to the old rules, restricted to dusk and dawn, between 9:00 p.m. and 5:00 a.m., as opposed to the more lenient 5:00 p.m. to 9:00 a.m. period set in the 1890s.[191]

Finally, bathers were caught in the broader effort to make the unruly environment of the island visible and governable.[192] Leaseholders had already made their way onto the western sandbar semi-officially, but in 1906 their lots were measured and documented.[193] The city stepped in to regulate what was allowed on the sandbar and added washrooms for the use of "campers," as the cabin owners were called.[194] There were calls for more policing on the western sandbar and better lighting on the bridge that stretched across to it from Hanlan's Point.[195] Wolfgang Schivelbusch has discussed how light became an industrial product in the eighteenth century and how new streetlights helped illuminate dark city streets at night.[196] Schivelbusch argues the innovation allowed the leisure class, those with time and money, to engage in recreation at night, but streetlights were also a form of social control, stretching into spaces that had once been hidden in darkness.[197] On the island there were calls for lights to be turned on earlier in the season and left on until midnight rather than 11 p.m., to allow for the appropriate recreational, and monitored, use of the island.[198] The effort to stretch lighting out to the western sandbar went hand in hand with efforts to extend social control onto the sandbar.[199]

The entire island was incrementally transformed into parkland or leaseholds. The porous landscape bathers had immersed themselves in during the 1870s was transformed by filling in lagoons to create dry land or digging them out to create deeper channels. The result of this regimentation was that some lagoons were fenced off to prevent people from bathing or stumbling into them (see Figure 3.8). Long Pond had been a popular bathing space in the late nineteenth century but it was progressively deepened to serve as a channel for watercraft. Bathing in the space was discouraged and finally outlawed entirely as being too dangerous, a hazard that was, of course, created by the city's own actions.[200]

We do not hear about nude bathing on the western sandbar in the decades after 1906. It likely endured. The free bathing station on the sandbar remained for males only. Hugh Garner fondly recalled racing across the sandbar as a boy and shedding his clothes to bathe nude, a practice which continued into the 1920s.[201] However, while the provision for nude bathing in the designated space remained on the city's books until 1930, the lack of complaints and charges against people after 1906 suggests if men were still bathing in the nude, they were doing so in insufficient numbers to draw attention to themselves.[202] Construction of the island airport in the 1930s likely disrupted any nude bathing that remained on the island but, as discussed in the epilogue, a new generation of nude bathers claimed Hanlan's Point after the 1950s.

Anthony Giddens suggests "place ballets" of social activity become embedded in the physical environment and constitute a locality.[203] And so it had been on the western sandbar where the longstanding public use of the area for nude male bathing had held on even as a new clothed heterosocial system of bathing was emerging. But the nude bathing space depended on the repetition of that activity and on the public's complicity in looking away. Pictures of boys bathing at the free bathing site on the western sandbar taken by the

Globe in 1897, as it endorsed the city's new free bathing program, were a rare moment when a nude bathing space was photographed on the island.[204] By the beginning of the twentieth century nude bathing on the island was finally becoming both an oddity and a spectacle when it did occur, which led to its being driven out.

Spectatorship was even viewed with suspicion at the Wiman Baths. Despite the efforts to promote it as a resort space, men and women were still learning how to be looked at. That ambivalence helps explain why the space has been erased from Toronto's visual memory, save for images of the bathing structure itself taken long after its heyday. There was little expectation before the 1890s that people would or could be taking pictures of people. The camera is a powerful tool: it creates a "visual culture" that valorizes moments that have

Figure 3.10. Hanlan's Point beach on a Sunday, 1911. Image courtesy of City of Toronto Archives.

been photographed and erases objects that are not photographed.[205] When "Common Sense" ran off a list of optical instruments that he did not want in use at the Wiman Baths in 1883 he did not include cameras because there was little expectation they would be turned towards the beach.[206] Similarly, while the *Toronto Island Guide* was filled with photographs of buildings and promenading spaces, the only image of bathers in the 1894 publication was an artistic rendition—not a photograph—of properly suited young girls.

This lack of a visual culture to define and defend nude and even early clothed bathing spaces like the Wiman Baths on the island meant that when Toronto photographer William James started snapping pictures in the early twentieth century he was able to overwrite the island as a space used by nude male bathers, transforming it with images of bathing suit–clad boys and girls bathing together at the beach. One place ballet seamlessly superseded another. The rambunctious crowds that James displays playing on the shoreline are clothed, with no hint of nudity. By the time James snapped his pictures of people at Hanlan's Point, the social prohibition against taking pictures of people at the beach had declined: James was able to move into spaces and moments in a way that would have been frowned upon just a few years before.[207] The island's beaches were also included on postcards, suggesting how they were one part of a replicable and coherent international language of recreation spaces.[208] The replicable nature of the beach was not lost on contemporaries; as one writer noted to a female friend on a postcard of Centre Island: "This picture is like Buffalo. Do you remember when we were swimming along Niagara Street . . . ?"[209] The camera helped erase the nude bathers from the visual legacy of Toronto Island.[210]

Popular culture and the full embrace of heterosocial amusement space played a role in the erasure of vernacular bathing as well. Rather than a space on the margin, the western sandbar was brought into a direct relationship with the Hanlan's Point Amusement Park. Hanlan's Point ran a series of advertisements in 1910 flogging its "Delicious bathing, delightful temperature," noting, "There is no better nor safer bathing spot than off the sandbar."[211] Hanlan's reflected Coney Island and Blackpool in marrying the beach with the amusement park. Similarly, Scarboro Beach, a new amusement park on the city's eastern shoreline, opened in 1907 and advertised its beach and bathing facilities as a key part of the experience.[212] The beach was not a novelty any more. It carried a coherent and consistent set of cultural markers, and by the early twentieth century Torontonians knew them well.[213]

4

THE DON RIVER AND THE BATHING BOY

Albert Petrie, age nineteen, slipped in behind the Rosedale Train Station to bathe in the Don River on Saturday, 14 June 1913. An orphan, Petrie lived in a boarding house run by Mrs. George Thom at 63 St. James Avenue, just west of the Don River, and worked at Hope's Bird Store on Queen Street West. He had joined thirteen-year-old Gordon Thom and a number of other boys and young men for a swim. On that warm spring day, Petrie stepped into a deep hole in the stream bed and slipped beneath the water.

"Albert was used to the water and we never expected any trouble until we saw him go down," Thom told the *Star*, suggesting how Petrie was expected to *know* the river and have a feel for where its dangers lurked. "We were frightened and yelled out to the brakeman on a train that was passing. He ran down, only taking off his shoes, and dived three or four times. At last he got the body, and he and another brakeman and two other men worked over the body for a long time."[1]

The image of a rail worker racing to the river, kicking off his shoes, and diving in to rescue a drowning teenager is probably the best example one might find of the melding of industry and recreation in Toronto.[2] The Don River was a borderlands space, the ragged edge between nature and development. The clanging of trains mingled with the sound of rushing water and the screech of brakes signalled trouble along the river.

This chapter will demonstrate how the distinctive physical and social environment of the Don River between 1890 and 1930 fetishized the swimming hole as a pre-modern oasis and enabled and prolonged vernacular bathing. While the formal organization of the beach was beginning to dominate the rest of Toronto's waterfront and its riparian spaces, the Don River crystallized as a space where boys, and men, might still bathe in the nude. It is within the Don that vernacular bathing demonstrates its properties most clearly. "Vernacular," as I have suggested, refers to an experience or a language that is produced within the local environment. The vernacular bathing space could be rendered knowable only through the acquisition of an embodied sense of space and practice and a learned physical routine.[3] Bathers needed to understand how the Don River behaved and the hybrid, industrial and natural, riparian environment that surrounded them.[4] Sensory stimuli and perception were critical for the assessment of danger in murky waters. The soundscape alerted swimmers to the threat of trains but also the potential assistance of industrial workers.[5] People bathed in a world that echoed, stank, and tasted of the nineteenth century, and they shared their experiences to create a collective knowledge of the spaces.[6] This embodied experience created distinct "locales" in the Don River, defined by ballets of movement and social activity within them.[7]

I am borrowing Don River historian Jennifer Bonnell's description of "the middle Don" as a hybrid space between industry and nature, where "old and new political economies overlapped."[8] But while Bonnell argues that the Don shifted "from a central position in the geography and material life of the early settlement, to a polluted and reviled periphery in the latter half of the nineteenth century,"[9] I suggest that the presence of boys bathing created a nostalgic gloss over the middle Don that cloaked the river's hazards. How Torontonians thought about nature and the city is key to understanding this space. Nature, as William Cronon has argued, was seen by turn-of-the-century North Americans as invigorating, in contrast to the "confining, false, and artificial" urban setting.[10] City and nature—humanity and nature—became a dualism.[11] But the Don—mingling mill dams, railroad tracks, and flowing waters—was a borderland space that confounded efforts to imagine a binary.[12]

The middle Don is both a place and a temporal moment, focused between 1890 and 1930, within which a vibrant vernacular bathing culture was able to survive. The time period is framed by Toronto's decision to channel the lower Don River in the 1880s—which drove recreational users out of that portion of the river, and yet enabled bathing in the middle and upper reaches—and the 1930s, when growing levels of pollution drove bathers out of the middle Don. Geographically, the middle Don stretched north from Riverdale Park and the newly channelled lower Don to roughly the forks of the river a few kilometres upstream. It straddled the boundary between the city of Toronto and the adjacent county of York, and was within reach of city dwellers and workers. Industry was close enough that a brakeman could be called on to rescue Albert Petrie in 1913. While nude bathing was driven out of most public spaces in Toronto in the early twentieth century, it lingered in the middle Don into the 1920s, enabled by working-class independence, middle-class indulgence, and the hybrid environment of the Don.

The bathing boy held the middle Don together as a "natural" environment, lending his discursive innocence to the river to help it override its industrial nature and sanction it as moral heterosexual terrain.[13] It's within the Don River that we see most clearly how Toronto's middle class was entranced by the presence of the youthful bodies that cavorted in the river and crafted them as "folk" figures and a "romantic antithesis" to the urban and industrial life.[14] This folk-making enabled bathing to continue, but constrained who could claim a space in the river: they needed to be perpetually boys and perpetually innocent. The Don was also an opportunity for middle-class men in the early twentieth century to vicariously relive their childhood experiences and the embodied sense of masculinity that came with them.[15] For working-class boys and men, bathing within the Don was considered a key moment of identity formation, to be held up in contrast to the effete middle-class bathing spaces. The Don River thus was a space where gender and sexuality were performed, produced, and verified.[16] This performance was not, as Judith Butler has taken pains to point out, a simple matter of a subject "acting" like a man or woman, but rather one's gender, one's subjectivity, being produced through the discourse that names it.[17]

The construction of bathing boys as pre-modern folk flattened the identities of people in the Don River, turning people in the river into a collection of "boys." But the Don was never so simple. Men who drowned in the river

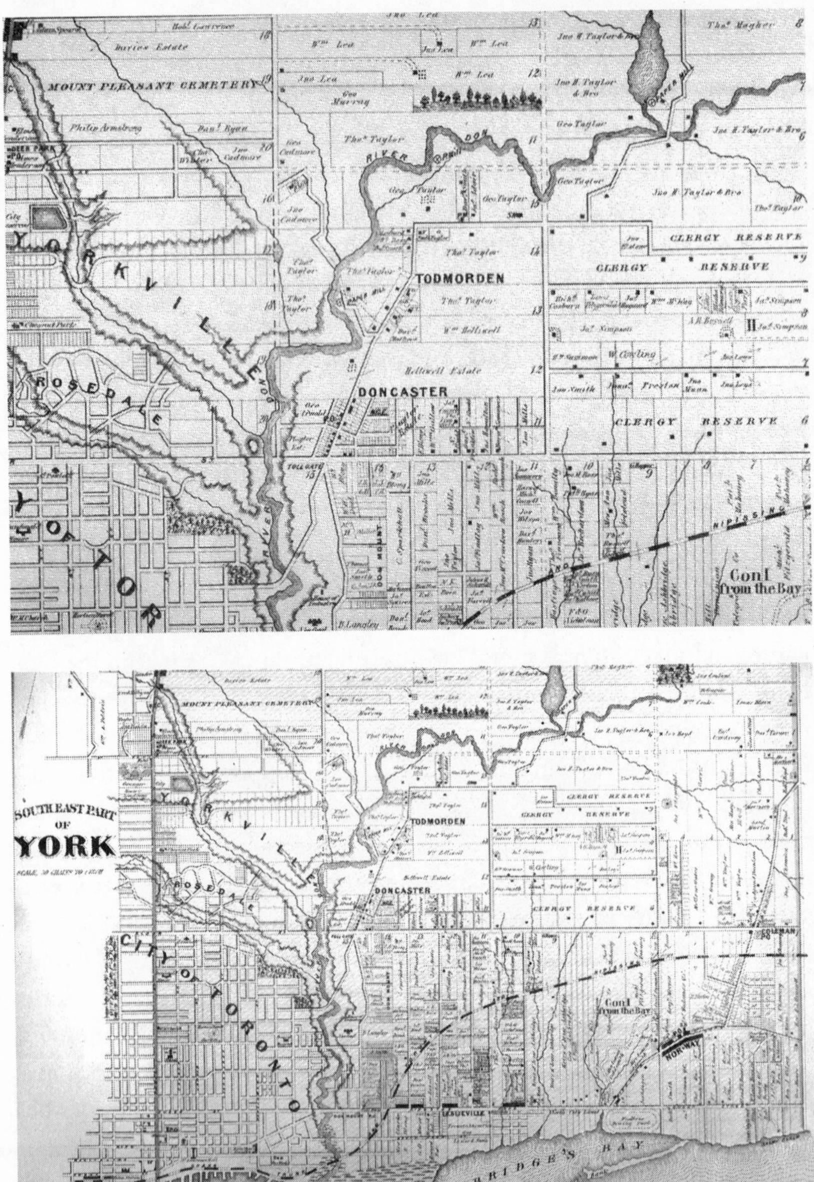

Figure 4.1. The middle Don stretches between Riverdale Park in the south and the forks of the Don in the north.

Figure 4.2. The principal branches of the Don River and land ownership in the valley, 1878.

were predominantly working class. But the conscious effort by working-class writers such as Hugh Garner to see bathing in the Don as a working-class experience erased the middle-class boys that used the city's popular free bathing station. The fixation on boys erased women and girls from the valley. Females appear in documentary evidence of Don River drownings only in the 1920s, but that does not mean females were not in and around the river. Women could recall bathing in the river as children and men, recalling their boyhood, could remember that at times girls joined them. The valorization of the boyhood experience of the Don also relied on editing men out of the picture and erasing the mixed-age groups that had bathed in the river.[18]

In the discourse surrounding the Don River we can see efforts to create the bathing boy as an emblem of nostalgia. Cartoons, pictures, and commentary worked to distill its bathers into the "essential character" of an embodied relationship with an idyllic swimming hole, even though the tangible experience of being in the Don was less romantic.[19] Photographers, such as William James, used pictures to weave a narrative of youthful innocence.[20] James locked in the character of the river and the bodies within it and promoted the idea that Canadian identity was joined to nature.[21] Autobiographies from Gordon Sinclair and Garner, and regional histories from George Rust-D'Eye and Colleen Kelly, portrayed bathing as a working-class experience.[22] Toronto's newspapers used bathers in the Don to signify health or the changing of the season, and as the antithesis to the Sunnyside boardwalk. Skinny-dipping in the Don became a regional myth, immortalized in print and pictures, and reflected in government documents that, as late as 1997, benchmarked the potential swimmability of the river as a mark of its health.[23]

Setting: Creating the Middle Don

The Don River is just thirty-eight kilometres long and flows south from the Oak Ridges Moraine, a hilly and sandy soiled legacy of the last ice age that divides the drainage basin of Lake Ontario from Lake Simcoe. Glaciation around the Great Lakes has given the Don a deep valley, which defines its riparian zone and its influence on the urban environment.[24] The river has three principal tributaries, which meet seven kilometres north of Lake Ontario: the East and West Don and Taylor-Massey Creek. Never large, the Don carried more water 100 years ago than it does today; the steady

Figure 4.3. Castle Frank, from the Don Valley, c. 1796. After a drawing by Elizabeth Simcoe, 1880. Image courtesy of Toronto Public Library.

removal of tree coverage and drainage of marshes has reduced the river's base flow, while urbanization has left it vulnerable to flash floods.[25]

Early settlers describe an idyllic river. Elizabeth Simcoe, wife of John Graves Simcoe, Upper Canada's first lieutenant governor, romanticized walks and canoe trips along the river in her diary and in sketches from 1793 to 1795. The Simcoes built Castle Frank, a summer retreat, to overlook the valley. As Simcoe, who drew many sketches of the Don River, notes in her diary, "I take no sketches of a place I never wish to recollect."[26] Toronto clergyman and historian Henry Scadding was born in England in 1813 but spent his formative years after 1821 along the river and describes how, "in the spring and summer, a pull up the Don, while yet its banks were in their primeval state was something to be enjoyed. After passing certain potasheries and distilleries that at an early period were erected a short distance northward of the bridge, the meadow land at the base of the hills began to widen out."[27] From there a paddler entered a wooded wonderland.

The lower reaches of the river were being industrialized in Scadding's earliest recollections. European beliefs that Ashbridge's Bay marsh at the mouth of the Don was an unhealthy source of miasma and ague pushed residential development away from the river but opened the door for breweries, distilleries, tanneries, and candle- and soap-makers, industries that were too loud, smelly, or waste-intensive for other areas of the city.[28] Industry shifted to institutional uses at Carlton Street, with the Don Jail and the House of Industry, a workhouse and residence of last resort for the poor, on the east bank, and the Necropolis and St. James Cemetery on the west.[29] The lower Don was the only section of the river that could be bridged economically, which meant traffic and the eyes that came with it were focused there.[30] Toronto's civic boundary stopped at Bloor Street until 1883, and thereafter the city pulled away from the river—and its unindustrialized portions—as it expanded northward.[31] This truncated relationship with the Don helped ensure that it was seen, as Bonnell describes it, as "polluted, dangerous, and disease-ridden" and industrial.[32] The water was already being referred to in the press as "questionable" in 1876. The *History of Toronto and County of York*, published in 1885, describes the Don as a "formerly a picturesque stream, but it has greatly diminished in size of late years and has been shorn of much of its ancient glory."[33]

The lower Don was a popular bathing space, despite its industrial nature, in the 1870s and 1880s.[34] However, development around the river, roads passing over it, and recreational use by boaters ensured there was little opportunity for the bathers to hide from the eyes around them. The *Globe* complained of an "infestation" of bathers near the Eastern Avenue bridge, making it unsafe "for any female to go near either in a boat or along the banks" in 1880. We can read the complaint another way: women moved along the Don and did see people bathing.[35]

The Don Improvement Project clarified the muddy relationship between bodies, the river, and industry in the 1880s by giving the lower Don an industrial form. Inspired by similar projects in New York and Cleveland, the project had four goals: to improve the sanitary condition of the river, to make the lower Don navigable, to create a corridor for the railway companies, and to create new land for industry.[36] The once serpentine lower Don would be given "as near a perfect straightening as the high banks would permit."[37]

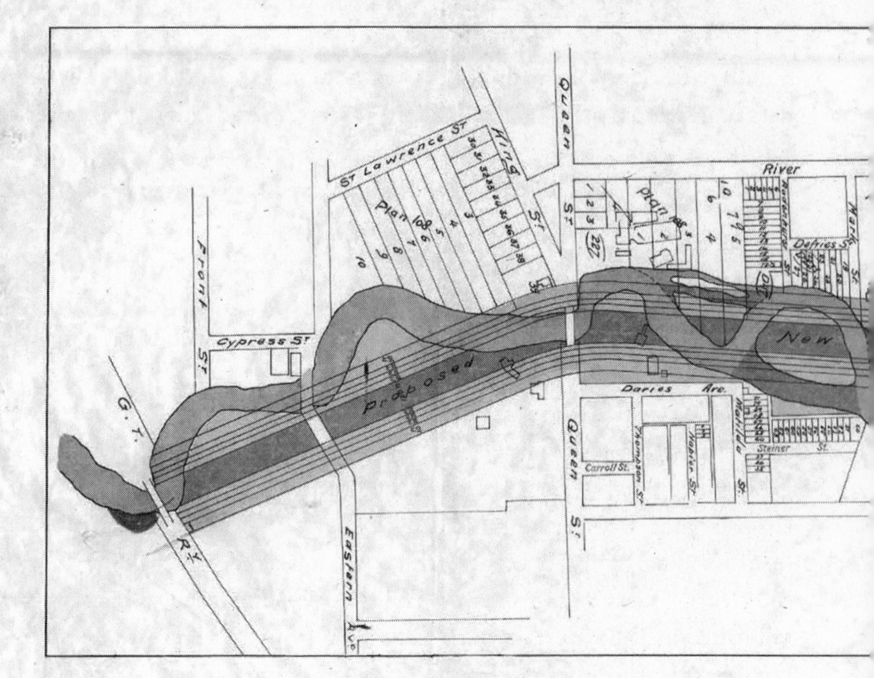

Channelization fulfilled few of the city's goals. Yes, the river was straightened and new land was created for industrial use. But a shallow channel, brought on by budget constraints, combined with low bridges, kept ships from navigating the new route.[38] Rail companies used the easier grade of the valley floor and banks of the new channel as a corridor into the city, but doing so hemmed in the river and ensured it could never be used for shipping.[39] Promoters had argued that straightening the river would increase its flow and allow it to draw pollution—a "cloacal effect"—out of the land around it.[40] But that logic meant the lower Don was treated as an open sewer, and indeed Torontonians voted down a plan in 1886 intended to reroute sewage away from the river, thus sealing its fate.[41] As the water in the lower Don soured there were discussions about dredging or enclosing the river.[42]

The Don Improvement Project severed the river's recreational relationship with Lake Ontario, yet that break also enabled the creation of a vibrant

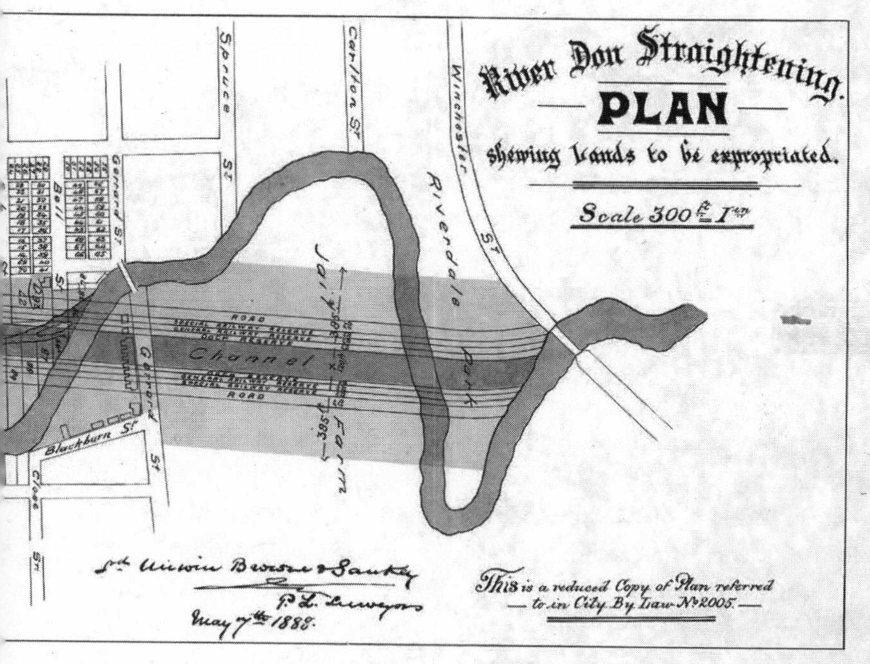

Figure 4.4. River Don Straightening Plan, 1886. Image courtesy of City of Toronto Archives.

vernacular bathing culture in the middle Don. Few people bathed south of Winchester Street and Riverdale Park after 1890.[43] The Don Rowing Club moved to Ashbridge's Bay.[44] Paddlers had little urge to come up the river and compete with bathers for space; bathers felt little inclination to look to the lower reaches of the river when they swam. The project isolated the middle Don and turned it into a space that most bathers reached on foot. While people bathing on Toronto's waterfront or in the less industrialized Humber River had to compete with other recreational users, they could claim the middle Don as their own.

The Hybrid Geography of the Middle Don

Development ended bathing in the lower Don, but when we look north we find a series of blended natural and semi-industrial bathing sites.[45] Some, like "Dunnett's swimming hole," in the West Don River near today's York University's Glendon Campus, were intimate, others such as Clay Banks on the eastern Don were large enough and popular enough to hold dozens of bathers.[46] In smaller creeks, inventive youth created their own ponds, as Don River conservationist and writer Charles Sauriol recalled doing on a scouting trip to Taylor-Massey Creek: "On that occasion we worked like beavers to build a dam of stones, branches and clay, and raised the creek waters about three or four feet which provided the happy experience of immersing oneself in water that was clear, cold and invigorating; the first time I was able to splash in water other than in a bath tub."[47]

Bathing spaces formed at the confluence of natural and constructed landmarks and created a human geography around the river.[48] They retained their popularity over generations, suggesting how their use became embedded in the social landscape of the city.[49] The Winchester Street Bridge, north of Riverdale Park, was the beachhead for bathing; it was popular enough that when the city debated extending restrictions against nude bathing across Toronto in 1879, the draft bylaw specifically excluded the Don River north of the Winchester Bridge.[50] (Previously restrictions against nude bathing during the day were limited to a section of the central waterfront.) And while the Don was included when the city updated its bylaw in 1880 to formally require the neck-to-knee bathing dress for daytime bathing, policing the river north of Winchester was not a high priority.[51] The Winchester bathing area, crowded on hot summer days, was easily visible from the bridge and intimately connected with the brickyards and urban environment. The water was deep enough for diving.[52] Sandy Banks was located near the present-day Bloor Street Viaduct, though it long predated the structure. In the 1870s Scadding listed the site as a "favourite bathing-place for boys, with a clean gravelly bottom, and a current somewhat swift";[53] 80 years later Sauriol noted it as well, suggesting how these bathing spaces were imprinted within Toronto's imagination. Yet even long-established sites such as Sandy Banks could be flagged as safe one year and dangerous the next, given the unpredictable environment of the Don.[54]

Millponds were among the most popular bathing spaces. The mill dams, ponds, and races used to drive the mills created micro-bathing environments. Historian W.H. Pearson recalled the charm of swimming in a millpond in Castle Frank Creek, a small tributary to the Don, in his 1914 history, and

Figure 4.5. "Dunnett's swimming hole": West Don River, c. 1900, slightly west of Bayview Avenue. Image courtesy of Toronto Public Library.

Figure 4.6. Winchester Street Bridge over the Don River, as reconstructed, 1909. Photo taken in connection with the construction of the Bloor Street Viaduct, 1910. Image courtesy of City of Toronto Archives.

credits the pond's warm temperature, writing, "This was a glorious bathing-place for the boys, because of its seclusion and the water being much warmer than that of the bay." [55] Today, Todmorden Mills hosts a museum and heritage village, but in 1795 it was known as Skinner's Mill and had been commissioned directly by Lieutenant Governor John Graves Simcoe to supply timber for York. The millpond was already a popular space for bathing in the 1830s when owner William Helliwell recorded bathing there in his diary.[56] By the late nineteenth century the Taylor family controlled the mills and most of the land in the middle Don. The Taylors rode an explosion in literacy and population growth that saw the publication of 172 newspapers across Ontario by 1870.[57] The family owned 4,000 acres along the river but did little to stop people from crossing their property to access the Don.[58] They also owned the mill at Todmorden and the Toronto Brickworks, which was acquired in the 1880s, and operated paper mills near Beechwood Drive and on the western Don, just north of the forks.[59] The three paper mills were known, appropriately, as the lower, middle, and upper mills, and each of them was a popular swimming space.[60] Even after the mills ceased to run on water, the dams remained, grandfathered into the landscape and the civic imagination, and continued to serve a recreational role. It would not be until 1933 that the last of them was removed.[61]

Within the middle Don, then, lay waters that were warmer than Lake Ontario, only moderately damaged by industrialization, filled with enticing infrastructure, and surrounded by land owned by only a handful of people, who did little to hinder bathing in the river. There was little incentive for Torontonians to turn a critical gaze on people bathing around these sites and clearly when such a gaze did fall on them it was approving or indifferent.

The Vernacular Bathing World

Bathing in the Don River, as the following series of vignettes suggests, required an embodied understanding of the hybrid environment, an oral culture that shared that knowledge, and a reciprocal system of watching out for fellow bathers. While the social use of these bathing spaces was sedimented into the landscape through generations of use, the embodied knowledge around them had to be renewed each spring as the river rewrote its physical environment. Many of these bathers were naked, others were dressed in trunks, but few wore a neck-to-knees bathing suit; the act of bathing nude was considered a formative experience.

Bathing spaces were busy and integrated into the urban and industrial environment. Herbert Currie, age fifteen, was surrounded by companions when he went swimming next to the Winchester Street Bridge on a Wednesday evening, 15 June 1881, and they raised the alarm when he went under. Their cries drew William Mulmer from an adjacent brickyard, who dove into the water with his clothes on to pull Currie out of a hole in the riverbed.[62] Currie's companions sent word of the incident back to his parents at 80 Gerrard Street East, west of the river, and the couple rushed to the scene, "having secured the services of Dr. Graham" in an effort to revive their son. When the effort failed, Policeman Thompson was on hand to help them bring their son home. J. Currie, the father, was a manufacturer of boots and shoes, which would confirm there were middle-class youth in the river. It would be tempting to say wealth helped the Curries secure a doctor, but doctors often headed to the river to lend a hand.[63] In this case, a stream of industrial workers, business people, police, and medical staff, both women and men, all flowed seamlessly to the Don.

Mill dams served as architecture for bathers to swim around or clamber on.[64] Don Valley Brickworks employees William Goddard and George Andrews headed to the lower dam for a noon-time swim on Friday, 5 July 1902.[65] Both from England, the two were boarding together in Todmorden at the home of George Wicklam.[66] The casualness of the swim is a reminder that, even as Toronto industrialized and workplace discipline increased, there were still moments when workers could duck out for a swim.

It may have been Goddard's first time in the Don; the *Globe* noted he had been in Canada only a few weeks, could not swim, and was not familiar with the river.[67] The two headed into the water and Andrews floated on a raft into the middle of the stream. But when Goddard waded in, he sank into a fifteen-foot-deep hole and went under. After failing to rescue Goddard on his own, Andrews returned to the brickworks to secure help from J.B. Millar, the company's superintendent, and three other workers, George Ball, James Burgess, and William Ford. A "number of lads" bathing nearby joined the recovery effort, but it would be a long two hours before they were successful.[68] The lower dam was in the news again a month later: on a Monday afternoon eight-year-old William J. Buchanan of Todmorden tumbled off it and drowned in the deep pond at its base.[69]

The groups that converged on the Don relied on an embodied understanding of its environment, but it was not always enough to save them. Frank Slater, age twenty-two, formerly of England, had been in Canada for about eighteen months working as a driver for John Klees, when he headed to the middle dam on a Sunday afternoon in early September 1900. Roommates Thomas Jarvis and Thomas Stanburry joined him. They were familiar with the river and as they waded in, Slater remarked prophetically that he had almost drowned there once before. Moments later he tumbled into a hole and went under. Stanburry and Jarvis struggled to save him, but he was pulled from their grasp and went under again. The two headed to shore and caught the attention of a passerby, Thomas Petrie, and collectively they were able to pull Slater's body from the river and summon Drs. Sneath and Vernon, who unsuccessfully attempted to resuscitate him.[70]

Trains added to the Don's hybrid landscape, creating noise and smoke, as they were shunted from one track to another.[71] Charles Sauriol vividly recalled the sound of the steam engine whistling in the background as he walked in the valley.[72] Rail lines helped isolate the river from the rest of the community and maintain its role as a male space. Bathing within it meant dipping into a natural setting one moment and dealing with industrial interruptions the next. For example, Toronto writer Gordon Sinclair recalled skinny-dipping in the river, adding that "when a train would go by on the Canadian Northern, we would either kneel in the water, or stand with our hands in front of ourselves."[73] Sinclair's description portrays the boys as icons of innocence.[74]

The death of Willie Wildbore in 1907 demonstrates the dangers of a hybrid space. Wildbore lost his life just after noon on Thursday, 8 August 1907, when he was struck by a CNR passenger train north of the Winchester Bridge.[75] Wildbore had been bathing there, despite his father's admonishments not to, with Fred Martin and Alberta and Norman Dwight, who all lived just east of the river. Wildbore had left for home before the others, but when Martin heard the warning blast of the train whistle and the screech of brakes that followed, he pulled on his clothes and raced up to find his friend had been struck and killed. The inquest that followed looked at the relationship between bathers and the railroad. Wildbore was deaf, and it was speculated that his deafness hindered his ability to know the space and hear the train coming.

The bathers were not supposed to be there: the Don was fenced north of the Winchester Bridge, but during the inquest it was noted the wire fence had been broken, and people were still using the river. The river-hugging line made interactions between the CNR and bathers routine and dangerous. "The foliage is considerably in our line of view, and it is often difficult to see people on the track at a distance ahead," conductor James Campbell told Coroner Young, while indicating the rail company knew where the popular bathing spaces were.[76] The inquest did not blame the rail company for the accident, but did call on municipal authorities to prevent boys from bathing in the vicinity of the Don flats, and also called for the erection of fencing along the rail lines from the point where they entered the city to the Queen Street crossing.

Finally, the Don River represented a polymorphous space filled with different groups. A handful of friends might head down together and come across others in the river; sometimes the groups merged and other times they kept to themselves. Ethnic communities carved out their own spaces in the river. Cristo Tonny, age twenty-one, and Vasil Nikola Poleff, age nineteen, were bathing just north of Riverdale Park with a group of Macedonians on a Thursday afternoon in June 1911. It was the middle of a heat wave and the river was just a few blocks away from their home in the working-class neighbourhood north of the Gooderham and Worts distillery.[77] Tragedy struck when Poleff dazed himself diving into the water and then pulled Tonny down as he struggled to steady himself. "The rest of the party raised an outcry and brought Benjamin Kirk and John Petrie to the spot."[78] The two recovered Tonny and Poleff, and while it was too late to save Tonny, Dr. W.T. Hamilton had arrived on the scene and attempted, unsuccessfully, to revive Poleff. The Don offered a space for the Macedonians to bathe together; as such they were part of a collective experience and could call on others for help. In this case documentary evidence shows how the Macedonian community made space in the river, but similar spaces would have been carved out in the Don, upper Humber River, and along the waterfront by ethnic and racial communities.

It is tempting to imagine that ethnic differences dropped away in the Don and a communal ethos emerged, but when we look closer we can see schisms of age and ethnicity. The communal atmosphere was a romantic projection on the space; it was also a necessity brought on by the need for safety in a shared environment.[79] We get a sense of how Poleff remained Macedonian, rather than Canadian, when a troop of Boy Scouts arrives and forms a cordon around Hamilton to help him focus on his work. The *Globe*, dividing the "us" of Anglo institutions from the "them" of ethnic others, looked on approvingly: "For a moment it looked as if they would have their work cut out, for the remainder of the Macedonians were excited. Even after the arrival of the police, the Scouts stood guard."[80] Hamilton described their work as "simply splendid." How the Macedonians felt about being cordoned off is not stated.

Securing the Don

The fact that the Macedonians were able to call for and receive help demonstrates how security in the middle Don rested on a system of reciprocity. This was rooted in the same system of mutual support that Bettina Bradbury argues underpinned nineteenth-century working-class communities.[81] People in and around the river shared warnings of dangers and risks, even if they did not know each other. People walking nearby knew they were part of the security system and dove in to help. A passing brakeman attempted to rescue Albert Petrie, brickyard worker William Mulmer responded to cries of help when Herbert Currie went under, and so on.[82] Doctors living or working around the Don joined in the effort to save lives. The expectation that people would watch over each other helps to explain the presence of youngsters bathing in the Don. Parents let their children go because they believed that other bathers would look out for them.[83]

The reciprocal safety system was so well known that people complained when it was abused by bathers. A speaker quoted in the *Daily Mail* in 1887 groused, "You know the number of boys, some of them, indeed, more than boys—young men, in fact—that live an amphibious life on the Don River, bathing, it would seem all the day long. I don't object to the bathing; there may be nothing wrong in that, but what I do object to—and this is my grievance—is that these youngsters impose on the passers-by, and sometimes, as I have said, give them very much annoyance."[84] His specific complaint was that the boys—or young men, in fact—were practical jokers crying wolf, ducking under the water to lure would-be—and often still dressed—rescuers into the stream, only to surface a few feet away.[85] The boys in the Don were committing several sins: they were drawing attention to themselves and disrespecting the reciprocal safety system.

Bathers were responsible for educating each other about the risks of the river and that shared responsibility created a distinct oral culture around it.[86] This collective knowledge offered a degree of safety but it had its limits: not everyone got the message or chose to listen. When Goddard dove into the Don near the Don Valley Brickyards, or when Michael Foley, age twenty-five, a recent immigrant from the United States described by onlookers as a "stranger in a bathing suit," drowned by the old beltline train station in 1908, their newness to the river was flagged as a warning sign.[87] Not yet members of the Don's collective experience, these newcomers had failed to learn, or could not yet read, the language of its space.[88] In contrast, when eight-year-old William J. Buchanan of Todmorden climbed up on the lower mill dam, fellow bathers warned him that it was a dangerous space, but he failed to listen.[89]

But could the Don River ever be known? It was a hybrid environment; the bathers faced dangers from the river's hydrological behaviour and from its industrial manipulation. The death of "little" Albert Francis North, age twelve, kicked off a discussion about the safety of the river.[90] North lived just east of the river, at 73 Lewis Street, and had drowned at the paper mill dam while bathing with neighbours Gordon and John Baker on a Monday afternoon in July 1906. The timing of the death is worth noting. Temperatures were in the high twenties and low thirties, which stirred up bathing issues across the city. The concerns raised with regard to the Don in 1906 were happening at the same time as the city was clamping down on nude bathing on Toronto Island and targeting sunbathers on the eastern waterfront.

While the chief coroner saw no reason for an inquest into North's death, the *Star*, reflecting public concern or trying to stir it up, felt otherwise and published an article focused on the Don and the drowning.[91] City and county police officers argued that the Don was an inherently dangerous space because it was unmappable. "I know the Don thoroughly," Sergeant of Detectives Duncan told the *Star*, in a turn of phrase that meant he understood its unknowability. "It is the most dangerous bathing spot in the neighbourhood of Toronto. Just above Winchester Street Bridge is the worst. There the river is full of deep holes scooped into the bank by the spring freshets. The water around is shallow, and boys slip suddenly into these deep spots, and are sucked down in an eddy." As Inspector Johnston pointed out, the Don rewrote its environment every year: "The trouble is that the character of the river bed is continually changing. Each spring old holes are filled up and new ones are created. Boys go there one summer and think they know the river. The next year there are deep holes where there were shallows the previous summer." The physical environment could change easily, but the social use of the river, settled into familiar spaces, was slow to adapt. The hybrid industrial/natural nature of the Don was accepted and hardly mentioned by police. One officer flagged the river as "foul," but the sewage that must surely have been in the water was not listed as a concern in 1906. As police and civic officials debated security within the Don, they agreed on one point: signage, which had been tried at the lower mill dam, whether intended to warn or restrict, would be universally ignored.[92]

Bringing the Beach to the Don

The city attempted to impose the logic of the beach on the Don when it included the river as one of three new free bathing stations in 1897. But there were challenges; the beach depended on a predictable environment, lifeguards to ensure safety, and rules for bathing. None of these were easy to achieve in the Don; the river was unpredictable and people were used to bathing without rules. They depended on each other for safety. When the property department sent Street Commissioner John Jones to find a suitable location for the bathing station he immediately raised red flags.[93] Jones wrote, "no part of that river is so level and free from holes as to be safe swimming ground for the boys."[94] But having said that he suggested that an area between Bloor and Winchester, near the traditional bathing space, be designated for bathing, and that with a "smart man" to patrol it the space would be "comparatively safe."[95] As with the rest of the new free bathing spaces in 1897, the Don continued the vernacular practice of being male-only and allowing nude bathing: the boys would not be forced to wear a bathing suit. The *Star* announced the new area with the headline, "Safety in the Don" and promoted the surveillance and lifesaving equipment the site would offer.[96]

Even under surveillance, the river was a dangerous and unknowable environment; holes could develop and divers struck stones in areas that had seemed safe the season before.[97] The city could not impose a predictable environment on the Don. Instead it was forced to work with the river: moving the bathing station upstream or down, depending on conditions. In 1908, the *Star* noted that the bathing station had been moved to "high banks" and that mothers were "advised not to allow their boys to continue to bathe at the sandy point about a quarter of a mile further north, a dangerous place." The use of local landmarks suggests how local knowledge was still critical and that being a mother around the Don required an intimate understanding of its landscape and bathing places.[98]

Even if the city could create a space of surveillance over one section of the Don, it had no ability to force people to use it. As Sergeant Miller complained in 1906, "The conduct of some of those who bathe up there is simply outrageous. The city already has a man there to keep the lads in order, but because he makes them behave themselves, they go outside of the city limits up to Taylor's Mills, and at the brickyards."[99] Unlike the "reform parks" that emerged in the twentieth century, the city could never control the physical environment of the free bathing area, had only limited control of the bathers, and no ability to lock the gates at the end of the day.[100]

The free bathing station attempted to impose an artificial schedule on the Don. Henceforth the city, not the temperature of the water or the joy of a hot spring day, would "open" the bathing season. But the challenge was convincing people to swim within the window of safety that the city offered. Just one day before the opening of the free bathing station in 1898, Harry Burt, age eleven, the son of a fruit seller, drowned in the Don on 30 June at the Winchester Street bridge—the traditional bathing space.[101] Andrew Forrest, age fourteen, of 446 Jones Avenue, was seized with a cramp and drowned in twelve feet of water at "the baths" on Monday, 6 July 1914, just five minutes after the guard had left for the day.[102]

The Don's unique environment challenged efforts to standardize bathing facilities across the city. Ideally, the city wanted to open all its free bathing stations at the end of June.[103] But the natural bathing season started earlier in the Don, which was quicker to warm up than Lake Ontario. At times the city tried to adapt: it opened the Don's free bathing station a week early in 1912 because a cold spring had created pent-up demand for summer activities and pushed people towards the warmer environment of the river.[104] The river won out again in 1922 as the city remarked: "By far the most popular of the bathing stations is that stationed on the Don River. The water there is a good deal warmer than that of the lake, and consequently huge crowds have been attending since it opened a week ago."[105]

Free bathing attendance records demonstrate the popularity of the Don; in 1902, when there were 134,030 visits to the city's stations, the Don beat out Sunnyside, Fisherman's Island, and Toronto Island's western sandbar as the most popular space.[106] The Don pulled in 44,497 of the city's 130,000 free bathing visits in 1913—only slightly less than Fisherman's Island.[107] Those numbers only include visits recorded in the city's registry. They miss people who swam further up or down the river, which means the overall number of Don bathers would have been substantially higher. Some middle-class boys would have made use of the free bathing station, but press, pictures, and regional histories show bathing in the Don as a working-class experience.

Myth-Making in the Don

Bathing in the Don carried powerful symbolic meaning for middle-class and working-class Torontonians. For the middle class, it represented a gendered and nostalgic wellspring for resisting the industrializing city. For the working class, trips to the Don were remembered as an opportunity to hold themselves up against an effete middle class. The physical environment required communal behaviour to create security, but it was conscious myth-making from middle-class and working-class people that created a "folk" within the Don.[108]

We can see how the middle class was entranced by the Don when we look at efforts to straighten the river in 1887. The *Globe* sent a writer down to watch the progress. The writer was fascinated by the industrial transformation and described how the new channel chewed through land and old buildings alike, the future rewriting the past. But amid the chaos of construction, the writer noted, "all around are numerous small boys in the costume which antedated fig leaves, diving out of scows or jumping off the piles, regardless of dirt-dumpings or sun-skinned backs, laughing, shouting, swimming, and spluttering."[109] Construction made the river even more appealing by creating pools and diving platforms.[110] The *Globe* used the bathing boys as a symbol of a past that would be erased by a modern Don. The boys and their youthful bodies were a soothing sight in the midst of the disruption. The phrase "in the costume which antedated fig leaves" suggests how they represented a timeless element within the chaos; even though the old order was being torn apart and replaced, the simplicity of a boy bathing remained. Of course, this story tells us nothing of how or why the boys arrived at the Don. The complexity of the boys' lived experiences was distilled into symbolic representation.[111]

Vernacular bathing in these marginal spaces was described as a rite of passage for men. In an August 1889 *Globe* column "Observer" wrote, "In what utter contempt we would have held a bathing suit in the days of our free, exuberant boyhood on the farm." He went on to describe bathing in a mill race, "with its obstructing saw logs and its sawdust bottom," and swimming out to the dam and challenging others to follow. When Pearson reflected on a millpond in Castle Frank Creek in 1914, he added, "I have often greatly enjoyed a swim in it."[112] The use of the present perfect tense suggests Pearson had just stepped out of the pond, even though his swims in it would have happened decades earlier.[113] "Observer" believed that little had changed: "Canadian summers are hot, and Canadian streams inviting, and Canadian youth full of spirit and strong in self-reliance and not overly-disciplined."[114]

The naked boy symbolized spring and the breaking of winter's cold. As the *Star* reported in late April 1906, "Bathing in the Don River has begun already, as far as the small boy is concerned. Numbers of them took their first dip of the season yesterday, and they didn't bother about bathing suits."[115] The *Globe* looked towards the Don River for inspiration when it imagined a summer idyll in 1925 it, arguing, "Boys seek water as inevitably as water seeks its own level," and the "swimming holes" in the Don and elsewhere needed to be maintained "as reservoirs of civic health."[116]

The Don bathers provided a symbolic link with nature that could be held up against the acculturation within the rest of the city. The *Globe* tracked the annual Easter parade of spring fashion on the boardwalk at Sunnyside on 17 April 1927, an event that amounted to a heterosocial promenade of men and women.[117] But across town, the city's east end boys were more interested in a dive in the Don: "Passersby watched them from the Danforth viaduct as they splashed one another beneath an old bridge half a mile farther north. Of course, there was not a bathing suit in the party. The water was cold; it took quite a little courage to go on, but, knowing the punishment of the shirker, he would indeed have been brave who stayed out."[118] Spring was here, the latest fashions were on display, but the naked boy and an old swimming hole were eternally pure. The site was easily viewed for those who chose to look. The bathing boy provided a gloss of health to the swimming hole as much as the swimming hole did to the boy.[119]

Photographs of people bathing in the Don illustrate how the naked body was allowed to be displayed, but only in a particular way. Timing matters: nude bathing had been popular along Toronto's industrial waterfront in the nineteenth century, but technology advanced enough to capture active outdoor scenes emerged only in the 1880s, and taking pictures of popular activities such as bathing became common only after 1900. So our photo record tilts towards the Don, where nude bathing remained popular well into the twentieth century.[120] But the Don photographs display a careful narrative. Men appear at a distance, if at all. John Boyd Jr. gives us a rare image of men bathing by the lower dam on the Don River in 1915 and captures the full circuit, from men in a state of undress to a group gathered on the side of the river either completing or about to begin their swim. They might even be getting rousted out of the site by police, though it is hard to tell from the photo, and media coverage at the time does not mention a raid (see Figure 4.8). But Boyd's photograph is the exception; most of the pictures are of boys, and position the boys in an artistic fashion to highlight their youth and idyllic relationship with nature (see Figures 4.9 and 4.10).

Pictures of the bathing boy immersed in nature circulated throughout North Atlantic countries at the turn of the century and soothed men who feared that masculinity itself was under threat amid the industrializing urban environment.[121] But the bathing body was also caught in the turn-of-the-century tensions and prohibitions around sexuality. British artist Henry Scott Tuke focused on boys, bathing, and boats. Tuke's clientele were predominantly homosexual, but by keeping the boys chaste Tuke was able to open "a space in Victorian aesthetic culture in which the nude male figure could become the subject of a homoerotic discourse" and avoid the censure that figures such as Oscar Wilde had faced.[122] Capturing a familiar bathing moment, combined with artistic positions that limited the presentation of nudity—the boys were never seen from the front—ensured the chastity of the bathers. Artists like Tuke were able to avoid the critique that they were sexualizing youth by attaching their work to Greek artistic tradition and representing "the nude boy as no mere boy, but a kouros; a representation of the imperishable glory of the human spirit."[123] Late nineteenth-century romantics viewed the nude boy as part of nature and a representation of innocence, in contrast to the clothed female body, which represented culture and control.[124]

Our Don River photographs follow that trend by desexualizing the boys and portraying their innocence. William James snapped pictures around the Don River that vacillated between the humorous, pictures of naked boys on bikes, or the artistic, a lineup of boys watching swimming instructors at work (see Figures 4.11 and 4.12). The photographs essentialize the experience to boyhood, innocence, and nature; despite the industrial infrastructure around the Don, it is only the Prince Edward Viaduct that sneaks into the pictures.[125] James took multiple versions of bare-bottomed boys sitting along the Don over a number of years and they were distributed widely, even appearing in the *Toronto Star*. As someone who made his money through photography, he knew a money shot when he saw one. The James photographs have become iconic in Don River mythology, and a stock image in regional histories, such as *Cabbagetown in Pictures* and *Cabbagetown Remembered*; the pictures lock in the boyhood image of the Don and erase a more complicated reality.[126] (It is worth noting that some of the slightly older boys in Figure 4.12 are looking back at the photographer, suggesting self-consciousness or at least an awareness of how their image was being used.) Bathing boys were also included in postcards of the Don River, illustrating how they pervaded the public view of the Don; "Scenes from the Don," a postcard dated between 1906 and 1913, shows two boys skinny-dipping in the Don.[127]

Regional histories and autobiographies of the Don and adjacent Cabbagetown canonize the bathing experience as integral to the lives of working-class youth. As noted earlier, writers such as Hugh Garner and Gordon Sinclair remember the Don River as a bathing space for children.[128] Likewise historians such as Colleen Kelly and George Rust-D'Eye repeat and embellish those recollections, turning them into a mark of resistance and a formative part of working-class experience.[129] We can read Garner's experiences, in particular, as a conscious act of looking back at the middle-class gaze and using vernacular bathing as a critical component of identity formation. Garner describes how streetcars, part of the free bathing program, transported youth in the west to tony Sunnyside Beach, while in the east, youth on the Danforth were taken to the "Bloor Street viaduct where they rushed down the hill to the Don Valley to swim naked at the old Red Bridge

Figure 4.7. Boys swimming in the Don River at "Bare Ass Beach" in Riverdale, 1923. *Toronto Star* Photograph Archives, courtesy of Toronto Public Library.

Figure 4.8. Don Valley, scene at paper mill dam, July 1915.

Figure 4.9. "Old swimmin' hole," between 1920 and 1934.

Figure 4.10. "Police officer and (naked) boys on road" in this pre-1940 picture. Images courtesy of City of Toronto Archives.

Figure 4.11. Cycling beside the Don River, between Don Mills Road and Leaside, c. 1912.

Figure 4.12. Skinny-dipping in the Don River, c. 1909. William James returned to this site multiple times over the years to capture and sell almost identical images. For a similar image see *Toronto Star*, 10 August 1922, 11. Images courtesy of City of Toronto Archives.

over the Don." Garner added, "We Cabbagetowners and Riverdaleites didn't need a streetcar; we hiked up the Don Valley to the Red Bridge."[130]

Garner also recalled trips to the western sandbar on Toronto Island via the Queen Street streetcar and the SS *Luella*. Here the link between skinny-dipping and class is even more explicit. He notes, "We underprivileged kids, who felt nothing but pity for the Rosedale private schoolboys who had to wear bathing suits, used to disembark from the free car after a slow, song-filled ride."[131] Clothing in these stories was an artifice that the middle class had to endure, but one the working class could throw off. Rust-D'Eye uses Sinclair's experience to argue that for Cabbagetown "the most popular summer activity for boys was skinny-dipping" in the Don, even as he noted that "everyone who lived in Cabbagetown in those days was poor."[132] Colleen Kelly gives us a similar interpretation, with the Don serving as a "natural playground" for kids in the neighbourhood.[133]

The Limits of Innocence

People shed their clothes to enter the Don River, but this was no biblical Eden; they could never entirely shed the expectation that they should be wearing clothes. Even when they bathed, people were still tethered to their clothes. For example, a "lad" named Daley stripped down to bathe with a group of boys in the Don on an August afternoon in 1867.[134] Wading cautiously into the river, Daley looked back to see his companions tying knots in his clothes. Rushing back to stop them, he tumbled into a hole and nearly drowned before his friends managed to pull him out.[135] The vulnerable moment of undressing and stepping into the water was reflected in the often-repeated nineteenth-century political trope that the opposition had figuratively caught the government in the water bathing and had stolen their clothes.[136] Clothes could also symbolize loss: a pile of untended clothes was often a red flag that someone had drowned.[137]

The tension between shedding clothes and the need to return to them was part of the mythology of the Don. As a boy, Stan Wadlow, a native Cabbagetowner, East York politician, and author of *Life's Precious Memories*, disobeyed strict orders from his parents and went skinny-dipping in the Don. During his forbidden swim, Wadlow's pants were stolen and his mother—described as not happy about the situation—had to bring a replacement pair before he could make the trip home.[138] The moral here was that you better do a good job of hiding your clothes, but it also suggests that the boys tended to be a bit naughty.[139] In another case, the cleverness of a boy who had trained his dog to protect his clothes while he was in swimming was flagged.[140] Bathers knew they were circumventing bathing bylaws, which meant their catching sight of a police officer created a scramble to retrieve their clothes.[141] The police, in turn, knew they had to catch scofflaws in the buff. The *Star* joked about the situation in 1909, noting, "Boys who go in bathing in the Don in a nude condition will be arrested if the police can catch them. The aggravating part of it is that the boys nearly always leave their clothes on the other side of the river." The *Star* included a drawing of a boy standing in a bush while a policeman raged at him from the other side of the water (see Figure 4.13).

The mythology of bathing in the Don River also depended on policing identity and sexuality. Despite a visual legacy focused on boys engaged in innocent play, there were men in the Don as well. Descriptions of people bathing often flitted between calling them men and boys. When the *Star* quizzed police about whether bathing in the Don should be maintained, it stated the "majority" of those "who meet death in its treacherous root-meshed deep holes are youngsters ranging from 8 to 16": a silent acknowledgment that not everyone was a boy.[142] When our speaker groused to the *Daily Mail* about bathers crying wolf in the Don River, he made the same slippage, complaining about "the number of boys, some of them, indeed, more than boys—young men, in fact."[143] And when Coroner Young questioned CNR conductor James Campbell at the inquest into the death of Willie Wildbore, he asked, "Have you had much trouble up on the Don flats with boys?"[144] Campbell replied, "Young men and boys are accustomed to bathe in the river near the scene of the accident."[145] The answer was a subtle correction; there were more than just boys in the Don. These slippages were part of the effort to write men out, essentialize the innocence of the naked boy, and, from the mid-twentieth century on, retroactively question the sexuality of the men who swam in the river.[146]

Newspaper records of people bathing in the Don lay bare the human geography of the river. People over eighteen, with jobs, were typically swimming on weekends or in the evening, which means that while people of different ages swam in the same spaces, they often did so at different times. Men claimed the river near Rosedale Station, for example, on the weekend.[147] The more

Boys who go in bathing in the Don in a nude condition will be arrested if the police can catch them. The

aggravating part of it is that the boys nearly always leave their clothes on the other side of the river.

Figure 4.13. "Little of everything," *Toronto Daily Star*, 8 July 1909.

visible area north of the Winchester Bridge seems to have been popular with boys. The river near Todmorden saw a mix of men and boys, but the men often came out in the evening and weekends.[148] But even these trends had exceptions: William Goddard and George Andrews nipped over to the Don River for a swim at noon on a Friday. Cristo Tonny and Vasil Nikola Poleff were beating the heat when they took to the Don on a Thursday afternoon. Temperature blurred boundaries in the urban environment.

Distilling the Don experience down to the innocent bathing boy helped purify the swimming hole, but there were practical reasons for referring to the Don bathers as boys or sometimes as "young men, in fact."[149] Teenagers did not exist as a distinctive social group with its own behaviour patterns and expectations in the early twentieth century. Historians Mary Louise Adams and Cynthia Comacchio argue the modern usage of adolescence, what we think of today as teenagers, did not emerge until the 1920s.[150] This lack of terminology made it difficult to get a linguistic grip on males on the cusp between boyhood and manhood.

Marital status and class played a role in separating men from boys at the turn of the century. The people who bathed within the Don environment were almost entirely young unmarried men.[151] Bathing in the Don with the boys represented an activity for men who lingered in the prolonged bachelorhood before marriage.[152] Looking at Hamilton, Craig Heron has noted working-class men usually did not marry until their mid-twenties and spent the intervening years between childhood and marriage in a "a vibrant leisure-time culture of young bachelorhood."[153] The Don River was part of that culture. While we see middle-class teenagers and boys bathing in the Don, nearly all the men bathing in the river were working class. Lack of affordable recreational activities elsewhere likely helped drive them to the river.[154] But their presence in this boyhood space blurred the line between men and boys, and their continued participation in a homosocial culture that eschewed the presence of women also raised questions about their sexuality, particularly in retrospect.[155]

The mingling of men and boys was problematized in the twentieth century as urban development increased the visibility of the bathing areas and as policing of gender and sexuality became more rigid. Mixed-age groups that had once been considered normal now became suspect. The free bathing program was officially limited to boys under sixteen years of age to manage the mingling of men and boys. Free bathing also created a social space for youth; the dense proximity of youngsters was probably as discouraging to men as the steady glare of a city worker looking over them.

Don River conservationist Charles Sauriol demonstrates, through a casual reference to his own youth, how men in the Don could be othered. On the back of a picture of the Clay Banks Swimming Hole, Sauriol wrote, "After an hour in the water we would run along the bank to the tents and stand in front of the cooking fire to warm up—no bathing suits, everyone nude—but when a 'dirty guy' showed up, the boys ran him out."[156] The caption was probably jotted down one day when Sauriol was leafing through his photo collection. It suggests a sexual threat within the mixing of boys and men in the Don River. But the timing of the caption also suggests shifting views on homosexuality. Sauriol made a conscious effort to retroactively write in this policing effort and attach it to the bathing space; it's an effort that reflected mid-twentieth-century suspicions of male nudity, suspicions that argued a homosocial space might also be a homosexual space. It may well be that Sauriol and the boys did chase out any "dirty guys" who showed up. But in stating that they did, Sauriol retroactively ensured his own heterosexual performances were unblemished. In doing so, he also turned every adult male who might be around the Don into a potential homosexual predator.[157] The narrative becomes even more complex because Sauriol, by his own recollection, would have been at least fifteen years old when he was warming up around the fire.[158] Today we would call him a teenager. But looking back at the experience decades later, Sauriol mythologizes the experience to boyhood, just as photographs of the period have, and just as news media at the beginning of the twentieth century did.

Sinclair also treats the presence of men bathing in the Don as aberrant. "Once or twice each summer men would come among us," Sinclair writes, "some wearing bathing suits down to their knees and some wearing none. But when the men began to mingle with us hairless boys, the police would usually come and tell them to go away. We had never heard the word homosexual, but thinking back on it now, I suppose that is what was on the police's mind."[159]

The concern over homosexual encounters might well have been on the mind of the police. As Steven Maynard has shown, criminal case records in Ontario indicate that men pursuing sex with boys did seek them out in the ravines and parks of the city at the turn of the century.[160] Authorities would have known of the possibility of sexual encounters between men and boys. Sinclair does not specify where he was swimming, but if he is recalling swimming in the free bathing area, boys under sixteen were officially discouraged from entering the space.[161] But Sinclair is also implanting his contemporary interpretation of homosexuality onto his early twentieth-century experiences in the Don. While he had not heard the word *homosexual* in 1910, he certainly had by 1966 and was ready to apply it retroactively to the men, all the men, who swam in the Don, labelling them as potential homosexual predators, on the basis of their nudity and proximity to children.

Women have been all but removed from these vernacular bathing spaces. The dearth of female drownings in the Don (the first I came across was in the late 1920s) suggests they were in the river far less often than men. But this was also a discursive effort: conceiving the Don as a distinctive space for undressed male bodies depended upon a successful effort to erase women. The archival record suggests women and girls were moving in and around the river. Artistic works of the Don River, such as *Lady Pellatt Fishing,* tell us they were there, as both artists and subjects.[162] Photographs tell us they were there.[163] Postcards tell us they were there viewing the valley. On a postcard entitled "The Race, Don Valley," writer "WRS" identified "one of our honeymoon scenes, and typical of the beauty spots of the Northland" in a note to Mrs. L.H. Saunders in New Jersey.[164] Gordon Sinclair recalls the presence of girls in the Don: "Once a group of girls about our own age or even younger came swimming as we were . . . in the raw. They caused a measure of interest but not really a stir, until their parents came to take them away."[165] We can take Sinclair at his word and accept that sometimes girls did swim in the river.[166] But he's also, once again, desexualizing the experience of being in the Don: the boys were too young and innocent to think anything of girls being among them.

North of the middle Don, the gendered geography of the river likely became even more complicated. Joy Mollenhauer recorded her personal recollections of growing up along the west Don River, near the current site of York University's Glendon Campus, in the early twentieth century, describing the river as her park. Mollenhauer noted the boys and girls each had their own swimming holes and recalled how "we went in one cold May 14th in heavy serge bloomers (our school uniform) and had trouble drying them without confessing to our mothers." During picnic and school events, she notes that everyone waded into "the clear Don River."[167] Mollenhauer's recollections suggest the girls did not have the same luxury to strip down that the boys had, but they did have a physical relationship and emotional connection with the river.

The introduction of the free bathing system and the surveillance that came with it set the stage for the emergence of a heterosocial bathing culture in the Don River; but it was still an incremental process. The free bathing program started in 1897 as a male-only endeavour and continued to allow nude bathing. The Don was still listed as a boys-only space in 1910, though bathing suits were now required.[168] James's photos taken through the 1910s and early 1920s show that swimming lessons were still in the nude.[169] By 1925 the *Globe* was pointing out that the "girls share equally with the boys in this daily adventure."[170]

Vernacular bathing in the middle Don relied on a precarious balance between nature and industry, visibility and invisibility, men and boys. If the Don had been too environmentally pristine, middle-class excursionists would have continued to paddle or stroll up its length, and their gaze would have penetrated these isolated swimming holes and revealed the men within them. Instead, the Don remained at the edge of their vision, occluded enough that it was possible to imagine the innocence of the swimming hole within its reaches, people it with innocent bathing boys, and create a rich mythology around bathing in the river, albeit one that relied on excluding men by age and females entirely. If the Don had been too isolated, vernacular bathing and the reciprocal safety regime that underpinned it would never have been able to protect the bathers within the river. The Don needed to be visible enough that people strolling along its banks, crossing its bridges, or working next to it could dive in and rescue people. Finally, if the Don had been as despoiled as declensionist narratives of it suggest, the bathers, fully capable of moving and working around polluted spaces, would never have been in the river to begin with.

Pollution, along with new expectations of safety and hygiene, conspired to pull bathers out of the river from the 1920s on. In 1925 the *Globe* fretted in "A Summer Idyll Urbanized" that the city's swimming holes were under threat from pollution, and during the 1920s city council faced increasing calls to clean up the river.[171] But as the city's commissioner of works pointed out succinctly in 1924, 1927, and again in 1928, without an interceptor sewer line to pull waste away from the river, its condition could not be improved. As he bluntly put it, "I see no possibility of making the Don a beauty spot similar to the Humber."[172] The city's free bathing station in the Don was closed in 1928.[173] Bathers were pushed up the river, as bathing spaces closed and once-popular infrastructure, such as the Don Valley Paper Mill dam, was removed for safety reasons.[174] Semi-treated sewage from the growing suburban population around Toronto was the greatest threat to the river, and by 1949 the amount of semi-treated sewage flowing into the river was nearly double the normal summer water flow.[175] Still, the upper river remained popular with bathers well into the 1950s, and memories of bathing in the river remained part of the mythology for people like Charles Sauriol, who worked to "reclaim" the Don.[176] The potential for the river to return as a bathing space was even floated in the Don Watershed Regeneration Council and the Toronto and Region Conservation Authority's "Turning the Corner" report card in 1997, which asked, "Will children swim in the Don again?"; it quoted survey respondents saying, "I used to swim there as a kid" as part of a call for environmental action.[177]

The loss of the free bathing station in the middle Don in 1928 was keenly felt, as letter writer "SALOP" told the *Star*: "I am a working woman with a family of five boys and have been four years in Toronto out from the old country. For the first two summers during the holidays I packed the kids off each day to bathe in the Don at Red Bridge." But she noted that space was closed to bathing in 1927, and a bathing space further up was closed in 1928 because of sewage problems. "Is there any other place the kids can go?" she asked. "What I want is a place on the streetcar line where they can spend the afternoon stripped and playing in and out of the water. It is a great health to them and a great relief to me."[178] For SALOP, the river represented a communal space to send her children; she had faith, and at times that faith was clearly misplaced, that the Don and the people along it would care for them.

5

HUMBER RIVER ENCOUNTERS

The spotlight was on the Humber River in 1911. Toronto developer Robert Home Smith revealed a vision for the river that would see a new housing development stretch out along its banks, while parkland would fill the valley.[1] The Humber Valley Surveys was billed as the largest land development project to date in Toronto and included 800 acres spread over 6.5 kilometres along the river.[2] Home Smith had quietly purchased land from more than seventy different owners to put the project together, but he wanted the city of Toronto to come in as a partner. The city would get 105 acres from Home Smith to use for parkland and in return extend its boundaries westward to a point 600 feet past the Humber and build a boulevard along the river.[3] The project was announced at the height of the Laurier boom: the period between 1900 and 1913 when immigration and economic growth across Canada exploded and Toronto's population during the previous decade nearly doubled to over 375,000 people by 1911. Toronto's growth had also been driven by annexing suburban territory, a process that peaked between 1905 and 1912. The Humber Surveys would add to that expansion.[4] Home Smith and his supporters on council called it a win/win proposal; the river bottom land was unsuitable for housing development but turning it into city-owned park space ensured it would be controlled and beautified. Home Smith's own development, as he frankly admitted, would also benefit.[5] The *Globe* endorsed the project: "In the matter of natural beauty the Humber Valley is richly endowed, and the carrying out of Mr. Smith's project will secure to the citizens of Toronto perpetual access to it under *ideal conditions* for enjoying its picturesque attractions."[6]

The Humber Boulevard would use islands as landing pads as it leapt back and forth across the river.[7] It would define the physical appearance of the river and manage how people moved and behaved while they were in the valley.[8] Travellers would shuttle along the boulevard in carriages or automobiles and its route would divide the river into a main channel for motorboats and rowboats and a second for more sedate travel in canoes.[9] Notably, there was no space allotted for bathers in this new civic vision.

The Humber represents a socio-ecological counterpoint to the Don River.[10] Straightening and industrializing the lower Don River had isolated the middle reaches of the river, driving out other recreational users and creating a borderland oasis within which a lively vernacular bathing culture thrived. But with the Humber River a quite different social dynamic evolved. The Humber was only lightly touched by industry: it was poised on the edge of the urban environment rather than centred within it. Male vernacular bathers had to compete for space with men and women who used the river as an aquatic promenade on warm summer evenings, canoeing up and down its lower reaches in a sedate courtship ritual.[11] While in the Don the bathing boy was valorized as a symbol of masculine vitality and was used to purify the moral terrain of the valley, in the Humber the bathing man was targeted for a rough aberrant masculine performance, in contrast to the genteel masculine performance of the men paddling up the river.[12]

The effort to create "ideal conditions" in the Humber River hinged on using the boulevard as a form of moral architecture to improve the river's use as an aquatic promenade while driving out the boisterous male bathing culture. The boulevard would make the river visible so that people could manage their own behaviour and police the behaviour of others in the valley.[13] The effort to promote canoeing in the Humber and push out nude bathing was already well under way by the early twentieth century, but the boulevard discussion helps reveal the competition over space.[14] Critics of men bathing in the river portrayed the tension as a contest between middle-class people in canoes and working-class bathers over what the natural environment of the river should mean and how it should be used.[15] But the Humber denies us easy boundaries. People canoeing included working-class and white-collar workers who had saved up enough money to participate in the courtship ritual. Some of the bathers were working class; they made their way to the Humber from working-class neighbourhoods such as Toronto Junction. But many of the bathers were middle class; they headed over to the Humber from Toronto, paddled up the stream, and then dove in for a swim, which meant that men and boys could be appropriately paddling one moment and then inappropriately skinny-dipping the next.[16]

Setting

The Don and Humber Rivers act as bookends for Toronto. Like the Don, the Humber is a short river, topping out at just 100 kilometres, with its headwaters in the Niagara Escarpment and the Oak Ridges Moraine. The Humber Valley had been a critical trade conduit between Lake Ontario and Lake Simcoe prior to European contact and remained a critical fur trade corridor during the early stages of colonization. The Humber owes its pedigree as an excursion space for Toronto's settler elite to Elizabeth Simcoe, who recorded plans in her diary on 25 June 1796 to canoe up the river and spend the day listening to music.[17] By the mid-nineteenth century Torontonians were boarding the steamship *Hero*, which promised to take groups of up to eighty people to "try the lake breeze and cool spots about the Humber."[18] The authors of the *History of York County* in 1885 noted the Humber "is a good deal resorted to by picnickers and holiday makers during the summer season."[19] The river competed with Toronto Island and Victoria Park and Kew Beach on Toronto's eastern shoreline for Torontonians looking to escape the heat and the smoke of the city and enjoy a natural setting.[20] Excursions were more than just a chance to commune with nature: the picnics and community events created space for courtship in a period when men and women did most of their social networking in closed social groups.[21]

The Humber's role as a vernacular bathing space was also well established by the mid-nineteenth century and bathers competed for space with excursionists. "Eye-Witness" railed against "gangs of boys of all ages, numbering a score or two," bathing near the Humber "during all hours of the day, and in full view of every passerby" in 1877.[22] The bathers were making a spectacle of themselves: "ladies and children enjoying the air of the Humber cannot venture to walk along the beach, or even on the road, without being insulted by this indecent exposure, aggravated as it is by the cries and jeers of these young rascals, whose morals certainly will not be improved by this practice."[23] "Eye-Witness" argued that something must be done or the excursionists would be driven away: the "proprietors of the steamers and of the Humber hotels should for their own interests, take the matter in hand."[24]

The Aquatic Promenade

Something new was happening in the Humber River by the turn of the century. In the summer of 1900 the *Toronto Star*'s Elmina Elliot Atkinson, who wrote under the pen name Madge Merton, reported how one of "Toronto's good-hearted hostesses" chaperoned a picnic on the Humber River with a twist. Rather than packing one large lunch and eating around a picnic table the hostess packed thirteen baskets for thirteen people, including lunch and a book in each, and after the group paddled up the Humber most of the participants paired up: joining their picnic baskets together and taking turns reading the books. They all came back together at the end of the day and paddled home.[25] The picnic suggests that courtship was a chaperoned affair, but it also demonstrates how expectations were changing; people could couple up and yet maintain propriety in a public space like the Humber. Increasingly, they did not even need a hostess any more. Couples paddled up the Humber on their own, surrounded and secured by other couples doing the same.

The association of the canoe with courtship at the start of the twentieth century ensured the popularity of the Humber River as a leisure space. Courtship had been a carefully managed affair: done in the shelter of the home or within the secure confines of one's social group, be it familial, ethnic, religious, or work-related. But the growing participation of women in the workforce and the urban environment pushed courtship into new commercial spaces; theatres, beaches, and amusement parks emerged to provide public space for men and women to meet and mingle.[26] The Humber was just one more space where couples could court, but rather than promenading on a boardwalk, they could rent a canoe or pleasure craft and take a paddle up the river.

Historians have focused on the canoe as a mode of transportation that romanticizes nature and encourages people to see Canada's natural setting as a space for rejuvenation.[27] Taking that romantic view, of returning nature as a form of recreation, has led writers to valorize the canoe as a symbol of Canada.[28] Recent historical work has raised concerns about this process of valorization. Not only does it frame nature as a space for consumption, it erases Indigenous people—removing them from the landscape to create an Edenic setting—or portrays them as the embodiment of nature, and thus just one more aspect of the scenery to be admired.[29] Using the canoe as a national icon raises similar challenges; it becomes a piece of Indigenous art and technology that settlers can appropriate to form an embodied relationship with their adopted land.[30] Misao Dean suggests what's at stake when she writes, "The ideology of the canoe allows Canadians like me to construct an identity in which subjectivity and nationality form a seamless whole, and each seems to both confirm and contribute a satisfying depth to the other."[31]

The focus on the canoe as a tool of settler colonization has tilted research towards its role in wilderness trips, sports clubs, or summer camps.[32] But the Humber River gives us an opportunity to see how the canoe and the colonial imagery around it becomes sexualized. That link between the canoe and romantic interludes hovers like a ghost in the historiography, with writers coyly repeating the quote, attributed to Pierre Berton, that "a Canadian is someone who knows how to make love in a canoe."[33] But the quote seems to both open and close off the discussion with little follow-up on how men and women co-opted the canoe as a technology for coupling.[34] Perhaps the ability of nature and the symbolically laden canoe to create romantic settings is too obvious. It was certainly clear to canoe manufacturers, for whom filling the liveries of rental companies within urban settings or attached to amusement parks was a lucrative market.[35]

Diane Beasley discusses the courting experience in her work, adopting the term "girling" to describe the practice of young men and women using a canoe to capture private time together in the public space of a river or lake.[36] Urban canoeing peaked in the late nineteenth century and was already in decline by the 1920s.[37] But during its peak rental companies lined the mouth of the Humber River and nearby Sunnyside Beach. Walter Dean, Octavius Hicks,

Figure 5.1. Humber River, Weston. William Arthur Johnson, 1871. Image courtesy of Toronto Public Library.

Figure 5.2. The aquatic promenade, Humber River. Image courtesy of City of Toronto Archives.

T.N. Devins, the Orr Brothers, and Maw's boathouses rented hundreds of canoes and provided livery services for private owners.[38]

Couples turned trips up the Humber River into an aquatic promenade on warm summer evenings. David Scobey has described how promenading in nineteenth-century New York enabled a genteel middle class to define class and gender roles, and set the tone for mixed-gender socialization. Promenading included elaborate social cues and expectations for behaviour.[39] The same logic was at work with the Humber. The aquatic promenade had its own set of cues and codes for courtship on the river, entry was moderated through the expedient of renting or owning a canoe, and people paddled knowing they were being watched by others.

The promenade was a space where gender and sexuality were performed, produced, and verified, but in this case it was other paddlers doing the verification.[40] Masculine and feminine roles were repeated and solidified. This ballet of gender expectations, of how one should *be* male or female, stood out in high relief when breached by boisterous boaters or the undisciplined bodies of vernacular bathers.[41] The rambunctious groups of men bathing in the river performed their own competing performances of rough masculinity and at times, mirroring working-class efforts that historian Craig Heron has described in the urban environment, took pleasure in puncturing the courtship atmosphere in the Humber.[42] For middle-class observers, the aberrant displays of bathers only confirmed the respectable masculinity of the men sedately paddling with a female companion.

The Humber promenade was a sensuous affair. It took its cue from new public spaces such as the boardwalk, the dance hall, and the amusement park, where encounters between men and women were foundational to the experience.[43] As a postcard writer told a female friend in 1906, "This is a swell place to spend a day. It is just like Coney Island."[44] The Humber River, of course, lacked the intensity of Coney Island but its role was similar, with commercial infrastructure that enabled men and women to meet in public, and a set of cultural expectations, reinforced with photographs and postcards, that encouraged flirtation and courtship.

Visual, written, and material culture modelled the parameters and routine of the aquatic promenade and are emblematic of the conscious effort to impose meaning on the space.[45] Postcards marketed a trip up the Humber as a romantic interlude and laid out the steps of the journey.[46] Canoeists set

Figure 5.3. Boat livery and restaurant, Humber River, 1910. Image courtesy of City of Toronto Archives.

Figure 5.4. Views of a sedate Humber River, 1900–43. Image courtesy of City of Toronto Archives.

Figure 5.5. William Gamble Mill, Humber River, west side, north of Bloor Street West. Attributed to George Edward Alexander Robinson, 1905. Image courtesy of Toronto Public Library.

out from liveries along the Humber Bay. Some couples lingered in the bay but most travelled up the river and used the ruins of the William Gamble Mill, which had burned down in 1881, as a romantic destination point.[47] Postcards of the Old Mill played up its reputation, one even including a poem by John M. Campbell, entitled "The Old Humber Mill," that described the river and mill as a "lover's ground."[48] Robert Home Smith added a tea room to the Old Mill site in 1914 to tap the popularity of the space.

People used postcards to capture and share their Humber promenade experience.[49] In a postcard to Miss Laura Bray, dated 4 June 1906, the writer comments, "wouldn't you like to be taking a trip up this clear sparkling river?"[50] And "CWR" spelled out the expectation of a paddle up the river to Miss Hazel Macpherson in 1908 when she wrote: "Bert Stokes and myself reached the old mill on the Humber by means of a rowboat from Sunnyside yesterday afternoon. We had a nice time but had to come back too soon."[51] And, on a postcard of the mill, "Maggie" wrote, "Dear Katie. How are you getting along? I am having a lovely time do you know this place. I was up here last night for a canoe ride."[52] A working-class man used most of the space on his mill-themed postcard to complain about Toronto, but at the end added: "Saw mill."[53] As succinct as the comment was, it illustrates how he felt that having reached the mill was worth reporting.

Renting a canoe and paddling on the Humber was a way of punching up for Torontonians. It was not within reach of Toronto's poorest citizens, who struggled to buy food. But for working-class people who had saved money, or for a growing class of white-collar workers, this was a way to spend an evening or an afternoon out and acquire some of the "trappings and signs" of gentility.[54] The Humber was a space where being middle class was performed, even if the financial background of the people doing the performance varied. A canoe was that generation's equivalent of getting a car, and the river was their lovers' lane. The *Star* noted the trend at Long Branch, west of the Humber, in 1903: "Canoeists are gaining numbers gradually, and already they boast a presentable fleet. The fortunate young men who own canoes are decidedly the most popular."[55]

The appeal and danger of a trip up the Humber River are illustrated by a double drowning that took place on 5 July 1908. George Farley, described as a tall athletic man in his twenties, worked as a manager with the Parker Dye Works. Still a bachelor, Farley lived with his mother and sister. At around 7 p.m. on a Sunday, he rented a canoe from Maw's Boathouse at Sunnyside and set out for a paddle in the company of a woman, dressed in summer apparel. They "were apparently well acquainted and were laughing and chatting as they paddled out on the water."[56] One of the boatmen at Maw's told the *Globe*, "I had no misgivings about them as I saw at once he was an expert canoeist: we can nearly always tell after we have seen them make a stroke or two." He added, "The canoe they had out was of our own make and is good and steady."[57] The last statement suggests how these canoes were built with sedate promenading in mind.[58] The couple was out for a couple of hours before the boathouse received word that something had gone wrong. At some point after 9 p.m., the canoe upended, and both occupants drowned; it was dark enough in the bay that no one saw the accident and the night was filled with enough "laughter" and noise that any sounds of a struggle were lost. Although this was ostensibly a playful space, enabled by a vibrant commercial sector, there were always risks when people paddled away from the docks.

This courtship culture drew regulation to the Humber. Karen Dubinsky and Carolyn Strange have demonstrated how a moral panic emerged around gender and sexuality in the period between 1880 and 1920 as Toronto strained under social and economic transformation.[59] Industrialization drew women into the workforce and turned them into a public presence in the growing urban environment. Middle-class reformers were unsettled by the presence of young single women on the streets of Toronto and fretted that they were engaged in illicit sexual activities, behaviour that could threaten the moral health of the nation and even, through immoral couplings, degrade the white race itself.[60] The state, social welfare agencies, and the law stepped in to police single working women who were visiting dancehalls and amusement parks, or, in this case, going for a canoe trip.[61] The Humber could not escape their gaze.

We get an explicit example of policing along the Humber River in 1916 when the County of York used a police boat to tighten its "grip on the traffic on the Humber."[62] Police targeted speeding motorboats and rowdyism, but paid "special attention to young women and girls who frequent the river every day, and stay out on the water till all hours in the morning with undesirable characters."[63] The arrest of a twenty-year-old girl, who was reported to have been on the Humber for several days and nights, was played up as the prequel of an upcoming purge. The girl, whose name is not given, was described as an "inmate" of the Alexandra Industrial School who had broken her parole. The industrial school, located in Toronto's east end, had been created in 1893 to serve as a reformatory school for wayward girls and while girls were supposed to be released from the school at age sixteen, some remained under its control into their twenties.[64] It appears the same constables, Robert Dennis and Robert Wilkins, were tasked with running the patrol boat each night, and kept an eye out for familiar faces. This is one of the rare moments when we see how the gaze of civic authorities rested on the Humber. In the midst of a river filled with hundreds of people, proper policing would reveal which women were in the Humber for appropriate courtship and which were not. It's hard to imagine that the policing described here was consistently maintained, but this example illustrates how surveillance washed over some bodies more thickly than others.

And yet as much as regulatory forces might have wanted to target women in the Humber, economic and cultural forces saw their presence there as entirely justified. The river was given over to young men and women, booths along the shore sold them lemonade and ice-cream, and businesses rented them canoes. The aquatic promenade was a gendered liminal space held in dynamic tension; it could never be fully policed, yet it was never fully free. In 1909, a police constable was canoeing with a lady (wife, date, or friend, we are not told) and was knocked into the river by the wake of a motorboat. The dunking set off a discussion about the dangers of high-speed boats in the river, but we can read it another way: when the police were not chasing down potentially wayward women in the Humber Valley, they were on the river courting them.[65]

Vernacular Bathing on the Aquatic Promenade

Vernacular bathing was part of the Humber River's fabric. But while the *Globe* granted the river a place in the "Summer Idyll" in 1925, the swimming hole was more often peopled with men rather than children, and more often seen as a problem than a romantic pre-modern space.[66] While bathers in the Don faced little competition for space, the mix of bathing and promenading on the Humber ensured conflict. There was a hierarchy at work here as well: paddling was a respectable masculine performance, whereas for men (in contrast to boys), bathing nude in the twentieth century was not.[67]

The problem was not simply that men were bathing in the Humber but that they were choosing to do so in such a public fashion, disrupting the routine of the aquatic promenade, and showing no shame for their activity. As the *Globe* phrased it in 1896, in reference to an incident involving five young men who were pulled before a magistrate, "Many complaints have been made of the *conduct* of young men, who go bathing in the Humber."[68] At least three of the men, hailing from Toronto and Toronto Junction, earned a one-dollar fine for their swim.[69] Similar language was repeated after a 1899 raid on the river: "To bathe in the pellucid depths of the Humber and swim about therein in nature's garb is a great temptation to the youth of the western city limits. Warnings have been repeatedly voiced, but seemingly, without in the least intimidating the unadorned marauders of the river's bank."[70] The fact eleven names were collected during the raid—seven of them false—suggests an effort to push bathers out of the river. But the term *marauding* suggests the true crime was not swimming but disrupting the heterosocial space on the Humber. Finally, two constables visited the river in 1905 and secured "a long list of names, some of which are incorrect, of boys swimming in the river without bathing suits. A large number of persons whose names were taken were naked, and others were using profane language to persons paddling up the river."[71] The transgression was in engaging with the people in canoes, making it impossible for the paddlers to look away.

The bathers' disruptive actions were spelled out by "Decency" in a letter to the *Star* in 1904. The letter began by saying, "I wish to call attention to the lack of self-respect and an appreciation of the ordinary rules of decency evidenced by a number of men (?) who frequent the Humber River on Sunday afternoons and use it as a bathing place."[72] "Decency" flagged the picturesque setting of the river and noted its popularity with Torontonians before going on to say that while out for a stroll on Sunday afternoon "near the bend in the river, where a small refreshment stand is located, I observed about twenty well matured men in swimming without bathing suits."[73] The group of bathers compounded their crime by not immersing themselves in the water as a launch, filled with two ladies and two gentlemen, went by, and "to make matters worse, the party in the launch were compelled to put up with such indecent remarks as 'Come in and have a swim; the water's fine,' and others unnecessary to mention."[74] The bathers needed to be compelled "to do two things—equip themselves with bathing suits, and *learn to mind their own business.*" He finished by noting there were many "other ladies and their escorts around this bathing place" and called for police intervention.[75]

"Decency," whose name proclaims his own sense of moral high ground, returns us to the theme of surveillance and exposure that we saw in "the letter from "Eye Witness," and demonstrates how the bathers were being targeted for an aberrant display of masculinity. The language used by "Decency" suggests the bathers' behaviour even stripped them of their right to be called men, in contrast to the respectable "gentlemen" and "escorts" who were plying the river with female companions in canoes and pleasure craft. Participation in the Humber relied upon self-governance; that is, proper decorum, gender behaviour, and dress. These men, whatever their profession, failed to measure up.[76] Visibility, once again, matters. The bathers were near a gathering place, drawn together in a group rather than splashing about in seclusion, and had the temerity to draw attention to themselves by speaking directly to the people in the river instead of keeping their mouths shut and ducking into the water. They were, in other words, challenging the genteel middle-class paddlers for spatial control of the river.[77]

When we look at these critiques of people bathing in the Humber we see nothing of *Toronto the Good*'s chaste boy, who appropriately hid his nakedness when he felt eyes upon himself.[78] Indeed, there was nothing of the boy in these "well matured men." Whereas the Don River's supporters infantilized the people in that river to create a moral terrain and essentialized the bathing boy as part of a pure relationship with nature, the critics of bathing in the Humber ensured its bathers received no such absolution.

The inquest into the drowning death of seventeen-year-old James Furniss in 1910 demonstrates how bathing in the Humber was a safety and moral concern. After considering the circumstances of Furniss's death, the inquest recommended three things: that bathing be banned south of Bloor Street, motorboats be restricted to five miles per hour in the river to prevent them from tipping canoes, and a patrol boat be assigned to the river to enforce both restrictions.[79] There were safety concerns. O. Hicks, who was credited with thirty-five years in the district, argued it was "dangerous whether they could swim or not, on account of the weeds." The excessive speed of motorboats was flagged, although that appears to have had nothing to do with this drowning. F.F. Reeves groused that property owners "should have some protection from the bathers, who had to trespass upon their land to get to the water."[80] There were also moral concerns. Charles Nurse, who had lived by the river all his life and who was often called in to recover drowning victims, said "since bathing [had] become so popular there decent people could not go picnicking as they used to," and that he considered the river to be "morally and physically dangerous."[81]

But while the inquest focused on the behaviour and threat represented by people bathing in the river, Furniss and his friends had started their trip in a canoe. They had enjoyed a Sunday paddle upstream and Furniss had only dipped into the water when they stopped at the second bend in the river, what was "familiarly known as 'the swimming hole.'"[82]

Authorities viewed canoeists and bathers as discrete groups, but in practice the lines blurred; a canoe was often the platform from which to take a swim. The experience of Arthur Poyntz Smyth, age twenty-two, demonstrates how busy the Humber could be and the diversity of users. Smyth, who worked as a clerk in the Eaton's Company Store, lived with his widowed mother and sister at 562 Bathurst Street. Of the four companions who joined him on Sunday, 17 July 1904, one of them boarded with the Smyth family, another lived in the same building, and the others, Milton Dedmon, 280 Bathurst Street, and Arthur Poyntz, 426 Queen Street, lived reasonably close by. The group rented a boat at 11:00 a.m. and rowed upstream to Deadman's Point, about a mile north of the river's mouth, where there were already several "boys" swimming. They could easily have been one of the groups that "Decency" had fretted about. Perhaps seeking a space of their own, Smyth's group paddled further upstream and then piled out of the boat and clung to its sides as Charles Traynor, the only skilled swimmer among them, pulled the boat across the river. Finally, exhausted, Traynor swam for the shore and the others clambered back into the boat but Smyth, clutching the boat's rudder, went under without warning. When he resurfaced, a passing canoeist, whose presence suggests how busy the river was, grabbed Smyth's arm and tried unsuccessfully to pull him up. Traynor made several dives to try to save him but it was an hour before Smyth was recovered.[83]

Critics suggest men bathing in the Humber were doing so in large groups and thumbing their noses at other people on the river in a deliberate moment of rebellion against the genteel use of the Humber.[84] But when we investigate these groups, the pattern is similar to what we have seen in the Don River; people headed out individually or in small groups and it was only from those smaller groups that larger, more boisterous, gatherings formed at popular spaces on the river and impressed their presence upon its social space. The use of space *was* being contested in the Humber, but these were spontaneous groups brought on by hot weather.

While the Humber was idealized as a space for romance, it was also a space where men got together with friends for a paddle, a picnic, or a swim.[85] Other articles welcoming spring blended boating and bathing as the *Star* did in 1908 when it noted that the "water was quite warm and a number of the sterner sex took advantage of the favorable conditions for their initial swim of the season."[86] When we look at reports of people who drowned in the Humber we find that some of them were local bathers, drawn to the river on a hot day, but many had made the trek from Toronto.[87] The Don River acted as a regional pool for local people, but the Humber was a destination point for middle-class bathers. And while there were working-class people bathing in the Humber, there were also students and white-collar workers, which means the efforts to control activity in the river were as much about the middle class policing itself as it was about policing the working class.[88] Despite the criticism they faced and public efforts at enforcement, people bathing in the Humber faced the typical one-dollar fine when they appeared in court, suggesting that the legal system was not prepared to be more aggressive.

The civic and media glare suggests conflict, but bathers, boaters, campers, and walkers probably managed to harmoniously coexist more often than not. The valley was actively promoted as a space for women to walk or paddle, suggesting how multiple uses—multiple presentations of the body—could occupy the same space.[89] In 1901 Atkinson's "Madge Merton Women's Page," with no hint that the Humber or the bathers in it were a moral threat, described how "this sleepy little river coaxes you into some of the peacefulness which seems to brood over it and its valley"; it recommended walks along the Humber or in High Park to letter writer "Mary B." instead of car rides or bustling about in the city.[90] When Parkdale friends George Dean and Leslie Ecker, both age seventeen, camped along the Humber River, undressed, and took what for Dean would turn out to be a fatal swim in the river in 1908, they were peacefully being watched by J.B. McComisky and his wife, who were camping nearby.[91]

But unlike in the Don River, the bathing boy is never canonized as a folk figure or as a symbol of class resistance in the Humber River. Regional histories flag the Humber as a popular canoeing and bathing space, going so far as to identify a geography of bathing that included popular places such as Dead Man's Hole south of the Old Mill and the presence of boys diving from trees into the river.[92] We get glimpses of nude bathing from F.D. Cruikshank and J. Nason, describing how in Weston "one of the chief worries of the village constable in these days was to keep the boys in bathing suits," and from May Irvine Knapp, who lends a rare female voice when she recalls growing up in Weston at the beginning of the twentieth century and swimming in the Humber.[93] But throughout the descriptions, the bathers and canoeists merge into a nostalgic tableau, with little mythologizing around, and no nostalgic pictures of, the bathing boy.[94]

The Boulevard: A Hard Edge in a Fluid Environment

The Humber Boulevard was envisioned as a tool to bring order and clarity to the fluid environment of the Humber River: it would expose marginal behaviours such as nude bathing and help police people canoeing on the river. Boulevards were a favourite tool of the City Beautiful movement, which peaked between 1900 and 1910. City Beautiful evolved from the parks movement, epitomized by Frederick Law Olmsted's New York Central Park.[95] Olmsted believed nature could act as a "curative and spiritual force"[96] for people hemmed in by the urban environment.[97] Central Park was created as a natural oasis in New York, but from there Olmsted envisioned boulevards as sinuous lanes of parkland stretching through the rest of the city.[98]

City Beautiful took Olmsted's environmental framework and merged it with the social, moral, and economic priorities of the Reform Era in an effort to "refashion cities into beautiful, functional entities."[99] Advocates believed the city was an organic element that could be moulded to uplift—with a nod to Darwinian social theory—the working class.[100] Nature would not be overwritten but rather used as a tool to reshape people and the urban environment.[101] City Beautiful advocates believed that ugliness led to social disorder and economic loss, while beauty would lead to moral order and commercial profit."[102] A boulevard would draw cleansing nature through the city and raise property values along the way. But there were limits to what nature could do. In one of the movement's formative works, *The Improvement of Towns and*

Cities, Charles Mulford Robinson argued that, "If commerce must rule on the city water-front, it were better that the shore line be made richly urban than allowed to become degraded nature," suggesting the movement's hostility to spaces that blended industry and nature.[103] City Beautiful advocates looked at the Don River and saw degraded nature and a space that was irrevocably lost, but they imagined that the Humber, a still viable "natural" environment, could be saved. Vernacular bathing had been able to survive in the degraded nature of the Don, but it had no place in the ordered environment that City Beautiful advocates envisioned in the Humber.

The Toronto Guild of Civic Art's 1909 *Report on a Comprehensive Plan for Systematic Civic Improvements in Toronto* provided a model for the Humber River Boulevard and demonstrates Toronto's City Beautiful vision.[104] Toronto had already built a boulevard through the Rosedale ravine in 1895; city council had contemplated a more elaborate system in the following years, but the push for a city-wide scheme got a boost from the Guild of Civic Art.[105] The guild saw Toronto's natural environment as raw material that could be reshaped and improved.[106] W.A. Langton led off the report by writing, "The lake shore, the Island, the rivers Don and Humber, the ridge, the numerous ravines, the facilities for outings both by land and water which make the city such a pleasant abode in summer, all these are *features which can easily be spoiled for want of timely recognition and incorporation in an inviolable plan.*"[107] The moral and physical environment of the Humber would be ruined without proper control.

The guild's report demonstrates how activities such as bathing would be removed. The guild used pictures from other communities to demonstrate how Toronto could be reworked and to allow Torontonians to imagine themselves looking down on an ordered environment.[108] A picture entitled "A Riverside Drive Both Useful and Beautiful" showed a river stripped of its riparian boundary and instead framed by the hard edge of a boulevard. The river's role was reduced to providing a picturesque view for people travelling on the road or in the water. But there was no riparian space in between for bathing; the river would soothe the eye but not the body.[109] Enveloping a space within the City Beautiful structure meant folding it within a middle-class set of values: the images were not merely instructional but intended to change the realm of what was deemed possible. It was not just that one did not go skinny-dipping from the new boulevard, but that the nude body disappeared entirely from the civic imagination. City Beautiful historian William Wilson demonstrates this process when he uses "before and after" pictures of a City Beautiful project. The "before" picture shows a naked bather standing along an undeveloped riverbank. In the "after" picture, the naked body has been removed and the riverbank given a hard edge.[110] Wilson's casual, and unremarked, inclusion and removal of the naked body suggest how even late twentieth-century writers used the naked body as a trope to represent the past and unfinished spaces.

Humber Boulevard promoter Robert Home Smith's name runs through the effort to establish a boulevard system in Toronto. Not only was he a member of the guild, he was one of five inaugural commissioners on the Toronto Harbour Commission and helped drive its 1912 waterfront development plan, which envisioned "a system of waterfront driveways, bridle-paths and walks across the entire 11 miles of waterfront."[111] We will see in the next chapter how the Harbour Commission reshaped Toronto's waterfront and created a new Lake Shore Boulevard along the Humber Bay. But Home Smith was the glue that held everything together: he envisioned his new housing development linking to the Humber Boulevard, which would plug into the new Lake Shore Boulevard being developed by the Harbour Commission as called for by the Guild for Civic Art.[112] Home Smith believed in the aesthetic elements of the City Beautiful movement—aspects such as lot size, design features, and picturesque sites are threaded throughout his Humber Surveys housing development—and the ability of the built environment to set a moral tone and enhance profitability.[113] Toronto's developers often used buildings covenants, which remained legal until 1950 in Canada, to exclude buyers based on race and ethnicity. But historian Richard Harris argues that Home Smith relied on price point and advertising that plugged an "Angliae pars Anglia procul," or "A bit of England far from England," to draw a British clientele rather than direct racial covenants. City Beautiful guidelines set a financial benchmark as to who could move into his development; they also ensured that nature would be perpetually at the homeowner's doorstep, albeit with a "trespass-proof fence" to keep intruders out of the housing development, and "adequate police protection to prevent damage to the trees, etc." in the new park space.[114] Contemporaries did not fail to note that Home Smith would profit from linking his personal projects to civic projects like the development of Lake Shore Boulevard.[115]

The Policing Boulevard

City politicians and the media embraced the Humber River Boulevard in 1911 because they believed it would provide a new way to police and protect the moral and physical environment of the valley. The media imagined it would end the unacceptable juxtaposition of bathing and courtship: "In future this water-course will be again turned into a beautiful and pleasurable summer picnic resort where self-respecting visitors may paddle their friends from the lake-front to the old mill without having to pass gangs of nude, uncouth men and boys who are not content with causing embarrassment, but pass rude gibes and seek to make it uncomfortable for unsuspecting boaters."[116] The *Star* was more concise about what was at stake when it ran a picture of the Humber filled with canoes titled "Protection for Boating along the Humber"; the accompanying text read, "Again the necessity of police protection along the Humber arises. Young people in canoes are frequently insulted by rowdies along the banks, and there is little restraint on those who choose to go in bathing without clothing. The Humber is too close to civilization to permit this district to go longer without an adequate police patrol."[117] The last line speaks to the effort to wrap the Humber in Toronto's civic gaze, though the joy of the Humber, even for couples paddling up the stream, was that it existed precisely at the edge of the city.

A boulevard would also police behaviour on the aquatic promenade itself. A reporter from the *Star* took a jaunt on the river on Sunday, 21 May 1911, just a few days after Home Smith's proposal made headlines, and noted, "From the Humber bridge to the Old Mill the river was dotted all the way by young men and their lady friends. An effort to count the number of small boats in the river proved discouraging, but it is safe to say that it was well over the thousand mark, and that no accidents were reported seems more a streak of luck than any good management, as the promiscuous paddling hither and thither of canoes regardless of any idea of regulations of boat traffic, made it seem at times as if an accident was inevitable."[118] The busy courting space demanded control and order. The *Star* article went on to add, "At about four o'clock yesterday afternoon a gang of rowdies in a gasoline launch, in the center of which could be seen a keg of beer, came down the river, and one bibulous occupant held aloft a glass of this stuff, flaunting it in the faces of all whom they passed."[119] Policing schemes had been discussed for the Humber before and fallen through but now it was time to step up: "No argument is stronger than this fact for the city's acceptance of Mr. Home Smith's offer and the annexation of the Humber district to the city in order that some law and order could be enforced."[120]

The boulevard could also protect the natural environment of the Humber River, ensuring the hybrid development of the middle Don was not replicated.[121] As the *Globe* described it, "The Humber River from the lake to Bloor Street is an ideal boating stream—deep, sluggish, meandering, and picturesque. The Don, a somewhat similar stream for about the same distance into the country, has been lost for recreation purposes by being irremediably industrialized. There has always been a danger that the Humber valley would be *vandalized* a similar way."[122] As council debated the costs of upholding its side of the agreement and building a road, Alderman Robert Yeomans argued, "We do not want an open sewer in the west as we have in the east in the form of the Don River . . . We are only committed to an expenditure of $125,000 during the next five years on a roadway. Even if the total cost of the roadway is $1,000,000 I would vote for the scheme."[123]

The *Globe* referred to the project as "The Humber Valley Improvement" in a direct, though likely unconscious, reference to the Don River Improvement project. While the Don was straightened for industrial use, the Humber would embrace an improved version of its natural shape: "The river is quite navigable and very meandering. The length of the channel will be very much increased by the formation of alternative cuts suitable for light craft, while the deeper and wider reaches will accommodate motor boats and launches."[124] Home Smith's plan to quarry stone from the upper reaches of the river would allow boats to travel further upstream, and the erection of a number of cement dams would moderate spring flooding and tweak its appeal as a natural setting. The valley was "unmarred" by railways, thanks to the high banks on either side,[125] in obvious contrast to the Don, which had been breached by multiple rail lines. But the promotion of the cement dams illustrates how this was not an effort to possess a Humber untouched by man, but rather an improved Humber.[126]

There are erasures at work within these comparisons to the Don River. The middle Don remained a vibrant recreation space for working-class men and boys and at times the city even cast a nostalgic gaze upon the boys. But their presence is ignored when the Don is compared to the Humber; in that conversation the Don is an industrial space, vandalized, and "lost for recreation purposes."[127] Toronto could look indulgently upon boys bathing in the Don but not when it turned towards the Humber.

The Limits of Intervention

Seasoned city watchers would have known that despite the enthusiasm shown for the Humber River Boulevard in 1911 there was reason to be skeptical the city would follow through on the project. Toronto had traditionally washed its hands of responsibility for people using the Humber and its moody bay, repeatedly turning down efforts to create a lifesaving service to patrol the area and arguing that because it fell outside the city's limits it likewise fell outside the city's responsibility.[128] Mayor Joseph Oliver was blunt when challenged on the issue in 1909: "We might as well try to patrol the Muskoka Lakes, because Toronto people rent canoes there."[129] Annexation had been discussed before, with the *Globe* suggesting that the city claim the Humber, illuminate the river channel, and place buoys at dangerous points.[130] The lights would mimic the "morality lights" that were being installed in public parks, and thus draw the Humber into the controlled urban environment.[131]

This time interest in annexing the valley fizzled as Toronto's boom came to an end in 1912, leaving the city hesitant to take on the cost of developing new areas.[132] Even as the Humber scheme was being launched, the city solicitor and the assessment commissioner expressed skepticism about its viability; they highlighted the cost of putting in roads and readying the valley land for development and doubted there was enough demand for high-class residential property in the city.[133] In the short term, they were right: the First World War slowed sales.[134] City staff also argued that annexing territory up to and beyond the Humber would be an awkward fit for the city because it would be left with land sandwiched between High Park and the Humber River.[135] In the end, Swansea, the village within that space, did not become a part of Toronto until 1967.

While plans for annexation fell through, the city did develop a portion of the Humber Boulevard. However, the final product was quite different than initially envisioned. In the heady days of spring 1911 city council members had toured the valley and imagined a boulevard cutting through the heart of it. By fall reality was setting in. Alderman Daniel Chisholm expressed the

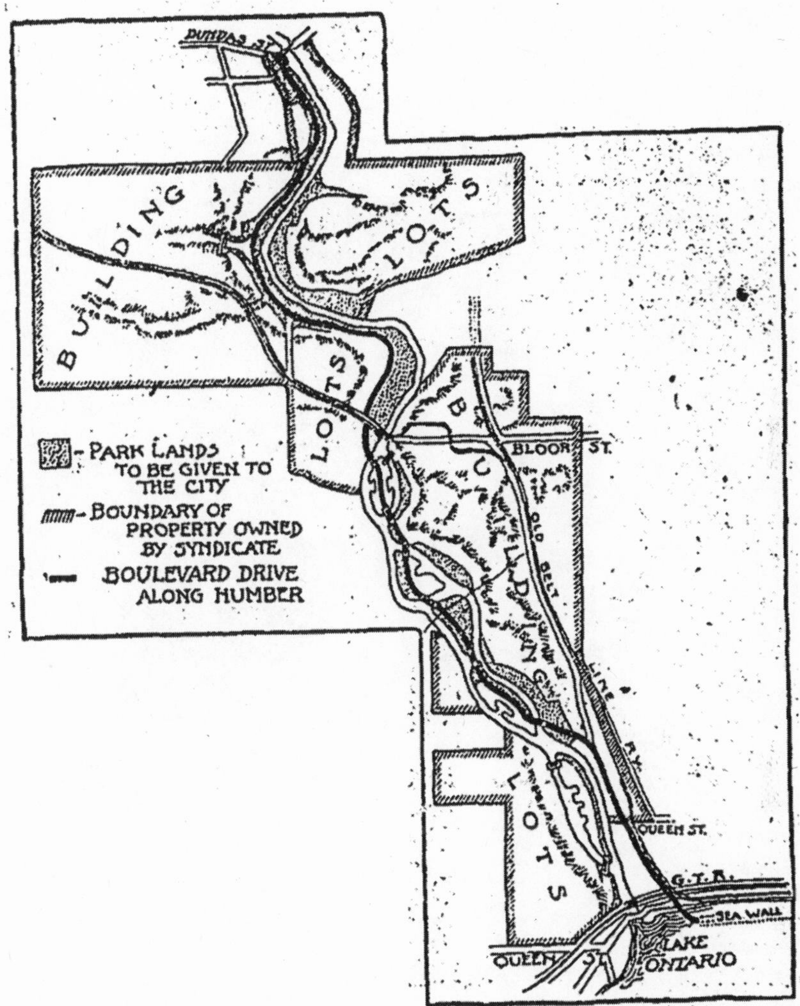

Figure 5.6. "Humber River Project Means Civic Beauty," *Toronto Daily Star*, 19 May 1911, 18. The original version of the Humber Boulevard envisioned a remodelled Humber River.

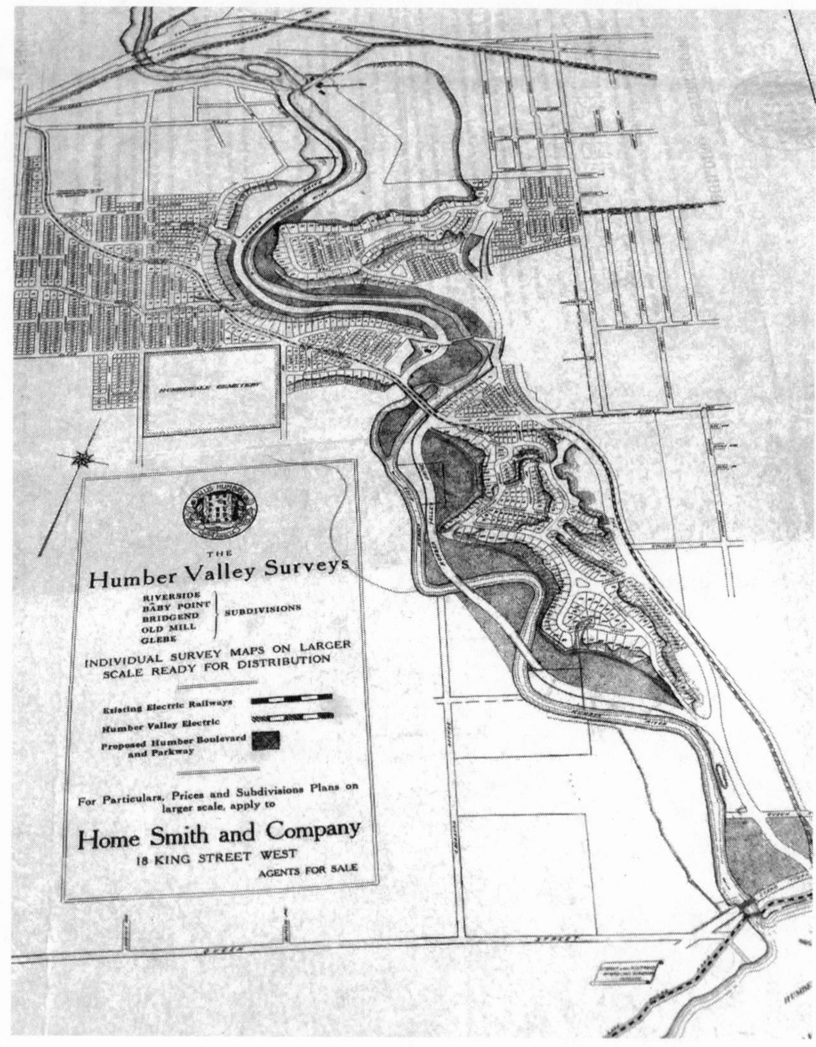

Figure 5.7. The Humber Valley Surveys as originally proposed imagined multiple river crossings. Image courtesy of City of Toronto Archives.

***Figure* 5.8.** Humber Boulevard, 1913.

***Figure* 5.9.** Humber Boulevard Tea Garden, 1917. Images courtesy of City of Toronto Archives.

Figure 5.10. Bathers and cars in the Humber River, 1922. Image courtesy of City of Toronto Archives.

challenges the city faced this way: "When we went up the Humber in boats . . . what appeared to be good land was pointed out to us. But the other day when the party visited the Humber we went up on a hill and were surprised to see that there was only a fringe of five or six feet of land, behind which was a swamp. We saw two boys in a boat where we had been told there was solid land."[136]

When a survey of the project was produced the boulevard hugged the sides of the river instead, crossing at only two points before joining existing roadways (see Figure 5.7). Through a series of negotiations, the Humber Boulevard was shifted even further from the "valley to the heights" on the east side of the river. While the initial plan had talked about five bridges over the river (see Figure 5.6), the final version settled for one.[137] Rather than a new road leap-frogging back and forth across the river, the city linked a short stretch of new road with existing roads such as Riverside Drive to create a "boulevard."[138] Practicality and parsimony trumped aesthetics.[139] The dialling down of the Humber River Boulevard project is a microcosm of the fate of the City Beautiful movement: elaborate projects fell through, and proponents focused on more modest changes to zoning codes, subdivision regulations, and local ordinances to shape the urban environment: social organization overtook moral organization.[140]

Middle-Class Victory

Proponents of the Humber River Boulevard still won in the end. The modified boulevard provided a practical link to the new housing division, a promenading space for Toronto's citizens, and a new gaze over the valley. The Old Mill bridge was used in postcards and advertisements to portray the picturesque setting of the valley.[141] Home Smith's effort to create a romantic ambience on the site worked: by 1914 pictures of the Old Mill figured in advertisements for the Humber Valley Surveys, and advertisements and postcards for the Old Mill Tea Garden at the Humber River and Bloor proliferated.[142] Home Smith's tea garden served 150,000 customers a year by 1921.[143] The romantic atmosphere of the Humber was reflected in a song published in 1924 by James M. MacGregor, the "Glen Warbler," entitled "When Roses Are Blooming in June," with lyrics about lads and lasses singing, laughing, and canoeing.[144]

We see the boulevard functioning as intended on a warm spring day in April 1915 when a line of motorists reached from the Lake Shore Road up the Humber Drive to Lambton.[145] On Sundays and holidays in 1916 drivers were backing up at the temporary bridge over the Humber River. With its completion in 1917 the Humber Boulevard was among amenities such as the island, lakeshore, and city parks listed as places to go to on a Sunday or a holiday. The *Globe* noted, "This is a new and popular district, many beautiful homes going up."[146]

The car and promenading spaces such as the Humber Boulevard created their own problems for a society keen on regulating behaviour. York County council reeve Thomas Griffith called for a tighter watch on automobile traffic in York township in 1915. "Some automobiles," Griffith said, "traveled too fast over the country roads. Others did not travel fast enough—in fact, in some places did not travel at all when they should have been traveling."[147] The article

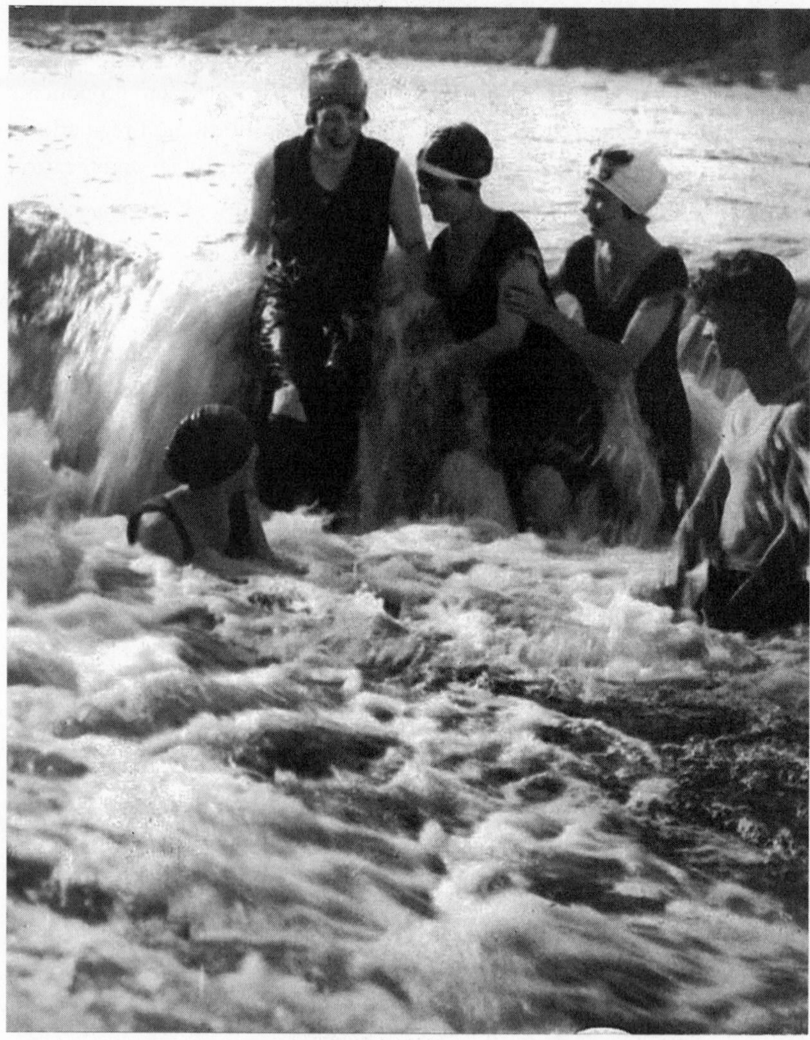

Figure 5.11. Bathers at the Humber River dam near the Old Mill, c. 1912. Image courtesy of City of Toronto Archives.

went on to say, "Inferences were left to the councilmen, but language was not spared in condemning the obvious immorality and other offences against the law as practiced by city joy-riders in portions of the township favored by them." Griffith's call for more policing to protect pedestrians, "especially ladies, travelling the highways after night," received nods of approval from representatives of Etobicoke, New Toronto, and other communities on the outskirts of Toronto. The car was well on its way to replacing the canoe by 1915 as space for private coupling, and, unlike the canoe, the car could not be limited to a discrete aquatic promenade along the Humber River.[148] The *Star* argued in 1921 that the "river should be cleared of motor-driven craft, the driveway properly lighted, and supervision of language and conduct inaugurated."[149] Instead of using the boulevard to discipline the river, lights and policing would be added to the boulevard to discipline the people using it.

Toronto's boulevards, which included the new Lake Shore Boulevard on the waterfront, were created as the automobile was emerging as a transportation technology, but the ramifications of that new technology were not yet clear.[150] Home Smith saw the car as only part of the solution in 1912 and hoped to set up his own streetcar line into the subdivision.[151] City Beautiful advocates saw controlled order when they imagined cars moving on a boulevard; they did not imagine the mix of speed and congestion that vehicles would bring.[152] By the 1920s the potential to move quickly—just a twenty-minute trip by car between the subdivision and downtown Toronto using the boulevard system—was a key selling point for the Humber Surveys.[153] Sold as scenic drives, boulevards soon became high-speed routes through the city.[154]

The automobile altered the environment of the Humber River in ways the promoters of the boulevard never imagined; people literally drove into the water supported by a firm bedrock river bottom. On a busy Saturday in August 1923, the drive was lined with hundreds of cars and the river filled with motorists taking a plunge. Drivers used their vehicles as change rooms and gave themselves and their cars a wash.[155] "Sunday, the bathers and neighbors claim, sees this retreat on the Humber drawing large crowds of motorists and bathers, the number of visitors to the pool is said sometimes to amount to one thousand in one day."[156]

The beach arrived at the Humber River, bringing bathing suits, public heterosocial bathing, and a security and surveillance system. As we will see in the next chapter, the Toronto Harbour Commission expanded Toronto's lifesaving service to cover the Humber River. The commission also completed the seawall on the bay's shoreline after 1912 and while its principal role was protecting the shoreline from erosion it was expected it would provide some shelter for recreational boaters.[157] When Stanley Sorrell was swimming near the Wanita Tea Rooms south of Bloor Street in 1921, he was seized with what was believed to be heart weakness and went under.[158] But he was quickly pulled out by James Trotter, a friend, and Harold Hall, both of whom had some training in first aid. Together they helped Sorrell regain consciousness and when the lifesaving crew arrived minutes later, he was on the road to recovery. The training received by citizens and quicker response times from the lifesaving unit had a significant impact on saving lives in the city.[159] The Humber was deep enough to allow lifeguard crews to reach bathers in trouble. In contrast, the Don remained out of reach; because it was too shallow for patrol boats, lifeguard crews had to paddle up the Don in a rowboat or hop into a car and drive to the scene.[160]

The new bathing culture brought men and women together and supplanted the old nude male bathing culture in the Humber River. But there is no distinctive moment when skinny-dipping in the Humber ends. Photographs from as early as 1912 show male and female teenagers in bathing suits in the river, and men, women, and young children wading in the shallow stretches of the stream (see Figure 5.11). The lower Humber was also used as a location for long-distance swimming races in the 1920s, turning the space of the river into a stage for athletic performance.[161]

However, we cannot trust photographs to give us the complete story of what was happening in the Humber River because according to the visual culture of the Humber, nude bathers were never there to begin with. Photographers like William James, who visited the Don River so often, did not memorialize the Humber River in the same manner.[162] Even into the 1920s, when the dominance of a new bathing culture in the Humber seems clear, there were still complaints in the newspapers from paddlers about the "lack of proper supervision by the police to curb the scores of boys and young men bathing in the river," youngsters who were, as usual, clothed inappropriately and drawing attention to themselves.[163] When the *Globe* waxed eloquent in 1925 about the potential loss of hidden spaces where boys skinny-dipped it included the Humber as well as the Don.[164] People bathing nude and wearing bathing suits were likely still sharing the Humber River in the 1920s, but using distinct spaces.

The Humber River was a space where the middle class constructed its identity through courtship and canoeing, while in the Don River it was the working class that used the space to construct its identity through idealizing the bathing boy. Bathing in the Humber did not play the same role in identity formation as it did for people growing up adjacent to the Don. That dichotomy helps explain how bathers are remembered in each river. Bathing was simplified in the Humber to races, the novelty of cars in the river, and pictures of bathing-suit-clad youth clambering on the dams.[165] The vernacular bather has not been entirely erased, and slips into some regional histories, but was never canonized as part of the Humber's history, at least not in the lower part of the river, where Torontonians focused their gaze.[166] While the Humber was peripheral to the city of Toronto, it was not a marginal space in the way that industrialization had transformed the Don. Instead it was imagined as a natural refuge from urban congestion. Bathing in the Don was a routine part of Toronto life; the regulatory gaze of the city slid over it entirely or embraced it. In contrast, the social, economic, and civic effort to create the Humber as a promenading space for men and women ensured that rambunctious nude men and boys were not embraced as part of an acceptable Humber experience.

6

SUNNYSIDE AND THE BEACH

The Toronto Harbour Commission opened the Sunnyside Bathing Pavilion and Amusement Park on the shore of Humber Bay, south of High Park, on 28 June 1922, "Ushering Toronto to the Threshold of her Newer Era." The *Globe* showed a crowd of adults in front of the new facility's grand entrance and announced, "Thousands of citizens of what was, not so long ago, mere 'Muddy York' yesterday thronged the shoreline at Sunnyside to witness the official opening of the magnificent boulevard and bathing pavilion."[1] The *Telegram* estimated that between 30,000 and an eye-popping 100,000 people turned out for the event: the latter number, just under one in five people in Toronto, was almost certainly an exaggeration.[2] Flanked by Toronto Harbour Commission chairperson Robert Home Smith and chief engineer E.L. Cousins, Toronto Mayor Charles A. Maguire "figuratively turned the key that opened the door for Torontonians to enjoyment of privileges and pleasure such as have been known heretofore only at great coastal resorts."[3] The new pavilion had room for 7,700 clients and opening night included tours between 6 p.m. and 9 p.m., with the first bathers expected to hit the water at 9 p.m.[4]

More than just a ribbon cutting for a building, the ceremony marked the official opening of the "new" Sunnyside Beach and Amusement Park, and the boardwalk that bound them together. The reference to Muddy York evoked a sense of progress; there would be nothing muddy about this new beach.

The bathing pavilion's elaborate entrance represented a conscious effort to show that patrons were moving from the cultural space of the city to the liminal space of the beach, a space where they could escape the rules and routines of everyday life (see Figure 6.1).[5] The beach is a lucrative boundary line between land and water and between the cultural trappings of the city and the rejuvenating natural energy of the lake.[6] Historians have detailed how beaches and amusement parks evoked the "carnivalesque" by the end of the nineteenth cenury: a term that draws on the European carnival tradition in which participants temporarily overturn the rules of everyday life and indulge in food, drink, and sex.[7] Boundaries were rarely ever truly upended, but the beach emerged as a space where it was imagined they *could* be, and the infrastructure around them was built to tap that energy.[8]

By the 1920s Sunnyside drew on a settled international language of beaches and amusement spaces. The carnivalesque had long since been commercialized at places such as Coney Island, in New York, and Blackpool, in Britain, to create what Gary Cross and John Walton refer to as an "Industrial Saturnalia": a play space for harried citizens of the industrial city.[9] Hanlan's Point on Toronto Island and Scarboro Beach on the city's eastern shoreline had proven there was a market for beachside amusement parks in Toronto. Sunnyside was part of this new courtship infrastructure that turned fun and the potential for social encounters into just one more commodity to be packaged and sold.[10] Unlike the Wiman Baths on Toronto Island, where the rules of behaviour between men and women were still in a state of flux, people walked onto Sunnyside with a clear set of expectations. The Toronto Harbour Commission set the stage; the crowd had only to enter and play their part as willing performers.[11] In this chapter, we will see the effort the commission put into trying to manage that performance and the limits of its control.

The harbour commission's redevelopment of Toronto's waterfront, launched in 1912, envisioned the rationalization of Toronto's waterfront into discrete industrial, commercial, and recreational sections.[12] It imagined a grand boulevard, Lake Shore Boulevard, pulling the entire waterfront

Figure 6.1. The Sunnyside Bathing Pavilion, 2021. The pavilion was intended to act as a portal to the beach. Image courtesy of Ryan Masters.

Figure 6.2. A look at a rough-hewn Sunnyside Beach prior to redevelopment in 1911. Image courtesy of City of Toronto Archives.

together. Marginal areas that had lingered on Toronto's waterfront would be erased and given new purpose. Toronto's historians have concentrated on the industrial and commercial aspects of the commission's 1912 plan.[13] I focus here on the recreational aspects of that plan, showing how the effort to create an amusement space at Sunnyside was a contingent affair. The harbour commission had always envisioned a recreational component with its plan but getting drawn into managing a beach, a bathing pavilion, and an amusement park were elements that emerged during the development process to meet public demand and to provide revenue for the commission. (The Toronto Harbour Commission still exists today as PortsToronto; it manages the Billy Bishop Toronto City Airport on Toronto Island and the Port of Toronto.)

In its role as waterfront manager, the harbour commission was drawn into managing the behaviour of individuals.[14] It expanded the Life Saving and Police Patrol Service to cast a net of surveillance over the entire waterfront and worked to push bodies towards the contained and controlled space of the beach.[15] The bathing pavilion was sold as a liminal play space but in practice it, not unlike the Wiman Baths, operated as a panoptical space where people's performances were measured.[16] The push for control included drawing up new rules for bathing suits and listening to new medical expertise around hygiene that promoted using chemicals such as chlorine to cleanse the bathing environment.[17]

The harbour commission's plans were never entirely successful: space, people, and place are not easily controlled. The commission imagined that it could replace the embodied relationship people had with the environment—the vernacular system that depended on people sharing knowledge of the hazards they found on an imperfect beach—with the industrial order of a manufactured beach. But new dangerous spaces emerged during construction of the beach and the environmental forces of Lake Ontario ensured that even a constructed beach could never be completely predictable.[18] Redeveloping the harbour was intended to erase old marginal spaces and create a new seamless industrial landscape, but when development lagged, bathers moved in and co-opted the underutilized new spaces for their own uses. The new Lake Shore Boulevard was supposed to allow orderly movement along the waterfront, but establishing an amusement park next to it ensured tension between drivers and recreational users. Finally, the harbour commission attempted to control the moral tone of Sunnyside, weighing in on the look and feel of the beach, the boardwalk, and the amusement park in an effort to create an environment that would instill middle-class values. But the need to turn a profit pushed the commission to give in to popular culture. Patrons and concessionaires reworked the amusement park into a symbol of working-class frivolity, and the commission could not afford to object.[19] At Sunnyside we can also see how Toronto's increasingly diverse population pushed into the new public spaces, remaking them as boundary spaces where people of different ethnicities rubbed shoulders.

The Setting: A Beach in Need of a Makeover

People had bathed in the nude along Sunnyside Beach in the nineteenth century, but by the 1890s nude bathing was restricted to a discrete space between Bathurst and Dufferin Streets, near the mouth of Toronto harbour, and by the early 1900s even that space appears to have gone into disuse. (Officially the nude bathing space remained in the city's books until 1930.)[20] The Parkdale Waterworks at the end of Roncesvalles Avenue was designated a bathing space for "men, boys, and women and children" in 1893 and a free bathing station was added in 1897.[21] The Sunnyside Bathing Pavilion would eventually be built just east of the Parkdale bathing area, suggesting how popular bathing areas were reinvented for each generation. Beyond the beach, Sunnyside's social life already included boathouses, dancehalls, concession spaces, and a lively canoe rental trade whose clientele paddled up the Humber River.[22]

Turn-of-the-century Sunnyside did not fit the postcard vision of what a beach should look like. The shoreline was prone to erosion. Railway tracks isolated the rough-looking beach and left little room for bathers to loll on the sand.[23] Hydro poles dotted the shore. When the Toronto & Niagara Power Company wanted to run a power line along the beach at Burlington Bay in 1913, Hamilton West Member of Parliament T.J. Stewart, argued, "It will spoil our beautiful beach," to which Toronto & Niagara Power Company general manager Robert John Fleming replied "We want only three towers ... There are already fifty at Sunnyside, and they do not interfere with bathing." "Surely," Mr. Stewart replied, "you would not compare Burlington Bay with that dirty, filthy hole they call Sunnyside?"[24] Sunnyside was both a recreation space and a corridor along the lake, which ensured that rail lines, hydro lines, and the harbour commission's new boulevard competed for space with recreational users. That competition would come to a head in the 1950s when Toronto demolished the Sunnyside Amusement Park to make space for the Gardiner Expressway.

But at the beginning of the twentieth century, the different users of the lakeshore managed to work together. Bathers paddled around the hydro towers and adapted as new roads encroached on their bathing spaces (see Figures 6.3 and 6.4).[25] The Grand Trunk Railway, for example, expropriated a section of the beach in 1911—including the property used by Brooker's bathhouses and the city's free bathing service—to elevate its tracks.[26] Faced with the new rail line and needing to ensure access to Lake Shore Road, the city built an overpass that curved directly across the face of the beach. But through it all the bathers remained.[27] While construction was supposed to have closed off bathing, harbour commission secretary A.C. Lewis pointed out in a 30 July 1912 letter to the city that "hundreds of boys still use the beach just east of Sunnyside Avenue for bathing purposes; as many, in fact, still use it as are conveyed daily to your supervised swimming-stations."[28] A William James photograph shows girls and boys swimming around the base of the overpass and using the bridge as a viewing deck to take in the scene (see Figure 6.5). As with the Don River, bathers needed to have an intimate understanding of the hybrid environment and any holes that lurked below the water to ensure their safety.[29] Despite its ramshackle nature, Sunnyside was Toronto's most popular bathing space when the harbour commission announced its redevelopment plan in 1912.[30]

Defining the Expectations of a Beach

The idea of how a beach should operate was still being refined in Toronto in the run-up to 1912. Sunnyside's bathing stations included a mixture of social venues: some catered only to men, some only to women, while others offered mixed bathing. Bathing had also established itself on Toronto's eastern waterfront; there a residential and cottage community had emerged and tumbled onto the beach by the 1890s.[31] Balmy Beach, Kew Beach, and pleasure parks such as Munro Park offered private and semi-public bathing facilities for residents, campers, and patrons.[32] While some bathhouses on

Figure 6.3 Bathers at Sunnyside Beach, c. 1909.

Figure 6.4. Bathers co-opted the stone bases of the hydro towers for their own use, c. 1909. Images courtesy of City of Toronto Archives.

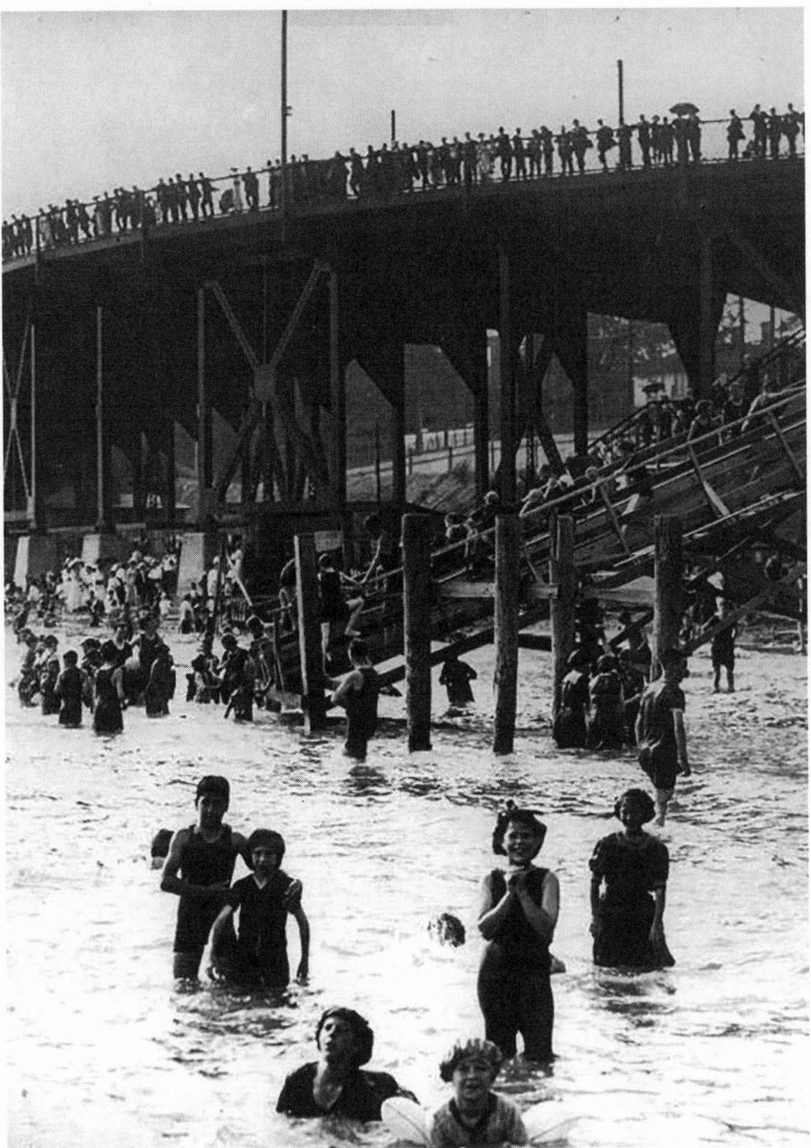

Figure 6.5. "Bathers at Sunnyside," c. 1910–12. Image courtesy of City of Toronto Archives.

Figure 6.6. Kew Beach bathing pavilion, 17 July 1915. The residential landscape merged with the east beaches. Image courtesy of City of Toronto Archives.

Figure 6.7. "The Robert Simpson Company Limited," *The Globe*, 17 July 1907.

Figure 6.8. "The Robert Simpson Company Limited: A Summer Sale at Simpson's," *The Globe*, 4 June 1910.

the eastern beaches only serviced men, women, or discrete groups, it was expected that everyone would share the sand.[33]

At times, Toronto's old guard still fought the emerging beach experience. Police took the names of "the reclining Venuses and their attendant Mars," who were having a "sand bath" after their swims at Kew and Balmy Beach during a warm stretch in 1906. Their sin was that they remained in their bathing togs and were lounging on the beach after their swim. Interviewed by the *Star*, the bathers were bemused by the restrictions. As one bather aptly put it, "They are doubtless making 'fish of one and flesh' of another."[34] Dressed in a legal two-piece suit, another groused, "What could they charge us for?" to which his companion replied, "Felony—stealing a nap," while "yawning and digging his toes into the sand."[35] With references to Venuses and Mars drying in the sun, lounging on the beach, and naked toes digging into the sand we get a sense of how bathing had become not just a hygienic or athletic endeavour, but a sensual one as well.

The Lord's Day Act made bathing on Sunday illegal in 1845, but police had often looked the other way and by the turn of the century the idea of outlawing public bathing on a Sunday was viewed with bemusement by the press. The Lord's Day Alliance made one last futile effort in 1915 to shut down bathhouses renting towels and suits at Kew Beach on Sunday, but it was quickly rebuffed by Toronto's police commissioners.[36]

The emerging commercial bathing culture promoted its sensual aspects and sold the beach as a space for mixed-gender play.[37] Torontonians were still debating what a beach should look like at the Wiman Baths in 1882, but by the twentieth century all they had to do was open a newspaper. Newspaper display advertisements allowed deep-pocketed department stores such as Eaton's and Simpson's to paint an image of what a bathing experience should look like (see Figures 6.7 and 6.8).[38] The advertisements displayed women in bathing suits, and often included men appraising female bathers.[39]

Struggles still existed behind those images. Cartoons at the turn of the century joked about how new women's bathing suits, complete with a skirt and stockings, represented the "height of fashion" and demonstrated the male gaze that rested on women's bodies when they bathed.[40] But the *Star*'s Elmina Elliot Atkinson, author of the Madge Merton column for women, suggested questions of modesty and fashion intertwined for women. While short sleeves were becoming popular for bathing suits, Atkinson argued middle-class women fought the change because they feared being seen with tan lines off the beach. "If people would only tell the truth it wouldn't be so bad. But they won't. They won't say, 'We wear long sleeves because we want to look well in the evening dress,'" Atkinson argued. "What they will say will be, 'It's so much more modest,' and they'll eye the woman in short sleeves until in self-defence she must follow the fashion."[41]

Advertisements for men recognized that the appeal of nude bathing still lingered and spelled out tangible reasons why they should suit up instead. A Simpson's ad in 1907 suggested, "Can you keep cool without a bathing suit these days? If so it must be after dark. If you want to see the nice assortment of bathing suits you should come to the Men's Store" (see Figure 6.7).[42] The image included men and women mingling on a beach, implying that putting on a suit and bathing with women during the day was far better than swimming unclothed with the boys at night.[43] Nude male bathing did not simply fade away: men were drawn into the new mixed-gender space of the beach.[44] Beach infrastructure appeared throughout the display advertisements; for instance, a 1910 advertisement showed a bathing pavilion nearly identical to the one the harbour commission would open in 1922 (see Figure 6.8).[45] The Hollywood film industry often gets credit for creating our image of the beach, but newspapers, photographs, and men and women simply sharing the sand did most of the leg work.[46] By the beginning of the twentieth century, the language of what a beach should be was in place, the tools to promote it existed, the harbour commission merely had to build it.[47]

Building a New Waterfront

The Toronto Harbour Commission was created by the federal government in 1911 from the bones of the city's Harbour Trust, which had managed the affairs of Toronto's harbour since 1850.[48] The Harbour Trust had lacked the authority or financial clout to make substantial changes to Toronto's harbour.[49] But the Toronto Harbour Commission would be different. It had the authority to manage the harbour and develop the waterfront. The commission would "walk on water" by filling in the lake to create new land, selling that land, and then using the profits to finance further work.[50] Commissions were creatures of the Reform Era. They were created to bypass direct political control: a board appointed by the city, Toronto's

Board of Trade, and the federal government would have the authority to get work done in a businesslike fashion.[51] Race and class fears drove the push for commissions in Toronto and elsewhere, with Canada's Anglo elite fearing that new ethnic and class alliances were corrupting local politicians and challenging their control.[52] In Toronto, the push for a harbour commission came from the Board of Trade, which was looking for a new tool to develop the dilapidated waterfront; it bullied Toronto's city council to sign on. The new commission won public endorsement in a referendum on 2 January 1911.[53] The city appointed three of the five commissioners and the federal government appointed two, drawing on recommendations from the Board of Trade for one of those appointments.[54] But after the appointments were made the harbour commission had the ability to act as a quasi-independent entity.

The harbour commission was given the tools to reshape the physical space of the waterfront and oversee its moral environment. The city transferred publicly owned waterfront land to the commission and gave it the ability to buy or expropriate the private land that remained.[55] Toronto Island was not part of the deal, though the commission was given control of its lagoons.[56] The commission was also given control of the city's lifesaving infrastructure in 1911, leading to the creation of a new lifesaving and police patrol. Initially, responsibility for the force was shared with the federal government, but in 1919 the commission took direct control of the force. Previously Toronto had relied on volunteers, the most famous of which was Toronto Island's Captain William Ward, who had managed the city's lifeboat on Ward's Island. Ward and his team of volunteers were credited with saving 160 lives. But Ward's focus had been on boaters and the merchant marine.[57] The commission envisioned a force that could patrol the harbour, enforce its bylaws, and manage the behaviour of people swimming along the waterfront.[58] It did not, however, get control of the city's free bathing stations; those spaces, and the lifeguards who staffed them, remained under city control.

The harbour commission initially expected to spend $19 million over ten years on three projects: filling in Ashbridge's Bay to create an industrial park, redeveloping the central waterfront into a commercial port, and creating new recreational space on the western waterfront for boat clubs and other recreational users driven out of the central waterfront.[59] Dreams of redeveloping the Sunnyside strip to improve bathing, protect the shoreline, and to lay out

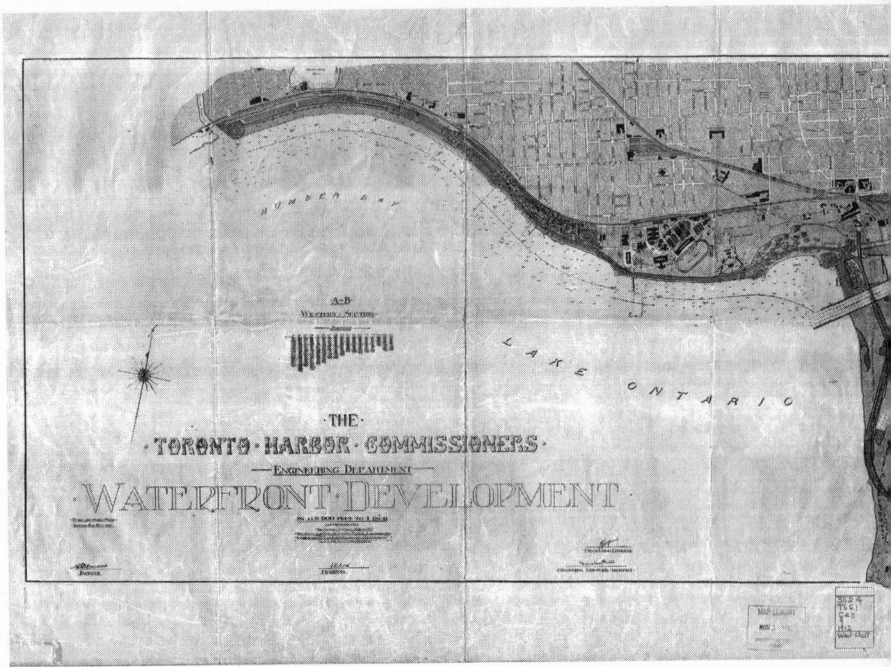

a lakeshore boulevard had long circulated in Toronto.[60] Robert Home Smith was already purchasing land along the Humber River, before the harbour commission received the green light, and imagining how his development could plug into a new waterfront boulevard. Toronto's middle-class elite was ready for change.

The 1912 waterfront plan blended utility and aesthetics, underpinned with a sense of moral order (see Figures 6.9 and 6.10). It would create distinct industrial, commercial, and recreational spaces, but a boulevard would run the length of the entire waterfront and pull everything together. As it reviewed the harbour plan, the *Toronto News* wrote, "In a comparatively brief space of time the whole waterfront from Victoria Park to the Humber River is to be transformed from a disgraceful state of neglect into eleven miles of utility and beauty."[61] The harbour commission's repeated use of terms such

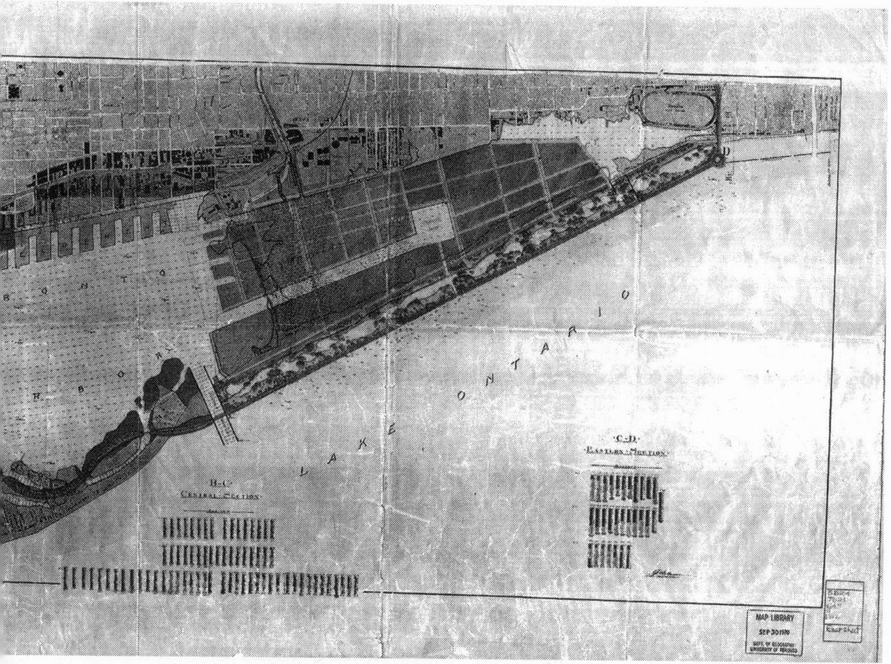

Figure 6.9. The Toronto Harbour Commission Waterfront Plan, 1912. It envisioned recreational spaces on Toronto's western waterfront, commercial docks in the harbour, and a new industrial district with a turning basin in Ashbridge's Bay, at the mouth of the Don River. A new boulevard would sweep across the waterfront, including across the island, and pull the entire project together. Image courtesy of University of Toronto.

as "disgraceful," "utility," and "beauty" suggests how it had bought into Charles Mulford Robinson's argument that "if commerce must rule on the city waterfront, it were better that the shore line be made richly urban than allowed to become degraded nature."[62] City Beautiful thinkers, as I have noted in the discussion of the Humber, associated "ugliness with social disorder and economic loss, and beauty with moral order and commercial profit."[63] Toronto's central waterfront had become degraded nature; development would cleanse it.[64]

The harbour commission would clarify how people used the waterfront. It proudly proclaimed that the entire harbour would be dredged to a uniform depth of thirty feet.[65] The new harbour would be composed of hard edges—land or deep water—with no marginal space in between.[66] It would act as a seamless transfer point, with the wharves connected to road and rail transportation corridors that would whisk the seaborne goods, like blood through a vascular system, into the city and beyond.[67] Recreational users had no place in this vision. The boat clubs decamped to Toronto Island or Sunnyside. The dilapidated docks and semi-industrialized spaces that had provided space for bathing were buried as the old waterfront was pushed south into the bay. And just as significant was the intellectual removal of the bathers; they are never shown in the "before" pictures of the central waterfront and never imagined in the pictures of the project in progress.[68]

The 1912 plan was created in consultation with Frederick Law Olmsted Jr., son of Central Park developer Frederick Law Olmsted and a revered designer and City Beautiful advocate in his own right. It included a boulevard intended to run the length of Toronto's waterfront.[69] The boulevard, as originally planned, ignored the distinct elements of the waterfront and replaced them with a corridor from which people might view, but never touch, nature. *Financial Saturday Night* captures this utilitarian aspect through the imaginary eyes of "Cap," as he takes in the changes on Fisherman's Island and contrasts them with the spaces he had known: "Where Cap had stood on a soggy beach was a noble paved boulevard, wide as Spadina Avenue, with a fine belt of young trees fringing an artificial lagoon to the north, and a concrete retaining wall to the south."[70] Consistent pavement would replace the indeterminate nature of a beach, and where nature was planned it would be improved and displayed.[71] On the western shore, the new Lake Shore Boulevard treated Sunnyside Beach as window dressing. The plan even severed the pedestrian connection with the beach by placing the boardwalk north of the boulevard. When it was suggested the new breakwater might block the view of the lake, the harbour commission pointed out it was low enough that people would still be able to see the lake from the boulevard; the visual experience of people on the beach was not considered.[72] The City Beautiful–inspired plan, on paper at least, did not imagine an embodied relationship with the lake.

Making Adjustments

Everything did not go according to plan. The harbour commission adjusted the 1912 plan based on fiscal realities, the need to work with Toronto's distinctive physical and human environment, and the need to please local

Figure 6.10. Sunnyside, Toronto, 1926. The Sunnyside Amusement Park sat in the middle of the waterfront traffic corridor, resulting in conflict between drivers and people trying to reach the amusement park and the beach. Image courtesy of Toronto Public Library.

users of the waterfront. The plan to deepen and rebuild the harbour went ahead, but the commission squabbled with Toronto's railway companies over who should pay for building a viaduct. The viaduct was a critical component in opening the harbour for commercial use: without it the corridor of rail lines laid down in the nineteenth century would continue to hamper access to the new waterfront. The financial stand-off delayed the building of the viaduct until 1930. That delay was critical; it hindered efforts to create a commercial waterfront. There were other challenges as well. Efforts to develop commercial and industrial land were hampered by the pre– and post–First World War depression in Canada and the war itself.[73] Stymied elsewhere, the commission turned its attention to finding ways to extract profit from the western waterfront, a space over which it had full control.[74]

Olmsted's boulevard could have been placed on any waterfront. It too underwent revisions. Plans to run it across Toronto Island and across the face of a newly redeveloped Ashbridge's Bay were delayed and eventually dropped. And even on the western waterfront, the harbour commission needed to rework it to adapt to Toronto's distinct geography and to take into consideration Torontonians' relationship with their lake. Recreational bathing was ingrained and seen as a healthy activity, so a space had been earmarked at the end of Roncesvalles Avenue where people had traditionally bathed.[75] Significantly, that space was highlighted with heavy black type—a last-minute addition to ensure people knew their established bathing space had not been forgotten—when the harbour commission's illustrations ran in Toronto's media.[76] Harbour commission survey engineer Norman D. Wilson critiqued the "Omstead plan" [*sic*] in 1915, arguing it separated pedestrian traffic from the beach, had "No satisfactory solution for bathing houses and boathouses," and put a boulevard between the children's playground and the beach.[77] There was little consideration for how people might interact with, or even reach, the water in Olmsted's plan. Wilson called for placing a set of recreation buildings directly adjacent to the beach and suggested building a "Winter Swimming Tank."[78] Alfred Chapman, the commission's head architect, reflected Wilson's focus when he made changes to the western waterfront plan in 1915. Chapman's revisions pulled the recreation and boardwalk spaces towards the new beach, which he anticipated with industrial precision would be exactly 110 feet wide.[79] Wilson and Chapman were both born and raised in Toronto and each played a role in localizing Olmsted's original plan.

The Sunnyside Amusement Park emerged as a contingent addition, intended to raise money for a cash-strapped harbour commission, from a similar process of negotiation. The 1912 plan included a "Reservation for Amusement Features," complete with sketches of a Ferris wheel, on the western side of the development, but gave no hint as to how it might be accessed by rail, road, or foot.[80] With construction already under way in 1915, Chapman identified a space between Keele Street and Roncesvalles Avenue for an amusement park, which, when "properly equipped, in such a situation, would undoubtedly produce a great revenue."[81] The amusement park was squeezed into an available space along the boulevard to pull in needed revenue and outflank private operators planning to build next to Sunnyside.[82] The contingent approach of finding space for the amusement park meant it sat as a knot in the middle of a traffic corridor across the waterfront, leading to traffic congestion as automobile use increased in Toronto. That precarious position

Figure 6.11. Making land for the boulevard, Sunnyside, looking east, c. 1920. Image courtesy of City of Toronto Archives.

sowed the seeds of its destruction in the 1950s when it was bulldozed to make way for the Gardiner Expressway, a major highway which further severed the city from the lakeshore.[83]

Unknowing Space

Rebuilding Toronto's waterfront created a dangerous and unknowable environment while work was in progress, and the completed waterfront included hard lines and boundaries that had to be mediated by signage or surveillance. The dredge became emblematic of the transformation, with the *Globe* describing how work drew "the intense delight of huge crowds who watch intently enormous mouthfuls of muck disappearing into the gullets of the monsters."[84] But even as the dredge churned, recreational use of the waterfront continued, creating a dangerous mix of industrial-scale work and human-scale use.[85] Prior to construction, Sunnyside Beach had a gentle slope, and bathers had enough experience with the beach to warn each other about potentially dangerous spaces.[86]

Construction created the worst of both worlds; bathers could no longer rely on embodied knowledge and shared experience, and the harbour commission had yet to create the predictable environment that a manufactured beach promised.[87] When Theresa Cummings, age fifteen, drowned while bathing at Sunnyside in 1916 during a hot spell, the city and news media blamed the harbour commission, arguing she had stepped from a shallow beach into dredged terrain.[88] The commission denied her death was linked to its work, but argued it could not guarantee a consistent bathing environment during construction.[89] Signs ordered for the waterfront stated, "while the beach is under construction it is impossible to maintain a uniform beach, and anyone bathing does so at his own risk."[90] Considering a female had just died along the waterfront, the gendered expectation built into the signs seems even more striking.

The *Star* argued the waterfront was now under the harbour commission's authority and should be closed during construction.[91] But even the commission recognized the limits of its power in 1916 and refused to shut down bathing, certainly not in the middle of a hot summer. As commission chief engineer E.L. Cousins phrased it, "You can imagine the wail that would have been raised if there had been no bathing there during the past hot weeks."[92]

Building a waterfront created new hazards. Storm sewers were extended with the shoreline, and, while the harbour commission planned to extend them beyond the breakwater, initially they poured out overflow within it, carving trenches under water that claimed the lives of bathers in 1920 and 1921.[93] The hazard was enough that the city passed a resolution stating, "the newly formed beach on the lake at Sunnyside has been declared dangerous in many places."[94] The resolution drew a cranky response from the harbour commission, which argued, "there is no reason why this beach should be declared more dangerous than any of the City beaches and, at the present time, danger signs are placed at the outlets of all the storm overflow sewers."[95]

The new harbour was, by design, dangerous for anything other than its intended use as a harbour. The spaces where bathers had paddled in shallow water around dilapidated wharves became a regulated environment of hard edges and a consistent depth of thirty feet. When Willie Beach, of 94 Peter Street, and his dog fell into the bay at the foot of Bathurst Street in 1925, seventeen-year-old Thomas O'Brien jumped in and saved his life. But the new shore offered no purchase for climbing out of the water; O'Brien had to keep himself and the boy afloat until two employees of the Dufferin Construction Company pulled them out with a rope. Beach was safe by the

Figure 6.12. Lookout tower, 1920. Image courtesy of City of Toronto Archives.

time the lifesaving patrol arrived, but the crew did rescue his exhausted dog, which, the crew noted in its report, had been gamely keeping Beach afloat until O'Brien arrived.[96]

Managing Bathers

The harbour commission did more than just reshape land; it expanded Toronto's lifesaving service to create an integrated system of surveillance to manage harbour activity and bathers along the new waterfront. Lifesaving stations and lookout towers were set up along the western channel, the Humber River, and Scarboro Beach; a new eighty-foot tower was built along the eastern channel to provide a "commanding view of the Bay and Lake Front south of the Shore line from Gibraltar Point to Victoria Park Point" (see Figure 6.12).[97] A phone network with an operator on duty twenty-four hours a day linked the lifesaving stations.[98] Meticulous records tracked the day-to-day activities of lifeguards and enumerated rescues and deaths. Boats gave the patrol reach, with a speedboat available "for emergency calls, where speed means lifesaving."[99] The web of protection was rounded out with 138 lifesaving appliance stands "equipped with ladders, buoys, pike poles, hooks and in some cases, drags."[100]

The lifeguard system was a disciplinary tool intended to protect people but also to train them in how to behave along the new waterfront.[101] The lifesaving records tracked drownings, people out of place, and unusual activities: when someone drowned the lifeguards questioned why their surveillance had missed it.[102] Throughout the nineteenth and early twentieth century, it had fallen to newspapers to explain what had gone wrong when people drowned in Toronto: the newspapers often interviewed people to find out. Now it fell to the lifeguards to explain what went wrong and newspaper coverage relied on their expertise. Efforts to increase the strength of the security net were ongoing with new substations added to fill in remaining gaps.[103] The lifesaving patrol even mused about the day when alarms could be installed at each of the 138 lifesaving appliance systems, allowing people to draw an immediate response from a mobile patrol.[104]

Signage was part of the new security system. The commission created a new beach on Olympic Island (part of Toronto Island), but just outside the designated bathing area the lakebed, by design, dropped rapidly into the freshly dredged harbour. The boundary was managed by fencing and "Danger Deep Water" signs, deterrents the harbour commission counted on people to respect. But people did not always follow the rules. Horace Buzzacort, age thirteen, of 49 Wright Avenue, strayed outside the safe bathing space in 1920 and drowned. The frustration in the lifesaving crew's report on the drowning, which noted the safety procedures and that a safe zone was "plainly defined," is palpable.[105]

Despite the efforts to create a seamless net, it was still a precarious system. The performance of the telephone network that held it together varied from day to day.[106] Bathers found—or sought out—holes in the net. When Ashley Reith, age nine, of 4 Robinson Place, and George Coblick, age five, of 4 Robinson Terrace, were found drowned near the Alexandra Yacht Club in 1928, it was noted the boys had been seen earlier bathing along the shoreline but had evaded the lifeguard boat and could not be seen from a nearby watchtower.[107] The people in the towers could not accurately judge just what they were seeing every time either. What appeared to be an overturned canoe on 5 July 1925 was revealed to be an "old log with sea gulls on it" when a patrol arrived to investigate.[108]

While Sunnyside Beach was the harbour commission's signature recreational space, it seeded the waterfront with supervised "Safe Bathing" areas. The designated spaces were an effort to focus bathing in designated areas and a tacit recognition that laying a net of surveillance over the entire waterfront was untenable: "At present time it is absolutely impossible to maintain a competent patrol covering the 42 miles of shore line where at many points bathing can only be indulged in at considerable risk."[109] The challenge flexed and swelled with the temperature and humidity. As the 1921 report put it, "It has always been a problem as how best to keep urchins from frequenting the most dangerous part of the harbor front during the hot weather."[110]

In theory, the safe bathing areas represented an effort to remove the vernacular bathing spaces people had carved out on the waterfront and replace them with the authority and wisdom of the harbour commission. But in practice, many of the new "safe" bathing spaces were in familiar places. For example, in 1921 the "Old Fort" safe bathing area was located between Bathurst Street and Strachan Avenue, near where Torontonians had traditionally swum on the west end of the bay.[111] The safe bathing areas allowed Toronto's ethnic communities to carve out spaces of their own along the waterfront, just as the Macedonians had done along the Don River. This sort of territorialization by ethnic communities did not go unnoticed. The lifesaving crew noted in 1923 that the Old Fort beach "has become very popular with the foreign population living in that neighbourhood."[112] The "foreign population" is not identified in the report, but the crew almost certainly meant members of Toronto's Jewish community for whom the Old Fort Beach would have been readily accessible from the Jewish neighbourhood around Spadina Avenue.[113]

People resisted the industrial logic the harbour commission was trying to imprint on the waterfront. The new industrial park in Ashbridge's Bay, for example, included a shipping channel and turning basin but the new infrastructure was underutilized and, in a familiar tradition, became a marginal territory that could be co-opted by recreational users. Life Saving and Police Patrol reports show numerous groups of youngsters and young adults bathing in the space, swimming across the channel, and making it their own.[114] The ship channel provided a space for small groups to gather out of sight of the prying eyes of lifeguards but was close enough to Cherry Beach that the lifesaving crew could be summoned if someone got into trouble.[115]

Lifeguard captain A.P. Saunders wrote in 1923, "The ideal condition would be attained if it was possible to restrict bathing to the protected bathing areas alone." He acknowledged the "idea is a trifle too dramatic to put into force in Toronto for the present," but added, "I hope to see it in successful operation here some day in the future."[116] By the 1930s, the harbour commission did have the tools it needed to push bathers out of industrial spaces. The city made bathing in the harbour's industrial sections illegal in 1930; the harbour commission followed in 1932, with Bylaw 20 giving the commission the authority to outlaw bathing in the industrialized sections of the harbour.[117] The new bylaw, endorsed by the courts, enshrined in law what the Toronto Harbour Commission had hoped to achieve with its 1912 plan: the clear division of Toronto's waterfront into recreational and industrial spaces. An amendment in 1934 added Toronto Island's lagoons and the breakwater along the Humber Bay shoreline to the list of forbidden spaces.[118]

The new lifesaving system forced bathers to conform to the rules and regulations laid down by the harbour commission. But it did save lives. When we look at the City of Toronto's annual police report records in the period between 1895 and 1935 we find that, despite a growing population, the average number of people who drowned per year drops by about one-third—from an average of about twenty people a year to fewer than thirteen people a year—after 1918, when the harbour commission expanded lifesaving services. But even with a more rigorous lifesaving system in place, weather still played a critical role in the number of people who died on the waterfront in any given year, with a hot summer drawing more people to the water or a stormy day increasing risk, as the commission noted in 1931, when a long warm summer led to more drownings.[119]

Surveilling the Body

Emboldened by its efforts to control where people bathed in the 1930s, the harbour commission turned its sights directly on the bodies of bathers, with a push to regulate bathing suits. The commission could police what people wore at the Sunnyside Bathing Pavilion but had no authority beyond its gates.[120] In pitching for more authority from the federal government, harbour commission general manager J.G. Langton argued that the commission's act of incorporation, which gave it authority over the harbour, should extend to the bodies rowing, boating, or bathing in its waters. Langton pointed to the distinctive environment of the harbour, where people still swam in close proximity to commercial docks and within the turning basin, as justification for the change, noting, "As you are fully aware of the local conditions in this Port for swimming and boating I think you will appreciate that we are confronted with problems different from that of any other Harbour Commission." In other words, because people were paddling or swimming in its territory, the harbour commission believed it had a right to decide how those bodies should appear: men choosing to wear trunks were considered the primary problem. The commission, which had been created to enact a multi-million-dollar transformation of Toronto's waterfront, would now turn its attention to the cut of people's bathing suits for the "public good."[121]

The federal Department of the Marine, which oversaw the Toronto Harbour Commission, came on board and A.R. Tibbits, the supervisor of harbour commissions, even offered his opinion on how to define a proper chest-covering bathing suit in the bylaw to ensure that shirtless men were brought to heel. (The bathing costume should be "suspended from the shoulders of the wearer and covering the major portion of the torso of the body." However, it "may have limited portions cut away to allow direct exposure to the sun." Specifying the torso be covered was critical, Tibbits argued, otherwise the bylaw "might permit trunks to be worn if the flimsiest of suspenders were attached." Boys under twelve would not be covered by the bylaw.) But Tibbits also cautioned, "In these days it seems as though a certain amount of latitude must be allowed the public in the exposure of nakedness," hoping the bylaw would manage a balance.[122] The commission unrolled its new bylaw on 19 June 1934, sending copies to the chief constable, aquatic clubs, and local newspapers.[123] Reviews were mixed: Toronto's police gave the new policy a positive response, but the *Star* openly mocked it, arguing lifeguards would be too busy appraising bathing suits to rescue people.[124] Early efforts to enforce the bylaw were met with complaints from bathers about the heavy hand of the commission.[125] And even the commission's solicitor, who was ready to go forward with charges against over a dozen "boys"—they were likely teenagers, although their ages are not included in the archival material—for bathing in the now off-limits ship channel, did not think the charges would stick if he tried to prosecute "these lads for swimming in scant garb."[126]

The new bylaw was enacted in 1934; by 1935 efforts at enforcement were already breaking down. Toronto learned the same lesson that other resorts across the North Atlantic were learning: bathing suits were getting smaller, people were already exposing more skin, and society no longer had a problem with it.[127] When we look at bathing suit advertisements between the turn of the century and the 1930s we can see hemlines on men and women marching upwards from the knees to the thighs, and tops becoming smaller for women and disappearing for men. As a police sergeant on duty told the *Star*, "People aren't as strait-laced as they used to be."[128] Tom Nichols, a lifeguard at Sunnyside, was philosophical about the failing efforts to convince men to keep their tops on, and the chaste bathing boy lurked in his comments: "Russia and Japan have nude bathing, and they aren't any worse morally than we are. The minute you put a bathing suit on a child you create a sex-consciousness it will never overcome." He added, "You can't enforce a law that hasn't public support."[129] By the end of the year the harbour commission threw in the towel. Toronto police had already stepped back from active enforcement, and attempts to charge people ended in "a warning or on suspended sentence."[130] E.L. Cousins, now general manager of the commission, acknowledged the "turmoil" created by the law, and after talking with sports associations and Dr. A.G. Hall, International Outdoor Health Association, the commission finally accepted that swimming trunks, which had been in use since the nineteenth century, were part of the "modern trend."[131]

But the commission was still worried about propriety and in 1936 amended the bylaw to read, "No person shall bathe, swim or wash the person in any of the waters of the Port and Harbour of Toronto except when wearing a proper bathing suit sufficient to prevent indecent exposure of his or her person."[132] The bylaw mirrored Toronto's Bathing By-law no. 12774. Cousins argued the words "indecent exposure" were key: "These words would have some meaning before a Magistrate on any prosecution because of analogous provisions in the Criminal Code."[133] Cousins is not specific about which provisions he is referring to, but new attitudes towards and definitions of nudity were emerging under the law.

The federal government had recently added a new tool that brought the nude body into the Criminal Code in a way it had never been before.

Section 205 (A) was introduced in 1931 as a direct effort to address the tactics of the Sons of Freedom sect of the Doukhobors, which included ritual stripping during legal proceedings or protest marches.[134] Indecency had been part Canada's Criminal Code since the nineteenth century, carrying a summary conviction fine of fifty dollars or up to six months in jail.[135] But the 1931 revision added a specific clause dealing with nudity: singling out people who appeared nude with one or two other people in public places—the focus on the Doukhobors was clear—and people who had the "intent" to parade while nude, or who had just done so. The addition also raised the stakes for those charged by setting the punishment at up to three years in prison.[136] Conservative Minister of Justice Hugh Guthrie said bluntly during debate over the legislation that the longer jail term was intended to punish Doukhobors who ignored the law.[137]

In its effort to target Doukhobors, the new law redefined what nudity and indecency meant. Previously charges for nudity could be laid under parts of the Criminal Code covering indecency, the word that likely caught Cousins's attention, but the focus of that law was on people performing an indecent act rather than on nudity or bathing.[138] The amendment made the presentation of nudity itself a crime but defined nudity in terms of a person who is "so scantily clad as to offend against public decency or order."[139] As legislators noted, it was not the same definition found in a dictionary, which equated nudity to nakedness and defined it as a complete lack of dress. The Canadian Parliament had created a law with the potential to target bathers, both dressed and undressed. As Liberal MP and former justice minister Ernest Lapointe suggested, "I am quite sure some judges would find that a certain bathing suit does not accord with public morality, whereas others would find the same costume absolutely correct."[140] The Senate agreed and amended the law so that the decision was not left up to individual judges; prosecution could only proceed with "the consent of the attorney general of the province in which the alleged occurred."[141] The amendment ensured Section 205 (A) was a difficult offence to use against nude bathing, let alone people in a bathing suit.

The Bathing Pavilion

The Sunnyside Amusement Park and the Sunnyside Bathing Pavilion represented the face of the harbour commission's new waterfront, a space

Figure 6.13. The Sunnyside Bathing Pavilion, displayed for the camera, showcased the beach as a public space, 1924.

Figure 6.14. Sunnyside, children's bathing beach, 6 August 1925. Images courtesy of City of Toronto Archives.

where the effort to attract a clientele competed with the effort to control how that clientele behaved. The $400,000 bathing pavilion was expected to set the tone for the entire recreation area. As chairman of the harbour commission in 1923, Home Smith argued it would "be such a model of excellence as to make possible the holding of concessionaires and others to the same high standard."[142] The pavilion was modelled after a facility at Lynn Beach, Massachusetts, but Alfred Chapman was responsible for its distinctive design.[143] Chapman used a Italian Renaissance design on the beach side of the building, while he drew on Byzantine influences for the commanding Lake Shore Boulevard entrance.[144] Those that passed through the entrance could walk up a flight of stairs to a terrace, which offered refreshments and a view of the beach.[145] Change rooms were open to the elements, but women had dressing booths covered by canopies while the men made do with benches. The "boys" had their own entrance and change room, separated from the men's change room by a six-foot-high metal fence.[146] Admission cost twenty-five cents for adults and fifteen cents for children; bathing suits and towels could be rented and the facility included laundry facilities to ensure a steady supply of both.[147] Other services included hairstylists, and first aid rooms for people who were injured.[148]

The swimming hole was not forgotten. The development's original kiddie pool deliberately mimicked a natural bathing space (see Figure 6.14).[149] Comics in the news media took the image even further to envision the kiddie pool as a primordial space.[150] However, the rustic nature of the pool drew criticism from Toronto's chief medical officer Charles Hastings, who complained the pool did not drain properly, leaving the water within it in a stagnant and foul condition. The original kiddie pool was replaced by the 1930s with a shallow round cement pool, a standardized model that would become a familiar sight in parks for decades.[151]

The bathing pavilion, more than any other place on the waterfront, represents the space where the harbour commission had the tools to achieve the control over behaviour and comportment that it yearned for.[152] The pavilion included a proprietary relationship with the beach, with an area 1,200 feet long and 225 feet wide fenced in for the exclusive use of the pavilion's patrons.[153] An attendant activated a shower as people headed from the change room to the beach to ensure that everyone was cleansed before diving in. Two-piece bathing suits, with an upper shirt that draped over a set of shorts or skirt, were mandatory in the pavilion.[154] However, that did not stop the Murray-Kay Company from greeting the opening of the pavilion with an advertisement for its "popular one-piece suits."[155]

The pavilion's clientele was expected to include "bank clerks, stenographers, and junior bookkeepers" and mothers who could "bring their children and leave them confidently all day to the care of the attendants and life guards."[156] Paying to get into the pavilion lent it "a form of exclusiveness" but it was an exclusiveness that had to be fortified by the sharp eyes of lifeguards who also served as boundary keepers because there were "always rank outsiders who try to get into the social swim by way of the lake front."[157] Drowning was not expected to be a concern in the secured bathing area, but if people did need to be rescued efforts to resuscitate them would be handled discreetly "in a private room set apart for the purpose, under the direction of a trained nurse."[158]

The city's media participated in setting the tone for Sunnyside when the bathing pavilion opened in 1922. The *Globe* argued readers needed to rethink how they imagined a beach: "Regulations are irksome, yet unregulated bathing would be fatal to the permanent success of the project. Those who picture children in bathing suits, running hither and thither at will at all hours and on every part of the beach will have to revise their ideas. There will be ample facilities for children and adults as well. But they will be regulated facilities."[159] The use of the word "project" suggests how this was an effort to uplift and transform the bathing experience.

Controlling the tone of the resort included banning cameras from the bathing pavilion.[160] The *Star*'s women's column endorsed the rule against cameras, arguing it was necessary to maintain middle-class propriety in the dressed-down space of the beach: "Those of us, however, who are humbly conscious of our elbows and of how we look from the side, and of how much we owe to the hairdresser, will be very glad we cannot be caught inadvertently by a wandering camera man, and exhibited wherever the illustrated sections of Sunday papers penetrate."[161] Pictures of people splashing in the water *were* a popular fixture in Toronto's newspapers and bathing beauty contests would become a staple of the Sunnyside Amusement Park experience.[162] But the harbour commission hoped the bathing pavilion would be above the fray. The viewing deck at the pavilion suggests bathing was an activity worth watching, but only for those who were invited into the controlled social confines of the resort. Perhaps ironically, banning cameras from the bathing pavilion has diminished our memory of the pavilion in that images of the tony resort the commission hoped to created were rarely captured on film.[163] Instead we are left with photographs from special events when the ban was ignored and crowds were photographed in front of the pavilion.[164]

We can also see how the bathing pavilion was caught between serving a twentieth-century beach culture that saw the sand as a space to suntan and socialize and a nineteenth-century bath house culture focused on the hygienic role of bathing. There was a limited amount of beach in front of the pavilion, which meant that on a busy day sunbathers were pushed onto the lawn. The harbour commission's new beach was almost utilitarian, with limited space for sunbathing or socializing. For that we can blame the initial City Beautiful–inspired plan that had treated the beach as a visual space for people travelling along the boulevard, rather than a physical space for recreational users. But there were also structural issues: the commission owned the water lots along the shoreline and had to work within their boundaries, which limited the space available for building a beach. Even when it decided to extend the beach and create more space the commission was hemmed in by the offshore seawall.[165]

The seawall itself was built to fortify the shoreline and create a sheltered space for bathers and boaters. The harbour commission even promoted the idea that an enclosed bathing area would raise the frigid Lake Ontario water temperature by as much as 15°F and create a more inviting environment.[166] By the 1930s the commission was quietly admitting that the seawall appeared to have no impact on temperature.[167] The seawall was one more intervention intended to reshape the waterfront; once again the commission discovered there were limits to what that intervention could do.

The bathing pavilion treated the lake like a pool: patrons showered as they left the change rooms to ensure a hygienic environment. Patrons with the clear intention "to adorn the sands" rather than the water were showered just the same.[168] The mandatory shower reflected the logic that a bathhouse was a tool for cleansing people rather than a space for socializing. The *Star* even suggested the lake water in front of the pavilion be chlorinated to provide maximum hygienic security. "It is impossible to imagine bathing being conducted under more sanitary conditions—the bathers given preliminary baths, the water chlorinated, the bathing suits sanitized," the *Star* argued, before admitting, "It is a heroic attempt but it must have its discouraging phases. Supposing for instance that a group of unsterilized boys were to go in swimming immediately upstream."[169]

Despite the exuberant coverage in the *Star*, it is not clear that the harbour commission ever did chlorinate the lake water in front of Sunnyside; if it did the process was probably short-lived. The commission's archival material on Sunnyside does not mention the process, and chlorinated water was not used as a draw in advertisements for the bathing pavilion. However, Toronto's medical health officer Charles Hasting was floating the idea of chlorinating public bathing stations throughout the city in 1924.[170] According to Hastings, "chlorination has been found to be a most effective safeguard, especially in those locations where the water is not open and does not circulate freely."[171] He told the *Star*, "We have been doing that all along in connection with private baths."[172] By "private baths" Hastings likely meant pools, but chlorinating outdoor bathing water had been used at a beach in Washington, DC, in 1922.[173] The chlorination discussion illustrates how new medical definitions of hygiene based on the chemical composition of water and pollution and efforts to create a sterilized environment now guided the operation of a bathing space. It was this same logic that would push the city to "close" the Don River in the 1920s and which led to the closure of Sunnyside's first kiddie pool.[174]

Adding a pool to Sunnyside in 1925 was a logical next step, given the discussion around water quality, chlorination, and temperature. The new Sunnyside Bathing Tank—known today as Sunnyside Gus Ryder Outdoor Pool—gave the harbour commission full control over the bathing environment. Its development had been discussed as early as 1915. By the 1920s, Toronto already had a mix of public and private pool facilities. The city-owned Harrison Baths, which included a pool and shower facilities, had opened in 1909 on Stephanie Place just north of Queen Street. The Harrison Baths were a creation of the Reform Era intended to provide a cleansing space for working-class people who did not have their own shower or bathing facilities at home.[175] By the 1920s, they were a popular recreational space with community and school groups using the pool, but their hygienic use remained important; in fact 120,000 used the facility's showers in 1920.[176] A better model for the Sunnyside Bathing Tank was the High Park Mineral Springs, opened in 1913, which had expanded over the years to become a popular recreational pool.[177] Pools had relied on circulating their water to provide a hygienic environment but by the 1920s chlorination was becoming the system of choice.[178]

Building the Sunnyside Bathing Tank was a financial necessity for the harbour commission owing to a series of cold summers: a profitable waterfront demanded a consistent bathing experience that only a pool could offer (see Figure 6.15).[179] The new bathing tank opened on 30 July 1925, but while the pool was intended to offer a secure, hygienic, and managed environment, manufacturing a bathing environment created new risks. The pool's impact on the bodies of Torontonians was apparent immediately, with records showing cut toes and fingers, bruised arms and knees, sprained backs and wrists, scraped feet, hips, and hands, and bruised heads from diving into the shallow end of the pool.[180] People used to swimming in a lake needed to adjust to the hard edges of the "bathing tank." The persistence of bruises, abrasions, and cuts through 1926 and 1927 suggests the distinctive dangers of bathing in a cement structure.[181] We do not have specific numbers for injuries in the pool itself, but we can make comparisons. In 1927, with the bathing tank included in the numbers, the lifesaving patrol dealt with 447 instances where first aid needed to be dispensed to bathers. But in 1928, when the Sunnyside Pavilion was given its own nurse, the number of minor injuries handled by the lifesaving patrol dropped to 117.[182] Clearly, most of the injuries were happening in the pool.

The Outside Looking In

The city's free bathing program had been created in 1897 to give Toronto's boys—and eventually girls—a safe place to swim. While the harbour commission's lifesaving force managed the waterfront the free bathing program remained under direct city control. At Sunnyside it had an itinerant existence, moving up and down the shoreline, its location dictated by environmental conditions and the harbour commission, which preferred to keep "free bathers" away from paying customers.[183] The free bathing station challenged the commission's efforts to set the tone of Sunnyside; it was thrown together every year and many of its working-class patrons jumped the fence and penetrated the bathing pavilion. They were the "unsterilized boys" and girls that the *Star* had fretted about.

Figure 6.15. The Sunnyside Bathing Tank opened in 1925 to provide a predictable bathing environment. Image courtesy of Toronto Public Library.

Figure 6.16. The free bathing station at Sunnyside, 1924. It was just down the shoreline from the Sunnyside Bathing Pavilion, and the harbour commission laboured to keep the two groups separate. Image courtesy of City of Toronto Archives.

The free bathing station and the pavilion were snug up against one another in 1924 and a Toronto Transit Commission photograph shows bathers along the shoreline with the wooden clapboard fencing that surrounded the bathing space serving double duty as a clothes rack, in contrast to the neat lockers bathing pavilion clients could expect. Beyond the wooden fence is the rail fencing of the Sunnyside Bathing Pavilion running into the water and, further down the shoreline, the pavilion itself. We can see "free bathers" tumbling out of their area and literally climbing the railings of the exclusive bathing pavilion space (see Figure 6.16). Harbour commission general manager J.G. Langton griped in a 21 March 1928 letter to city property commissioner D. Chisholm that "it is extremely difficult to control free bathers from making their way to the paid enclosure and bathing tank."[184] With the bathing season approaching, Langton suggested the free bathing station be moved east of the Sunnyside development to keep the free bathers out of the paid space; he also recommended its relocation because "the temporary building erected is not in keeping with the surroundings of the Amusement area."[185] The ramshackle appearance of the free bathing station and its penny-poor patrons did not fit the image the commission was trying to create at Sunnyside.

The laid-back nature of the free bathing spaces and their ad hoc construction is brought home by the complaints that the harbour commission, and even the city's own staff, directed towards them. Toronto's chief medical officer Charles J. Hastings complained about the condition of the free bathing station washroom in 1922, and about how the beach was "strewn with garbage and refuse." It was, Hastings wrote, "not in keeping with the rest of the surroundings in this vicinity."[186] In 1928, the commission complained that male free bathing station attendants were "misbehaving with young ladies."[187] The complaint raised sharp concerns with property commissioner D. Chisholm, who quickly demanded details.[188] And in another case harbour commission general manager J.G. Langton complained that men were changing in open sight, thanks to the thrown-together nature of the bathing station.[189] A set of permanent free bathing structures—"in keeping with the Sunnyside development"—was finally established in 1929 east of the bathing pavilion; the low-slung buildings, which blended in with the beach rather than standing out, met with the approval of the harbour commission.[190] The use of streetcars to ferry free bathers to Sunnyside would continue until 1950.[191]

Perhaps ironically, Torontonians were more likely to see free bathers than bathing pavilion patrons when they opened their newspapers. While photographers were forbidden in the bathing pavilion they had no trouble visiting the free bathing beach at Sunnyside, pictures of which appeared liberally in Toronto's media.[192] Postcards captured the laid-back atmosphere of the free bathing spaces as well.[193] Popular images of Toronto's free bathing program focus on smiling, happy children riding a streetcar to the beach or queuing up along the side of the road, waiting for their ride home.[194] But there was always a mixture of young adults among the crowd at the free bathing beaches.

The Poor Man's Riviera

The Sunnyside boardwalk and amusement park represented the harbour commission's final intervention on the waterfront, one in which its effort to create order clashed with the desire of the crowd to create their own experience. Reflecting the ethos of the City Beautiful movement, the commissioners imagined that public space, properly managed and defined, would model behaviour for Toronto's increasingly ethnic and racially diverse population.[195] Engineer E.L. Cousins outlined the commission's goals in a presentation to the Hamilton Harbour Commissioners in 1919: "If proper forms of amusement are provided for the people in general their energies are accentuated thereby, which, indirectly, is in the interest of the individual from an earning capacity viewpoint as well as from the viewpoint of output in so far as industry and commerce is concerned."[196]

The effort to create the ideal environment drew the harbour commissioners into the minutiae of setting up a resort. They weighed in on the design and clientele of the Sunnyside Pavilion, which—not to be confused with the bathing pavilion—was built to be a high-class dancing and refreshment establishment, even suggesting what type of silverware the facility should use. As the Sunnyside Amusement Park was under development, the commissioners attempted to control its built form, selected its colour patterns, and were quick to voice their concerns when the product did not measure up.[197] Robert Home Smith groused, in a 10 September 1923 letter to chief engineer and manager E.L. Cousins, that the United Cigar Company had painted its location red and strung up illuminated signs—complete with unsightly iron support trusses—over the boardwalk: "I do not wish to be hypercritical, but

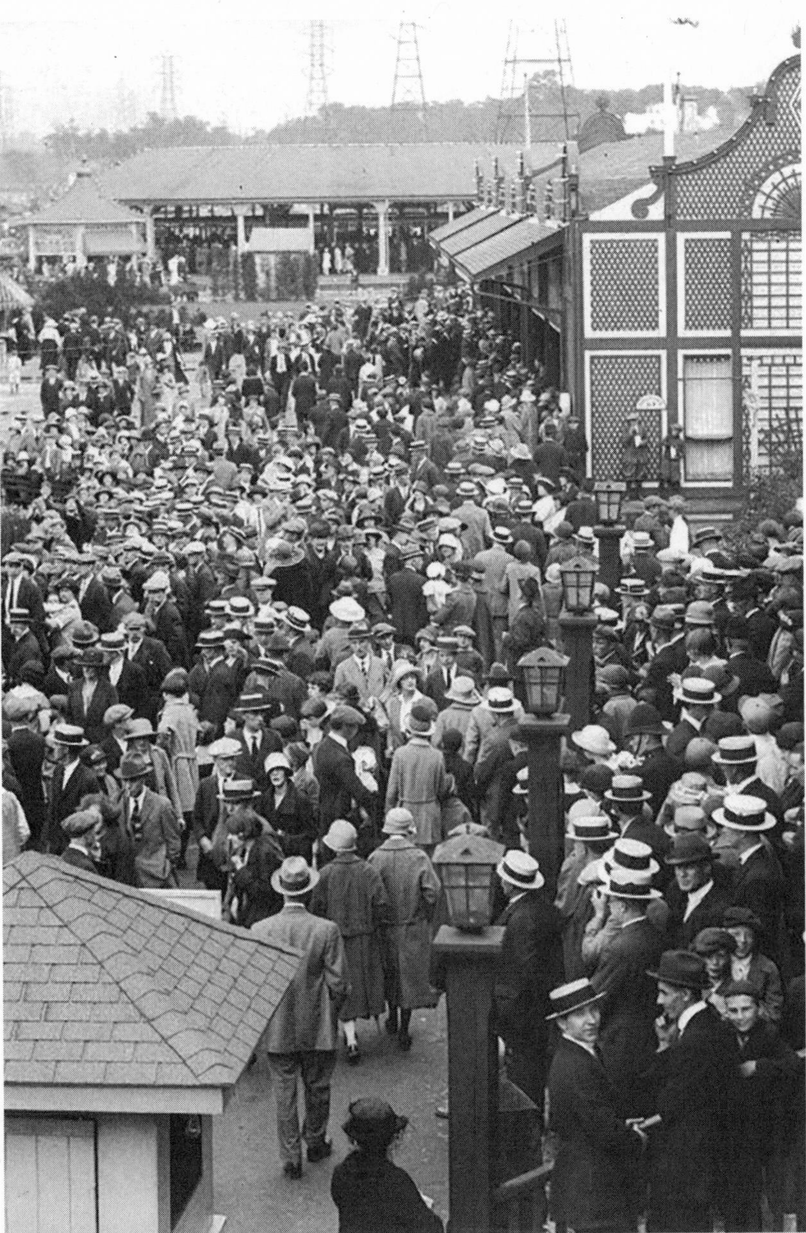

Figure 6.17. "Sunnyside, crowd in amusement area, looking west," *Globe and Mail*, 1 July 1924. Note the consistent design in the amusement park's pavilions. Image courtesy of City of Toronto Archives.

I would point out that they have pretty well ruined the two pavilions and there does not seem to be much to be gained in our spending time and money and good taste in the erection of buildings if the whole effect is to be spoilt. Don't make any mistake about it, I am mad."[198]

We see moments where the effort to create order and a more genteel setting seems to have paid off. Toronto's traditional Easter Parade had predated the Sunnyside redevelopment but quickly made the new boardwalk its own. The city's tonier class showed off the city's latest fashions on Easter weekend providing, as the *Globe* noted, a stark contrast to the irreverent boys bathing in Toronto's Don River.[199] And pictures of Sunnyside in the 1920s reveal a well-dressed crowd. People did let their hair down when they went to the resort, but they saw it as a public outing and dressed up accordingly.[200]

But the collective memory of Sunnyside is that rather than being uplifted, Toronto's working-class people made the space their own. The harbour commission had set the stage, but its need to attract a crowd and turn a profit limited its ability to control the performance.[201] Sunnyside is remembered for the crush of people drawn by the special events that were held at the beach, the crowds of people that thronged the amusement park, and the men and women who flirted and displayed themselves as they strolled along the boardwalk.[202] The working-class ethos of the resort led it to be nicknamed "the poor man's Riviera,"[203] a name that became so entwined with the space that even the harbour commission used it decades later in a retrospective on its work.[204] The phrase demonstrates the collective effort needed to turn Sunnyside into a space of class resistance.[205] Sunnyside became the poor man's Riviera not only through the experience of people who went there in the 1930s and 1940s but through the retelling of their experiences.[206] The phrase is all the more telling because Sunnyside was not the only poor man's Riviera. The same sort of construction—using the terms "poor man's Rivieras" or "people's playgrounds" to democratize the spaces—has taken place around Coney Island, Manitoba's Winnipeg Beach, and at other resorts across North America and Europe.[207]

The notion of a poor man's Riviera reflected the ability of working-class people to take part in the excitement. Not by going to a place such as the Sunnyside Pavilion, although even it was renamed Club Top Hat and became less exclusive by the 1940s.[208] And not by taking part in the Easter parades, which owed their exclusivity to the time of year as much as to the fashion on display, but by joining thousands of others to stroll the boardwalk in the heat of summer and take in the events at Sunnyside. Those events included beauty contests, launched in the 1920s, during which women displayed themselves for men.[209] And they included mass spectacles such as the burning of ships off the shoreline, including the *John Hanlan* and the *Lyman Davis*.[210] Sunnyside's amusement park depended on a taste for the carnivalesque. But it was merely a taste. As John K. Walton has argued, class boundaries and societal norms were being flirted with, but not overturned when people went out to the beach.[211] Amusement parks were never as carnivalesque as their promoters liked to suggest or as patrons wanted to believe: the excitement was contained within a commercial infrastructure that profited from it.[212] Sunnyside depended on a mix of clientele with full wallets, and its businesses marketed their goods at prices they thought their clients could afford. The poor were not co-opting the beach; they were a critical component of it.

Sunnyside does give us a window into how Toronto managed its growing ethnic diversity in the early twentieth century. In the United States, ethnically diverse Europeans mingled at resorts and the process helped create a sense of whiteness among them. This process stands out most clearly in places like Atlantic City, where African Americans played a subservient role—pulling a white clientele up and down the boardwalk in carts—and provided visual contrast to an ethnically diverse white crowd.[213] This same process was at work in Toronto in the early twentieth century with the pervasive use of blackface in vaudeville shows: white performers and a white audience shared the experience of imagining black people as an object of amusement and a racial other.[214] But we should not think of different ethnic groups folding seamlessly into a white majority in early twentieth century Canada. Canada's different ethnic communities maintained the cohesiveness of their communities through religious, cultural, and community groups: they created and were pushed into distinctive neighbourhoods and spaces of their own.[215] But there were also boundary spaces where the different ethnic communities rubbed shoulders with each other and with the dominant Anglo-Saxon group: Sunnyside was one of those boundary zones.[216]

Pervasive anti-Semitism in Canada ensured that Jewish people, Toronto's largest non-Anglo-Saxon ethnic group throughout the early twentieth century, asserted their presence when they walked on Sunnyside's boardwalk. Changing demographics and Toronto's response to them explains the dynamics we see on the waterfront. Numbering in the hundreds at the end of the nineteenth century, Toronto's Jewish community had expanded to nearly 35,000 by 1921, or roughly 6.6 percent of the city's population. It was a small proportion compared with those of British origin, 85 percent of the population in 1921, but was significantly higher than any other ethnic group in Toronto.[217] When reform-minded British Torontonians fretted about the "foreign-born" and the survival of the white race in Canada they were often targeting Jewish people, who they continued to see as a race apart. Those attitudes turned ethnic enclaves within Toronto, such as the downtown Ward, which was dominated by Jewish people in the early twentieth century, into exotic spaces.[218]

Jewish people encountered a complicated geography of access and exclusion on Toronto's waterfront. They pushed through the active hostility of Toronto's British population to access the public space of Toronto Island, but were often excluded from hotels and boarding houses on the island.[219] Kew Beach was a draw for Jewish people who lived nearby, but on weekends it also attracted crowds of Jewish people from downtown Toronto who would hop on the streetcar and head east for a picnic or a day at the beach. As anti-Semitism in Toronto rose during the 1930s, the presence of Jews at the beach drew the attention of the pro-Nazi Beach Swastika Club in 1933 and led to a picnic being attacked by Swastika Club members. The dust-up was a prequel to the Christie Pits Riots on 16 August 1933, which saw thousands of Jewish and pro-Nazi rioters take to the streets.[220]

Sunnyside and other public spaces along the waterfront became places where Torontonians encountered difference. Privately run recreation facilities, such as pools, golf courses, hotels, and boarding houses, could and did police their boundaries to push Jewish people and other racial and ethnic groups away from recreational facilities.[221] But Sunnyside had been designed as public space by the Toronto Harbour Commission, and it needed to turn a profit. The commission and the businesses within its zone were loath to turn away paying customers and in fact turned Sunnyside into a draw for the Jewish community. As Sam "The Record Man" Sniderman described it, Sunnyside "was the focal point of our courting and social activities from April to September. And, with the Toronto Islands somewhat out of bounds to many of us, Sunnyside was our only chance for a holiday resort and a respite from the city's hot months of July and August."[222] Like Sunnyside,

Manitoba's Winnipeg Beach served the Jewish community. The Canadian Pacific Railway created Winnipeg Beach at the beginning of the twentieth century and remained both its patron and promotor. The corporate giant's involvement and interest in turning a profit ensured that Winnipeg Beach was open to Jewish people even as official and unofficial covenants kept them out of other resorts around Lake Winnipeg.

But the fact that it was designed as public space did not mean Sunnyside was above the fray. The visible presence of Jewish people clearly concerned contemporaries. Toronto South Member of Parliament Dr. Charles Sheard reported the popularity of the resort to Canada's Parliament in 1925 but felt it worth noting that "Sunnyside Park had attracted large numbers of citizens, but principally Hebrews. To such an extent that a sign had been put up by someone reading: 'We gave you Palestine. Let us have Sunnyside.'"[223] Similar signs, or at least rumors of such signs, have been reported at beaches across Canada throughout the early and mid-twentieth century and suggest the discomfort Anglo-Canadians felt about sharing their public spaces with others.[224] Toronto filmmaker Harry Rasky recalled childhood visits to the Sunnyside Bathing Tank where the number of Jewish people admitted into the pool were limited—a recreational quota—though he noted once people paid their dime and "were inside the turnstile gates, all were equal, more or less."[225] (Unsurprisingly, I have not come across mention of such a quota in the harbour commission's records on Sunnyside.) It is questionable whether the actual number of Jewish people at Sunnyside was as overwhelming as Sheard's comments or a quota on Jewish kids entering a pool would suggest. But to contemporaries it likely felt that way. By the 1920s the Jewish community was established in Toronto and had the income, the ability, and the interest in participating in public space as equals with the Anglo-Saxon community around them. They could and did make their presence known in the public space at Sunnyside in a way that they could not at restricted resorts, and a frustrated Anglo community, still uncomfortable with their presence, pushed back.

The Toronto Harbour Commission set out to recreate Toronto's waterfront in 1912 and divide it into a set of distinct uses: recreation, commerce, and industry. We typically measure the success of the commission in the number of hectares that were created for industrial use or on how profitable amusement areas such as Sunnyside were. But looking at the commission through the lens of an activity such as bathing suggests that one of its most critical roles was in transforming how Torontonians related to their natural environment. Over the course of decades, the commission untethered the bathing body from the marginal spaces of the waterfront and pushed it into managed recreation spaces along the waterfront. The commission actively sought to contain people within the bathing beach and to a large degree succeeded—to the point where even if people chose to swim in one of the lagoons, or off the docks in Toronto, they could not help but feel they were doing something outside the norm.

CONCLUSION

Bathing on the Ragged Edge

Toronto's waterfront, rivers, and island were awash with naked bodies throughout the nineteenth and early twentieth centuries. The undressed body was a visual fact of urban life, creating a distinctive human geography across the urban environment that waxed and waned with the seasons and the temperature. If the bathers were not naked they were wearing trunks, which were illegal for bathing until the 1930s and yet readily available in stores. The bodies were mostly young men and boys—teenagers, though that word was not yet in use—but could include young girls, who slipped into bathing spaces with young boys or carved out spaces of their own. This undressed Toronto was hardly a secret. A *Globe* reporter found bathers lined up when he strolled along the waterfront in 1887. When a brickyard worker drowned in the Don River in 1902, friends and fellow bathers joined in the rescue attempt, suggesting a popular and well-frequented bathing space.[1] In looking at Canadian laws, Bob Tarantino argues, "The laws on nudity offer a telling encapsulation of our response to nudity and sex. When the Criminal Code was originally enacted in 1892, public nudity was so rare and the social stigma attaching to it so profound that it was not even thought necessary to address a separate section of the law to the matter."[2] But in fact, it had been quite the opposite. In the late nineteenth century, public nudity had been so common along the lakefront and rivers of cities such as Toronto that there was hardly any social stigma attached to it. The naked body was part of the urban fabric, something men *and* women walking along the waterfront or along the Don or Humber Rivers expected to see. It was only as the nude bathing body disappeared from public view that the social stigma around it became more profound.

These bathing spaces thrived along the city's ragged edges, hybrid spaces where industry had failed to completely take hold and hints of nature remained. These were spaces that Toronto's vernacular bathers could take up and remake for their own uses. Rob Shields's concept of social spacialization provides a useful tool for thinking about the presence of these undressed bodies in an urban environment.[3] The swimming hole was a conscious space of embodied use, sedimented into the urban landscape through repeated use and the support, indulgence, or indifference of people around it. Some of these bathing spaces on the Don River existed for generations. Others, like those on the central waterfront, evolved or were sustained by industrialization. The moat of railyards and flotsam of log booms enabled bathing spaces by cloaking the space from other users.

When we look at the waterfront as a series of embodied encounters, Toronto's waterfront and the Don River valley come alive as rich incubators of identity formation for both the working class and a middle class conflicted by urbanization and industrialization. By looking at these spaces through the lens of their embodied use, we can dispense with the idea that they were too polluted, too industrial, or too crowded to have acted as a space for recreational pleasure. Our culturally defined interpretations of pollution do not hold for people in the nineteenth century who embraced and used the sticky, smelly, and potentially dangerous physical environment around them.

These vernacular bathing spaces were perpetuated, and yet also erased, by the nostalgia of the middle class and the limitations of liberal technologies of governance intended to control the urban landscape. As I have suggested, with a nod towards the work of Jackson Lears and Ian McKay, Toronto's middle class looked upon the bathing experience through a nostalgic gloss.[4] Bathing allowed Toronto's men to recall their own experiences and their own embodied relationship with the city's lakeshore and riparian spaces. It was a foundational experience for building masculinity and a comforting anti-modernist balm for the deleterious effects of industrial change. And the nostalgia around it turned the Don River into a powerful tool for crafting working-class identity well into the twentieth century. Toronto's civic, legal, and intellectual leaders were quite willing to tell people to avert their eyes from the swimming hole and let the boys be, leaving the bathers caught in a liminal moment between being seen and not seen.

This indulgence came with a price. It flattened the experience to the innocence of boys in a swimming hole, writing out men, excluding women, and distilling the participants into a white Anglo-Saxon essence. The slippages around the use of man or boy, and the efforts of writers such as Charles Sauriol and Gordon Sinclair to insulate their memories of youthful bathing against the incursion of men, suggest the challenges of discursively removing the men. It may well be that the turn-of-the-century swimming hole was never as pure and chaste a homosocial environment as contemporaries wanted it to be, a question that is all the harder to answer given the fluidity of sexual identities at the turn of the century. But these efforts to retroactively police the memory of the space suggest more about how a nude all-male bathing environment might be seen in the mid-twentieth century than how it was seen decades earlier.

The effort to establish Toronto as a modern, ordered city depended on technologies such as the map and the photograph to render the urban space both visible and knowable and to instruct residents in its proper ordering. We might expect that these technologies would have caught the undressed body in their web and held it up for inspection and removal. But rather than recording an image of the urban environment as it was, these technologies rendered it as it was supposed to be. It was a modernist vision that erased the bathing body as something that had no place within a modern waterfront. This expulsion, paradoxically, allowed such spaces to continue to exist by leaving them off the map and outside the camera lens. Rather than clarifying our vision of the past, these technologies have blinded us to the presence of the undressed body by ensuring it was never seen. The Don River was an exception to this rule: within that space a visual legacy of the swimming hole was constructed that played up its whimsy and the chaste youths within it. The imagery of the Don created a formative myth for working-class men who grew up around the river and the locus of the middle class's nostalgic gaze. Once again, this construction excluded as much as it included; however, the visual legacy of the Don wasn't completely controlled, and pictures that slip through of men bathing in the river reveal the more complicated setting.

Adopting the Beach

I have treated the beach as a tentative and contested attempt to manage bathing in Toronto by containing and training men and women in a new set of embodied practices. Toronto provides an ideal venue for studying the beach because, as a product, system, and set of technologies, it had to be transplanted into the settler community. It was not enough to have a strip of sand on the shoreline; people had to be taught how to use the beach. John Fiske provides the best language for thinking about a beach, suggesting how it operates as a text, as a collection of symbols and practices, for how people navigate the body's movement between culture and nature.[5] While the language of the beach circulated internationally in the nineteenth century, its cultural heft was neither so strong nor so coherent as to simply impose itself on Toronto's waterfront. Rather, Torontonians wrestled with the idea of what a beach should mean: Should men and women be divided, or mixed together? Should the city use bathing machines or allow people to bathe in the open air? The beach was adopted because it answered a series of challenges that vernacular bathing could not. The bathing suit solved the problem of managing the body so that men and women could bathe together. Setting aside discrete bathing areas that were staffed by lifeguards created a safer bathing environment than the old swimming hole, an improvised place where people had relied on each other for help and knowledge about unpredictable stream beds and semi-industrial spaces. But replacing one system with the other was an incremental process that took decades and in the meantime the vernacular and the beach operated in tandem in some spaces and blurred in others.

The effort to establish the Wiman Baths on Toronto Island makes this process visible. At the baths, patrons and critics wrestled with the bathing suit as a new technology for managing the mixing of men and women. It was not enough to wear a bathing suit; men and women—but particularly men who had enjoyed the privilege of nudity in public space—had to be trained in how to behave within a bathing suit. While the bathing suit was designed to cloak the body, it also served to eroticize it by hugging and accentuating the anatomy of men and women. Men actively resisted this process and the challenge to their privilege that it represented.

The same geography that had enabled vernacular bathing—in some spaces—impacted the ability to create a beach in Toronto. The beach was predicated on the ability to secure and police an environment. The Don River could never be so thoroughly managed. Its environment was constantly shifting, which meant that the best the city could hope for was to establish a zone of surveillance. And even then, bathers could avoid regulation by heading upstream. On Toronto Island, efforts to establish Turner's Baths as a middle-class bathing space were frustrated by the long-standing use of the western sandbar as a nude bathing space, use that was abetted by an indulgent city council. The best that Turner's could hope for in the 1890s was a stalemate with nude bathing allowed to continue behind a fence down the shoreline from the bathhouse. Vernacular bathers even held on along the industrial waterfront, ensuring that when the city established its free bathing system in 1897 its ferries stopped directly at popular old bathing spaces along the docks to collect the youngsters and take them to Toronto Island. The nostalgia of Toronto's men towards the bathing boy, and practical challenges of trying to suit up working-class boys, also ensured the boys were initially allowed to bathe in the nude and that girls were initially excluded.

The Toronto Harbour Commission's effort to redevelop Sunnyside represents the high tide of beach making in Toronto. The commission literally built a beach, expanded the city's lifesaving program to stretch across the entire waterfront, and even tried to police the form and style of people's bathing suits. By the time the commission started its work in 1912, the international language of the beach was settled: comics, advertisements, pictures, and stories all circulated a clear articulation of what a beach should look like and how it was a space for men and women to socialize rather than simply bathe. Everyone knew what a beach was. The harbour commission had merely to build it.

In the end the vernacular bathing space needed to be cast aside so that men and women could bathe together and so that bathing spaces could be integrated into a commercial entertainment system. But the process took decades and was contested by bathers, the people charged with making the laws, and the people in charge of enforcing them. However, Toronto was not done with nude bathing. It would re-emerge in the twentieth century at Hanlan's Point beach, the old western sandbar, and at secluded spaces along the city's eastern waterfront. But as a modern nude bathing area, Hanlan's Point does not challenge the expectation that people should be wearing a bathing suit; rather it depends on the creation of a contained space where they do not.

EPILOGUE

Recrafting the Bathing Body

The Don River and Toronto Island's western sandbar—today's Hanlan's Point—were two of the most popular spaces for vernacular bathing in the nineteenth and early twentieth centuries, earning acceptance and even indulgence from Toronto's city councillors. However, since that time the two spaces have had very different fates. At Hanlan's Point nude bathing has moved from the margin to the centre, with legalized nude bathing helping to turn the beach into a tourist destination. The Hanlan's Point Clothing Optional Beach demonstrates how rules and social expectations at a beach can be used to manage nude bodies and how those rules continue to be circumvented and challenged. In the Don River, the bathing body's link with nature is slowly being erased in Toronto's public memory and a new icon has been co-opted to promote the river's natural environment.

Hanlan's Point: The Undressed Beach

Toronto launched the Hanlan's Point Clothing Optional Beach, on what had been known as old western sandbar, as a test project in 1999 and confirmed it as a permanent site in 2002. The decision turned what had been an isolated and predominantly queer space into one of the city's most popular beaches and, along with Vancouver's Wreck Beach, one of only two legal nude beaches in Canada. Today, the space is unquestionably popular. On busy weekends the clothing optional area is filled while the adjacent clothing required portion sits vacant; even people who do not strip down want to be where the crowd is. But in valorizing the undressed body, Hanlan's Point is not an updated version of the swimming hole filled with young boys, but rather an effort to contain the sexuality of undressed male and female bodies.

Nude bathing at Hanlan's Point in the twenty-first century depended on the remarginalization of the "western sandbar" in the twentieth century and the recovery of a nude bathing space that had been lost at the beginning of the twentieth century. Nude bathing on the western sandbar had been erased by the end of the 1920s. While discrete nude spaces for children remained in the early 1920s, men had been driven out, at least as a visual presence, in the first decade of the twentieth century.[1] On paper, Toronto's bylaws allowed nude bathing on Toronto Island and designated waterfront spaces until 1930, but we should not assume the existence of those laws meant the spaces were still being used. When the city finally updated its bathing bylaw in 1930, the discovery of old rules that allowed nude bathing was greeted with bemused surprise, suggesting the habit had fallen out of practice.[2] The construction of the Toronto Island Airport in 1937 and 1938 tore up the northern portion of the western sandbar, filled in the lagoon, and disrupted the former bathing spaces next to it.[3] Aerial photographs of the island in 1950 reveal extensive cottage development along the western side of the island, and an area still shorn of trees around the airport.[4] There was little marginal territory for vernacular bathers to claim and during the 1930s and 1940s the nude body dropped out of sight along Toronto Island's western shoreline.[5]

The nude beach that emerged after the 1950s was driven by a different logic of bathing, one focused around sexuality and the potential for sexual encounters. A queer Hanlan's Point emerged by the 1950s with the southern tip of the beach, near Gibraltar Point, becoming a popular hangout for gay people vacationing at Centre Island.[6] The gay community was drawn to the island for the same reason other Torontonians were: it was a cheap, convenient place to get out of the city and yet offered its own playful atmosphere.[7] This early gay beach was probably integrated into the heterosocial beach around it in the 1950s. Gibraltar Point was a popular swimming space, with its own bathhouse at the time, and was in close proximity to the island's cottage community.[8] As Ed Jackson suggests in *Any Other Way: How*

Toronto Got Queer, Hanlan's Point's journey from beach to queer space to queer nude beach was evolutionary: the queer community found the space and then reshaped it for their own ends, aided by the removal of cottages on the western side of the island in the 1960s as part of a broader effort to drive out the island's residential community and create a larger regional park. Metro Toronto's decision to remove the cottages helped remarginalize the western sandbar once again.[9] Gordon Brent Ingram has noted Wreck Beach also has its roots in gay cruising spaces of the 1940s before emerging as a nude space by the 1970s.[10] The gay community played trailblazer when it came to establishing nude beaches, with the heterosexual community following in their footsteps and expanding the space.[11]

The queer nature of Hanlan's Point came out in 1971 when Toronto's gay community held a picnic—an early precursor of future Gay Pride events—at the beach.[12] By that time Hanlan's Point had joined Cranberry Flats, along the Saskatchewan River south of Saskatoon, and Wreck Beach, Vancouver, as part of an established circuit of gay beaches across the country.[13] Hanlan's Point's notoriety as a nude beach was also being paraded in the press in the 1970s, fuelled by complaints that nude bathers were "taking over the beach."[14] The geography of where the queer space was on Hanlan's Point varied. The *Body Politic* directed people cruising for sex to the southern end of the beach, near Gibraltar Point, in 1974, but an examination of complaints made in 1975 indicates that the nude section had settled near the island airport at the beach's northern end, too near in some cases, with airport manager Jerry Thornton noting, "our only concern is that sometimes they come on to the runway and we have to shoo them off."[15]

The sexual nature of the space reverberated through the 1970s, with accusations that nude beach goers were guilty of sexual improprieties and Toronto's media acknowledging publicly that the beach was a queer space.[16] Police laid a round of charges in 1975; they used the city's bathing bylaw—rather than the Criminal Code charge of public nudity—but immediately ran into a problem. The city's bathing bylaw was focused on policing what people wore when they bathed. It did not apply to people who had not yet gone in the water; suntanning in the nude fell into a legal grey zone, resulting in most of the cases being thrown out of court.[17] There were mixed couples on the docket in 1975, but the numbers suggest this was predominantly a male space: of the sixty-two summonses handed down, only three targeted women.[18]

The cat and mouse game of enforcement continued over the next twenty-five years until the city, with prodding from the gay community and advocacy from city councillor/gay community member Kyle Rae, legalized the clothing optional beach in 1999.[19] There were hiccups as the city's police force struggled to accept the beach's new designation. By designating Hanlan's Point as a clothing optional space the city was setting aside its own bathing bylaw. But faced with the loss of one tool, Toronto police responded by resurrecting and attempting to enforce the Toronto Harbour Commission's Bylaw #20, which had been created in the 1930s to stop men from bathing in swimming trunks.[20] Police recognized, as had been the case in 1975, that the bylaw would still allow people to sunbathe in the nude and took to warning beachgoers that they could strip down, but not step into the water. The absurd effort lasted only a few days before the police accepted the new reality.[21]

The city's endorsement of Hanlan's Point as a clothing optional beach in 1999 was an effort to both valorize and contain the nude body. Making nudity legal within a defined area set off a debate over just what sort of space the beach would be, a debate still raging in 2006 and summed up neatly by the *Globe*'s John Barber when he wrote, "Is this beach a semi-institutionalized kind of 'queer space'—one of those generally out-of-view nooks where gay men cruise and have sex? Or is it plain public space?"[22] Mariana Valverde and Miomir Cirak argue the goal was containment: gay pride marchers had been threatening to strip down and march naked in Toronto's annual gay pride parade. Hanlan's Point could serve as an outlet for acceptable nudity.[23] (Ultimately, nudity has become a feature of the gay pride parade as well.) Rae argued in 1998 that a legal Hanlan's Point would end the harassment of gay people at the beach.[24] But as the new clothing optional system was launched he was careful to add, "It's going to be a beach for everyone to use,"[25] suggesting how its role as a "queer space" would be impacted. Proponents imagined a space that would include the surveillance and control of a public beach, while keeping the nude experience.

For groups such as the Hanlan's Beach Naturists, creating a nude beach for everyone meant creating a beach that was free of sexuality, queer or straight. Stepping onto the newly christened clothing optional space, the naturists presented beachgoers with their "Free Beach Etiquette" flyer, which called for "no overt, erotic, or hidden sexual activity. Nude is not lewd, but combined with sex, undermines our public image. Sexual activity belongs in the bedroom, not on the beach or nearby public areas."[26]

The Hanlan's Beach Naturists reflected the attitudes of social nudism, a movement that emerged in Germany at the start of the twentieth century and then crossed to North America. Mary-Ann Shantz has detailed the evolution of the movement in Canada, where the number of clubs, particularly in British Columbia and Ontario, took off in the postwar period.[27] Social nudism drew on the same anti-modernist attitudes that valorized the bathing boy and the swimming hole, and imagined nudity as a chaste activity. Social nudists embraced nature to counter the industrialization they saw happening around them and dreamed of a lifestyle entirely free of the constraints of clothing.[28] The early Canadian movement consciously drew on "Summer Idyll" sentiments and childhood memories of skinny-dipping in the swimming hole by publishing articles and letters that recalled its members' own youthful experiences.[29] The retroactive effort to make these links was a tactical way for the movement to prove nudism was not an alien European habit but rather rooted in the Canadian experience.[30] But drawing on the male vernacular experience also meant appealing disproportionately to men, which challenged a movement marketing itself as a mixed-gender experience and created fears among members that their sexuality, should they be surrounded predominantly by other nude men, would be questioned.[31] Nudists faced the same need to ensure that their nudity was seen as pure and chaste, as Charles Sauriol and Gordon Sinclair did when they reflected on their experiences swimming in the Don River. Even successfully recreating the swimming hole into a heterosocial space sexualized it and opened the movement to accusations it was little more than a sex club, accusations that clubs answered with strict rules to control any signs of sexual activity. The proliferation of such rules, of course, suggested that sexual urges remained in a nude setting.[32]

When social nudists walked onto Hanlan's Point they saw a space that needed to be contained and controlled.[33] Dave Fleming, the founder of the Hanlan's Beach Naturists, argued Hanlan's Point needed to follow "European-style" rules and strictly avoid any hint of sexual activity on or near the beach. This was not just a case of being a prude, Fleming suggested, but a necessity to ensure the city did not turn against the beach and scrap the pilot project.[34] Peter A. Simm, a lawyer for Totally Naked Toronto Men

Enjoying Nudity and a key advocate for winning official clothing optional status for the beach, acknowledged public sex could threaten the beach's new legal status. But at the same time, queer and heterosexual beachgoers who did not subscribe to the naturists' chaste approach to nudity felt targeted by the effort to create a platonic beach space.[35] And in turn, Fleming and the Hanlan's Beach Naturists felt targeted by beachgoers who made no secret of their dislike for having their behaviour critiqued and judged.[36]

In the end, Hanlan's Point has emerged as part of a public beach bathing system. Though some bathers skip the bathing suit, the beach remains contained and surveilled by lifeguards during the day. The popularity of the beach on a hot summer day imposes a convivial conformity on beachgoers. As Pau Obrador Pons argues, the ability of people to police each other increases on a nude beach; people police their own gaze and the gaze of others in an effort not to sexualize the people around them, a form of self-regulation the Hanlan's Beach Naturists' list of instructions was trying to lay out explicitly.[37] Just as patrons at the Wiman Baths learned to bathe under the surveillance of their fellow bathers, people at Hanlan's Point appraise and critique each other's performances and engage in a conscious form of not looking.[38] In other words, people are taught not to stare.

And yet, Hanlan's Point is not a platonic space either. While the public creates and enforces social codes on the most visible spaces of the beach, sex and sexuality have not been severed from the body. Flirtation remains on the beach and the cruising space remains, as queer men pad along the paths amid the trees behind the beach seeking sexual encounters, and straight and queer couples alike settle in to watch the sunset.[39] On busy days the publicly contained face of the beach and its more sexualized hinterland operate in a silent and nearly discrete tandem, while on quiet days the randier use of the beach slides onto the shoreline and into public space.

The Don River: From Bathing Bodies to the Canoe

While Hanlan's Point has rediscovered the nude body, albeit in a new way, vernacular bathing and the embodied relationship with the Don River it represented has been replaced with a new effort to see the Don as a reclaimed natural space: an effort best facilitated by the canoe.

Despite the disappearance of bathing in the upper Don River by the 1960s, the myth of the bathing boy maintained a tenacious hold on Toronto's civic imagination, with pictures and stories of his exploits appearing in regional histories of the Don River and Cabbagetown.[40] Conservationist Charles Sauriol, who advocated for the preservation and protection of the Don Valley, considered bathing in the river an intimate and embodied part of experiencing it.[41] That relationship with the river pushed Sauriol to help launch the Don Valley Conservation Association in 1947; he later joined the Metropolitan Regional Conservation Authority in 1957 and continued to serve the conservation movement in one way or another until his death in 1995.[42]

The embodied relationship with the Don River that Sauriol represented was still recognized when the Don Watershed Regeneration Council and the Toronto and Region Conservation Authority considered the state of the river in 1997. The conservation authority's "Turning the Corner" report card centred on bathing in its description of a healthy environment and considered swimmability as one of the benchmark goals of the rehabilitation process. The report began by asking, "Will children swim in the Don again?" and then challenged people's perceptions of the river by noting that in dry conditions portions of the upper Don were safe for swimming. German Mills Creek and the Upper West Don, areas fed by groundwater, had fecal counts as low as 20 fecal coliform bacteria per 100 millilitres of water—a level considered "well within the province's limit of 100 fecals/100 ml for safe swimming."[43] But, the report warned, during wet weather it was a different matter entirely: stormwater "routinely" brought bacteria counts throughout the river to levels of more than 100,000 fecal coliforms per 100 millilitres and that "if there were swimming holes on the Don, they would be posted [to warn of hazardous bathing conditions] by health authorities, just as the beaches at the lakefront are posted."[44] Semi-treated sewage had been the predominant pollution problem for the Don River in the mid-twentieth century, but by the twenty-first the primary issue was storm sewer water, with the hardened urban landscape incapable of diverting or filtering runoff water entering the river.[45] But "Turning the Corner" held out hope that people could one day bathe in the Don again, envisioning the river being safe for swimming during dry weather in 2010 and returning to a "natural level of bacteria in both dry and rainy conditions by 2030."[46]

"Turning the Corner" spoke to two audiences, an older audience that remembered being in the river—"I used to swim there when I was a kid," one respondent was quoted as saying—and a younger audience that saw the river as irredeemably polluted.[47] For the first audience, the bathing boy represented a language of recovery that resonated within them; for the second, speaking in terms of bathing was a tool to demonstrate the Don had been—*and could again be*—a healthy environment.

The "Beyond Forty Steps" report in 2009 demonstrates the limits of regional myths and the reliance upon new systems of knowledge to measure the value of a space. In contrast to "Turning the Corner," which centred on the bathing experience, "Beyond Forty Steps" addressed the idea only briefly in a section entitled "Bacteria," where it pointed out the river is unable to meet provincial guidelines intended to protect swimmers in even the most likely of spots—the Upper East Don River which draws water directly from the Oak Ridges Moraine aquifer.[48] While "Turning the Corner" laid out a timeline in 1997 for when people might bathe in the Don again, the 2009 plan made no attempt to suggest they ever would.[49] The practical reality of pollution levels in the Don likely contributed to the report's focus, but it also represents the culmination of the century-long effort to contain bathing in discrete and manageable spaces.

"Beyond Forty Steps" did more than just erase bathing from the Don's future, it retroactively withdrew it from the past as well: the cultural history of people bathing in the river, which remained foundational for the 1997 report, is not discussed at all in the 2009 report.[50] Rather than viewing the Don as a hybrid space, "Beyond Forty Steps" takes a declensionist narrative, suggesting the Don was once a pristine wilderness that needs to be reclaimed. As the report notes, "The Don has been subjected to more than two hundred years of settlement and degradation."[51] The bathing experience within the middle Don, which had blended industry and nature, has no place in a narrative that is trying to reclaim and protect a natural environment. Whereas swimmability was considered a benchmark for success to people with an embodied experience with the river, it has no role when the river's health is dictated by, and reduced to, statistical benchmarks for water quality.[52] Swimming as an activity that people might indulge in within the Don has also been overlooked by the Don Valley's use as a park space, one within which the river is to be admired and photographed but certainly never bathed in and hardly touched.[53]

The Toronto and Region Conservation Authority has turned to the canoe, rather than the bathing body, to model the Don River's environmental health and provide an anti-modernist gloss for encountering it. The annual Paddle the Don event raises awareness and funds for conservation, and deploying the canoe allows people to engage with the environment and have an anti-modern moment without having to immerse themselves in the river. In other words, it is a technology that allows people to have a relationship with the river.[54] There is an irony here: a bathing culture thrived in the Don River during the nineteenth century precisely because the hybrid middle Don was too shallow and inaccessible for canoeing.[55] Today the conservation authority overcomes the challenge of a shallow stream by releasing water from the G. Ross Lord Dam to raise river levels just enough for people to canoe down a 10.5-kilometre route.[56] So once a year, the conservation authority "provides a unique opportunity for people to paddle the Don River" and through that experience raises awareness of it as a natural environment.[57] This presentation of the river for the event is thus predicated on its status as a hybrid environment, built by man and nature, proving that the middle Don lives on. Nature does not always cooperate; for example, in 2017, the river swelled with heavy spring rains and the conservation authority was forced to cancel the event. The capricious Don gets to have the last word when it comes to how people use or interpret its environment.

NOTES

Introduction

1 "A Summer Idyll Urbanized," *The Globe*, Tuesday, 25 August 1925, 4.

2 Ibid.

3 I borrow the terms heterosocial (mixed-gender) and homosocial (single-gender) from Kathy Peiss. They are not intended to denote sexuality. See Kathy Peiss, *Cheap Amusements: Working Women and Leisure in Turn-of-the-Century New York* (Philadelphia: Temple University Press, 1986), 4–5. For a look at the turn-of-the-century idealization of boyhood and its potential for promoting commercial culture see Woody Register, *The Kid of Coney Island: Fred Thompson and the Rise of American Amusements* (New York: Oxford University Press, 2001).

4 Anthony Giddens refers to these social spaces as "locales," which are defined by the social activity within them. See Anthony Giddens, "Time, Space and Regionalisation," in *Social Relations and Spatial Structures*, ed. Derek Gregory and John Urry (London: Macmillan , 1985), 271–72; Rob Shields, *Places on the Margin: Alternative Geographies of Modernity* (New York: Routledge, 1991), 57. On moral environments, see David Bell and Gill Valentine, *Mapping Desire: Geographies of Sexualities* (New York: Routledge, 1995).

5 Richard Rutt, "The Englishman's Swimwear," *Costume* 24, no. 1 (1990): 69.

6 Douglas Booth, "Nudes in the Sand and Perverts in the Dunes," *Journal of Australian Studies* 21, no. 53 (1997): 170.

7 John Fiske, *Understanding Popular Culture* (Boston: Unwin Hyman, 1989), 11, 14.

8 Henry Scadding, *Toronto of Old: Collections and Recollections Illustrative of the Early Settlement and Social Life of the Capital of Ontario* (Toronto: Adam, Stevenson, 1873), 80–81; Frances N. Mellen, "The Development of the Toronto Waterfront during the Railway Expansion Era, 1850–1912" (PhD diss., University of Toronto, 1974), 31–32.

9 Ken Greenberg, "Toronto: The Urban Waterfront as a Terrain of Availability," in *City, Capital and Water*, ed. Patrick Malone (London and New York: Routledge, 1996), 197. For similar views on the destruction of the waterfront as an amenity, see Gene Desfor, Michael Goldrick, and Roy Merrens, "Redevelopment on the North American Water-frontier: The Case of Toronto," in *Revitalizing the Waterfront: International Dimensions of Dockland Redevelopment*, ed. B.S. Hoyle, D.A. Pinder, and M.S. Husain (London: Belhaven Press, 1988), 96; James O'Mara, "Shaping Urban Waterfronts: The Role of Toronto's Harbour Commissioners, 1911–1960," *Discussion Paper No. 13* (Toronto: York University, Department of Geography, March 1976), 25.

10 Mellen, "The Development of the Toronto Waterfront," 55; Thomas McIlwraith, "Digging Out and Filling In: Making Land on the Toronto Waterfront in the 1850s," *Urban History Review/Revue d'histoire urbaine* 20, no. 1 (1991): 22, 29.

11 Jennifer Bonnell, *Reclaiming the Don: An Environmental History of Toronto's Don River Valley* (Toronto: University of Toronto Press, 2014), 24–25.

12 Alain Corbin, *The Lure of the Sea: The Discovery of the Seaside in the Western World, 1750–1840*, trans. Jocelyn Phelps (Cambridge, UK: Polity Press, 1994), 59, 78, 82.

13 John Travis, "Continuity and Change in English Sea-Bathing, 1730–1900: A Case of Swimming with the Tide," in *Recreation and the Sea*, ed. Stephen Fisher (Exeter: University of Exeter Press, 1997), 8–13; John Travis, *The Rise of the Devonshire Seaside Resorts, 1750–1900* (Exeter: University of Exeter Press, 1993), 121.

14 Corbin, *The Lure of the Sea*, 59, 82, 83; Sarah Howell, *The Seaside* (London: Cassell and Collier Macmillan, 1974), 20–22.

15 See Rutt, "The Englishman's Swimwear," 70–72.

16 Rutt, 71, 72; Travis, "Continuity and Change," 8–13; Travis, *Devonshire*, 121.

17 Richard Allen, "The Social Gospel and the Reform Tradition in Canada," *Canadian Historical Review* 49, no. 4 (1968): 381–84; Paul Rutherford, "Tomorrow's Metropolis: The Urban Reform Movement in Canada, 1880–1920," in *The Canadian City: Essays in Urban History*, ed. Gilbert A. Stelter and Alan F.J. Artibise (Toronto: McClelland and Stewart Limited, 1977), 370–71.

18 Rutherford, "Tomorrow's Metropolis," 378–82. On the loss of the human environment, see John C. Weaver, "'Tomorrow's Metropolis' Revisited: A Critical Assessment of Urban Reform in Canada, 1890–1920," in Stelter and Artibise, *The Canadian City*, 404.

19 J.M.S. Careless, *Toronto to 1918: An Illustrated History* (Toronto: James Lorimer, 1984), 202.

20 Daniel T. Rodgers, "Worlds of Reform," *OAH Magazine of History* 20, no. 5 (2006): 51; Mariana Valverde, *The Age of Light, Soap, and Water Moral Reform in English Canada, 1885–1925* (Toronto: University of Toronto Press, 2008), 20–25, 134, 165–66.

21 For the Canadian historiography, see Alan Metcalfe, *Working-Class Physical Recreation in Montreal, 1860–1895* (Kingston, ON: Sports Studies Research Group, Queen's University, 1978), 11–12, 22; Robert S. Kossuth, "Dangerous Waters: Victorian Decorum, Swimmer Safety, and the Establishment of Public Bathing Facilities in London (Canada)," *International Journal of the History of Sport* 22, no. 5 (2005): 796–97. For efforts at regulation and resistance, see Rutt, "The Englishman's Swimwear," 71–72.

22 For the effort to create a hygienic America, see Suellen Hoy, *Chasing Dirt: The American Pursuit of Cleanliness* (New York: Oxford University Press, 1995); Richard L. Bushman and Claudia L. Bushman, "The Early History of Cleanliness in America," *Journal of American History* 74, no. 4 (1988); Andrea Renner, "A Nation That Bathes Together: New York City's Progressive Era Public Baths," *Journal of the Society of Architectural Historians* 67, no. 4 (2008); Katherine Ashenburg, *The Dirt on Clean: An Unsanitized History* (Toronto: A.A. Knopf Canada, 2007).

23 Renner, "A Nation That Bathes Together," 504; Ashenburg, *The Dirt on Clean*, 201. And see Valverde, *Age of Light*, 13–16.

24 Michel Foucault, "Governmentality," in *The Foucault Effect: Studies in Governmentality*, ed. Graham Burchell, Colin Gordon, and Peter Miller (Chicago: University of Chicago Press, 1991), 93; Michel Foucault, "The Subject and Power," in *Power: Essential Works of Foucault, 1954–1984*, ed. James D. Faubion (New York: The New Press, 2000), 341–43; Bruce Curtis, "After 'Canada': Liberalisms, Social Theory, and Historical Analysis," in *Liberalism and Hegemony: Debating the Canadian Liberal Revolution*, ed. Jean-François Constant and Michel Ducharme (Toronto: University of Toronto

Press, 2009), 193; Michèle Dagenais, "The Municipal Territory: A Product of the Liberal Order?" in *Liberalism and Hegemony: Debating the Canadian Liberal Revolution*, ed. Jean-François Constant and Michel Ducharme (Toronto: University of Toronto Press, 2009), 207.

25 Nikolas Rose, Pat O'Malley, and Mariana Valverde, "Governmentality," *Annual Review of Law and Social Science* 2 (2006): 86–87.

26 Curtis, "After 'Canada,'" 178, 190; Rose, O'Malley, and Valverde, "Governmentality," 83–85.

27 Patrick Joyce, *The Rule of Freedom: Liberalism and the Modern City* (New York: Verso, 2003), 2–4, 7, 11–12.

28 Rose, O'Malley, and Valverde, "Governmentality," 89; Curtis, "After 'Canada,'" 181–82; Patrick Joyce, *Freedom*, 2–4, 7, 11–12. For a fuller discussion and alternative approaches for thinking about a liberal subjectivity, see Jean-François Constant and Michel Ducharme, eds., *Liberalism and Hegemony: Debating the Canadian Liberal Revolution* (Toronto: University of Toronto Press, 2009).

29 Rose, O'Malley, and Valverde, "Governmentality," 88; Patrick Joyce, *Freedom*, 23. For quote see Curtis, "After 'Canada,'" 194.

30 Mitchell Dean, *Governmentality: Power and Rule in Modern Society* (London: Sage, 1999), 30–33.

31 Simon Gunn, "From Hegemony to Governmentality: Changing Conceptions of Power in Social History," *Social History* 39, no. 3 (2006): 713.

32 Shields, *Places on the Margin*, 63. Joy Parr, *Sensing Changes: Technologies, Environments, and the Everyday, 1953–2003* (Vancouver: UBC Press, 2010), 8–9.

33 Joy Parr, "Notes for a More Sensuous History of Twentieth Century Canada: The Timely, the Tacit and the Material Body," *Canadian Historical Review* 82, no. 4 (2001): 733. Geographers prefer the term lay geography; for example, see David Crouch, "Places around Us: Embodied Lay Geographies in Leisure and Tourism," *Leisure Studies* 19, no. 2 (2000): 63–76.

34 For a good description, see Tina Loo and Meg Stanley, "An Environmental History of Progress: Damming the Peace and Columbia Rivers," *The Canadian Historical Review*, Volume 92, Number 3, September (2011): 405–406.

35 Parr sees the same relationship with the St. Lawrence River and the community of Iroquois; see Parr, "Notes for a More Sensuous History," 725. Richard White captures the same embodied relationship between gillnetters and the Columbia River: Richard White, *The Organic Machine: The Remaking of the Columbia River* (New York: Hill and Wang: 1995), 41.

36 On how "noise" can be read as a mark of cultural distinction, see Peter Bailey, "Breaking the Sound Barrier," in *Hearing History: A Reader*, ed. Mark M. Smith (Athens: University of Georgia Press, 2004). See also Murray Schafer, "Soundscapes and Earwitnesses," in Smith, *Hearing History*.

37 Parr, *Sensing Changes*, 9–12, 20.

38 Mariana Valverde and Lorna Weir, "The Struggles of the Immoral: Preliminary Remarks on Moral Regulation," in *Moral Regulation and Governance in Canada: History, Context and Critical Issues*, ed. Amanda Glasbeek (Toronto: Canadian Scholars Press, 2006), 78.

39 Gunn, "From Hegemony to Governmentality," 714; Jonathan Crary, *Techniques of the Observer: On Vision and Modernity in the Nineteenth Century* (Cambridge, MA: MIT Press, 1992), 11–13; Sarah Bassnett, *Picturing Toronto: Photography and the Making of a Modern City* (Montreal: McGill-Queen's University Press, 2016), 4–6.

40 Anders Ekström, "Seeing from Above: A Particular History of the General Observer," *Nineteenth-Century Contexts* 31, no. 3 (2009): 187, 200.

41 Jae Emerling, *Photography: History and Theory* (New York: Routledge, 2012), 23, 34. Carol Payne and Andrea Kunard, *The Cultural Work of Photography in Canada* (Montreal: McGill-Queen's University

Press, 2011), xiv, xvii. Stuart Ewen, *All Consuming Images: The Politics of Style in Contemporary Culture* (New York: Basic Books, 1988), 25. See also James Opp, "Re-imaging the Moral Order of Urban Space: Religion and Photography in Winnipeg, 1900–1914," *Journal of the Canadian Historical Association* 13, no. 1 (2002). URI: id.erudit.org/iderudit/031154ar.

42 John Fiske, *Reading the Popular* (New York: Routledge, 2005), 7–9; John Fiske, *Understanding Popular Culture* (Boston: Unwin Hyman, 1989), 32–36. Michel de Certeau might describe this as a tactic but I think his approach is too ephemeral to capture the coherent spaces that bathers were able to collectively shape on Toronto's waterfront. See Michel de Certeau, *Practice of Everyday Life*, trans. Steven F. Rendall (Los Angeles: University of California Press, 1988), xix, 18.

43 Shields, *Places on the Margin*, 3.

44 Shields, 5–6. We see hints of similar bathing communities in Hamilton; see Ken Cruikshank and Nancy B. Bouchier, "The War on the Squatters, 1920–1940: Hamilton's Boathouse Community and the Re-Creation of Recreation on Burlington Bay," *Labour/Le Travail* 51 (Spring 2003): 17, 22.

45 Lynne Bell, "Unsettling Acts: Photography as Decolonizing Testimony in Centennial Memory," in *The Cultural Work of Photography in Canada*, ed. Carol Payne and Andrea Kunard (Montreal: McGill-Queen's University Press, 2011), 168.

46 Toronto's elite were not simply "slumming" when they looked at vernacular bathers but recalling their own embodied experiences. On slumming and popular culture, see Fiske, *Understanding Popular Culture*, 43–44.

47 William Cronon, "The Trouble with Wilderness: Or, Getting Back to the Wrong Nature," *Environmental History* 1, no. 1 (1996): 13–15. The curative role of the natural environment suggested that such spaces needed to be preserved for their ability to uplift people and drove the parks movement in the nineteenth century. For more on that, see S.B. Sutton, ed., *Civilizing American Cities: A Selection of Frederick Law Olmsted's Writings on City Landscapes* (Cambridge, MA: MIT Press, 1971), 2–13, 21, 35–7; Nancy Pollock-Ellwand, "Rickson Outhet: Bringing the Olmsted Legacy to Canada. A Romantic View of Nature in the Metropolis and the Hinterland," *Journal of Canadian Studies/Revue d'études canadiennes* 44, no. 1 (2010): 143–44; Peter J. Schmitt, *Back to Nature: The Arcadian Myth in Urban America* (New York: Oxford University Press, 1969), xv.

48 Michael Kimmel, *Manhood in America: A Cultural History*, 4th ed (New York: Oxford University Press, 2018), 102–15; Gail Bederman, *Manliness and Civilization: A Cultural History of Gender and Race in the United States, 1880–1917* (Chicago: University of Chicago Press, 1995), 16–22. See also John F. Kasson, *Houdini, Tarzan, and the Perfect Man: The White Male Body and the Challenge of Modernity in America* (New York: Hill and Wang, 2001); Robert W. Rydell, *All the World's a Fair: Visions of Empire at American International Expositions, 1876–1916* (Chicago: University of Chicago Press, 1987).

49 T.J. Jackson Lears, *No Place of Grace: Antimodernism and the Transformation of American Culture, 1880–1920* (Chicago: University of Chicago Press, 1994), xvii. Lears uses Sigmund Freud's *Totem and Taboo* to capture the ambivalence around modernity felt by the middle class. I would even extend that approach to the bathing body itself. See Sigmund Freud, *Totem and Taboo: Some Points of Agreement between the Mental Lives of Savages and Neurotics*, trans. James Strachey (London: Routledge and Kegan Paul, 1950), 34–35.

50 Lears, *No Place of Grace*, 4–5, 26–30. Kimmel, *Manhood*, 102, 125–26.

51 Marshall Berman gives us an excellent definition of modernity, suggesting how it was felt at the physical, mental, and spiritual level. See Marshall Berman, *All That Is Solid Melts into Air: The Experience of Modernity* (New York: Verso, 1982), 16. S.N. Eisenstadt offers a useful discussion for how modernity had to be interpreted and inscribed locally and how modernity is critical to creating new identities. S.N. Eisenstadt, "Multiple Modernities," *Daedalus* 129, no. 1 (2000): 1–4.

52 Freud provides a useful language for looking at the tension between the instincts of the individual and the dictates of society; see Sigmund Freud, *The Future of an Illusion*, trans. J.A. Underwood and Shaun Whiteside (London: Penguin, 2008), 1–20. On the troubling role of nature as therapeutic balm, see William Cronon, ed., *Uncommon Ground: Toward Reinventing Nature* (New York: W.W. Norton, 1995): 16–17, 24, 25, 37; Cronon, "The Trouble with Wilderness," 9. For a similar critique, see Martin V Melosi, "Humans, Cities, and Nature: How Do Cities Fit in the Material World?" *Journal of Urban History* 36, no. 1 (2010): 3.

53 Thomas Lekan looks at how the environment was used to fortify national identities in Germany. But vernacular bathing suggests how this process doesn't have to be tethered to nationalism. See Thomas M. Lekan, *Imagining the Nation in Nature: Landscape Preservation and German Identity, 1885–1945* (Cambridge, MA: Harvard University Press, 2004), 4–6, 12, 20.

54 Ian McKay, *The Quest of the Folk: Antimodernism and Cultural Selection in Twentieth-century Nova Scotia* (Montreal: McGill-Queen's University Press, 1994), 4–7, 11–12.

55 This quest for an embodied relationship with the land also drove the creation of the social nudist movement in Germany at the end of the nineteenth century. See Chad Ross, *Naked Germany: Health, Race and the Nation* (Oxford, UK: Berg Publishers, 2005), 1, 9, 15, 98.

56 Fiske, *Understanding Popular Culture*, 27–28.

57 Eric Kaufman and Oliver Zimmer suggest Canada's settlers could not consider the country their "natural" environment but could use the nature of the nation as a constituting force to rally around. See Eric Kaufmann and Oliver Zimmer, "In Search of the Authentic Nation: Landscape and National Identity in Canada and Switzerland," *Nations and Nationalism* 4, no. 4 (1998): 483, 495–96. Cameron White sees picnics as enactments of occupation in Australia: Cameron White, "Picnicking, Surf-Bathing and Middle-Class Morality on the Beach in the Eastern Suburbs of Sydney, 1811–1912," *Journal of Australian Studies* 27, no. 80 (2003): 102–3.

58 McKay, *Quest of the Folk*, 21. See also Sandwell, "Missing Canadians," 253, for a good discussion on how groups that fall out of the liberal order are imagined.

59 As Graham Seal suggests, a myth need not always "perpetuate the dominant ideology" and can be a form of resistance: Graham Seal, *Inventing Anzac: The Digger and National Mythology* (Perth: University of Queensland Press, 2004), 8.

60 For a look at working-class bathing in Montreal, see Metcalfe, *Working Class Physical Recreation*, 11–12, 22.

61 Fiske, *Reading the Popular*, 7, 15.

62 McKay, *Quest of the Folk*, 151; Seal, *Inventing Anzac*, 3–7.

63 Corbin, *Lure of the Sea*, 2, 14.

64 Corbin, 61–72.

65 S.B. Sutton., ed., *Civilizing American Cities: A Selection of Frederick Law Olmsted's Writings on City Landscapes* (Cambridge, MA, Massachusetts Institute of Technology, 1971), 2–13, 21, 65; Pollock-Ellwand, "Rickson Outhet," 137–83, 138.

66 Corbin, *Lure of the Sea*, 81, 270, 272; Travis, "Continuity and Change," 8–13.

67 Peter Ward, *Courtship, Love and Marriage in Nineteenth-Century English Canada* (Montreal: McGill-Queen's University Press, 1990), 64–69; Peiss, *Cheap Amusements*, 15–31; Beth Bailey, *From Front Porch to Back Seat* (Baltimore: Johns Hopkins University Press, 1988), 13.

68 As Peiss notes, working as a domestic servant remained a dominant field for women, but even women outside the industrial labour force could make use of the new leisure opportunities that were appearing. Peiss, *Cheap Amusements*, 36–42.

69 See Gary S. Cross and John K. Walton, *The Playful Crowd: Pleasure Places in the Twentieth Century* (New York: Columbia University Press, 2005); John F. Kasson, *Amusing the Million: Coney Island at the Turn of the Century* (New York: Hill and Wang, 1978); Register, *The Kid of Coney Island.*

70 Mike Filey, *I Remember Sunnyside: The Rise and Fall of a Magical Era* (Toronto: Dundurn, 1996), 5.

71 Barbaranne Boyer, *The Boardwalk Album: Memories of The Beach* (Erin, ON: Boston Mills Press, 1985), 42.

72 Bill Freeman, *A Magical Place: Toronto Island and Its People* (Toronto: James Lorimer and Company, 1999). See also Glenn Cochrane and Jean Cochrane, *The Beach: An Illustrated History from the Lake to Kingston Road* (Toronto: ECW Press, 2009).

73 Norbert Elias, *Power and Civility: The Civilizing Process: Volume 2*, trans. Edmund Jephcott (New York: Pantheon Books, 1982), 230, 232.

74 Or what Dean might refer to as problematizations: see Dean, *Governmentality*, 27.

75 Gunn, "From Hegemony to Governmentality," 713.

76 Fiske, *Reading the Popular*, 41.

77 Michel Foucault, "Questions of Geography," in *Power/Knowledge: Selected Interviews and Other Writings, 1972–1977*, ed. Colin Gordon (New York: Pantheon Books, 1980), 72–73.

78 Fiske, *Reading the Popular*, 76.

79 Fiske, 50–51.

80 Michael Immerso, *Coney Island: The People's Playground* (Rutgers, NJ: Rutgers University Press, 2002), 152–53, 167. On the emergence of gay space at Coney Island, see George Chauncey, *Gay New York: Gender, Urban Culture, and the Making of the Gay Male World, 1890–1940* (New York: Basic Books, 1994).

81 For Britain, see Cross and Walton, *The Playful Crowd*. For America and the role of race in shaping the amusement park experience, see David Nasaw, *Going Out: The Rise and Fall of Public Amusements* (Cambridge, MA: Harvard University Press, 1999); Bryant Simon, *Boardwalk of Dreams: Atlantic City and the Fate of Urban America* (New York: Oxford University Press, 2004). And for Australia, see Christine Metusela and Gordon Waitt, *Tourism and Australian Beach Cultures Revealing Bodies* (Toronto: Channel View Publications, 2012).

82 Royden Loewen and Gerald Friesen, *Immigrants in Prairie Cities: Ethnic Diversity in Twentieth-Century Canada* (Toronto: University of Toronto Press, 2009), 4–13.

83 Allan Levine, *Toronto: Biography of a City* (Madeira Park, BC: Douglas and McIntyre, 2014), 165.

84 See Paul Rutherford, *Victorian Authority: The Daily Press in Late Nineteenth-Century Canada* (Toronto: University of Toronto Press, 1982), 7–8.

85 See, for instance, "Suburban News: Bathing in the Don," *The Globe*, Thursday, 22 July 1880, 6; "Bathing and Swimming," *The Globe*, Thursday, 22 July 1880, 6.

86 Parr, "Notes for a More Sensuous History," 721. Parr demonstrated this approach by adding multimedia options to her work in *Sensing Changes*.

Chapter 1: Central Waterfront: Testing the Waters

1 Henry Scadding, *Toronto of Old: Collections and Recollections Illustrative of the Early Settlement and Social Life of the Capital of Ontario* (Toronto: Adam, Stevenson, 1873), 59.

2 John Ross Robertson, *Robertson's Landmarks of Toronto: Toronto from 1834 to 1908* (Toronto: John R. Robertson, 1908), 65, 332.

3 John Ross Robertson, *Robertson's Landmarks of Toronto: A Collection of Historical Sketches of the Old Town of York from 1792 until 1833 and of Toronto from 1834 to 1893* (Toronto: J. Ross Robertson, 1894), 183.

4 Scadding, *Toronto of Old*, 80.

5 Scadding, 80.

6 J.M.S. Careless, *Toronto to 1918: An Illustrated History* (Toronto: James Lorimer, 1984), 19.

7 Joseph Bouchette, *The British Dominions of North America; or a Topographical and Statistical Description of the Provinces of Lower and Upper Canada, New Brunswick, Nova Scotia, the Islands of Newfoundland, Prince Edward, and Cape Breton, Vol. 1* (London: Longman, Rees, Orme, Brown, and Green, 1831), 89.

8 Sally Gibson, *More Than an Island: A History of the Toronto Island* (Toronto: Irwin, 1984), 12–13.

9 Robertson, *Landmarks* (1908), 37.

10 Scadding, *Toronto of Old*, 75.

11 For a useful summary of the debate over Toronto's name, see Victoria Freeman, "'Toronto Has no History!': Indigeneity, Settler Colonialism and Historical Memory in Canada's Largest City" (PhD diss., University of Toronto, 2010), footnote 27, page 31.

12 C. Pelham Mulvany, *Toronto: Past and Present. A Handbook of the City* (Toronto: W.E. Caiger, 1884; Toronto: Ontario Reprint Press, 1970), 97.

13 John Ross Robertson, *Robertson's Landmarks of Toronto: A Collection of Historical Sketches of the Old Town of York from 1792 until 1833 and of Toronto from 1834 to 1914* (Toronto: J. Ross Robertson, 1914), 292. Robertson draws this from *The Oracle*, vol. 12 no. 15 (7 August 1802).

14 Freeman, "'Toronto Has No History!,'" 8–9, 46.

15 Careless, *Toronto to 1918*, 10–11.

16 Careless, 11.

17 Freeman, "Toronto Has No History!,'" 40.

18 Freeman, 70–71.

19 Freeman, 72–73. The $145 million land claim agreement also included compensation for the Mississauga's Brant Purchase Claim. In 1797 the colonial government had purchased 3450 acres of land from the Mississauga for 100 pounds near present-day Burlington to create a new land base for Mohawk Chief Joseph Brant and Loyalist members of the Six Nations. Once again, the Mississauga were underpaid for the land given up. See Donna Duric, "The Brant Tract Treaty, No. 8 (1797)," 28 May 2017, http://mncfn.ca/treaty8/. See also Treaty Texts—Upper Canada Land Surrenders, https://www.aadnc-aandc.gc.ca/eng/1370372152585/1370372222012#ucls6 (accessed on 16 July 2019).

20 Robertson, *Landmarks* (1908), 153.

21 Robertson, 157; Freeman, "'Toronto Has No History!,'" 72.

22 Freeman, "'Toronto Has No History!,'" 60.

23 Freeman, 72, 118.

24 Freeman," 4. Freeman is looking at the Toronto context but gives credit to Coll Thrush for his spelling out this process in Seattle. See Coll Thrush, *Native Seattle: History from the Crossing-Over Place* (Seattle: University of Washington Press, 2007), 12.

25 Freeman, "'Toronto Has No History!,'" 62.

26 For a good illustration of how these changes impacted Indigenous and Metis people, see Mary Jane Logan McCallum and Adele Perry, *Structures of Indifference: An Indigenous Life and Death in a Canadian City* (Winnipeg: University of Manitoba Press, 2018).

27 On this process, see Colin Coates, "Seeing and Not Seeing: Landscape Art as a Historical Source," in *Method and Meaning in Canadian Environmental History*, ed. Alan MacEachern and Willian J. Turkel (Toronto: Nelson Education, 2009), 151; Scadding, *Toronto of Old*, 50; William Henry Bartlett, *Fish-Market, Toronto* (1838), Toronto Reference Library: Baldwin Collection, call number JRR 1845 Cab IV (Bartlett), https://www.torontopubliclibrary.ca/detail.jsp?Entt=RDMDC-JRR1845&R=DC-JRR1845.

28 Edith G. Firth and Curtis Fahey, "Scadding, Henry," in *Dictionary of Canadian Biography*, vol. 13, University of Toronto/Université Laval, 2003, http://www.biographi.ca/en/bio/scadding_henry_13E.html (accessed 17 July 2019).

29 Scadding, *Toronto of Old*, 32.

30 Robertson, *Landmarks* (1908), 388. While still a peninsula in the 1840s, Toronto Island was often referred to as an island because accessing it by land was challenging: it required crossing the Don River and the marshy Ashbridge's Bay at the mouth of the Don.

31 Scadding, *Toronto of Old*, 163.

32 Scadding, 163.

33 Cameron White, "Picnicking, Surf-Bathing and Middle-Class Morality on the Beach in the Eastern Suburbs of Sydney, 1811–1912," *Journal of Australian Studies* 27, no. 80 (2003): 102–103.

34 Patricia Jasen, *Wild Things: Nature, Culture, and Tourism in Ontario, 1790–1914* (Toronto: University of Toronto Press, 1995), 16, 43, 50, 82. I have explored this idea in *Winnipeg Beach*, 105.

35 Edwin C. Guillet, *Toronto: From Trading Post to Great City* (Toronto: Ontario Publishing, Limited, 1934), 68; Robertson, *Landmarks* (1908), 36; Scadding, *Toronto of Old*, 31, 59. On nineteenth-century ports, see Glen Norcliffe, Keith Bassett, and Tony Hoare, "The Emergence of Postmodernism on the Urban Waterfront: Geographical Perspectives on Changing Relationships," *Journal of Transport Geography* 4, no. 2 (1996): 124; Ken Greenberg, "Toronto: The Urban Waterfront as a Terrain of Availability," in *City, Capital and Water*, ed. Patrick Malone (London and New York: Routledge, 1996), 197. For another example, see the description of the Freeland Soap Factory in Robertson, *Landmarks* (1894), 182–86.

36 Scadding, *Toronto of Old*, 62.

37 Ibid. John Ross Robertson, *Robertson's Landmarks of Toronto: Toronto from 1834 to 1898* (Toronto: John R. Robertson, 1898), 66, 68, 71; John Ross Robertson, *Robertson's Landmarks of Toronto: Toronto from 1834 to 1895* (Toronto: John R. Robertson, 1896), 675–77; "When Toronto Was Younger," *The Evening Star*, 21 April 1900, 2; John G. Howard, Chart of the North Shore of Toronto Harbour, 1846, in Robertson, *Landmarks* (1908), inset between 530 and 531.

38 For a good description of the baths, see Charles Anthony Joyce, "From Left Field: Sport and Class in Toronto, 1845–1886" (PhD diss., Queen's University, 1997), 229–30.

39 Joyce, "From Left Field," 230–31.

40 William Ormsby, "Rees, William," in *Dictionary of Canadian Biography*, vol. 10, University of Toronto/Université Laval, 2003–, http://www.biographi.ca/en/bio/rees_william_10E.html (accessed 24 March 2015). The bathing area is also mentioned in *William Rees, The Case of Doctor William Rees, Late Physician to the Provincial Lunatic Asylum, Toronto* (Quebec: Hunter, Rose, 1865), 4, http://static.torontopubliclibrary.ca/da/pdfs/37131055319479d.pdf. For more on Rees, see Danielle Terbenche, "'A Soldier in the Service of His Country': Dr. William Rees, Professional Identity, and the Toronto Temporary Asylum, 1819–1874," *Histoire sociale/Social History* 43, no. 85 (2010): 97–129.

41 Conyngham Crawford Taylor, *The Queen's Jubilee and Toronto "Called Back" from 1887 to 1847* (Toronto: William Briggs, 1887), 77.

42 Robertson, *Landmarks* (1908), 61.

43 "Police Intelligence," *The Globe*, 31 August 1850, 418.

44 Alain Corbin, *The Lure of the Sea: The Discovery of the Seaside in the Western World, 1750–1840*, trans. Jocelyn Phelps (Cambridge, UK: Polity Press, 1994), 59, 82, 83; Sarah Howell, *The Seaside* (London: Cassell and Collier Macmillan, 1974), 20–22. British restrictions were established in British common law in a legal case in 1809: see Richard Rutt, "The Englishman's Swimwear," *Costume* 24 no. 1 (1990): 70.

45 Britain adopted a similar approach: see Rutt, "The Englishman's Swimwear," 70. Australia's initial restrictions were set at the colonial level and then moved to local councils by the 1890s. See Christine Metusela and Gordon Waitt, *Tourism and Australian Beach Cultures Revealing Bodies* (Toronto: Channel View Publications, 2012), xviii, 1, 26.

46 Patrick Joyce, *The Rule of Freedom: Liberalism and the Modern City* (New York: Verso, 2003), 4. For Toronto's founding act, see "'AN ACT to extend the limits of the Town of York; to erect the said Town into a City; and to incorporate it under the name of the City of Toronto,' Fourth William IV, Chapter 23, passed on March 6, 1834," *The Revised Statutes of Upper Canada to the Time of the Union, 1797–1841, Revised and Published by Authority, Vol. II Local and Private Acts* (Toronto: Robert Stanton, Printer to the Queen's Most Excellent Majesty), 762. An act to establish a police force in the towns of York, Sandwich, and Amherstburgh passed 7 April 1817 included the beach in front of York but made no mention of bathing in *Statutes of The Province of Upper Canada* (Kingston, ON: Francis M. Hill, 1831), 210–11.

47 Toronto City By-law 4, section 12: Item 207, Friday, 30 May 1834, 81, Toronto City Council Minutes, 1834, TCA.

48 "An act to prevent the Profanation of the Lord's Day, in Upper Canada," *The Consolidated Statutes for Upper Canada* (Toronto: Steward Derbishire and George Desbarats, 1859), CAP. CIV, Section 6, 944.

49 Charles Anthony Joyce, "From Left Field," 27, 44.

50 See, for example, "Bathing," *The Globe*, Tuesday, 28 July 1857, 2.

51 *The Consolidated Statutes for Upper Canada* (Toronto: Stewart Derbishire and George Desbaras, 1859): municipal institutions, section 294: Nuisances 19, 600 and municipal institutions, section 282, 10 and 11, 594–95.

52 *The Consolidated Statutes for Upper Canada*, 1859, section 294, 19, 600.

53 Taylor, *The Queen's Jubilee*, 77.

54 Careless, *Toronto to 1918*, 100; Helen Boritch and John Hagan, "Crime and the Changing Forms of Class Control: Policing Public Order in "Toronto the Good," 1859–1955," *Social Forces* 66, no. 2 (1987): 308–10. For a class-based argument for police actions, see Allan Greer, "The Birth of the Police in Canada," in *Colonial Leviathan: State Formation in Mid-Nineteenth-Century Canada*, ed. Allan Greer and Ian Radforth (Toronto: University of Toronto Press, 1992), 24–42.

55 For the broader trend, see Howell, *The Seaside*, 20–22; John Travis, "Continuity and Change in English Sea-Bathing, 1730–1900: A Case of Swimming with the Tide," in *Recreation and the Sea*, ed. Stephen Fisher (Exeter: University of Exeter Press, 1997), 15; John K. Walton, "Respectability Takes a Holiday: Disreputable Behaviour at the Victorian Seaside" in *Unrespectable Recreations*, edited by Martin Hewitt (Leeds: Leeds Centre for Victorian Studies, 2001), 184. And on early reform efforts, see Jan Noel, *Canada Dry: Temperance Crusades before Confederation* (Toronto: University of Toronto Press, 1995), 218–22.

56 The Toronto police usefully filed annual reports with Toronto City Council each year from 1859 to 1955; these included what amounted to a state of the union address from the chief of police, outlining his areas of interest, and a list of infractions.

57 Chief Constable Annual Report, 1895, H.J. Grassett, chief constable, 21 January 1896, 14, Toronto City Council Appendix C, 1896, CTA.

58 Frank C. Draper, Chief Constable Annual Report for 1878, 3 February 1879, 20, Toronto City Council Appendix, 1879, CTA; Frank C. Draper, Chief Constable Annual Report for 1879, 21 January 1880, 26, Toronto City Council Appendix, 1880, CTA; Frank C. Draper, Chief Constable Annual Report for 1880, 24 January 1881, 34, Toronto City Council Appendix, 1880, CTA.

59 Police specifically mention charging people for indecent exposure for urinating in public in the 1879 and 1880 reports. Frank C. Draper, Chief Constable Annual Report for 1878, 3 February 1879, 20, Toronto City Council Appendix, 1879, CTA; Frank C. Draper, Chief Constable Annual Report for 1879, 21 January 1880, 26, Toronto City Council Appendix, 1880, CTA. It was specifically mentioned in the 1881 report that the police magistrate had refused to inflict a fine owing to the lack of public urinals. Frank C. Draper, Chief Constable Annual Report for 1880, 24 January 1881, 34, Toronto City Council Appendix, 1880, CTA.

60 This is stated explicitly by Hamilton Police Chief Hugh McKinnon when he was being questioned for the Enquiry into the Prison and Reformatory System of Ontario, 1891, but the process was the same in Toronto. See *Report of the Commissioners Appointed to Enquiry into the Prison and Reformatory System of Ontario, 1891* (Toronto: Warwick and Sons, 1891), 277.

61 Charles Pelham Mulvany, Graeme Mercer Adam, and C.B. Robinson, *History of Toronto and County of York Ontario* (Toronto: C. Blackett Robinson, 1885), 488. See also (No. 9) Report no. 3, Board of Administration, 2 March 1896, 71, Toronto City Council Appendix A, 1896, CTA.

62 Mulvany, Mercer Adam, and Robinson, *History of Toronto*, 488.

63 Williams described his duties to city council in 1889. He did get the raise: Item 625, Report no. 8, Committee on Property, 24 April 1889, 714, Toronto City Council Appendix, 1889, TCA.

64 For instance, "City News," *The Globe*, 27 July 1877, 4. For more on Williams, see Mulvany, Mercer Adam, and Robinson, *History of Toronto*, 488.

65 Conyngham Crawford Taylor, *Toronto "Called Back," from 1892 to 1847: Its Wonderful Growth and Progress* (Toronto: William Briggs, 1892), 52. James Bain, "When Toronto Was Younger," *The Evening Star*, 21 April 1900, 2.

66 Greenberg, "Toronto: The Urban Waterfront," 197. And for similar views on the destruction of the waterfront as an amenity, see Gene Desfor, Michael Goldrick, and Roy Merrens, "Redevelopment on the North American Water-frontier: The Case of Toronto," in *Revitalizing the Waterfront: International Dimensions of Dockland Redevelopment*, ed. B.S. Hoyle, D.A. Pinder, and M.S. Husain (London: Belhaven Press, 1988), 96; James O'Mara, "Shaping Urban Waterfronts: The Role of Toronto's Harbour Commissioners, 1911–1960," *Discussion Paper No. 13* (Toronto: York University, Department of Geography, March 1976), 25.

67 Peter G. Goheen. "Currents of Change in Toronto, 1850–1900," in *The Canadian City: Essays in Urban History*, ed. Gilbert A. Stelter and Alan F.J. Artibise (Toronto: McClelland and Stewart, 1977), 86. And we get a similar take in Michael Goldrick and Roy Merrens, "Toronto: Searching for a New Environmental Planning Paradigm," in *City, Capital and Water*, ed. Patrick Malone (London: Routledge, 1996), 219–39.

68 Scadding, *Toronto of Old*, 80–81; Frances N. Mellen, "The Development of the Toronto Waterfront during the Railway Expansion Era, 1850–1912" (PhD diss., University of Toronto, 1974), 31–32.

69 Mellen, "The Development of the Toronto Waterfront," 41, 45–46. For a look at Tully's plan, see Thomas McIlwraith, "Digging Out and Filling In: Making Land on the Toronto Waterfront in the 1850s," *Urban History Review/Revue d'histoire urbaine* 20, no. 1 (1991): 22.

70 "The Esplanade," *The Globe*, 2 August 1853, no. 366, 2.

71 Scadding, *Toronto of Old*, 80–81; Mellen, "The Development of the Toronto Waterfront," 31–32, 48–49.

72 Mellen, "The Development of the Toronto Waterfront," 54–55; McIlwraith, "Digging Out," 15.

73 "The Esplanade: Great Public Meeting of the Citizens Last Night," *The Globe*, 4 July 1855, no. 632, 2.

74 Scadding, *Toronto of Old*, 81.

75 Anders Ekström argues the elevated viewpoint helped educate the viewer into new ways of seeing and thinking: see Anders Ekström, "Seeing from Above: A Particular History of the General Observer," *Nineteenth-Century Contexts* 31, no. 3 (2009): 187, 200.

76 Patrick Joyce, *The Rule of Freedom*, 44.

77 On the ability of pictures to create order, see Sarah Bassnett, *Picturing Toronto: Photography and the Making of a Modern City* (Montreal: McGill-Queen's University Press, 2016), 5–6; Jae Emerling, *Photography: History and Theory* (New York: Routledge, 2012), 23, 34; and Jonathan Crary, *Techniques of the Observer: On Vision and Modernity in the Nineteenth Century* (Cambridge, MA: MIT Press, 1992), 11–13.

78 For a view of a pastoral Toronto waterfront, see Gooderham and Worts 1855, by William Armstrong, and additional images at the Distillery District Heritage Website, www.distilleryheritage.com/art.html.

79 On the ability of postcards to promote a liberal order, see Michael Lesy, *Dreamland: America at the Dawn of the Twentieth Century* (New York: The New Press, 1997), xi–xiii; and Mary Warner Marien, *Photography a Cultural History* (New York: Harry N. Abrahams, 2002), 170–72.

80 Lesy, *Dreamland*, xi–xii, xiii.

81 Leo Marx, *The Machine in the Garden: Technology and the Pastoral Ideal in America* (New York: Oxford University Press, 2000), 150, 166, 185–86, 226.

82 Marx, 186, 195–97.

83 Marx, 208. Jeffrey L. Meikle, "Leo Marx's The Machine in the Garden," *Technology and Culture* 44, no. 1 (2003): 158.

84 For a portrayal of this industrial sublime in industrial projects, see Richard White, *The Organic Machine: The Remaking of the Columbia River* (New York: Hill and Wang: 1995); David E. Nye, *American Technological Sublime* (Cambridge, MA: MIT Press, 1994); John F. Kasson, *Civilizing the Machine: Technology and Republican Values in America, 1776–1900* (New York: Grossman), 1976.

85 McIlwraith, "Digging Out," 30. He suggests that of an estimated 822,000 cubic metres of fill were required to complete the Esplanade, some 660,000 cubic metres came from the Ontario Terrace.

86 Mellen, "The Development of the Toronto Waterfront," 55; McIlwraith, "Digging Out," 22, 29.

87 Plates 4–11, Charles E. Goad, *Atlas of the City of Toronto and Vicinity*, March 1880, TCA.

88 Mellen, "The Development of the Toronto Waterfront," 343.

89 Careless, *Toronto to 1918*, 77–86; Mellen, "The Development of the Toronto Waterfront," 113, 117, 124.

90 On industrial change, see Craig Heron, "The Second Industrial Revolution in Canada, 1890–1930," in *Class, Community and the Labour Movement: Wales and Canada*, ed. Deian Hopkin and Gregory

Kealey (St. John's: Committee on Canadian Labour History, 1989). On storage, see Mellen, "The Development of the Toronto Waterfront," 108–109, 126, 131.

91 Jason Gilliland, "Muddy Shore to Modern Port: Redimensioning the Montreal Waterfront Time-Space," *Canadian Geographer/Le Géographe canadien* 48, no. 4 (2004): 453.

Chapter 2: The Central Waterfront: Vernacular Spaces

1 "Bathing in Public," *The Globe*, 10 August 1887, 5.

2 Climate data: Climate Data Online, 1840–2000. Daily Data Reports, Toronto Meteorological Observatory. Climate Data Online. Environment Canada, http://climate.weather.gc.ca/historical_data/search_historic_data_e.html: July, 1887.

3 This article does a good job of detailing how turn-of-the-century Torontonians responded to a heat wave: "Toronto's Hot Spell," *The Globe*, 28 June 1901, 10. Nineteenth-century citizens relied on the physical environment to cool down during heat waves, a situation made worse because industrial cities generated their own heat island effect. While it covers a different period, Eric Klinenberg's discussion of the 1995 Chicago heat wave offers a great window into the social and physical experience of an urban heatwave. See Eric Klinenberg, *Heat Wave: A Social Autopsy of Disaster in Chicago*, 2nd ed. (Chicago: University of Chicago Press, 2015). For the heat island effect in Toronto, see Tanzina Mohsin, "Greater Toronto Area Urban Heat Island: Analysis of Temperatures and Extremes" (PhD diss., University of Toronto, 2009); and P.G. Mackintosh and R. Anderson, "The Toronto Star Fresh Air Fund: Transcendental Rescue in a Modern City, 1900–1915," *Geographical Review* 99 (2009): 547–49.

4 "Bathing in Public," *The Globe*, 10 August 1887, 5.

5 Ibid. For the location of the wharf, see Plate 2, Charles E. Goad, *Atlas of the City of Toronto and Vicinity*, 2nd ed. (Toronto: Chas. E. Goad, 1890).

6 "Bathing in Public," *The Globe*, 10 August 1887, 5.

7 "Against Bathing Dresses," *The Globe*, 12 August 1887, 6.

8 Ibid. We will hear the phrase "Evil be to him who evil thinks," or "Honi soit qui mal y pense," again in Chapter 3.

9 Charles Anthony Joyce, "From Left Field," 168.

10 John Fiske refers to this creation of cultural spaces as excorporation: see John Fiske, *Reading the Popular* (New York: Routledge, 2005), 1–9; John Fiske, *Understanding Popular Culture* (Boston: Unwin Hyman, 1989), 15.

11 Rob Shields, *Places on the Margin: Alternative Geographies of Modernity* (New York: Routledge, 1991), 5, 47, 52–54, 57, 63, 77.

12 For the role of the reform movement in bathing in Canada, see Alan Metcalfe, *Working-Class Physical Recreation in Montreal, 1860–1895* (Kingston, ON: Sports Studies Research Group, Queen's University, 1978), 11–12, 22; Robert S. Kossuth, "Dangerous Waters: Victorian Decorum, Swimmer Safety, and the Establishment of Public Bathing Facilities in London (Canada)," *International Journal of the History of Sport* 22, no. 5 (2005): 797, 802. For international examples, see Sarah Howell, *The Seaside* (London: Cassell and Collier Macmillan, 1974), 20–22; Douglas Booth, *Australian Beach Cultures: History of Sun, Sand, and Surf* (London: Routledge, 2001), 31; Cameron White, "Picnicking, Surf-Bathing and Middle-Class Morality on the Beach in the Eastern Suburbs of Sydney, 1811–1912," *Journal of Australian Studies* 27, no. 80 (2003): 103; Christopher Love, *A Social History of Swimming in England, 1800–1918* (New York: Routledge, 2008), 20–21. On the goals and logic of the reform movement more broadly, see Ramsay Cook, *The Regenerators: Social Criticism of Late*

Victorian English Canada (Toronto: University of Toronto Press, 1997); Richard Allen, "The Social Gospel and the Reform Tradition in Canada," *Canadian Historical Review* 49, no. 4 (1968); Daniel T. Rodgers, "Worlds of Reform," *OAH Magazine of History* 20, no. 5 (2006): 49–54; Carolyn Strange, *Toronto's Girl Problem: The Perils and Pleasures of the City, 1880–1930* (Toronto: University of Toronto Press, 1995); Craig Heron, *Booze: A Distilled History* (Toronto: Between the Lines, 2003).

13 John F. Travis, *The Rise of the Devonshire Seaside Resorts, 1750–1900* (Exeter: University of Exeter Press, 1993), 19; Richard Rutt, "The Englishman's Swimwear," *Costume* 24, no. 1 (1990): 70–72. Robert Kossuth argues moral concerns usually trumped safety concerns in nineteenth-century London, Ontario, but even then there were sympathetic voices for the bathers: Kossuth, "Dangerous Waters," 800–4.

14 I will have more to say about the notion of the bathing boy as a folk figure in Chapter 4. For a useful discussion on folk people and the folk idea as a projection, see Ian McKay, *The Quest of the Folk: Antimodernism and Cultural Selection in Twentieth-century Nova Scotia* (Montreal: McGill-Queen's University Press, 1994), 4–7, 11–12; Graham Seal, *Inventing Anzac: The Digger and National Mythology* (Perth: University of Queensland Press, 2004), 3–7. I am borrowing the term "slippage" from Mariana Valverde; see Valverde, *Age of Light*, xiii–xiv.

15 We see similar patterns in England: Rutt, "The Englishman's Swimwear," 71, 72; Travis, *Devonshire Seaside Resorts*, 121; John K. Walton, "Respectability Takes a Holiday: Disreputable Behavior at the Victorian Seaside," in *Unrespectable Recreations*, ed. Martin Hewitt (Leeds: Leeds Centre for Victorian Studies, 2001), 184.

16 Mackintosh and Anderson use the number of days where the temperature failed to drop below 18°Cs (65°F) in July as their benchmark for change: Mackintosh and Anderson, "The Toronto Star Fresh Air Fund," 546.

17 Kossuth suggests parsimony trumped efforts to alleviate the heat-driven discomfort of bathers in London. But while parsimony held up efforts to improve bathing facilities in Toronto, temperature and discomfort did play a role in changing policy: Kossuth, "Dangerous Waters," 804–5.

18 Careless, *Toronto*, 200.

19 Careless, 17–19.

20 Careless, 138.

21 "Police Court: Caution to Bathers," *The Globe*, 10 June 1873, 1.

22 "About the City: Police Court Cases," *The Globe*, 6 August 1889, 8.

23 "City News," *The Globe*, 15 August 1867, 2.

24 "City News," *The Globe*, 5 June 1877, 4; "City News," *The Globe*, 2 August 1880, 6.

25 "City News," *The Globe*, 30 August 1877, 4.

26 Here and throughout the waterfront we can see John Fiske's notion of excorporation taking place, with bathers carving out spaces of their own: Fiske, *Understanding Popular Culture*, 15; Fiske, *Reading the Popular*, 1–9. We can also see, as Rob Shields suggests, how competition over meaning in some spaces emerges: see Shields, *Places on the Margin*, 61.

27 Catherine Brace, "Public Works in the Canadian City: The Provision of Sewers in Toronto 1870–1913," *Urban History Review/Revue d'histoire urbaine* 23, no. 2 (1995): 35–39.

28 Michael Moir, "Planning for Change: Harbour Commission, Civil Engineers, and Large-scale Manipulation of Nature," in *Reshaping Toronto's Waterfront*, ed. Gene Desfor and Jennefer Laidley (Toronto: University of Toronto Press, 2011), 31–35; Brace, "Public Works," 33–43.

29 See Maclear and Co., Plan of the city of Toronto, 1858, Toronto Public Library (TPL)/Toronto Referene Library (TRL), Baldwin collection, Ms1921.9; Brace, "Public Works," 35–39.

30 See A.A. Stewart, Secretary Toronto Swimming Club, "Swimming Baths," letter to the editor, *The Globe*, 30 July 1877, 2; and "The Awful Loss of Life by Drowning," *The Globe*, 8 July 1887, 4, which referred to "bathing from the wharfs (practically from sewage)."

31 See Katherine Ashenburg, *The Dirt on Clean: An Unsanitized History* (Toronto: A.A. Knopf Canada, 2007), 2–8.

32 "City News: Disgraceful Conduct," *The Globe*, 8 July 1878, 4. These fenced-in areas pop up across the waterfront: see, for example, Charles Anthony Joyce, "From Left Field," 231. A bathing space had also been created at Rees's Pier in 1862: "City News," *The Globe*, 25 July 1862, 2.

33 "City News: Disgraceful Conduct," *The Globe*, 8 July 1878, 4.

34 Item No. 160, By-law 1034, 15 November 1880, 608, Toronto City Council Appendix, 1880, CTA.

35 "Police Court: Bathing," *The Globe*, 4 August 1877, 8. Fines suggest bathing had not been eliminated entirely: "General News of the City: A Bathing Place for Boys," *The Globe*, 1 August 1882, 8; "About the City: Police Court Cases," *The Globe*, 6 August 1889, 8.

36 For quote, see Scadding, *Toronto of Old*, 62. See Frances N. Mellen, "The Development of the Toronto Waterfront during the Railway Expansion Era, 1850–1912" (PhD diss., University of Toronto, 1974), Fig. 1, p. 3; "Bathing Places," *The Evening Star*, 9 July 1897, 2. To map out the preservation of the Peter Street space, see Wadsworth and Unwin's map of the City of Toronto, 1872, Library Archives Canada, Local class no.: H1/440/Toronto/1872 (3 sections) Box number: 2000225124; and Thomas McIlwraith, "Digging Out and Filling In: Making Land on the Toronto Waterfront in the 1850s," *Urban History Review/Revue d'histoire urbaine* 20, no. 1 (1991): 21.

37 Shields, *Places on the Margin*, 52–53.

38 "A Plea for Public Bathing Accommodation," *The Globe*, 19 June 1876, 4.

39 Ibid. "Notes and Comments," *The Globe*, 26 June 1876, 2. Inspiration often came from New York or Britain. Indeed, there are references to New York bathing facilities as early as 1852: "Public Baths and Wash Houses," *The Globe*, 1 May 1852, no. 210, 2.

40 The temperature hit 30°C on 24 and 25 June, dipped to 25.6° on 26 June and then jumped back up to 30.6° when *The Globe* published on 27 June. See Climate Data Online, 1840–2000. Daily Data Reports, Toronto Meteorological Observatory, Climate Data Online, Environment Canada, http://climate.weather.gc.ca/historical_data/search_historic_data_e.html: June 1876; "City News Bathing on the Esplanade," *The Globe*, 27 June 1876, 4.

41 "City News: Bathing on the Esplanade," *The Globe*, 27 June 1876, 4.

42 Mellen, "The Development of the Toronto Waterfront," 62–63.

43 Mellen, 101, 225. See also *The Empire*, 8 November 1889.

44 Mellen, "The Development of the Toronto Waterfront," 38, 108.

45 McIlwraith, "Digging Out," 29.

46 The lumber trade peaked at 4,845,117 feet of lumber in 1856 but in 1876 Toronto still handled 729,000 feet: Mellen, "The Development of the Toronto Waterfront," 110.

47 McIlwraith, "Digging Out," 29; Brace, "Public Works in the Canadian City," 35–39. The Maclear Plan of Toronto's Sewers map shows that as well: Maclear and Co., 1858/1875; Moir, "Planning for Change," 27.

48 Charles Anthony Joyce, "From Left Field," 67, 167–68.

49 "City News," *The Globe*, 11 July 1881, 6.

50 "City News," *The Globe*, 14 August 1865, 2.

51 "Drowning Accident in the Bay," *The Globe*, 10 July 1876, 4.

52 Why a pike pole? Ebenezer Martin argued in his 1876 instructional guide for swimming that a drowning bather will instinctively grip a pole if it touches their hand, giving rescuers a chance to pull them up. Clearly, Jackson's friends hoped that would happen. See Ebenezer Martin, *Treatise on the Theory of Swimming Made So Easy That It Can be Reduced to Practice at Once* (Montreal: Lovell, 1876), 13.

53 "Drowning Accident in the Bay," *The Globe*, 10 July 1876, 4.

54 Ibid.

55 Ibid.

56 Archibald Taylor, "To the Editor of the Globe," *The Globe*, 11 July 1876, 3.

57 "Drowning Accident in the Bay," *The Globe*, 10 July 1876.

58 L.K., "Bathing," *The Globe*, 12 July 1876.

59 "Drowning Accident in the Bay," *The Globe*, 10 July 1876, 4; A.A. McKenzie, "The Accident at the Queen's Wharf," *The Globe*, 11 July 1876; Archibald Taylor, "The Accident at the Queen's Wharf," *The Globe*, 11 July 1876.

60 See Rutt, "The Englishman's Swimwear," 29.

61 "Bathing within City Limits," *The Globe*, 27 June 1868, 2. "Bathing on Sunday," *The Globe*, 30 June 1868, 1. "Police Court," *The Globe*, 1 July 1868, 2.

62 "Bathing on Sunday," *The Globe*, 30 June 1868, 1.

63 Ibid.

64 Climate Data Online. 1840–2000. Daily Data Reports, Toronto Meteorological Observatory, Climate Data Online, Environment Canada, http://climate.weather.gc.ca/historical_data/search_historic_data_e.html: June-July, 1868; "Provision for Public Bathing," *The Globe*, 30 July 1868, 2.

65 See bylaw 467, "A by-law for the regulation of the Streets, Sidewalks and Thoroughfares of the City of Toronto, and for the preservation of Order and suppression of Nuisances therein," Item 497, 26 October 1868, 133, Toronto City Council Minutes, 1868, TCA. The changes received little attention when they were implemented in the midst of a series of other bylaw revisions: "City Council," *The Globe*, 27 October 1868, 4.

66 "Provision for public bathing," *The Globe*, 30 July 1868, 2. Nearly identical comments would be repeated just a few years later: "Dangerous amusements," *The Globe*, 11 February 1873, 2.

67 "Provision for Public Bathing," *The Globe*, 30 July 1868, 2.

68 Charles Anthony Joyce, "From Left Field," 104–5.

69 "Answers to Correspondents," *The Globe*, 23 April 1870, 2.

70 This was initially proposed in 1879: Item 316, 17 March 1879, Toronto City Council Minutes, 1879, CTA. The initial attempt at amendment in 1879 was voted down: Item 581, 19 May 1879, Toronto City Council Minutes, 1879, CTA; Item 495, Report No. 16 of the Property Committee, 16 June 1879, 369, Toronto City Council Appendix, 1879, CTA.

71 Item 630, Monday, 31 May 1879, Toronto City Council Minutes, 1879, CTA. (No. 75) No. 1004. A bylaw, Item 400, 320, 31 May 1880, Appendix A, Toronto City Council, CTA; "City News: Bathing on the Esplanade," *The Globe*, 1 June 1880, 8.

72 "City News: Bathing on the Esplanade," *The Globe*, 1 June 1880, 6.

73 "City News: Bathing on the Esplanade," *The Globe*, 7 June 1880, 4.

74 Civic Affairs," *The Globe*, 1 June 1880, 6. Parsimony held up the construction of bathing infrastructure in London, Ontario, as well: Kossuth, "Dangerous Waters," 799–801.

75 Mitchell Dean, *Governmentality: Power and Rule in Modern Society* (London: Sage, 1999), 21–22.

76 "Notes and Comments," *The Globe*, 7 June 1880, 4.

77 "Bathing on the Esplanade," *The Globe*, 7 June 1880, 4. Note the letter appeared in the 7 June edition but was dated 3 June. Emphasis mine.

78 "City Council: The Bathing By-law," *The Globe*, 29 June 1880, 6. Bylaw 1034.

79 "City News," *The Globe*, 4 August 1880, 6.

80 Sally Gibson, *More Than an Island: A History of the Toronto Island* (Toronto: Irwin, 1984), 86; "Bathing Facilities," *The Globe*, 4 August 1880, 4.

81 Gibson, *More Than an Island*, 90–91; Charles Anthony Joyce, "From Left Field," 334–40.

82 On the gender divides within Toronto, see Carolyn Strange, *Toronto's Girl Problem*, 123.

83 "Civic Affairs: Bathing," *The Globe*, 15 July 1881, 8.

84 "City News: Bathing on the Esplanade," *The Globe*, 18 July 1881, 8.

85 Item 603, 5 June 1893, 176, Toronto City Council Minutes, 1893, CTA; Item 651, 19 June 1893, 193, Toronto City Council Minutes, 1893, CTA; By-law 3179, 19 June 1893, 274, Toronto City Council Appendix B, CTA; Bylaw 3179 amended bylaw 2449.

86 By-law 3179, 19 June 1893, 274, Toronto City Council Appendix B, CTA.

87 Item 671, 23 June 1893, 204, Toronto City Council Minutes, 1893, CTA; By-law 3183, 23 June 1893, 283, Toronto City Council Appendix B, 1893, CTA; Toronto Island: No. 3268 a by-law, 17 July 1894, 265, Toronto City Council Appendix B, CTA.

88 "City Council in Session: Bathing in the Nude," *The Globe*, Tuesday, 6 June 1893, 8.

89 "Ald. Crawford and the Boys—His bylaw gives them permission to take an old-time plunge," *The Empire*, June 1893, 3, col. 1; found in Peter Simm, "Enhance Toronto Tourism and Recreation: Restore Clothing-Optional Status to Hanlan's Point Beach." Brief submitted to Toronto City Council, April 1999, 12. Fonds 2, series 1143, item 4963, box 564020–folio 3. CTA.

90 "City Council in Session: Bathing in the Nude," *The Globe*, 6 June 1893, 8.

91 "Notes and Comments," *The Globe*, 21 June 1893, 6.

92 "Dogs Must Not Roam at Large," *The Evening Star*, 6 July 1894, 4.

93 "Narrow Escape from Drowning," *The Globe*, 4 August 1859, 2.

94 "The Drowning of Mr. Griffin," *The Globe*, 19 July 1878, 4; "Drowning Accidents," *The Globe*, 18 July 1878, 4; "Narrow Escape from Drowning," *The Globe*, 4 August 1859, 2.

95 "Proceedings and Scenes of Yesterday," *The Globe*, 15 August 1882, 3.

96 John Ross Robertson, *Landmarks of Toronto: Toronto from 1834 to 1814* (Toronto: J. Ross Robertson, 1914), 116.

97 Robertson, 118. Stonehookers were used for carrying stone: Andrew Armitage, "The Stonehookers of Lake Ontario," http://archive.li/qM8bE.

98 Norman Knowles, "Denison, George Taylor," in *Dictionary of Canadian Biography*, vol. 15, University of Toronto/Université Laval, 2003–, http://www.biographi.ca/en/bio/denison_george_taylor_1839_1925_15E.html (accessed 17 November 2015).

99 There are some cases directly attached to Denison's name: "Police Court," *The Globe*, 12 September 1878, 4; "Police Court," *The Globe*, 17 September 1881, 6. Others simply mention the police magistrate and could have been chaired by a different judge.

100 "Police Court: Bathing," *The Globe*, 4 August 1877, 8. And later fines suggest how bathing at the end of York and to the east did not end: "General News of the City: A Bathing Place for Boys," *The Globe*, 1 August 1882, 8; "About the City: Police Court Cases," *The Globe*, Tuesday, 6 August 1889, 8.

101 "Who Owns the Water?," *The Globe*, 17 August 1905, 5.

102 "A Mistaken Idea," *The Globe*, 12 August 1902, 12.

103 "Boy's Bathed, Clad in Nature's Garb," *The Toronto Daily Star*, 7 August 1902, 2.

104 "Never Argue with Police," *The Toronto Daily Star*, 11 August 1902, 1.

105 Ibid.

106 "Never Argue with Politics," *The Toronto Daily Star*, 11 August 1902, 3.

107 C.S. Clark, *Of Toronto the Good, a Social Study: The Queen City of Canada as It Is* (Montreal: Toronto Publishing Company, 1898), 187–88; Valverde, *Age of Light*, 83. For the emergence of dating, see Beth Bailey, *From Front Porch to Back Seat* (Baltimore: John Hopkins University Press, 1988), 4, 18.

108 Strange, *Toronto's Girl Problem*, 9. See also Valverde, *Age of Light*, 82–83.

109 Steven Maynard, "Through a Lavatory Wall: Homosexual Subcultures, Police Surveillance, and the Dialectics of Discovery, Toronto, 1890–1930," *Journal of the History of Sexuality* 5, no. 2 (1994): 1, 13. And we find that concern scattered throughout Clark, *Of Toronto the Good*, 83, 89–90.

110 Clark, *Of Toronto the Good*, 4.

111 "Family Matters," *The Globe*, 7 July 1894, 8.

112 Clark, *Of Toronto the Good*, 81.

113 Clark, 113.

114 W.D. Andrews, *Swimming and Life-Saving* (Toronto: William Briggs, 1889), 15.

115 Andrews, 15.

116 Andrews, 15.

117 Andrews, 15.

118 Martin, *Theory of Swimming*, 9–12.

119 T.W. Sheffield, *Swimming* (Toronto: Musson Book Company, 1909), 175–76.

120 Sheffield, 44.

121 Climate data: http://climate.weather.gc.ca/climateData/dailydata_e.html?timeframe=2&Prov=ON&StationID=5051&dlyRange=1840-03-01%7C2015-04-14&Year=1897&Month=7&Day=1.

122 "Death Due to a City By-law," *The Evening Star*, 8 July 1897, 7.

123 Ibid.

124 "Another Lad Drowned," *The Globe*, 8 July 1897, 10; "Where the People May Bathe," *The Globe*, 8 July 1897, 6.

125 "General News of the City: The Body Identified," *The Globe*, Friday, 9 July 1897, 10; "Slain by a by-law," *The Evening Star*, Thursday, 8 July 1897, 1. Fenton appears in the York Coroner records, though his name is misspelled: Feuton D., 1897, York County Coroner Investigations and Inquests. RG22-5895, microfilm reel 7606, Archives of Ontario.

126 "Slain by a By-law," *The Evening Star*, Thursday, 8 July 1897, 1.

127 "Bathing Places Needed," *The Evening Star*, Thursday, 8 July 1897, 4. Similar arguments with respect to "luxurious bath-tubs" would be repeated in other editorials: "A Pressing Need," *The Evening Star*, 10 July 1897, 4.

128 "Bathing Places Needed," *The Evening Star*, Thursday, 8 July 1897, 4. And in a few days it would be calling for five bathing spaces on the waterfront: "Toronto's Greatest Need," *The Evening Star*, 10 July 1897, 2.

129 "Bathing Places Needed," *The Evening Star*, 9 July 1897, 2.

130 "Toronto's Greatest Need," *The Evening Star*, 10 July 1897, 2.

131 "Bathing Places Needed," *The Evening Star*, 9 July 1897, 2. The phrase "mother of boys" is used in the letter, but that doesn't guarantee the letter was written by a female; men were often more than willing to speak for women.

132 See Gail Bederman, *Manliness and Civilization: A Cultural History of Gender and Race in the United States, 1880–1917* (Chicago: University of Chicago Press, 1995).

133 "A Pressing Need," *The Evening Star*, 10 July 1897, 4.

134 "Toronto's Greatest Need," *The Evening Star*, 10 July 1897, 2.

135 "Bathing Places Needed," *The Evening Star*, 9 July 1897, 2.

136 "Toronto's Greatest Need," *The Evening Star*, 10 July 1897, 2.

137 Howell, *The Seaside*, 105.

138 "Toronto's Greatest Need," *The Evening Star*, 10 July 1897, 2.

139 Originally published in the *Globe* "Notes and Comments," *The Globe*, 12 July 1897, 4. And dutifully quoted in "Bathing Places Needed," *The Evening Star*, 12 July 1897, 2.

140 "Notes and Comments," *The Globe*, 12 July 1897, 4.

141 See Annual Chief Constable Reports, Toronto City Council Appendix, 1896–98, CTA.

142 On the reach and limits of Victorian newspapers, see Paul Rutherford, *Victorian Authority: The Daily Press in Late Nineteenth-Century Canada* (Toronto: University of Toronto Press, 1982), 7–8.

143 Item 539, Tuesday, 13 July 1897, 182, Toronto City Council Minutes, 1897, CTA; Item 547, Tuesday, 13 July 1897, 183, Toronto City Council Minutes, 1897, CTA.

144 (No. 35), Board of Control Report no. 30, 22 July 1897, adopted by city council on 26 July 1897, 543, Toronto City Council Appendix A, 1897, CTA.

145 "City Hall Small Talk," *The Globe*, 13 July 1897, 8.

146 (No. 35), Board of Control Report no. 30, 22 July 1897, adopted by city council on 26 July 1897, 543, Toronto City Council Appendix A, 1897, CTA.

147 "Bathers in a Tug," *The Evening Star*, 14 July 1897, 2; "Shaw Loses It on a Tie Vote," *The Evening Star*, 14 July 1897, 2. For the quote, see "Swimming! Public Notice to the Boys of Toronto," *The Globe*, 19 July 1897, 6.

148 "With the Boys . . . on the Sandbar," *The Globe*, 31 July 1897, 4.

149 "The Happy Small Boy," *The Globe*, 15 July 1897, 9; "Swimming! Public Notice to the Boys of Toronto," *The Globe*, 19 July 1897, 6.

150 "With the Boys on the Bar," *The Evening Star*, 22 July 1897, 7.

151 Ibid.

152 Ibid.

153 Timing matters: news photography was just beginning in the late 1890s, thanks to advancements in technology and reductions in cost. See Ulrich Keller, "Photojournalism around 1900: The Institutionalization of a Mass Medium," in *Shadow and Substance: Essays on the History of Photography in Honour of Heinz K. Henisch*, ed. Kathleen Collins (Bloomfield Hills, MI: Amorphous Institute

Press, 1990), 283–86, 288; Mary Warner Marien, *Photography: A Cultural History* (New York: Harry N. Abrahams, 2002), 167–70. In contrast, the *Star* only showed line art of people heading over to the new bathing space: see "With the Boys on the Bar," *The Evening Star*, 22 July 1897, 7.

154 For the ability of photography to produce news events and meaning more broadly, see Ulrich Keller, "Photojournalism around 1900," 293–95. Jae Emerling, *Photography: History and Theory* (New York: Routledge, 2012), 34.

155 "With the Boys on the Sandbar," *The Globe*, 31 July 1897, 4.

156 E. McFarland, "The Development of Supervised Playgrounds," in *Recreational Land Use: Perspectives on Its Evolution in Canada*, ed. Geoffrey Wall and John Walsh (Ottawa: Carlton Press, 1982), 282–84. For more on St. Andrew's, see "The New Playground," *The Toronto Daily Star*, 12 August 1909, 14; Final Report of the Parks and Exhibition Committee, 6 January 1910, 158–59, Toronto City Council, 1909, Appendix A, CTA.

157 Galen Cranz, "Women in Urban Parks," *Signs: Journal of Women in Culture and Society* 5, no. 3, supplement, *Women and the American City* (1980): 579–80; Dominick Cavallo, *Muscle and Morals: Organized Playgrounds and Urban Reform, 1880–1920* (Philadelphia: University of Pennsylvania Press, 1981).

158 "With the Boys on the Sandbar," *The Globe*, 31 July 1897, 4.

159 McFarland, "The Development of Supervised Playgrounds," 292–94.

160 The Fresh Air Fund idea had been around in Toronto since 1888, but the *Star* formalized the program in 1901: Mackintosh and Anderson, "The Toronto Star Fresh Air Fund," 539–44.

161 The city had envisioned the program as contingent on the heat, but extended it to cover the entire summer, and voted on it again each year after that: (No. 35), Board of Control Report no. 30, 22 July 1897, adopted by city council on 26 July 1897, 543, Toronto City Council Appendix A, 1897, CTA.

Chapter 3: Toronto Island: Implementing a Beach

1 "The Wiman Baths," *The Globe*, 26 June 1882, 5.

2 On moral architecture, see Mitchell Dean, *Governmentality Power and Rule in Modern Society* (London: Sage, 1999), 12; Patrick Joyce, *The Rule of Freedom: Liberalism and the Modern City* (New York: Verso, 2003), 2–4, 7, 11–12; Nikolas Rose, Pat O'Malley, and Mariana Valverde, "Governmentality," *Annual Review of Law and Social Science* 2 (2006): 85–86, 88; Robert A. Campbell, *Sit Down and Drink Your Beer: Regulating Vancouver's Beer Parlours, 1925–1954* (Toronto: University of Toronto Press, 2001).

3 Elias wrote his views on the evolution of society decades before Michel Foucault, but as Bruce Curtis notes, we can, see governmentality at work in Elias's "civilizing process." See Norbert Elias, *Power and Civility: The Civilizing Process: Volume 2*, trans. Edmund Jephcott (New York: Pantheon Books, 1982), 230, 232; and Bruce Curtis, "After 'Canada': Liberalisms, Social Theory, and Historical Analysis," in *Liberalism and Hegemony: Debating the Canadian Liberal Revolution*, ed. Jean-François Constant and Michel Ducharme (Toronto: University of Toronto Press, 2009), 190.

4 Rob Shields, *Places on the Margin: Alternative Geographies of Modernity* (New York: Routledge, 1991), 52–54, 57.

5 John Fiske, *Reading the Popular* (New York: Routledge, 2005), 41.

6 Fiske, 50–51.

7 John Fiske, *Understanding Popular Culture* (Boston: Unwin Hyman, 1989), 11, 14.

8 Douglas Booth, "Nudes in the Sand and Perverts in the Dunes," *Journal of Australian Studies* 21, no. 53 (1997): 170.

9 Fiske, *Understanding Popular Culture,* 59–70, quote on 91. Or, in Foucauldian terms, the body becomes a technology of the self: see Christine Metusela and Gordon Waitt, *Tourism and Australian Beach Cultures Revealing Bodies* (Toronto: Channel View Publications, 2012), 25–26.

10 Fiske, *Reading the Popular*, 64. See also Michel Foucault, "Body/Power," in *Power/Knowledge: Selected Interviews and Other Writings, 1972–1977*, ed. Colin Gordon (New York: Pantheon Books, 1980), 57.

11 Fiske, *Reading the Popular*, 52. Catherine Horwood traces this process in Great Britain, but she envisions it taking place in the twentieth century. See Catherine Horwood, "'Girls Who Arouse Dangerous Passions': Women and Bathing, 1900–39," *Women's History Review* 9, no. 4 (2000): 653–73.

12 Sarah Bassnett has done an excellent job of demonstrating how photography helped navigate and direct the modernization of Toronto's cityscape and the people within it; we see that process at work in recreation spaces as well. See Sarah Bassnett, *Picturing Toronto: Photography and the Making of a Modern City* (Montreal: McGill-Queen's University Press, 2016), 4–6; Marita Sturken and Lisa Cartwright, *Practices of Looking: An Introduction to Visual Culture* (Oxford: Oxford University Press, 2009), 106–108.

13 Ulrich Keller, "Photojournalism around 1900: The Institutionalization of a Mass Medium," in *Shadow and Substance: Essays on the History of Photography in Honour of Heinz K. Henisch*, ed. Kathleen Collins (Bloomfield Hills, MI: Amorphous Institute Press, 1990), 283–86, 288; Gerry Badger, *The Genius of Photography: How Photography Has Changed Our Lives* (London: Quadrille, 2007), 38–41.

14 Sally Gibson, *More Than an Island: A History of the Toronto Island* (Toronto: Irwin, 1984), 38.

15 Gibson, 63.

16 Michael Moir, "Planning for Change: Harbour Commission, Civil Engineers, and Large-scale Manipulation of Nature," in *Reshaping Toronto's Waterfront*, ed. Gene Desfor and Jennefer Laidley (Toronto: University of Toronto Press, 2011), 31.

17 Nick Eyles, "Ravines, Lagoons, Cliffs and Spits: The Ups and Downs of Lake Ontario," in *HTO: Toronto's Water from Lake Iroquois to Lost Rivers to Low-flow Toilets*, ed. Wayne Reeves and Christina Palassio (Toronto: Coach House Books, 2008), 39.

18 *Toronto Island Guide* (Toronto: R.G. McLean, 1894), 18; Commissioner of Parks Report, Toronto Island Improvements, 15 December 1903, fonds 200, series 490, box 224914, file 1, Toronto City Archives; W.H. Pearson, *Recollections and Records of Toronto of Old: With References to Brantford, Kingston and Other Canadian Towns* (Toronto: W. Briggs, 1914), 112–13. See also John Ross Robertson, *The Diary of Mrs. John Graves Simcoe, Wife of the First Lieutenant-Governor of the Province of Upper Canada, 1792–6* (Toronto: W. Briggs, 1911) 179, on 30 July 1783.

19 Robertson, *Simcoe Diary*, 180, on 4 August 1793; John Ross Robertson, *Robertson's Landmarks of Toronto: Toronto from 1834 to 1908* (Toronto: John R. Robertson, 1908), 36.

20 Robertson, *Landmarks* (1908), 37. See, for example, Charles E. Goad lease renewal, fonds 200, series 768, subseries 2, file 36, dates of creation: 1900–1904, box 145254, folio 2, CTA.

21 Gibson, *More Than an Island*, 56.

22 Gibson, 72; Report no. 115, item 148, 8 August 1874, 201–202, Toronto City Council Appendix, 1874, CTA.

23 "City Council," *The Globe*, 12 November 1867, 1.

24 In 1903, for example, a leaseholder's plan to build a fence was disputed by a neighbour who argued it would block his right of way: DuVernet Ferguson & Jones letter, 5 August 1903, in Correspondence file re: Island leases, fonds 200, series 768, subseries 2, file 1, box 145247, folio 1, CTA.

25 Patricia Jasen, *Wild Things: Nature, Culture, and Tourism in Ontario 1790–1914* (Toronto: University of Toronto Press, 1995), 15–19.

26 *Toronto Island Guide*, 2.

27 Ibid., 25. Indigenous names continue to be used for island streets, and particularly on "Algonquin Island."

28 Jasen, *Wild Things*, 130.

29 Gibson, *More Than an Island*, 72–73.

30 "City Council," *The Globe*, 12 November 1867, 1.

31 Gibson, *More Than an Island*, 72.

32 "City Council," *The Globe*, 12 November 1867, 1 (132 feet broad to be precise).

33 "Narrow Escape from Drowning," *The Globe*, 4 August 1859, 2; "Drowning Accidents," *The Globe*, 18 July 1878, 4; "The Drowning of Mr. Griffin," *The Globe*, 19 July 1878, 4. See "Toronto's Only Fishing Village Must Go," *The Toronto Sunday World*, 22 February 1914, feature section, 1. See also "Fisherman's Island," Beaches Living Guide, Spring/Summer 2015, http://www.beachesliving.ca/pages/index.php?act=landmark&id=172 (accessed on 5 November 2017); Jillinda Greene, "The Long Lost Story of Fisherman's Island," *localmagazine.ca*, Summer 2011, vol. 2, http://localmagazine.ca/v2/wp-content/uploads/2011/07/FishermansIsland.pdf (accessed on 5 November 2017). Fisherman's Island, briefly called Gunsel's Island, was the remains of the peninsula that had attached to the island.

34 Robertson, *Landmarks* (1908), 35.

35 "City Police: Bathing," *The Globe*, 28 July 1857, 2.

36 Item 998, 43rd and final report of committee on property, 14 January 1879, 866, Toronto City Council Appendix, 1878, CTA.

37 As noted in Chapter 1, 1876 did feature an exceptionally hot summer: The temperature hit 30°C on 24 and 25 June, dipped to 25.6°C on 26 June, and then jumped backed up to 30.6°C when *the Globe* published on 27 June. Climate Data Online, 1840–2000, Daily Data Reports, Toronto Meteorological Observatory, Environment Canada: climate.weather.gc.ca. For the quote, see Gibson, *More Than an Island*, 83.

38 A.D. Stewart, "Communications: Swimming Baths," *The Globe*, 26 July 1877, 2.

39 Gibson, *More Than an Island*, 49.

40 We see outside examples being discussed in the newspapers: "Special Correspondence of the Globe," *The Globe*, 18 October 1851, 3. We can link the discussion with the broader commercialization of the beach that was happening across the north Atlantic: see Alain Corbin, *The Lure of the Sea: The Discovery of the Seaside in the Western World, 1750–1840*, trans. Jocelyn Phelps (Cambridge, UK: Polity Press, 1994), 263–78; Sarah Howell, *The Seaside* (London: Cassell and Collier Macmillan, 1974), 7, 17, 20–22.

41 Paterfamilias, "Communications: The Island," *The Globe*, 26 June 1876, 2.

42 "Communications: Bathing Machines," *The Globe*, 16 July 1868, 3.

43 "Bathing for Ladies," *The Globe*, 24 May 1875, 2.

44 "Bather," "Communications: Bathing for Ladies," *The Globe*, 24 May 1875, 2. *The Globe* endorsed the letter with an editorial of its own: "Bathing for Ladies," *The Globe*, 24 May 1875, 2.

45 Christopher Love, *A Social History of Swimming in England, 1800–1918* (New York: Routledge, 2008), 6, 20.

46 The issue was raised often at city council with little follow-through. Calls were made in 1873: Swimming baths, item 721, 19 August 1873, 168, Toronto City Council Minutes, 1873, CTA. In 1875 the calls were repeated and funding was proposed, but word of a new private operation caused

the city to back off: Bathing houses, erection of, item 388, 12 April 1875, 77; item 429, 19 April 1875, 85, Toronto City Council Minutes, 1875, CTA.; Bathing house, item 116, report no. 84, 1 June 1875, 208, Toronto City Council Appendix, 1875, CTA. The cycle repeated in 1876 when Dr. A.A. Riddell Coroner pointed to a recent drowning inquest and called for the "establishment of Bathing Houses in the Eastern and Western portions of the city." Bathing houses, establishment of, item 956, 12 June 1876, 179, Toronto City Council Minutes, 1876, CTA. Once again while funding was proposed, spending it was put off: Bathing houses, item 231, Committee on Finance and Assessment report no. 26, 4 August 1876, 258, Toronto City Council Appendix, 1876, CTA. Toronto would not have a civic bathhouse until 1909, when the Harrison Baths were opened. Parsimony did play a role in stunting the expansion of bathing facilities in Toronto, just as it did for London, Ontario: see Robert S. Kossuth, "Dangerous Waters: Victorian Decorum, Swimmer Safety, and the Establishment of Public Bathing Facilities in London (Canada), *International Journal of the History of Sport* 22, no. 5 (2005): 796–97.

47 Final Report: Wharves and Harbours, item 344, 8 January 1877, 585–86, Toronto City Council Appendix, 1876, CTA.

48 Item 764, 18 June 1877, 197, Toronto City Council Minutes, 1877; Item 166, Executive Committee of the Council, report no. 5 (but property committee manages), 18 June 1877, 220, Toronto City Council Appendix, 1877, CTA.

49 "City News," *The Globe*, 21 May 1877, 4.

50 Item 764, 18 June 1877, 197, Toronto City Council Minutes, 1877, CTA.

51 The nineteenth-century Goad's Fire Insurance maps relied on Unwin's legal framework while warning users that the location of buildings and waterlines was an estimate.

52 "City News," *The Globe*, 29 September 1877, 5.

53 "City News," *The Globe*, 1 July 1878, 4. In this case they were bathing "where they should not have been."

54 "Police Protection for the Island," *The Globe*, 15 July 1878, 2. In Australia such groups of bathing men were often referred to as larrikins: The "larrikin" symbolized the immoral and irreligious mob. See Cameron White, "Picnicking, Surf-Bathing and Middle-Class Morality on the Beach in the Eastern Suburbs of Sydney, 1811–1912," *Journal of Australian Studies* 27, no. 80 (2003): 105.

55 Climate data: climate.weather.gc.ca.

56 In addition, Chicago's parks were laid out in the 1860s and 1870s; see S.B. Sutton, ed., *Civilizing American Cities: A Selection of Frederick Law Olmsted's Writings on City Landscapes* (Cambridge, MA: Massachusetts Institute of Technology, 1971); and Michael P. McCarthy, "Politics and the Parks: Chicago Businessmen and the Recreation Movement, *Journal of the Illinois State Historical Society (1908–1984)* 65, no. 2 (1972): 158. Peter Clark argues the high tide of park making in Europe fell between 1880 and 1900: Peter Clark, ed., *The European City and Green Space: London, Stockholm, Helsinki and St. Petersburg, 1850–2000* (Aldershot, UK: Ashgate, 2006), 9.

57 David Bain, "John Howard's High Park: 'A Square Mile or Two of Rough Ground,'" *Ontario History* 51, no. 1 (2009): 7–10. J.M.S. Careless, *Toronto to 1918: An Illustrated History* (Toronto: James Lorimer, 1984), 147.

58 Gibson, *More Than an Island*, 88.

59 M. Jane Fairburn, *Along the Shore Rediscovering Toronto's Waterfront Heritage* (Toronto: ECW Press, 2013), 145, 154. On the role of pleasure gardens, see Galen Cranz, "Women in Urban Parks," *Signs: Journal of Women in Culture and Society* 5, no. 3, supplement, *Women and the American City* (1980): 579–80; Gibson, *More Than an Island*, 88.

60 In suburban areas of Australia undressed bathing bodies became an issue as promoters attempted to sell waterfront property: see Metusela and Waitt, *Tourism and Australian Beach Cultures*, 9.

61 (No. 160) No. 1034. A bylaw, item 835, 608, 15 November 1880, Toronto City Council Appendix A, 1880, Toronto City Archives. "City Council: Bathing," *The Globe*, 16 November 1880, 8.

62 Technically there were two bylaws passed in 1880: the island hadn't been included in bylaw 1004 but was captured in the amendment, bylaw 1034. See No. 1004, A bylaw, 320, 31 May 1880, City Council Appendix 1880 and (No. 160) No. 1034, A bylaw, item 835, 608, 15 November 1880, Toronto City Council Appendix A, 1880, CTA.

63 Fiske, *Understanding Popular Culture*, 91.

64 We see the island emerging as resort space during the 1880s: see Charles Anthony Joyce, "From Left Field: Sport and Class in Toronto, 1845–1886" (PhD diss., Queen's University, 1997), 336–37; Gibson, *More Than an Island*, 86–88.

65 Gibson, 86. "Bathing facilities," *The Globe*, 4 August 1880, 4.

66 "The Wiman Baths," *The Globe*, 26 June 1882, 5. A "peeler" is another name for a police officer, drawn from Bob Peel, who developed the foundation of the modern police force in London in the early nineteenth century. The term "bobbie" also comes from Peel's name. Thus nicknames were drawn from both his first and his last name.

67 "The Wiman Baths," *The Globe*, 26 June 1882, 5.

68 "City Council," *The Toronto Daily Mail*, 24 May 1881, 8.

69 Robert Craig Brown, "Wiman, Erastus," in *Dictionary of Canadian Biography*, vol. 13, University of Toronto/Université Laval, 2003–, http://www.biographi.ca/en/bio/wiman_erastus_13E.html (accessed 11 February 2016).

70 "The Wiman Baths," *The Globe*, 26 June 1882, 5.

71 Ibid.

72 Charles Anthony Joyce argues Wiman was trying to promote temperance and respectability: see Joyce, *From Left Field*, 334. On hygiene, see Suellen Hoy, *Chasing Dirt: The American Pursuit of Cleanliness* (New York: Oxford University Press, 1995), 64; Richard L. Bushman and Claudia L. Bushman, "The Early History of Cleanliness in America," *Journal of American History* 74, no. 4 (1988): 1219; Katherine Ashenburg, *The Dirt on Clean: An Unsanitized History* (Toronto: A.A. Knopf Canada, 2007), 175, 178; Andrea Renner, "A Nation That Bathes Together: New York City's Progressive Era Public Baths," *Journal of the Society of Architectural Historians* 67, no. 4 (2008): 505–506. The progressive movement would take an industrial approach to bathing, with bathhouses that focused on showering and cleansing workers as efficiently and quickly as possible. See Perry G. An, "Helping the Poor Emerge from 'Urban Barbarism to Civic Civilization': Public Bathhouses in America, 1890–1915," *Yale Journal of Biology and Medicine* 77 (2004): 133–35; and Renner, *A Nation That Bathes Together*, 510–12, 518, 519, 520.

73 "The Wiman Baths," *The Globe*, 26 June 1882, 5; "Ladies Who Would Swim," *The Globe*, 12 July 1882, 8. On McMaster, see Gina Feldberg, "Wyllie, Elizabeth Jennet," in *Dictionary of Canadian Biography*, vol. 13, University of Toronto/Université Laval, 2003–, http://www.biographi.ca/en/bio/wyllie_elizabeth_jennet_13E.html (accessed 14 February 2016).

74 Renner, *A Nation That Bathes Together*, 505.

75 John J. Withrow, "The Wiman Swimming Baths," letter to the editor, *The Globe*, 20 January 1882, 4 (note Withrow is referencing a letter published on 16 January).

76 For a good description of the Royal Floating Baths, see Charles Anthony Joyce, *From Left Field*, 229–30.

77 "Civic Affairs: Rules for the Wiman Baths," *The Globe*, 15 July 1882, 11.

78 "Ladies Who Would Swim," *The Globe*, 12 July 1882, 8.

79 "City News: The Women Swimming Baths," *The Globe*, 21 July 1882, 6.

80 Ibid.

81 "The Wiman Baths, *The Globe*, 2 September 1882, 14. For the quote, see "City News," *The Globe*, 27 August 1882, 14.

82 Charles Anthony Joyce, *From Left Field*, 339–40.

83 Item 596, Monday, 13 May 1889, Toronto City Council Minutes, 1889, CTA; "Public Baths," *The Toronto Daily Mail*, 11 June 1892, 6. *The Mail* noted the floating baths were being towed to a location near the island and lamented that better civic facilities were not being created by the city.

84 John J. Withrow, "The Wiman Swimming Baths," letter to the editor, *The Globe*, 20 January 1882, 4.

85 "The Wiman Baths," *The Globe*, Monday, 26 June 1882, 5.

86 On the site being left off the map, see "City Council," *The Globe*, 12 November 1867, 1.

87 "The Wiman Baths," *The Globe*, 26 June 1882, 5.

88 Ibid., 8.

89 Item 381, Committee on Property, report no. 11, John Irwin, chair, 28 April 1882, 263, Toronto City Council Appendix, 1882, CTA; Item 678, report no. 19, Committee on Property, John Irwin, chair, 28 July 1882, 553, Toronto City Council Appendix, CTA; Gibson, *More Than an Island*, 91. The 1910 Goad's atlas shows the baths on lot 40: see Charles E. Goad, *Atlas of the City of Toronto* 3rd ed. (Chas. E. Goad: Toronto, 1910), plate 44.

90 "Ladies Who Would Swim," *The Globe*, 12 July 1882, 8.

91 "The Wiman Baths, *The Globe*, Saturday, 2 September 1882, 14.

92 Item 1052, report no. 35, Property Committee, 16 December 1881, 855, Toronto City Council Appendix, 1881, CTA; Item 127, 30 January 1882, 29, Toronto City Council Minutes, 1882, CTA.

93 "Natatorial Frolics," *The Globe*, 24 July 1883, 6.

94 Gibson, *More Than an Island*, 91.

95 "The Wiman Baths," *The Globe*, 26 June 1882, 5; "Local News: The Wiman Baths," *The Globe*, 28 June 1883, 6.

96 "Free for All," *The Globe*, 24 July 1882, 6; "Where Cool Breezes Blow," *The Globe*, 7 August 1885, 2.

97 Howell, *The Seaside*, 55, 60, 66.

98 "Ladies Who Would Swim," *The Globe*, 12 July 1882, 8. On calls for female space, see "Toronto's Greatest Need," *The Evening Star*, 10 July 1897, 2.

99 "Ladies Who Would Swim," *The Globe*, 12 July 1882, 8.

100 "The Wiman Baths," *The Globe*, 26 June 1882, 8.

101 "Free for All," *The Globe*, 24 July 1882, 6.

102 "The Wiman Baths, *The Globe*, 2 September 1882, 14.

103 "Natatorial Frolics," *The Globe*, 24 July 1883, 6.

104 C. Pelham Mulvany, *Toronto: Past and Present. A Handbook of the City* (Toronto: W.E. Caiger, 1884; Toronto: Ontario Reprint Press, 1970), 264–65. On the tethering modernity to the mixing of genders, see Horwood, "Girls Who Arouse Dangerous Passions," 660. Mulvany, who was interested in the cultural "present" of Toronto as much as its past, is distinct among Toronto's nineteenth-century historians in devoting a substantial amount of space to the Wiman Baths. For John Ross Robertson

the baths seem to have been too contemporary to catch his interest. Scadding refers to the "free baths," though the island baths carried a fee for use: Henry Scadding and John Charles Dent, *Toronto: Past and Present: Historical and Descriptive: Memorial Volume* (Toronto: Hunter, Rose, 1884), 298.

105 Mulvany, *Toronto: Past and Present*, 264.

106 Mulvany, 265.

107 Charles Anthony Joyce, *From Left Field*, 336–38.

108 "Civic Affairs," *The Globe*, 15 July 1882, 11.

109 "Liquor Selling on the Island," *The Globe*, 14 April 1883, 8; Charles Anthony Joyce, *From Left Field*, 337–38; Gibson, *More Than an Island*, 90.

110 "City News," *The Globe*, 31 July 1882, 6.

111 "The Wiman Baths," *The Globe*, 26 June 1882, 5.

112 Michel Foucault, *Discipline and Punish: The Birth of the Prison*, trans. Alan Sheridan (New York: Vintage Books, 1995), 211–12.

113 Foucault, 200; Mitchell Dean, *Governmentality: Power and Rule in Modern Society* (London: Sage, 1999), 23.

114 Michel Foucault, "Two Lectures," in *Power/Knowledge: Selected Interviews and Other Writings, 1972–1977*, ed. Colin Gordon (New York: Pantheon Books, 1980), 78–105.

115 Michel Foucault, "The Subject and Power," in *Power: Essential Works of Foucault, 1954–1984*, ed. James D. Faubion (New York: The New Press, 2000), 331–34.

116 Foucault, *Discipline and Punish*, 210, 224; Fiske, *Understanding Popular Culture*, 91.

117 Michel Foucault, "Prison Talk," in *Power/Knowledge*, 74; Foucault, *Discipline and Punish*, 202–3, 208–9; Metusela and Waitt, *Tourism and Australian Beach Cultures*, 9.

118 Foucault, *Discipline and Punish*, 219–20; Shields, *Places on the Margin*, 60.

119 Elias, *The Civilizing Process*, 230, 232.

120 "Ladies Who Would Swim," *The Globe*, 12 July 1882, 8.

121 Ibid.

122 Fiske, *Reading the Popular*, 52.

123 "Bather," "Bathing for Ladies," *The Globe*, 24 May 1875, 2. (There's also an editorial on this same page taking up the argument.)

124 Advertisement, *The Globe*, 14 September 1864, 4; "Novelties," *The Globe*, 25 June 1880, 3.

125 "Gale's Shops," *The Globe*, 10 May 1879, 5; "Gentlemen's Bathing," *The Globe*, 18 June 1879, 3 (10 cents for men, 5 cents for boys).

126 See, for example, "The T. Eaton Co. Limited: Friday Bargains," *The Globe*, 11 July 1895, 4; "The T. Eaton Company," *The Globe*, 22 July 1899, 18; "John MacDonald & Co.," *The Globe*, 4 June 1900, 7.

127 "Markets and Health," *The Globe*, 16 July 1880, 6.

128 The beach is a linked and circulating set of commodities, but here we see the challenge on reaching agreement on just what commodity means: see Fiske, *Understanding Popular Culture*, 11, 14. For department stores, see Donica Belisle, *Retail Nation: Department Stores and the Making of Modern Canada* (Vancouver: UBC Press, 2011), 19–25.

129 Advertisements for bathing suits become more elaborate by the late 1880s but it's not until about 1900 that display advertisements with line art start to appear in the *Globe* and the *Toronto Daily*

Star. Photographs of bathers do not become common until the start of the twentieth century: see Keller, "Photojournalism around 1900," 283–86, 288; Badger, *The Genius of Photography*, 38–41.

130 In a Foucauldian sense, Toronto was at the edge of power networks: see Foucault, "Two Lectures," 96.

131 John Young, "Too Much Display at the Baths," *The Globe*, 17 July 1883, 4.

132 "Natatorial Frolics," *The Globe*, 24 July 1883, 6.

133 Ibid., 6.

134 "City Council: The Bathing By-law," *The Globe*, 29 June 1880, (No. 160) No. 1034, 6. A Bylaw, item 835, 15 November 1880, 608, Toronto City Council Appendix A, 1880, CTA; "City Council: Bathing," *The Globe*, 16 November 1880, 8.

135 Fiske, *Reading the Popular*, 64; Metusela and Waitt, *Tourism and Australian Beach Cultures*, 32–36. As a question of subjectivity, see Foucault, "Body/Power," 57.

136 "Natatorial Frolics," *The Globe*, 24 July 1883, 6.

137 "Decency and Morality," "The Wiman Baths," *The Globe*, 4 August 1883, 10.

138 Ibid.

139 "The Wiman Baths," *The Toronto Daily Mail*, 28 August 1883, 8.

140 Historians in Australia have flagged the same challenge: see White, *Picnicking, Surf-Bathing*, 104; Metusela and Waitte, *Tourism and Australian Beach Cultures*, 32–37.

141 "The Wiman Baths Humbug," *The Toronto Daily Mail*, July 23, 1883, 5.

142 Ibid. Emphasis in the original.

143 All of this paragraph is drawn from the same article: "The Wiman Baths Humbug," 5.

144 Keller, "Photojournalism around 1900," 284–86, 288.

145 "A Protest," *The Globe*, 2 August 1883, 6.

146 Ibid. Question mark is part of quote.

147 "Decency and Morality," "The Wiman Baths," *The Globe*, 4 August 1883, 10. This would be a literal example of Shields's description of certain behaviours being driven to the margins: see Shields, *Places on the Margin*, 60.

148 "Swimming and Bathing Facilities," *The Globe*, 21 August 1880, 8–9.

149 Corbin, *The Lure of the Sea*, 59, 82, 83. Sarah Howell, *The Seaside* (London: Cassell and Collier Macmillan, 1974), 20–22.

150 "Ladies Who Would Swim," *The Globe*, 12 July 1882, 8; "Where Cool Breezes Blow," *The Globe*, 7 August 1885, 2.

151 W.D. Andrews, *Swimming and Life-Saving* (Toronto: William Briggs, 1889), 13–14. See Gibson, *More Than an Island*, 92.

152 Mulvany, *Toronto: Past and Present*, 264–65.

153 "The Wiman Baths," *The Toronto Daily Mail*, 28 August 1883, 8.

154 Ibid. Similar complaints would be voiced about Turner's Baths: see "Toronto's Greatest Need," *The Evening Star*, 10 July 1897, 2.

155 "Natatorial Frolics," *The Globe*, 24 July 1883, 6. Emphasis in original. For an excellent discussion on the challenges of women occupying public space, see Iris Marion Young, "Throwing Like a Girl: A Phenomenology of Feminine Body Comportment, Motility, and Spatiality," in *On Female Body Experience: "Throwing Like a Girl" and Other Essays* (Oxford: Oxford University Press, 2005).

156 "The Wiman Baths," *The Globe*, 21 July 1883, 10.

157 "Where Cool Breezes Blow," *The Globe*, 7 August 1885, 2.

158 Metusela and Waitt, *Tourism and Australian Beach Cultures*, 120. See also Gill Valentine, "The Geography of Women's Fear," *Area* 21, no. 4 (1989): 385–90.

159 Moir, "Planning for Change," 41–44; "The Harbour Works," *The Globe*, 2 August 1883, 2.

160 "Where Cool Breezes Blow," *The Globe*, 7 August 1885, 2.

161 *Island Guide*, 10, 29.

162 Gibson, *More Than an Island*, 131.

163 Moir, "Planning for Change," 31. The western sandbar is not included in the Goad's Fire Insurance maps until 1910: prior to that a bridge was simply displayed as leading off the edge of the map.

164 Item 400, 27 March 1883, 77, Toronto City Council Minutes, 1883, CTA. See also item 298, report no. 9, Property Committee, 25 April 1883, 195, Toronto City Council Appendix, 1883; Item 438, Monday, 9 April 1883, 85, Toronto City Council Minutes, 1883, CTA; "Civic Committees," *The Globe*, 19 April 1883, 3.

165 Item 511, 7 May 1883, 105, Toronto City Council Minutes, 1883 CTA.

166 Item 536, 26 May 1884, 128, Toronto City Council Minutes, 1884; Item 378, no. 1372 by-law (no. 59), 26 May 1884, 229, Toronto City Council Appendix, 1884, CTA. The fluid nature of the western sandbar was such that the lease had to rely on longtitude and latitude measurements to define the space being leased. Item 378, no. 1372 by-law, (No. 59), 26 May 1884, 229, Toronto City Council Appendix, 1884, CTA.

167 Gibson, *More Than an Island*, 93.

168 "West End Baths," *The Globe*, 4 May 1883, 4. The *Star* argued this was tactical; the ferry companies wanted to prevent a streetcar line from accessing the island: "The City Will Not Hurry," *The Evening Star*, 20 February 1897, 3.

169 For a demonstration of a middle-class clientele: "Bathing Facilities," *The Toronto Daily Star*, 19 July 1905, 11.

170 For new municipal act rules, see "Assembly Notes," *The Globe*, 7 April 1887, 4; and "Ontario Legislature," *The Globe*, 21 April 1887, 4, which gives us a clear sense that the increased controls over bathing *and* boathouses were to prevent "illegal or immoral" activities.

171 Report no. 9, Island Committee, 2 June 1905, adopted as amended 25 June 1905, pages 680–81, Toronto City Council Appendix A, 1905, CTA.

172 Shields, *Places on the Margin*, 52–53.

173 "Civic Property Committee: Where Bathers May Enjoy Themselves without Molestations," *The Globe*, 10 July 1891, 3. See also "Disciplining an Official," *The Globe*, 22 March 1888, 8; "General City News: The Island Baths," *The Globe*, 26 June 1896, 10.

174 "City Hall Jots," *The Evening Star*," 17 June 1896.

175 Douglas Booth, *Australian Beach Cultures: History of Sun, Sand, and Surf* (London: Routledge, 2001), 31.

176 "General Local News," *The Globe*, 22 July 1890, 8.

177 "Civic Property Committee: Where Bathers May Enjoy Themselves without Molestations," *The Globe*, 10 July 1891, 3.

178 Item 603, 5 June 1893, 176, Toronto City Council Minutes, 1893, CTA; Item 651, Monday, 19 June 1893, 193, Toronto City Council Minutes, 1893, CTA; By-law 3179, Monday, 19 June 1893, 274, Toronto City Council Appendix B, CTA; Adjusted slightly: Item 671, Friday, 23 June 1893, 204,

Toronto City Council Minutes, 1893, CTA. Bylaw 3183, Friday, 23 June 1893, 283, Toronto City Council Appendix B, 1893, CTA.

179 No. 3268 A bylaw, 17 July 1894, 265, Toronto City Council Appendix B, 1894, CTA.

180 "Civic Property Committee: Where Bathers May Enjoy Themselves without Molestations," *The Globe*, 10 July 1891, 3.

181 *The Toronto Island Guide*, 29.

182 "Topics of the Town," *The Evening Star*, 26 June 1896, 1.

183 "With the Boys on the Bar," *The Evening Star*, 22 July 1897, 7.

184 "Death Penalty for Poor Bully," *The Toronto Daily Star*, 16 July 1906, 2. As I noted in Chapter 1, Toronto police records of indecency charges include everything from bathing and public nudity to being caught urinating in public, so they are an imprecise tool for measuring the number of people fined for nude bathing. Having said that, the number of people fined for indecency in 1906 was 38, up from 25 in 1905, and 27 in 1907, suggesting that policing in 1906 did make a distinctive jump. See Chief Constable Reports, Toronto City Council Appendix C for 1906, 1907, 1908, CTA.

185 For temperatures, see: http://climate.weather.gc.ca/climateData/dailydata_e.html?timeframe=2&Prov=ON&StationID=5051&dlyRange=1840-03-01%7C2015-12-01&Year=1906&Month=8&cmdB1=Go#.

186 Robertson notes both the appearance of the sandbar and its submergence the next year. Robertson, *Landmarks* (1908), 37.

187 "The New Swimming Baths," *The Toronto Daily Star*, 12 October 1906, 9.

188 "May Stop Bathing," *The Toronto Daily Star*, 25 July 1906, 1.

189 "No More Sand Baths," *The Toronto Daily Star*, 23 July 1906, 5.

190 Orvar Löfgren, *On Holiday: A History of Vacationing* (Los Angeles: University of California Press, 1999), 222–23.

191 Amendment of bylaw 4305, Board of Control, Report no. 19, 30 July 1906, 979, Toronto City Council Appendix A, 1906, CTA.

192 Bruce Curtis, "After 'Canada,'" 178, 190; Rose, O'Malley, and Valverde, "Governmentality," 83–85.

193 Report no. 2, Island Committee, 12 February 1906, 133, Toronto City Council Appendix A, 1906, CTA.

194 Report no. 2, Island Committee, adopted 23 February 1903, 133–34, Toronto City Council Appendix, 1903, CTA; Report no. 6, Island Committee, adopted 4 May 1903, 417, Toronto City Council Appendix, 1903; Report no. 13, Final, Island Committee, (No. 29), 31 December 1903, 707–79, Toronto City Council Appendix B, 1903, CTA.

195 Report no. 11, Island Committee, 953, adopted 25 June 1906, Toronto City Council Appendix, 1906, CTA.

196 Wolfgang Schivelbusch, *Disenchanted Night: The Industrialization of Light in the Nineteenth Century*, trans. Angela Davies (Berkeley: University of California Press, 1988), 28.

197 Schivelbusch, 142, 186.

198 Report no. 10, Island Committee, 25 June 1906, 848, Toronto City Council Appendix A, 1906, CTA.

199 Report no. 11, Island Committee, 25 June 1906, 953, Toronto City Council Appendix, 1906; Item 61, 14 January 1907, 20, Toronto City Council 1907, CTA.

200 "Harbor Board to Water's Edge," *The Globe*, 9 August 1918, 12; "Lagoon Danger Spot for Young Children," *The Toronto Daily Star*, 26 July 1918, 5; "Stop Bathing at Long Pond," *The Globe*, 20 August 1918, 8.

201 "Excellent Opportunity," *The Globe*, 13 August 1910, 14; Hugh Garner, *One Damn Thing after Another* (Toronto: McGraw-Hill Ryerson, 1973), 10. On boyhood solidarity and finding spaces, see Craig Heron, "Boys Will Be Boys: Working-Class Masculinities in the Age of Mass Production," *International Labor and Working-Class History* 69 (2006): 13–14.

202 There was bemusement when it was discovered that nude bathing was still legal in the spaces in 1929: see "12,000 City bylaws May Be Consolidated," *The Globe*, 8 January 1929, 12; "City Is Growing Up According to News from Our Town Hall," *The Globe*, 14 June 1929, 16.

203 Anthony Giddens, "Time, Space and Regionalisation," in *Social Relations and Spatial Structures*, ed. Derek Gregory and John Urry (London: Macmillan, 1985), 271–72; Shields, *Places on the Margin*, 47, 53.

204 "With the Boys on the Sandbar," *The Globe*, 31 July 1897, 4.

205 See Payne and Kunard, *The Cultural Work of Photography*, xiv, xvii; and Jae Emerling, *Photography: History and Theory* (New York: Routledge, 2012), 34.

206 "The Wiman Baths Humbug," *The Toronto Daily Mail*, 23 July 1883, 5.

207 Keller, "Photojournalism around 1900," 293–95.

208 Jonathan Crary, *Techniques of the Observer: On Vision and Modernity in the Nineteenth Century* (Cambridge, MA: MIT Press, 1992), 11–13.

209 File 5010004, series 330, file 501, sheet 1 V, folder 20, box 158725, CTA.

210 On the camera's ability to focus our attention, see Michael North, *Camera Works: Photography and the Twentieth-Century World* (Oxford: Oxford University Press, 2005), 3–11.

211 "Just across the Bay," *The Globe*, 30 June 1910, 2; "Youngster's Sure of a Good Time at Hanlan's Point," 5 July 1910, 8; "Will Be Great Week," *The Globe*, 22 August 1910.

212 See, for example, "Cool Breezes at Scarboro," *The Globe*, 12 August 1907, 12; "Many Swimming Out," *The Globe*, 12 August 1909, 13.

213 Fiske, *Understanding Popular Culture*, 11, 14.

Chapter 4: The Don River and the Bathing Boy

1 "Albert Petrie Was Drowned in the Don," *The Toronto Daily Star*, 16 June 1913.

2 And for a similar railway/bather interaction, see "William Franklyn Drowns," *The Toronto Daily Star*, 27 June 1913.

3 Vernacular bathing requires both a cultural production of space, as Rob Shields suggests, and an embodied relationship with the physical environment, as Joy Parr suggests. See Rob Shields, *Places on the Margin: Alternative Geographies of Modernity* (New York: Routledge, 1991), 57, 63; Joy Parr, *Sensing Changing Technologies, Environments, and the Everyday, 1953–2003* (Vancouver: UBC Press, 2010), 8–9; Joy Parr, "Notes for a More Sensuous History of Twentieth Century Canada: The Timely, the Tacit and the Material Body," *Canadian Historical Review* 82, no. 4 (2001): 733.

4 Parr sees the same relationship with the St. Lawrence River and the community of Iroquois: Parr, "Notes for a More Sensuous History," 725. Richard White captures an embodied relationship between gillnetters and the Columbia River: Richard White, *The Organic Machine: The Remaking of the Columbia River* (New York: Hill and Wang, 1995), 41.

5 On how "noise" can be read as a mark of cultural distinction, see Peter Bailey, "Breaking the Sound Barrier," in *Hearing History: A Reader*, ed. Mark M. Smith, 23–35 (Athens: University of Georgia Press, 2004). See also Murray Schafer, "Soundscapes and Earwitnesses," in *Hearing History: A Reader*, ed. Mark M. Smith, 3–9 (Athens: University of Georgia Press, 2004).

6 Parr, *Sensing Changes*, 9–12, 20. Geographers use the term *lay geography* to describe how people create intimate understandings and meaning around place. See David Crouch, "Places around Us: Embodied Lay Geographies in Leisure and Tourism," *Leisure Studies* 19, no. 2 (2000): 63–76. On creating a shared oral culture, see John Fiske, *Understanding Popular Culture* (Boston: Unwin Hyman, 1989), 170–73. For a discussion of folklore traditions, see Graham Seal, *Inventing Anzac: The Digger and National Mythology* (Perth: University of Queensland Press, 2004), 3–7.

7 Anthony Giddens, "Time, Space and Regionalisation," in *Social Relations and Spatial Structures*, ed. Derek Gregory and John Urry (London: Macmillan, 1985), 271–72.

8 Jennifer Bonnell, *Reclaiming the Don: An Environmental History of Toronto's Don River Valley* (Toronto: University of Toronto Press, 2014), xxvi–xxvii. Bonnell gives a useful nod to Richard White's work, which looks at the middle ground as a space of negotiation and accommodation. See Richard White, *The Middle Ground: Indians, Empires and Republics in the Great Lakes Region, 1650–1815* (New York: Cambridge University Press, 1991).

9 Bonnell, *Reclaiming the Don*, 24–25.

10 William Cronon, "The Trouble with Wilderness: Or, Getting Back to the Wrong Nature," *Environmental History* 1, no. 1 (1996): 13–15. The curative role of the natural environment suggested that such spaces needed to be preserved for their ability to uplift people and drove the parks movement in the nineteenth century. For more on that, see S.B. Sutton, ed., *Civilizing American Cities: A Selection of Frederick Law Olmsted's Writings on City Landscapes* (Cambridge, MA: MIT Press, 1971), 2–13, 21, 35–7; Nancy Pollock-Ellwand, "Rickson Outhet: Bringing the Olmsted Legacy to Canada: A Romantic View of Nature in the Metropolis and the Hinterland," *Journal of Canadian Studies/Revue d'études canadiennes* 44, no. 1 (2010): 143–44; Peter J. Schmitt, *Back to Nature: The Arcadian Myth in Urban America* (New York: Oxford University Press, 1969), xv.

11 Cronon, "Trouble with Wilderness," 17.

12 Industry moved out to intertwine with the environment: see William Cronon, *Nature's Metropolis: Chicago and the Great West* (New York: W.W. Norton, 1991), xv, 7–8, 46–7. I use *borderlands* to describe the urban edge rather than the romanticized space of the suburbs: see John R. Stilgoe, *Borderland: Origins of the American Suburb, 1820–1939* (New Haven, CT: Yale University Press, 1988), 9.

13 Rob Shields, *Places on the Margin: Alternative Geographies of Modernity* (New York: Routledge, 1991), 52–3, 57. See also Mariana Valverde and Miomir Cirak, "Governing Bodies, Creating Gayspaces: Policing and Security Issues in 'Gay' Downtown Toronto," *British Journal of Criminology* 43 (2003): 102–21; David Bell and Gill Valentine, eds., *Mapping Desire: Geographies of Sexualities* (New York: Routledge, 1995).

14 Ian McKay, *The Quest of the Folk: Antimodernism and Cultural Selection in Twentieth-Century Nova Scotia* (Montreal: McGill-Queen's University Press, 1994), 4. On the ability to define the individual, see Michel Foucault, "Questions of Geography," in *Power/Knowledge: Selected Interviews and Other Writings, 1972–1977*, ed. Colin Gordon, 63–77 (New York: Pantheon Books, 1980); and Foucault, "Prison Talk," in *Power/Knowledge:*.

15 On attachment to nude bathing, see John Travis, "Continuity and Change in English Sea-Bathing, 1730–1900: A Case of Swimming with the Tide," in *Recreation and the Sea*, ed. Stephen Fisher, 3–35 (Exeter: University of Exeter Press, 1997). See also John K. Walton, "Respectability Takes a

Holiday: Disreputable Behaviour at the Victorian Seaside," in *Unrespectable Recreations*, ed. Martin Hewitt (Leeds: Leeds Centre for Victorian Studies, 2001), 184–85.

16 See Judith Butler, *Gender Trouble: Feminism and the Subversion of Identity* (New York: Routledge, 1990); and Butler, *Bodies That Matter: On the Discursive Limits of "Sex"* (New York: Routledge, 1993), for a discussion of the potential and limits of looking at gender as being produced through performativity.

17 Butler is suggesting we look to Michel Foucault's theory of power to consider how gender is produced. See Judith Butler, Lynne Segal, and Peter Osborne, "Gender as Performance: An Interview with Judith Butler," *Radical Philosophy* 67 (Summer 1994): 32–33, https://www.radicalphilosophy.com/interview/judith-butler.

18 The "child" was valorized in the twentieth century: see Jeroen J.H. Dekker, "Family on the Beach: Representations of Romantic and Bourgeois Family Values by Realistic Genre Painting of Nineteenth-Century Scheveningen Beach, *Journal of Family History* 28, no. 2 (2003): 280.

19 Shields, *Places on the Margin*, 47.

20 Nancy B. Bouchier and Ken Cruikshank give us a similar portrayal of the people who bathed next to Hamilton's boathouse community on Burlington Bay: Nancy B. Bouchier and Ken Cruikshank, "The War on the Squatters, 1920–1940: Hamilton's Boathouse Community and the Re-Creation of Recreation on Burlington Bay," *Labour/Le Travail* 51 (Spring 2003): 17, 22. Australian writers argued the nude body had to be clothed as part of the colonization process: see Cameron White, "Picnicking, Surf-Bathing and Middle-Class Morality on the Beach in the Eastern Suburbs of Sydney, 1811–1912," *Journal of Australian Studies* 27, no. 80 (2003); and Christine Metusela and Gordon Waitt, *Tourism and Australian Beach Cultures Revealing Bodies* (Toronto: Channel View Publications, 2012). On photography, see Marita Sturken and Lisa Cartwright, *Practices of Looking: An Introduction to Visual Culture* (Oxford: Oxford University Press, 2009), 106.

21 This urge to link the body with nature grew stronger in Canada after 1900 as a way to draw the country's increasingly diverse population together; it was a trend exemplified by the work of the Group of 7: Eric Kaufmann and Oliver Zimmer, "In Search of the Authentic Nation: Landscape and National Identity in Canada and Switzerland," *Nations and Nationalism* 4 no. 4 (1998): 495–96. On the ability of pictures to overtake reality, see Stuart Ewen, *All Consuming Images: The Politics of Style in Contemporary Culture* (New York: Basic Books, 1988), 25. I will discuss the specific use of James's photos below.

22 See Gordon Sinclair, *Will the Real Gordon Sinclair Please Stand Up* (Toronto: McClelland and Stewart, 1966); Hugh Garner, *One Damn Thing after Another* (Toronto: McGraw-Hill Ryerson, 1973); George H. Rust-D'Eye, *Cabbagetown Remembered* (Erin, ON: Boston Mills, 1984); and Colleen Kelly, *Cabbagetown in Pictures* (Toronto: Toronto Public Library Board, 1984).

23 Graeme H. Patterson describes a regional myth as a complex of symbols and images embedded in larger narratives with predictable rhythms. See Graeme H. Patterson, *History and Communications: Harold Innis, Marshall McLuhan, and the Interpretation of History* (Toronto: University of Toronto Press, 1990), 166. For government documents describing the swimmability of the Don River, see "Turning the Corner: The Don Watershed Report Card," Don Watershed Regeneration Council and the Metropolitan Toronto and Region Conservation Authority, May 1997, 1, 3.

24 Wayne Reeves and Christina Palassio, eds., *HTO: Toronto's Water from Lake Iroquois to Lost Rivers to Low-Flow Toilets* (Toronto: Coach House Books, 2008). See Ontario Department of Planning and Development, *Don Valley Conservation Report* (Toronto: ODPD, 1950), Chap. 1, p. 2. It pegs the age of the Don at about 20,000 years. The valley is 100 feet deep at York Mills.

25 Bonnell, *Reclaiming the Don*, 20. Postcards portray an agricultural or idealized natural Don. For the agricultural Don, see item 540031, file 54, "Views of the Don River and Don Valley," series 330, fonds

70, City of Toronto Archives (CTA). For a more natural setting, see item 540020, file 54, "Views of the Don River and Don Valley," series 330, fonds 70, CTA.

26 John Ross Robertson, *The Diary of Mrs. John Graves Simcoe, Wife of the First Lieutenant-Governor of the Province of Upper Canada, 1792–6* (Toronto: W. Briggs, 1911). The quote is on page 91. See Don trips on 223, 308.

27 Henry Scadding, *Toronto of Old* (Toronto: Adam, Stevenson, 1873), 227.

28 Bonnell, *Reclaiming the Don*, 25–26, 35; C. Pelham Mulvany, *Toronto: Past and Present. A Handbook of the City* (Toronto: Ontario Reprint, 1970; originally published Toronto: W.E. Caiger, 1884), 246; Rust-D'Eye, *Cabbagetown Remembered*, 121; Gunter Gad, "Location Patterns of Manufacturing: Toronto in the Early 1880s," *Urban History Review/Revue d'histoire urbaine* 22, no. 2 (1994): 125.

29 Charles E. Goad, *Atlas of the City of Toronto and Suburbs*, vol. 1 (Chas. E. Goad: Toronto, 1884), plate 28..

30 "The Northeast Barriers," *The Toronto Daily Star*, 24 September 1924.

31 A. Douglas Ford, city surveyor, City Annexation map, 1 January 1967, fonds 2032; Toronto Planning Board fonds, series 727; Toronto Planning Board maps and plans, box 200777, CTA.

32 Bonnell, *Reclaiming the Don*, 189.

33 "Bathing," *The Globe*, 24 June 1874. For "questionable waters," see "Public Baths," *The Globe*, 28 June 1876; Charles Pelham Mulvany, G. Mercer Adam, and Christopher Blackett Robinson, *History of Toronto and County of York*, vol. 1 (Toronto: C. Blackett Robinson, Publisher, 1885), 1:53. The hospital and the jail, rather than the upstream community of Yorkdale, were singled out as the largest sewage polluters in the Don in 1878—a telling example of how the city failed to see the impact that suburban pollution would have on the Don. Item 67, report no. 19, city engineer, 25 February 1878, 89, Toronto City Council Appendix, 1878, CTA.

34 We have evidence of settlers bathing there as early as 1802: John Ross Robertson, *Robertson's Landmarks of Toronto: A Collection of Historical Sketches of the Old Town of York from 1792 until 1833 and of Toronto from 1834 to 1914* (Toronto: John R. Robertson, 1914), 292. Robertson draws this from *Oracle* 12, no. 15 (1802). We can see this as a form of excorporation, with the working class taking up cultural tools for their own use: see Fiske, *Understanding Popular Culture*, 15. For bathing examples, see "City News: Inquest," *The Globe*, 3 October 1877; "Suburban News: Bathing in the Don," *The Globe*, 22 July 1880.

35 "Suburban News: Bathing in the Don," *The Globe*, 22 July 1880.

36 Bonnell, *Reclaiming the Don*, 55–56.

37 Redmond J. Brough, city engineer, report no. 35, Committee on Works, item 781, 24 September 1881, 665, Toronto City Council Appendix, 1881, CTA.

38 Bonnell, *Reclaiming the Don*, 64.

39 Item 1018, no. 186, President's Message, *Report on the Accommodation for Railways*, C. Sproatt, city engineer, 21 June 1889, 1122–25, Toronto City Council Appendix, 1889, CTA.

40 This is stated explicitly by city council as it is launching the project: item 1026, 3 October 1881, 290, Toronto City Council Minutes, 1881, CTA. Bonnell, *Reclaiming the Don*, 25. Mulvany uses the term *cloacal:* see Mulvany, *Toronto: Past and Present*, 246.

41 Don Improvement Vote: no. 148, item 992, 809, Toronto City Council Appendix, 1886, CTA. Interceptor sewage project vote: John Blevins, city clerk, no. 151, item 995, 8 October 1886, 821, Toronto City Council Appendix, 1886, CTA.

42 Item 788, 14 November 1898, 250, Toronto City Council Minutes, 1898, CTA.

43 There are examples in 1890: "Life Saving," *The Globe*, 11 July 1890, 5; "General Local News," *The Globe*, 10 July 1890, 8.

44 Committee on Works, report no. 25, Don Improvement, item 1313, 5 October 1887, 1311–12, Toronto City Council Appendix, 1887, CTA.

45 Spaces where the weak might carve out their own places. See Fiske, *Understanding Popular Culture*, 32–36.

46 Don Valley Conservation Authority (DVCA), *The Cardinal* (Summer 1953), Charles Sauriol Fonds, file 14, series 104, fonds 4, CTA. The *Cardinal* was launched by Charles Sauriol in 1951; it was a quarterly publication published by the Don Valley Conservation Authority. Toronto writer John Court has looked into William Judd's family and tracked the location of Dunnett's swimming hole: personal correspondence with the writer.

47 Sauriol refers to it as Silver Creek, which was another name for Taylor-Massey Creek; see Charles Sauriol, *Trails of the Don* (Orillia, ON: Hemlock Press, 1992), 16.

48 White, *Organic Machine*, 13–22.

49 Shields, *Places on the Margin*, 52–3.

50 Morgan Baldwin, chair, report no. 16, Committee on Property, item 495, 16 June 879, 369, Toronto City Council Appendix, 1879, CTA.

51 No. 75. No. 1004, A By-law, Robert Roddy, city clerk, 31 May 1880, 320, Toronto City Council Appendix, 1880, CTA. Nude bathing officially continued to be allowed in Toronto during evening hours until 1929, although in practice it was driven out of most public areas in the first years of the twentieth century: see "12,000 City By-Laws May Be Consolidated," *The Globe*, 8 January 1929; "City Is Growing Up According to News from Our Town Hall," *The Globe*, 14 June 1929, 16.

52 "Bathing Fatalities," *The Globe*, 17 June 1892.

53 Scadding, *Toronto of Old*, 242.

54 "Bathing Spot in Don," *The Toronto Daily Star*, 14 July 1908.

55 W.H. Pearson, *Recollections and Records of Toronto of Old: With references to Brantford, Kingston and Other Canadian Towns* (Toronto: W. Briggs, 1914), 117. Charles Sauriol ticks off the same mill pond when he's listing bathing spaces on the Don, though it seems clear he's drawing his information directly from Pearson. Sauriol, *Remembering the Don*, 64.

56 See 13 August 1831, 53; 21 August 1831, 43; 6 July 1833, 222, in William Helliwell, *The Helliwell Diaries: The Diaries of William Helliwell from 1830 to 1890* (Toronto: City of Toronto Museum Services n.d.). See Guthrie, *Don Valley Legacy*, 29, for a picture of Todmorden Mills.

57 Guthrie, *Don Valley Legacy*, 102.

58 For more on the family, see Guthrie, 15, 190–96.

59 Guthrie, 98, 102–3; Charles Sauriol, *Remembering the Don: A Rare Record of Earlier Times within the Don River Valley* (Scarborough, ON: Consolidated Amethyst Communications, 1981), 55.

60 DVCA, *The Cardinal* (Summer 1953), Charles Sauriol Fonds, file 14, series 104, fonds 4, CTA. Charles Sauriol has a list of "swimming holes" in the *Cardinal* that match the primary research I have completed in the newspapers.

61 "Dynamite Removes Old Swimming Hole," *The Globe*, 27 May 1933, 13. Sauriol, *Remembering the Don*, 57.

62 "Fatal Drowning Accident," *The Toronto Daily Mail*, 15 June 1881, 8.

63 Ibid.

64 While we'd assume the deep water lay behind the dam, news coverage suggests the deep pool was below, or at the base of the dam.

65 "The Don's Victim," *The Globe*, 5 July 1902, 28.

66 "Drowned while Bathing in Don," *The Toronto Daily Star*, 5 July 1902, 17.

67 "Don's Victim," *The Globe*.

68 Ibid.; "Drowned while Bathing in Don," *The Toronto Daily Star*.

69 "Drowned at the Mill Dam," *The Globe*, 12 August 1902, 12.

70 "Drowned in the Don," *The Globe*, 3 September 1900, 12. Petrie lived at 78 River Street but was walking along the riverbank at the time.

71 Don Valley, abatement of smoke nuisance, item 807, 17 July 1914, 351–52, Toronto City Council Minutes, 1914, CTA.

72 Sauriol, *Trails of the Don*, 29, 86, 234.

73 Sinclair, *Will the Real Gordon Sinclair*, 11.

74 Famed muckraker Christopher St. George saw similar innocence and chastity when he looked at boys bathing. See Clark C.S. Clark, *Of Toronto the Good, a Social Study: The Queen City of Canada as It Is* (Montreal: Toronto Publishing, 1898), 113. See also Rust-D'Eye, *Cabbagetown Remembered*, 26.

75 "Would Fence In Railway Tracks," *The Toronto Daily Star*, 13 August 1907, 10. This was a traumatic accident; Wildbore's body was cut in two by the wheels of the train.

76 Ibid. The story used the names CNR and Canadian Northern Ontario Railway interchangeably: the companies were likely sharing tracks in 1907.

77 "Drags Comrade to Watery Grave," *The Globe*, 23 June 1911, 9. The heat had topped out at 33°C on 22 June 1911: "King's Coronation Cause of Rejoicing: Heat Was Oppressive," *The Globe*, 23 June 1911, 8.

78 "Drags Comrade to Watery Grave," *The Globe*.

79 Fiske, *Understanding Popular Culture*, 172–73; Seal, *Inventing Anzac*, 3–7.

80 "Drags Comrade to Watery Grave," *The Globe*.

81 Bettina Bradbury, *Working Families: Age, Gender, and Daily Survival in Industrializing Montreal* (Toronto: Oxford University Press, 1993).

82 "Albert Petrie Was Drowned in the Don," *The Toronto Daily Star*; "Fatal Drowning Accident," *Toronto Daily Mail*.

83 See, for example, *Globe*, "General News of the City: A Small Boy Drowned," 6 July 1897, 10.

84 "Current Chit-chat," *The Toronto Daily Mail*, 4 August 1887, 6.

85 "Current Chit-chat," 6.

86 Oral culture is part of creating a folk experience. See Seal, *Inventing Anzac*, 3–7; Fiske, *Understanding Popular Culture*, 173.

87 "The Don's Victim," *The Globe*. 5 July 1902, 28; "Was Drowned in the Don," *The Globe*, 20 July 1908, 12.

88 As I have suggested, a folk culture developed within the Don River Valley; one that included sharing information about conditions within the river. People who were not yet part of the informal Don River network were at risk. For more on systems of knowledge within folk cultures see Fiske, *Understanding Popular Culture*, 172–73. On learning a language of space, see Shields, *Places on the Margin*, 63.

89 "Drowned at the Mill Dam," *The Globe*.

90 "Got beyond His Depth," *The Globe*, 24 July 1906, 12; "Small Boy Drowned in the Don River," *The Toronto Daily Star*, 24 July 1906, 7.

91 For the extended conversation, see "Shall the Bathing in the Don River Be Prohibited?," *The Toronto Daily Star*, 24 July 1906, 1.

92 Ibid. For efforts to use signage, see "Drowned at the Mill Dam," *The Globe*.

93 Board of Control Report No. 30, 22 July 1897, 543, Toronto City Council Appendix A, 1897, CTA.

94 "City Hall Small Talk," *The Globe*, 13 July 1897, 8.

95 Ibid.

96 "Delayed by Red Tape," *The Toronto Daily Star*, 20 July 1897, 2.

97 "Strikes Head Diving and Is Paralyzed," *The Globe*, 30 July 1913, 6.

98 "Bathing Spot in Don," *The Toronto Daily Star*, 4 July 1908, 15.

99 "Shall the Bathing in the Don River Be Prohibited?," *The Toronto Daily Star*, 24 July 1906, 1.

100 Cranz, "Women in Urban Parks," 579–80.

101 "Lad Drowned," *The Toronto Daily Star*, 1 July 1898, 1. "General News," *The Globe*, 1 July 1898, 1.

102 "Took Cramps and Drowned," *The Toronto Daily Star*, July 7, 1914, 2.

103 This is particularly true on the waterfront, where the ferry had to be budgeted for and rented each year with a set daily fee.

104 "To Patrol the Don to Protect Bathers," *The Toronto Daily Star*, 20 June 1912, 2.

105 "North Winds Chill Waters," *The Globe*, 15 July 1922, 13.

106 "At Free Bathing Stations," *The Globe*, 12 August 1902, 12; "Local Briefs," *The Globe*, 4 September 1902, 14.

107 The Sunnyside free bathing station was temporarily closed in 1913 as a result of construction along that beach, though people continued to use it. "Multitude of Bathers Used Public Stations," *The Globe*, 5 September 1913, 5.

108 Rob Shields has suggested how different social groups can create antithetical place-myths within a space, but here we can see how the working class and middle class combined, though for different reasons, to shape the image of the Don: see Shields, *Places on the Margin*, 60–61.

109 "A Scene at the Don," *The Globe*, 14 July 1887, 5.

110 And perhaps the ultimate example of space being co-opted for new purposes: see Fiske, *Understanding Popular Culture*, 15, 32–36.

111 Shields, *Places on the Margin*, 262.

112 Pearson, *Recollections and Records*, 117.

113 The millpond would have existed from the mid to late nineteenth century: see *The Don Valley Conservation Report*, 1950, Chapter 2, "Land Settlement," 143, 160.

114 "Swimming: In the Old Mill Race in the Country," *The Globe*, 3 August 1889, 16.

115 "Happenings in Toronto: Bathing in Don," *The Toronto Daily Star*, 30 April 1906, 3.

116 "A Summer Idyll Urbanized," *The Globe*, 25 August 1925, 4.

117 "Colorful Fashion Parade Attracts to Boardwalk Dense Throngs of People," *The Globe*, 18 April 1927, 10.

118 "Boys of East End Hold Fashion Parade," *The Globe*, 18 April 1927, 10.

119 For a similar treatment of boys bathing, see Bouchier and Cruikshank, "War on the Squatters," 17–22.

120 Photography became cheap enough and popular enough to capture public scenes after the late 1880s, and we see it being taken up by newspapers, including in Toronto, by the start of the twentieth century. See Gerry Badger, *The Genius of Photography: How Photography Has Changed Our Lives* (London: Quadrille, 2007), 38–41; Mary Warner Marien, *Photography: A Cultural History* (New York: Harry N. Abrahams, 2002), 167–70.

121 Michael Kimmel, *Manhood in America: A Cultural History*, 4th ed. (New York: Oxford University Press, 2018), 125–26.

122 For quote, see Julia F. Saville, "The Romance of Boys Bathing: Poetic Precedents and Respondents to the Paintings of Henry Scott Tuke," in *Victorian Sexual Dissidence*, ed. Richard Dellamora (Chicago: University of Chicago Press, 1999), 254, 272; Jane Stevenson, "Nacktleben," in *Changing Bodies, Changing Meanings: Studies on the Human Body in Antiquity*, ed. Dominic Montserrat (New York: Routledge, 2003), 205.

123 Stevenson, "Nacktleben," 206.

124 Stevenson, 207.

125 For an example of the photograph not simply capturing an event, but creating it, see Ulrich Keller, "Photojournalism around 1900: The Institutionalization of a Mass Medium," in *Shadow and Substance: Essays on the History of Photography in Honour of Heinz K. Henisch*, ed. Kathleen Collins, 293–95 (Bloomfield Hills, MI: Amorphous Institute, 1990).

126 Shields, *Places on the Margin*, 47; Kelly, *Cabbagetown in Pictures*, 20; Rust-D'Eye, *Cabbagetown Remembered*, 25.

127 Item 540015, file 54, Views of the Don River and Don Valley, series 330, fonds 70, date of creation circa 1906–13, CTA.

128 Sinclair, *Will the Real Gordon Sinclair*, 11.

129 On resistance, see John Fiske, *Reading the Popular* (New York: Routledge, 2005), 7.

130 Garner, *One Damn Thing after Another*, 10. Garner does not provide an exact year for these recollections, but given that he was born in 1913 they likely stem from the early 1920s.

131 Garner, 13–14.

132 Rust-D'Eye, *Cabbagetown Remembered*, 26–28.

133 Kelly, *Cabbagetown in Pictures*, 5, 18.

134 "Nearly Drowned," *The Globe*, 15 August 1867, 2. No age given.

135 Ibid.

136 The trope comes from a specific statement in the British Parliament but was used often in the late nineteenth century. For more on political tropes around bathing, see Julia F. Saville, "Nude Male Alfresco Swimmers: The Prehistory of a Nineteenth-Century Republican Trope," *Word and Image: A Journal of Verbal/Visual Enquiry* 25, no. 1 (2009): 56–74.

137 See, for example, "Find Boy's Clothes on Banks of Don," *The Globe*, 2 August 1922, 13.

138 Kelly, *Cabbagetown in Pictures*, 20.

139 Kelly, 20.

140 "The Children's Circle," *The Globe*, 10 July 1897, 7.

141 "Public Swimming Baths," *The Globe*, 15 July 15, 1879, 2.

142 "Shall the Bathing in the Don River Be Prohibited?," *The Toronto Daily Star*, 24 July 1906, 1.

143 "Current Chit-chat," *The Toronto Daily Mail*.

144 "Would Fence In Railway Tracks," *The Toronto Daily Star*.

145 Ibid.

146 I'm borrowing the term *slippage* from Mariana Valverde; see Mariana Valverde, *The Age of Light, Soap, and Water Moral Reform in English Canada, 1885–1925* (Toronto: University of Toronto Press, 2008).

147 "William Franklyn Drowns," *The Toronto Daily Star*, 27 June 1913, 1.

148 "Was Drowned in the Don," *The Globe*, 20 July 1908, 12.

149 "Current Chit-chat," *The Toronto Daily Mail*.

150 Cynthia R. Comacchio, *The Dominion of Youth: Adolescence and the Making of a Modern Canada, 1920–1950* (Waterloo, ON: Wilfrid Laurier University Press, 2006), 2; Mary Louise Adams, *The Trouble with Normal: Postwar Youth and the Making of Heterosexuality* (Toronto: University of Toronto Press, 1997), 43.

151 George Lang, age 24, was an exception that proves the rule; though married, his family was still in Scotland: "Feat Cost Him His Life," *The Globe*, 26 June 1905, 12.

152 Craig Heron, "Boys Will Be Boys: Working-Class Masculinities in the Age of Mass Production," *International Labor and Working-Class History* 69 (Spring 2006): 19–20. For more, see Woody Register, *The Kid of Coney Island: Fred Thompson and the Rise of American Amusements* (New York: Oxford University Press, 2001).

153 Heron, "Boys Will Be Boys," 20.

154 Alan Metcalfe, "Working-Class Physical Recreation in Montreal, 1860–1895," *Working Papers on the Sociological Study of Sports and Leisure* 1, 2 (1978).

155 Heron, "Boys Will Be Boys," 15.

156 Photographs of the Clay Banks swimming hole near Bill Hill 1939, file 96, folio 61, series 80, fonds 4. Caption contained with photo.

157 And in this I agree with George Chauncey when he argues that in early twentieth-century New York, boundaries around male sexuality were not as thickly set as they would be by the mid-twentieth century. See George Chauncey, *Gay New York: Gender, Urban Culture, and the Making of the Gay Male World, 1890–1940* (New York: Basic Books, 1994).

158 Sauriol, *Trails of the Don*, 16, 23.

159 Sinclair, *Will the Real Gordon Sinclair*, 11.

160 Steven Maynard, "'Horrible Temptations': Sex, Men, and Working-Class Male Youth in Urban Ontario, 1890–1935," *Canadian Historical Review* 78, no. 2 (1997): 216, 233.

161 "Bathers in a Tug," *The Evening Star*, 14 July 1897, 2.

162 See *Lady Pellatt Fishing*, watercolour by Lena [Colleyna] Morgan, 1906, Call number E 5-109f, TPL/TRL: Baldwin Collection.

163 See, for example, "Humber River: Alice under Tree Near Mill," item 3416, John Boyd Sr. photographs, series 393, Alan Howard fonds, 20 September 1913, CTA. My thanks to Rudy Limeback for drawing my attention to this photograph.

164 Item 540001, Views of the Don River and Don Valley file 54, series 330, fonds 70, circa 1906–13, CTA.

165 Sinclair, *Will the Real Gordon Sinclair*, 1.

166 There are similar recollections of girls bathing in the Humber River: see Marjorie Mossman, "Weston," in *The Villages of Etobicoke*, ed. Etobicoke Historical Board (Weston, ON: Argyle Printing, 1986), 108.

167 Joy Mollenhauer, "This Was My Park." Typescript, recollections of Lawrence Park neighbourhood/subdivision from 1914, n.d. (c.1975). North District Lawrence Park Local History Vertical Files. My thanks to John Court for bringing this file to my attention.

168 "Time Table for Free Cars to the Swimming Holes," *The Toronto Daily Star*, 2 August 1910, 10. (And no mention that bathing dresses were required for the western sandbar.) "Excellent Opportunity," *The Globe*, 13 August 1910, 14.

169 See Figure 8 and "He Who Would Swim Must First Learn on Shore," *The Toronto Daily Star*, 10 August 1922, 11.

170 "Free Fares Handed to 50,000 Children in Bathing Season," *The Globe*, 29 August 1925, 47.

171 "A Summer Idyll Urbanized," *The Globe*, 25 August 1925, 4.

172 Report no. 3 of the Committee on Works, 10 February 1928, 252, Toronto City Council Appendix A, 1928, TCA.

173 The closure gets little mention in the Toronto's City Council minutes. The Don simply ceases to be included as a bathing station in 1928: see report no. 12 of the Committee on property, 11 June 1928, 1170–71, Toronto City Council Appendix A, 1928, CTA.

174 "Dynamite Removes Old Swimming Hole," *The Globe*.

175 Bonnell, *Reclaiming the Don*, 122; Ontario Department of Planning and Development, *Don Valley Conservation Report* (Toronto: ODPD, 1950). part 6: 15.

176 On swimming in the 1950s, see Charles Sauriol, "Swimming Holes in the Don," *The Cardinal* (Summer 1953), Charles Sauriol Fonds, file 14, series 104, fonds 4, CTA. On Sauriol, see Bonnell, *Reclaiming the Don*, 114. For Sauriol's relationship with the river, see Jennifer Bonnell, "An Intimate Understanding of Place: Charles Sauriol and Toronto's Don River Valley, 1927–1989," *Canadian Historical Review* 92, no. 4 (2011): 607–36.

177 "Turning the Corner: The Don Watershed Report Card," Don Watershed Regeneration Council and the Metropolitan Toronto and Region Conservation Authority, May 1997, 1, 3, 4.

178 "Bathing Places," *The Toronto Daily Star*, 14 June 1928; Item 36, Bathing General 1916–58, no. 101.G.1, vol. 1, RG 313, folder 10, box 53, TPAA. Today the biggest threat to the river is from stormwater runoff: see "Don River Watershed Plan: Beyond Forty Steps," Toronto and Region Conservation, 2009, v. As Bonnell notes, Metro Toronto had removed a number of overburdened sewage treatment plants from the river between 1956 and 1965; see Bonnell, "An Intimate Understanding of Place," 625.

Chapter 5: Humber River Encounters

1 "City May Have Parkway along the Humber River," *The Globe*, 17 May 1911, 8; "A fine boulevard drive and a parkway along the Humber River," *The Toronto Daily Star*, 16 May 1911, 1.

2 "Humber River Project means civic beauty as well as private utility," *The Toronto Daily Star*, 19 May 1911, 1. Richard Harris writes that Home Smith's land acquisition was primarily west of the Humber and included some 3,000 acres: the Humber project was just part of Home Smith's development plans. See Richard Harris, *Unplanned Suburbs: Toronto's American Tragedy, 1900 to 1950* (Baltimore: Johns Hopkins University Press, 1996), 189.

3 Report no. 17 of the Board of Control, 9 June 1911, 929–31, Toronto City Council Appendix A, 1911, CTA.

4 After slow growth between 1891 and 1901 Toronto's population jumped from 208,040 in 1901 to 376,538 in 1911, driven in part by annexations that added a fresh ring of suburbs to the city. See

J.M.S. Careless, *Toronto to 1918: An Illustrated History* (Toronto: James Lorimer, 1984), 179, 201, table V. See page 161 for the annexations.

5 "Humber River Project Means Civic Beauty," *The Toronto Daily Star*, 19 May 1911, 18.

6 "The Humber Valley Improvement," *The Globe*, 26 May 1911, 6. Emphasis mine.

7 "Humber River Project Means Civic Beauty," *The Toronto Daily Star*, 19 May 1911, 18; "The Humber Valley Playground," *The Globe*, 24 June 1912, 6.

8 "Humber River Project Means Civic Beauty," *The Toronto Daily Star*, 19 May 1911, 18. And on "controlling reckless motoring on both land and water," see "The Humber Valley Improvement," *The Globe*, Friday, 26 May 1911, 6.

9 "Humber River Project Means Civic Beauty," *The Toronto Daily Star*, 19 May 1911, 18; Humber River Plan: fonds 200, series 724, file 1, subdivision plans, dates of creation: [c. 1910–40], box 200760, folio 1, CTA.

10 Gene Desfor and Jennefer Laidley, eds., *Reshaping Toronto's Waterfront* (Toronto: University of Toronto Press, 2011), 9.

11 We can think of this as a competition between two spacializations of the river: see Rob Shields, *Places on the Margin: Alternative Geographies of Modernity* (New York: Routledge, 1991), 52–54.

12 On rough versus respectable masculinity see Mary-Ellen Kelm, "Manly Contests: Rodeo Masculinities at the Calgary Stampede," *Canadian Historical Review* 90, no. 4 (2009) 711–51: 735–36; and Stephen Meyer, "Work, Play, and Power: Masculine Culture on the Automotive Shop Floor, 1930–1960," in *Boys and Their Toys: Masculinity, Class, and Technology in America*, ed. Roger Horowitz (New York: Routledge, 2001), 13–16. On working-class masculinities, see Craig Heron, "Boys Will Be Boys: Working-Class Masculinities in the Age of Mass Production," *International Labor and Working-Class History* 69 (Spring 2006): 6–34.

13 Mitchell Dean, *Governmentality: Power and Rule in Modern Society* (London: Sage, 1999), 12, 23. As Michel Foucault suggests, this process was both individualizing and totalizing: Michel Foucault, "The Subject and Power," in *Power: Essential Works of Foucault, 1954–1984*, ed. James D. Faubion (New York: The New Press, 2000), 331–34.

14 Or "forced into the wilderness," as Shields would term it: see Shields, *Places on the Margin*, 60.

15 For a Canadian demonstration of this process, see Robert McDonald, "'Holy Retreat' or 'Practical Breathing Spot'?: Class Perceptions of Vancouver's Stanley Park, 1910–1913," *Canadian Historical Review* 65, no. 2 (1984): 153; Elizabeth Baigent, "'God's Earth Will Be Sacred': Religion, Theology, and the Open Space Movement in Victorian England," *Rural History* 22, no. 1 (2011): 39, 46.

16 Cameron White has noted moments when Sydney police were rousting what they assumed to be working-class nude bathers out of public spaces only to discover that they were "respectable" people instead: see Cameron White, "Picnicking, Surf-Bathing and Middle-Class Morality on the Beach in the Eastern Suburbs of Sydney, 1811–1912," *Journal of Australian Studies* 27, no. 80 (2003): 105.

17 Plans that were scuttled when the Simcoes' young son Francis came down with a fever: John Ross Robertson, *The Diary of Mrs. John Graves Simcoe, Wife of the First Lieutenant-Governor of the Province of Upper Canada, 1792–6* (Toronto: W. Briggs, 1911), 191, 332.

18 John Ross Robertson, *Robertson's Landmarks of Toronto: Toronto from 1834 to 1895* (Toronto: John R. Robertson, 1896), 915.

19 Charles Mulvany, Pelham, G. Mercer Adam, and Christopher Blackett Robinson, *History of Toronto and County of York*, vol. 1 (Toronto: C. Blackett Robinson, Publisher, 1885), part II, 53.

20 Patricia Jasen, *Wild Things: Nature, Culture, and Tourism in Ontario, 1790–1914* (Toronto; University of Toronto Press, 1995), 127; Galen Cranz, "Women in Urban Parks," *Signs: Journal of Women in*

Culture and Society 5, no. 3, supplement, *Women and the American City* (Spring 1980): 579–80, 586. For a good description of Victoria Park and Kew Beach, see M. Jane Fairburn, *Along the Shore: Rediscovering Toronto's Waterfront Heritage* (Toronto: ECW Press, 2013).

21 Dale Barbour, *Winnipeg Beach: Leisure and Courtship in a Resort Town, 1900–1967* (Winnipeg: University of Manitoba Press, 2011). See also Beth Bailey, *From Front Porch to Back Seat* (Baltimore: Johns Hopkins University Press, 1988).

22 "Bathing in the Humber," *The Daily Globe*, 27 July 1877, 2.

23 Ibid.

24 Ibid.

25 Madge Merton, "Madge Merton's Page," *The Toronto Daily Star*, 14 July 1900, 11.

26 The literature on the emergence of a consumer culture for courtship at the turn of the twentieth century is extensive. A good start includes Gary S. Cross and John K. Walton, *The Playful Crowd: Pleasure Places in the Twentieth Century* (New York: Columbia University Press, 2005); David Nasaw, *Going Out: The Rise and Fall of Public Amusements* (Cambridge, MA: Harvard University Press, 1999); John F. Kasson, *Amusing the Million: Coney Island at the Turn of the Century* (New York: Hill and Wang, 1978); Kathy Peiss, *Cheap Amusements: Working Women and Leisure in Turn-of-the-Century New York* (Philadelphia: Temple University Press, 1986); Bailey, *From Front Porch to Back Seat*, 4, 18.

27 On the nature/urban binary, see Jasen, *Wild Things*, 14–17. On the canoe as an entry point to nature, see Shelagh Grant, "Symbols and Myths: Images of Canoe and North," in *Canexus: The Canoe in Canadian Culture*, ed. James Raffan and Bert Horwood (Toronto: Betelgeuse Books, 1988); and C.E.S. Franks, "Canoeing: Towards a Landscape of the Imagination," in Raffan and Horwood, *Canexus*.

28 John Jennings and James Raffan capture the celebratory ethos in John Jennings, Bruce W. Hodgins, Doreen Small, eds., *The Canoe in Canadian Cultures* (Toronto: Natural Heritage/Natural History Inc., 1999).

29 For example, see Jocelyn Thorpe, *Temagami Tangled Wild: Race, Gender, and the Making of Canadian Nature* (Vancouver: UBC Press, 2012), 5–7; Bryan S.R. Grimwood, "'Thinking Outside the Gunnels': Considering Natures and the Moral Terrains of Recreational Canoe Travel," *Leisure/Loisir* 35, no. 1 (2011): 49–69; Beverly Haun-Moss, "Layered Hegemonies: The Origins of Recreational Canoeing Desire in the Province of Ontario," *Topia: Canadian Journal of Cultural Studies* 7 (April 2002): 39–55.

30 See Bruce Erickson, *Canoe Nation: Nature Race and the Making of a Canadian Icon* (Vancouver: UBC Press, 2013).

31 Misao Dean, *Inheriting a Canoe Paddle: The Canoe in Discourses of English-Canadian Nationalism* (Toronto: University of Toronto Press, 2013), 8–15.

32 Historians such as Lisa McDermott have turned the focus towards the experiences of female canoers, but still work with the same idea of a canoe trip involving an excursion into nature: see Lisa McDermott, "Exploring Intersections of Physicality and Female-Only Canoeing Experiences," *Leisure Studies* 23, no. 3 (2004): 283–301. And see, for example, William C. James, "Canoeing and Gender Roles," in Raffan and Horwood, *Canexus*, 27–43. On sports associations, see Jessica Dunkin, "Producing and Consuming Spaces of Sport and Leisure: The Encampments and Regattas of the American Canoe Association, 1880–1903," in *Moving Natures: Mobility and the Environment in Canadian History*, ed. Ben Bradley, Jay Young, and Colin M. Coates (Calgary: University of Calgary Press, 2016).

33 James Raffan exchanged letters with Berton about the quote; Berton noted it did not originate with him, but he had lost the original attribution and had given up trying to debunk the connection. See James Raffan, "Being There: Bill Mason and the Canadian Canoeing Tradition," in *The Canoe*

in *Canadian Cultures*, ed. John Jennings, Bruce W. Hodgins, and Doreen Small (Toronto: Natural Heritage/Natural History, 1999), 17.

34 See Raffan, "Being There." Along with citing Berton, James Benidickson points out the practical challenges of making love in a canoe: James Benidickson, *Idleness, Water, and a Canoe: Reflections on Paddling for Pleasure* (Toronto: University of Toronto Press, 1997), 12–14. Liz Newbery uses the quote to circle back to the idea of canoeists using their experiences to create Canadian subjectivity; see Liz Newbery, "Paddling the Nation: Canadian Becoming and Becoming Canadian in and through the Canoe," *Topia: Canadian Journal of Cultural Studies* 29 (Spring 2013): 136–37.

35 For the canoe's use in amusement parks and advertisements focused on courtship, see Ken Brown, *The Canadian Canoe Company and the Early Peterborough Canoe Factories* (Peterborough: Cover to Cover, 2011), 15, 99, 141–43. See also James Raffan, *Bark, Skin and Cedar: Exploring the Canoe in Canadian Experience* (Toronto: HarperCollins, 1999), 189, 195, 201.

36 Diane Beasley, "Walter Dean and Sunnyside: A Study of Waterfront Recreation in Toronto" (MA thesis, University of Toronto, 1994), 23. Ken Brown uses the same term in his work: see Brown, *The Canadian Canoe Company*, 141–43. On the commoditization of love, see Eva Illouz, *Consuming the Romantic Utopia: Love and the Cultural Contradictions of Capitalism* (Los Angeles: University of California Press, 1997), 56.

37 Beasley, "Walter Dean and Sunnyside," 1–2.

38 Beasley, 20, 30. For a sense of the number of canoes and companies available on or near the Humber, see "350 boats Destroyed in Fire at Humber," *The Toronto Daily Star*, 7 March 1917, 1.

39 David Scobey, "Anatomy of the Promenade: The Politics of Bourgeois Sociability in Nineteenth-Century New York," *Social History* 17, no. 2 (1992): 224–25.

40 See Judith Butler, *Gender Trouble: Feminism and the Subversion of Identity* (New York: Routledge, 1990); and Judith Butler, *Bodies That Matter: On the Discursive Limits of "Sex"* (New York: Routledge, 1993), for a discussion of both the potential and the limits of looking at gender as being produced through performativity.

41 And in this, as I have been suggesting throughout, it is most useful to think of these spaces as a series of competing, in this case, or compliant space ballets. See Shields, *Places on the Margin*, 53–54.

42 Craig Heron gives some of the best descriptions of this working-class identity making in his "Boys Will Be Boys," 15.

43 Scobey, "Anatomy of the Promenade," 227.

44 Views of the Humber River 1900–43, file 490043, fonds 70, series 330, file 49, folder 28, sheet 7R, box 158719, CTA.

45 Shields, *Places on the Margin*, 47; John Fiske, *Understanding Popular Culture* (Boston: Unwin Hyman, 1989), 45.

46 On the role of postcards and photography in creating these spaces, see Michael Lesy, *Dreamland: America at the Dawn of the Twentieth Century* (New York: The New Press, 1997), xi–xiii; Mary Warner Marien, *Photography: A Cultural History* (New York: Harry N. Abrahams, 2002), 170–72.

47 Jasen, *Wild Things*, 10–11.

48 For a more industrial view of the mill, see Views of the Humber River 1900–43, file 490040, fonds 70, series 330, file 49, folder 28, sheet 6V, box 158719, CTA. A more scenic view: Views of the Humber River 1900–43, file 490039, fonds 70, series 330, file 49, folder 28, sheet 6V, box 158719, CTA; With poem, dated 1907: Views of the Humber River 1900–43, file 490052, fonds 70, series 330, file 49, folder 28, sheet 8R, box 158719, CTA.

49 Marien, *Photography*, 170–72.

50 Views of the Humber River 1900–43, file 490051, fonds 70, series 330, file 49, folder 28, sheet 8R, box 158719, CTA.

51 Ibid.

52 Views of the Humber River 1900–43, file 490040, fonds 70, series 330, file 49, folder 28, sheet 6V, box 158719, CTA.

53 Ibid.

54 Beasley, "Walter Dean and Sunnyside," 18.

55 "Canoes Popular at Long Branch," *The Toronto Daily Star*, 25 July 1903, 16.

56 "Man and Woman Meet Death in Humber Bay," *The Globe*, 6 July 1908, 1. For a look at Maw's boat-house, see Maw's Boat House, Lakeshore Road at Sunnyside, James Salmon Collection Fonds 1231, item 2125, 28 July 1911, CTA.

57 "Man and Woman Meet Death in Humber Bay," *The Globe*, 6 July 1908, 1.

58 See Beasley, "Walter Dean and Sunnyside," 40–44. The advertisement on page 44 shows a couple sitting in a Dean canoe that's being advertised for its enhanced safety features.

59 Karen Dubinsky, *Improper Advances: Rape and Heterosexual Conflict in Ontario, 1880–1929* (Chicago: University of Chicago Press, 1993), 35. See also Jeffrey Weeks, *Sex, Politics and Society: The Regulation of Sexuality since 1800* (London: Longmans, 1981). For more on moral panics, see Mary Louise Adams, *The Trouble with Normal: Postwar Youth and the Making of Heterosexuality* (Toronto: University of Toronto Press, 1997), 56.

60 Carolyn Strange, *Toronto's Girl Problem: The Perils and Pleasures of the City, 1880–1930* (Toronto: University of Toronto Press, 1995), 210; Dubinsky, *Improper Advances*, 18, 161, 167. See also Mariana Valverde, *The Age of Light, Soap, and Water: Moral Reform in English Canada, 1885–1925* (Toronto: McClelland and Stewart, 1991). The approach laid out by Strange and Dubinsky was adopted in Canada in works such as Tamara Myers, *Caught: Montreal's Modern Girls and the Law, 1869–1945* (Toronto: Toronto University Press, 2006); and Carolyn Strange and Tina Loo, *Making Good: Law and Moral Regulation in Canada, 1867–1939* (Toronto: Toronto University Press, 1997).

61 Strange, *Toronto's Girl Problem*, 27; Dubinsky, *Improper Advances*, 36. See also Michel Foucault, *The History of Sexuality: An Introduction* (New York: Vintage, 1978), 31, 92–104; Chris Weedon, *Feminist Practice and Poststructuralist Theory* (Oxford: Basil Blackwell, 1987).

62 "Girl Arrested at Humber," *The Toronto Daily Star*, 15 July 1916, 2.

63 Ibid.

64 Strange, *Toronto's Girl Problem*, 132.

65 "A Policeman Was Ducked in Humber," *The Toronto Daily Star*, 15 September 1909, 9.

66 "A Summer Idyll Urbanized," *The Globe*, 25 August 1925, 4.

67 Fiske would refer to this as the subordinated challenging efforts by the dominant class to control the meaning of the river: see John Fiske, *Reading the Popular* (New York: Routledge, 2005), 1–9.

68 "Local Briefs," *The Globe*, 23 July 1896, 10. Emphasis mine.

69 "Bathers Fined," *The Toronto Daily Star*, 24 July 1896, 2.

70 "Bathing in Nature's Garb," *The Globe*, 14 July 1899, 10.

71 "A Raid on the Humber Bathers," *The Toronto Daily Star*, 26 June 1905, 1. There are other examples: "Severe Censure on South York Schools," *The Toronto Daily Star*, 13 June 1906, 11.

72 "Nude Bathing in the Humber," *The Toronto Daily Star*, 23 August 1904, 4. The question mark is in the original text.

73 Ibid.

74 Ibid.

75 Ibid. Emphasis mine.

76 Dean, *Governmentality*, 12.

77 Heron, "Boys Will Be Boys," 15.

78 C.S. Clark, *Of Toronto the Good, a Social Study: The Queen City of Canada as It Is* (Montreal: Toronto Publishing Company, 1898), 113.

79 "Stop Bathing in the Humber," *The Toronto Daily Star*, 19 July 1910, 7.

80 "To Prohibit Bathing," *The Globe*, 19 July 1910, 8.

81 Ibid.

82 "Humber River and Bay Claim Two More Victims," *The Globe*, 11 July 1910, 8. Furniss's name is spelled Furness in the early accounts of his drowning and then Furniss in the reports coming out of the inquest.

83 "Drowned in the Humber," *The Globe*, 18 July 1904, 10.

84 Heron, "Boys Will Be Boys," 15.

85 For example, "A Canoe Upset 2 Men in Water," *The Toronto Daily Star*, 11 June 1908, 1; "Young Man's Fatal Dive," *The Globe*, 25 July 1910, 6.

86 "Parks Crowded on a May Sunday," *The Toronto Daily Star*, 18 May 1908, 2. The temperature on 17 May 1908, was just above 21°C; see Historic Climate Data: http://climate.weather.gc.ca/climate-Data/dailydata_e.html?timeframe=2&Prov=ON&StationID=5051&dlyRange=1840-03-01%7C2015-12-14&Year=1908&Month=5&Day=01.

87 For some local encounters, see "Waters Near Toronto Claim 2 More Victims," *The Toronto Daily Star*, 9 July 1912, 8; "One Drowned in the Don, Another in the Humber," *The Globe*, 9 July 1912, 8; "Drowned in the Humber," *The Globe*, 16 June 1900, 18; "Boy Drowned," *The Toronto Daily Star*, 16 June 1900, 16.

88 As Cameron White has found in Sydney, bathers who were assumed to be working class "larrikins" often turned out to be middle-class bathers: White, "Picnicking," 106.

89 The Humber would have predominantly been policed by York County: policing likely was ramping up. When we look at Toronto's police reports we find that by the period after 1910, police were routinely charging over 30 people a year for indecency, a catch-all category that could include undressed bathing, being naked in a public space, or even being caught urinating in public. See police reports in Toronto City Council Appendix, CTA.

90 "Madge Merton's Page," *The Toronto Daily Star*, 7 September 1901, 12. The river received similar treatment in "Madge Merton's Page," *The Toronto Daily Star*, 19 October 1901, 12.

91 "Drowned Bathing in Humber River," *The Toronto Daily Star*, 23 June 1908, 1.

92 Esther Heyes, *Etobicoke: From Furrow to Borough* (Etobicoke: Borough of Etobicoke Civic Centre, 1974), 119; Ron Fletcher, *The Humber: Tales of a Canadian Heritage River* (Toronto: RWF, Heritage Publications, 2006), 4–5.

93 F.D. Cruikshank and J. Nason, *History of Weston* (Toronto: University of Toronto Press, 1983), 22. May Irvine Knapp is quoted in Marjorie Mossman, "Weston," in *The Villages of Etobicoke*, ed. Etobicoke Historical Board (Weston, ON: Argyle Printing, 1986), 108.

94 Weston Historical Society, *A Pictorial History of Weston* (Toronto: University of Toronto Press, 1981).

95 William H. Wilson, *The City Beautiful Movement* (Baltimore: Johns Hopkins University Press, 1989), 9. Olmsted designed Central Park with Calvert Vauxhas, but Olmsted is generally viewed as the visionary behind the project.

96 Nancy Pollock-Ellwand, "Rickson Outhet: Bringing the Olmsted Legacy to Canada. A Romantic View of Nature in the Metropolis and the Hinterland," *Journal of Canadian Studies/Revue d'études canadiennes* 44, no. 1 (2010): 144. See also Wilson, *The City Beautiful Movement*, 11–12, 65.

97 David Schuyler, *The New Urban Landscape: The Redefinition of City Form in Nineteenth-Century America* (Baltimore: Johns Hopkins University Press, 1986), 182, 185, 195; Wilson, *The City Beautiful Movement*, 11–12. The familiar urban/nature binary is at the heart of Olmsted's concerns; for more on that, see William Cronon, "The Trouble with Wilderness: Or, Getting Back to the Wrong Nature," *Environmental History* 1, no. 1 (1996): 7–28. See also Peter J. Schmitt, *Back to Nature: The Arcadian Myth in Urban America* (New York: Oxford University Press, 1969).

98 S.B. Sutton, ed., *Civilizing American Cities: A Selection of Frederick Law Olmsted's Writings on City Landscapes* (Cambridge, MA: Massachusetts Institute of Technology, 1971), 74, 83; Schuyler, *The New Urban Landscape*, 125.

99 Wilson, *The City Beautiful Movement*, 1, 17. On the link to the reform era, see Emily Talen, *New Urbanism and American Planning: The Conflict of Cultures* (New York and London: Routledge Taylor and Francis Group, 2005), 113; Jon A. Peterson, "The City Beautiful Movement: "Forgotten Origins and Lost Meanings," *Journal of Urban History* 2, no. 4 (1976): 429–30.

100 Wilson, *The City Beautiful Movement*, 1, 17, 48, 73, 78, 79, 81, 85; Richard E. Foglesong, *Planning the Capitalist City: The Colonial Era to the 1920s* (Princeton: Princeton University Press, 1986), 124. And in this they held much in common with turn-of-the-century medical practitioners who believed that health was environmental. See Felix Driver, "Moral Geographies: Social Science and the Urban Environment in Mid-Nineteenth Century England," *Transactions of the Institute of British Geographers, New Series*, 13, no. 3 (1988): 275–76. On the link with Darwin, see Wilson, *The City Beautiful Movement*, 79–81; Peterson, "Forgotten Origins," 429–30.

101 On high modernism, see Christopher Dummitt, *The Manly Modern: Masculinity in Postwar Canada* (Vancouver: UBC Press, 2007), 12. And for a full discussion, see James C. Scott, *Seeing Like a State: How Certain Schemes to Improve the Human Condition Have Failed* (New Haven, CT: Yale University Press, 1999).

102 John S. Pipkin, "'Chasing Rainbows' in Albany: City Beautiful, City Practical 1900–1925," *Journal of Planning History* 7, no. 4 (2008): 328.

103 Charles Mulford Robinson, *The Improvement of Towns and Cities or The Practical Basis of Civic Aesthetics* (New York: G.P. Putnam's Sons, 1901), 17.

104 For earlier discussions, see "For a Boulevard on the Waterfront," *The Toronto Daily Star*, 16 January 1906, 1. For the Guild of Civic Art, see John C. Weaver, "The Modern City Realized: Toronto Civic Affairs, 1880–1915," in *The Usable Urban Past: Planning and Politics in the Modern Canadian City*, ed. Alan F.J. Artibise and Gilbert A. Stelter (Toronto: Macmillan of Canada, 1979), 60–61.

105 "The Rosedale Drive," *The Toronto Daily Star*, 30 July 1895, 2. See also "The Rosedale Drive," an identically named article on the same page. Toronto Guild of Civic Art Fonds, fonds 1015, box 146634, SC 15, box 1, file 3, *Report on a Comprehensive Plan for Systematic Civic Improvements in Toronto*, 1909, "A Foreword," CTA.

106 Toronto Guild of Civic Art Fonds, fonds 1015, box 146634, SC 15, box 1, file 3, *Report on a Comprehensive Plan for Systematic Civic Improvements in Toronto*, 1909, "A Foreword," CTA.

107 Toronto Guild of Civic Art Fonds, fonds 1015, box 146634, SC, 15 box 1, file 3, *Report on a Comprehensive Plan for Systematic Civic Improvements in Toronto*, 1909, W.A. Langton. Emphasis mine.

108 Sarah Bassnett, *Picturing Toronto: Photography and the Making of a Modern City* (Montreal: McGill-Queen's University Press, 2016), 56–69. See also Jonathan Crary, *Techniques of the Observer: On Vision and Modernity in the Nineteenth Century* (Cambridge, MA: MIT Press, 1992), 11–13.

109 Toronto Guild of Civic Art Fonds, fonds 1015, box 146634, SC 15 box 1, file 3, *Report on a Comprehensive Plan for Systematic Civic Improvements in Toronto*, 1909, CTA.

110 Wilson, *The City Beautiful Movement*, 131.

111 Toronto debated a boulevard system in 1909 through 1912; see, for example, item 68, 11 January 1909, page 14, Toronto City Council Minutes, 1909, CTA; Report no. 2, Committee on Parks and Exhibition, Boulevards and Park Driveways, page 152, Toronto City Council Appendix A, 1910, CTA; Item 157, 14 February 1910 (Letter of support from Toronto Guild of Civic Art.), 43, Toronto City Council Minutes, 1910, CTA. For media coverage, see "Boulevard to Girdle Toronto," *The Toronto Daily Star*, 24 January 1910, 1. Again from 1912: Report upon Park Distribution, Parkways, and Main Boulevard System, page 3, fonds 200, series 490, file 2, box 224914. For the Toronto Harbour Commission, see Toronto Harbour Commission, Public Affairs Department, *Toronto Harbour, the Passing Years* (Toronto: Toronto Harbour Commissioners, 1985), 25; James O'Mara, *Shaping Urban Waterfronts: The Role of Toronto's Harbour Commissioners, 1911–1960, Discussion Paper No. 13* (Toronto: York University, Department of Geography, March 1976), 34–35.

112 Weaver, "The Modern City Realized," 63. See also Carolyn Whitzman, *Suburb, Slum, Urban Village: Transformations in Toronto's Parkdale Neighbourhood, 1875–2002* (Vancouver: UBC Press, 2009), 120–21.

113 On design elements: "Humber River Project Means Civic Beauty," *The Toronto Daily Star*, 19 May 1911, 18. There is some debate over how altruistic Home Smith was: see Kevin Plummer, "Historicist: A Monument to His Dreams," *The Torontoist*, 8 May 2010: http://torontoist.com/2010/05/historicist_a_monument_to_his_dreams/.

114 Richard Harris, *Creeping Conformity: How Canada Became Suburban, 1900–1960* (Toronto: University of Toronto Press, 2004), 88–89. See also Denise Harris, "The Kingsway," http://www.etobicokehistorical.com/the-kingsway.html (accessed on 10 December 2015). On fencing, see Report no. 17 of the Board of Control, 9 June 1911, 929–31, Toronto City Council Appendix A, 1911, CTA.

115 James H. Gunn, *Robert Home Smith 1877–1935: A Brief Biography and Some Highlights: The Unique Life of an Early 20th Century Canadian Businessman* (New Bern, NC, 20 April 1986; edited and corrected October 1986), 9–10: Research Subject Reference File, Robert Home Smith folder, Ports Toronto Archives (PTA).

116 "Unsightly Bathing to Be Prohibited: Authorities Will Restore Decency on the Humber," *The Globe*, 23 June 1913, 8.

117 "Protection for Boating along the Humber," *The Toronto Daily Star*, 25 June 1913, 7.

118 "Danger on Humber River, Carelessness in Boats," *The Toronto Daily Star*, 22 May 1911, 2.

119 Ibid.

120 Ibid.

121 "The Humber Boulevard," *The Toronto Daily Star*, 17 May 1911, 8.

122 "The Humber Park and Boulevard," *The Globe*, 17 May 1911, 6. Emphasis mine.

123 "City Council Makes Some Changes in the Big Humber Valley Project," *The Toronto Daily Star*, 17 October 1911, 7.

124 "The Humber Valley Improvement," *The Globe*, 26 May 1911, 6.

125 "The Humber Boulevard," *The Toronto Daily Star*, 26 May 1911, 8.

126 "Does Government Own the Humber?" *The Toronto Daily Star*, 5 June 1911, 1.

127 "The Humber Park and Boulevard," *The Globe*, 17 May 1911, 6. Emphasis mine.

128 The issue was raised numerous times: see Board of Control report no. 16, E.A. MacDonald, mayor, chairman, 26 April 1900; adopted as amended 30 April 1900, 403, Toronto City Council Appendix A, 1900, TCA. "Not the City's Job to Guard Humber Bay," *The Toronto Daily Star*, 25 June 1909, 10.

129 "No Patrol of Humber Waters," *The Toronto Daily Star*, 30 July 1909, 1.

130 "The Humber River and Bay," *The Globe*, 9 July 1908, 4.

131 Mary Louise Adams, "Almost Anything Can Happen: A Search for Sexual Discourse in the Urban Spaces of 1940s Toronto," *Canadian Journal of Sociology/Cahiers canadiens de sociologie* 19, no. 2, *Special Issue on Moral Regulation* (1994): 228. On lights and the urban environment, see Wolfgang Schivelbusch, *Disenchanted Night: The Industrialization of Light in the Nineteenth Century*, trans. Angela Davies (Berkeley: University of California Press, 1988), 134.

132 The addition of North Toronto in 1912 ended the annexation boom. There would be a couple of small additions in 1914, but no substantial additions for another 50 years. See Harris, *Unplanned Suburbs*, 41.

133 Report no. 19 of the Board of Control, 5 July 1911, 1097, Toronto City Council Appendix A, 1911, CTA.

134 Ross Paterson, "The Development of an Interwar Suburb: Kingsway Park, Etobicoke," *Urban History Review* 13, no. 3 (1985): 228.

135 Report no. 19 of the Board of Control, 5 July 1911, 1097, Toronto City Council Appendix A, 1911, CTA.

136 "City Council Makes Some Changes in the Big Humber Valley Project," *The Toronto Daily Star*, 17 October 1911, 7. The article doesn't specify when the trip up the Humber in boats was made, though city council members had toured the site in spring: "Take in 1,000 feet west of Humber," *The Toronto Daily Star*, 17 May 1911.

137 "McBride Hurls Challenge at Attacking Newspaper," *The Toronto Daily Star*, 11 July 1916, 5. For more discussion around the changes, see "Humber Boulevard Scheme Changed," *The Toronto Daily Star*, 4 July 1916, 1; "Home Smith Satisfied with Humber Changes," *The Toronto Daily Star*, 12 November 1912, 4. For a map of the changes to the project, see "Proposed Humber Boulevard Drive," *The Toronto Daily Star*, 5 July 1916, 2.

138 Parks and Exhibition Committee, S. Ryding, chair, 21 December 1915, adopted 27 December 1915, 1302–1303, Toronto City Council Appendix A, 1915, CTA.

139 Walter van Nus suggests the First World War, the collapse of the land boom, and a need for low-cost housing after the war helped knock the shine off the City Beautiful movement in Toronto: see Walter Van Nus, "The Fate of City Beautiful Thought in Canada, 1893–1930," *Historical Papers* 101 (1975): 198–204.

140 Wilson, *The City Beautiful Movement*, 287–90. The shift from "City Beautiful" to "City Practical" has been noted by historians, but John S. Pipkin notes the planning element was always part of City Beautiful, even if early supporters put more focus on aesthetic needs than later planners. See Pipkin, "Chasing Rainbows," 330. On growth of city planning, see Robert Freestone, "Reconciling Beauty and Utility in Early City Planning: The Contribution of John Nolen," *Journal of Urban History* 37, no. 2 (2011): 257, 271–72; Peterson, "Forgotten Origins and Lost Meanings," 430. On the emergence of social organization, see Peter D. Norton, *Fighting Traffic: The Dawn of the Motor Age in the American City* (Cambridge, MA: MIT Press, 2008).

141 "Humber Valley Surveys," *The Toronto Daily Star*, 1 May 1914, 24. For a look at the bridge and surrounding site in a postcard, see With the Bridge: Views of the Humber River 1900-1943, file 490071, fonds 70, series 330, file 49, folder 28, sheet 10V, box 158719, CTA.

142 "Humber Valley Surveys," *The Toronto Daily Star*, 1 May 1914, 24; "Old Mill Tea Garden," *Toronto Daily Star*, 8 April 1921, 27. (Where a full-course chicken dinner was available for $1.50.)

143 Report no. 5, Board of Control, passed 20 March 1922, 294, Toronto City Council Appendix A, 1921, CTA.

144 James M. MacGregor, "When Roses Are Blooming in June," *The Toronto Daily Star*, 28 June 1924, 6.

145 "Parks Patronized," *The Toronto Daily Star*," 19 April 1915, 2.

146 "Toronto Day Is Biggest Holiday," *The Globe*, 7 August 1917, 8.

147 "Immorality Rife in County of York: Toronto Joy-Riders Blamed for Giving County Unsavory Reputation," *The Toronto Daily Star*, 27 November 1915, 11.

148 For more on the social transformation of courtship during the twentieth century, see Bailey, *From Front Porch to Back Seat*.

149 "Policing the Humber," *Toronto Daily Star*, 15 June 1921, 6.

150 For a useful look at the social and environmental changes brought on by the automobile, see Stephen Davies, "Reckless Walking Must Be Discouraged": The Automobile Revolution and the Shaping of Modern Urban Canada to 1930," *Urban History Review* 18, no. 2 (1989): 123–38.

151 "The Proposed Humber River Railway," *The Toronto Daily Star*, 4 January 1912, 2. This was discussed fairly extensively between Home Smith and the city.

152 There were 535 automobiles registered in Ontario in 1904, 31,724 in 1914, 155,861 in 1920, and 303,736 in 1925: Davies, "Reckless Walking," 124.

153 "Humber Valley Surveys," *The Toronto Daily Star*, 1 May 1926, 7.

154 Peter W. Moore, "Zoning and Planning: The Toronto Experience, 1904–1970," in *The Usable Urban Past: Planning and Politics in the Modern Canadian City*, ed. Alan F.J. Artibise and Gilbert A. Stelter (Toronto: Macmillan of Canada, 1979), 324–25.

155 "Motorists Become Mermen at Limpid Roadside Pools," *The Globe*, 13 August 1923, 11.

156 Ibid. See "Up the Humber on That Hot Day Last Week When Even the Car Had to Be Cooled Off," *The Toronto Daily Star*, 14 July 1926, 19, for a picture of cars in the river.

157 "The Sea Wall Project," *The Globe*, 24 July 1906, 12. "The Humber River and Bay," *The Globe*, 9 July 1908, 4. The seawall was completed by the Toronto Harbour Commission after 1912.

158 For the location of the Wanita Tea Room, see Robert Given, The Old Mill Inn, http://www.etobicokehistorical.com/the-old-mill.html (accessed on 20 December 2015).

159 "Struggle with Death in Humber River," *The Toronto Daily Star*, 20 June 1921, 3.

160 Monday, 21 August 1922, Main Station, August 1922, 5, Life Saving and Police Patrol Annual Report, 1922, 1840-L-1-1, RG 7/1 box 1, PTA. For rowboat, see 6 August 1924 extracts from the log of the Life Saving and Police Patrol Department for the month of August, page 2: Life Saving and Police Patrol Annual Report, 1924, 1840-L-1-1, RG 7/1 box 1, PTA.

161 "Random Notes on Current Sports," *The Toronto Daily Star*, 16 August 1924, 10.

162 On photography's ability to both produce and erase, see Carol Payne and Andrea Kunard, *The Cultural Work of Photography in Canada* (Montreal: McGill-Queen's University Press, 2011), xiv, xvii; Jae Emerling, *Photography: History and Theory* (New York: Routledge, 2012), 34.

163 "Need Police at Humber," *The Toronto Daily Star*, 8 June 1925, 17.

164 "A Summer Idyll Urbanized," *The Globe*, 25 August 1925, 4.

165 Who uses the river and defined its space has become simplified. See Shields, *Places on the Margin*, 60.

166 Richard Anderson, "The Dustbins of History: Waste Disposal in Toronto's Ravines and Valleys," in *Toronto's Water from Lake Iroquois to Lost Rivers to Low-flow Toilets*, ed. Wayne Reeves and Christina Palassio (Toronto: Coach House Books, 2008), 77. Anderson writes that bathing continued into the 1940s and portrays the bathers as rambunctious teenagers.

Chapter 6: Sunnyside and the Beach

1 "Ushering Toronto to the Threshold of Her Newer Era," *The Globe*, 29 June 1922, 11.

2 "Sunnyside Recreation Resort Now Bids the Wide World Welcome," *The Evening Telegram*, 29 June 1922, Research Subject Reference File: Sunnyside Folder, Toronto Port Authority Archives.

3 "Ushering Toronto to the Threshold of Her Newer Era," *The Globe*, 29 June 1922, 11.

4 "Official Opening of Sunnyside Beach: "Toronto's Lake Shore Playground," *The Globe*, 27 June 1922, 15.

5 For a discussion of liminal moments in Toronto, see Ian Radforth. *Royal Spectacle: The 1860 Visit of the Prince of Wales to Canada and the United States* Toronto: (University of Toronto Press, 2004), 68; and Keith Walden, *Becoming Modern in Toronto: The Industrial Exhibition and the Shaping of a Late Victorian Culture* (Toronto: University of Toronto Press, 1997), 25. The concept of liminality has been defined by Victor Turner as a ritual moment when people cross from one realm of being into another, a moment that ends when they return to their regular lives. See Victor Turner, *The Ritual Process: Structure and Anti-Structure* (New Brunswick, NJ: AldineTransation, 2008), 94–95.

6 John Fiske, *Reading the Popular* (New York: Routledge, 2005), 44–45.

7 Mikhail Bakhtin, *Rabelais and His World* (Bloomington: Indiana University Press, 1984), 7–10.

8 John K. Walton, "Respectability Takes a Holiday: Disreputable Behaviour at the Victorian Seaside," in *Unrespectable Recreations*, ed. Martin Hewitt (Leeds: Leeds Centre for Victorian Studies, 2001), 176.

9 Gary S. Cross and John K. Walton, *The Playful Crowd: Pleasure Places in the Twentieth Century* (New York: Columbia University Press, 2005), 6, 61–62.

10 John F. Kasson, *Amusing the Million: Coney Island at the Turn of the Century* (New York: Hill and Wang, 1978), 4, 8, 23–26; Woody Register, *The Kid of Coney Island: Fred Thompson and the Rise of American Amusements* (New York: Oxford University Press, 2001), 10–15.

11 Fiske, *Reading the Popular*, 41–45, 50–51;. John Fiske, *Understanding Popular Culture* (Boston: Unwin Hyman, 1989), 11–14, 23–27.

12 Tom Wickson, *Reflections of Toronto Harbour: 200 Years of Port Activity and Waterfront Development* (Toronto: Toronto Port Authority, 2002), 14.

13 For example: Gene Desfor and Jennefer Laidley, eds., *Reshaping Toronto's Waterfront* (Toronto: University of Toronto Press, 2011).

14 On governance, see Mitchell Dean, *Governmentality: Power and Rule in Modern Society* (London: Sage, 1999), 30–33; and Eva Lovbrand and Johannes Stripple, "Governmentality," in *Critical Environmental Politics*, ed. Carl Death (New York: Routledge, 2014), 115.

15 On visibility and governance, see Nikolas Rose, Pat O'Malley, and Mariana Valverde, "Governmentality," *Annual Review of Law and Social Science* 2 (2006): 87; Simon Gunn, "From Hegemony to Governmentality: Changing Conceptions of Power in Social History," *Social History* 39, no. 3 (2006): 713.

16 On the role of the panopticon as a force for control and subjectivity, see Gunn, "From Hegemony to Governmentality," 717; Michel Foucault, "Questions of Geography," in *Power/Knowledge: Selected*

Interviews and Other Writings, 1972–1977, ed. Colin Gordon (New York: Pantheon Books, 1980), 72–73; Michel Foucault, "Truth and Power," in *Power/Knowledge*, 119.

17 As I have suggested, the bathing suit was a technology for ordering oneself: see Gunn, "From Hegemony to Governmentality," 709; Dean, *Governmentality*, 12. While I look at hygiene under the rubric of bathing we can of think of it as one part of an ensemble of techniques, technologies, and rationales coming into play, not all of which necessarily had the same goal: see Michel Foucault, "Governmentality," in *The Foucault Effect: Studies in Governmentality*, ed. Graham Burchell, Colin Gordon, and Peter Miller (Chicago: University of Chicago Press, 1991), 93, 95, 102; Michel Foucault, "The Subject and Power," in *Power: Essential Works of Foucault, 1954–1984*, ed. James D. Faubion (New York: The New Press, 2000), 342–43.

18 On the tenacity of relationships with place, see Rob Shields, *Places on the Margin: Alternative Geographies of Modernity* (New York: Routledge, 1991), 52–53, 60–61.

19 Fiske, *Understanding Popular Culture*, 27–38.

20 Carolyn Whitzman, *Suburb, Slum, Urban Village: Transformations in Toronto's Parkdale Neighbourhood, 1875–2002* (Vancouver: UBC Press, 2009), 83; "Bathing in the Humber," *The Daily Globe*, 27 July 1877, 2. On the nude bathing space: Item 603, 5 June 1893, 176, Toronto City Council Minutes, 1893, CTA; Item 651, 19 June 1893, 193, Toronto City Council Minutes, 1893, CTA; By-law 3179, 19 June 1893, 274, Toronto City Council Appendix B, 1893, CTA.

21 Whitzman refers to this land being sold for industrial use, but it is clear the lakeshore was co-opted for bathing: Whitzman, *Suburb*, 91. See Toronto City Council for setting up: Report no. 12 of the committee of property, 11 May 1893, 251, Toronto City Council Appendix, 1893, CTA. The specific mention of mixed bathing comes in 1897, but may have been in place earlier: "Bathing Place at Old Parkdale Pumping Station," Report no. 12 of the Committee on Property, 3 June 1897, 442, Toronto City Council Appendix A, 1897, CTA. The bathhouse at Roncesvalles would last into the twentieth century: See "Cramp Paralyzed Him," *The Globe*, 6 June 1908, 24. When John W. Bates drowned at the Roncesvalles Baths in 1908 it was stated that his had been the first drowning at the baths in their 16 years of operation, even though up to 2,000 people used them on a busy day.

22 "Knights of Pythias," *The Globe*, 16 July 1896, 5; "Thefts at Sunnyside Dance," *The Globe*, 22 March 1906, 10.

23 James Salmon portrays a bathhouse with little beach behind it: Sunnyside Bathing Beach, fonds 1231; James Salmon Collection, item 572, 28 July 1911, CTA. Alan Howard gives us similar pictures which show little beach and people sitting up against a stony terrace: Sunnyside—crowd on beach, fonds 1548, Alan Howard Fonds, series 393, item 1133, 3 August 1914, CTA.

24 "Wishes on One Pole May Be the Order," *The Globe*, 19 March 1913, 7. Fleming went on to serve as a Toronto harbour commissioner after 1921.

25 See also Bathers, Sunnyside Beach, William James Family Fonds 1244, item 194A, 19––, CTA.

26 "Toronto's Western Entrance," *The Globe*, 13 April 1911, 6. See also "The Railway Crossing at Sunnyside," *The Globe*, 13 May 1911, 6. For the facilities to be removed, see "Grand Trunk May Build the Bridge," *The Globe*, 29 May 1911, 9; and "Hundreds of Boats Must Be Moved," *The Globe*, 26 August 1911, 9.

27 This is an example of people co-opting a semi-industrialized environment and repurposing it for their own uses: see Fiske, *Reading the Popular*, 1–9; Fiske, *Understanding Popular Culture*, 15.

28 Letter to D. Chisholm, property commissioner, City of Toronto, from A.C. Lewis, secretary, Toronto Harbour Commission, 30 July 1912, in RG 313, box 53, folder 12, Bathing –Sunnyside Free Bathing Area 1912–1935, no. 101.S.2, vol. 1, PTA.

29 "Paralysed while Diving," *The Globe*, 5 August 1901, 10.

30 At least among the free bathing station numbers. "Free Bathing Popular," *The Globe*, 31 July 1906, 8.

31 Victoria Park was opened in 1878; Kew Beach was opened in 1879. M. Jane Fairburn, *Along the Shore: Rediscovering Toronto's Waterfront Heritage* (Toronto: ECW Press, 2013), 145, 154.

32 For a sense of social networking on the eastern beaches, see "General News of the City: Balmy Beach," *The Globe*, 9 July 1897, 10.

33 "General News of the City: Brotherhood of St. Andrew," *The Globe*, Wednesday, 26 May 1897, 12; "Two Drowning Accidents," *The Globe*, Thursday, 2 July 1903, 1.

34 "No More Sand Baths," *The Toronto Daily Star*, 23 July 1906, 5.

35 Ibid.

36 "Back to the Old Law," *The Globe*, 15 July 1903, 12; "Sunday Bathing Stopped by Lord's Day Alliance," *The Globe*, 26 July 1915, 7; "Controllers Irate at Sunday Action," *The Toronto Daily Star*, 26 July 1915, 3; "Sunday Dip in Lake Must Be Permitted," *The Globe*, 27 July 1915, 7; "Bathing a Necessity and Therefore Legal," *The Globe*, 28 July 1915, 7. For a broader discussion of changing Sunday laws, see Christopher Armstrong and H.V. Nelles, *The Revenge of the Methodist Bicycle Company* (Toronto: Peter Martin Associates Limited, 1977); and John Wigley, *The Rise and Fall of the Victorian Sunday* (Manchester: Manchester University Press, 1980).

37 A useful range of works on the topic includes Kasson, *Amusing the Million*; Kathy Peiss, *Cheap Amusements: Working Women and Leisure in Turn-of-the-Century New York* (Philadelphia: Temple University Press, 1986); David Nasaw, *Going Out: The Rise and Fall of Public Amusements* (Cambridge, MA: Harvard University Press, 1999); Bryant Simon, *Boardwalk of Dreams: Atlantic City and the Fate of Urban America* (New York: Oxford University Press, 2004); Cross and Walton, *The Playful Crowd*; and Dale Barbour, *Winnipeg Beach: Leisure and Courtship in a Resort Town, 1900–1967* (Winnipeg: University of Manitoba Press, 2011).

38 Display advertisements appeared in newspapers in the 1880s but became a daily and influential feature by 1900. See Donica Belisle, *Retail Nation: Department Stores and the Making of Modern Canada* (Vancouver: UBC Press, 2011), 47, 58–70; Douglas Booth, "War off Water: The Australian Surf Life Saving Association and the Beach," *Sporting Traditions* 7, no. 2 (1991): 144–45.

39 "The Robert Simpson Company: Ladies Bathing Suits," *The Toronto Daily Star*, 16 June 1903, 6.

40 "On the Beach," *The Toronto Daily Star*, 18 August 1900, 1.

41 "Madge Merton," *The Toronto Daily Star*, 18 August 1900, 19.

42 "The Robert Simpson Company," *The Globe*, 17 July 1907, 3.

43 For other examples of this theme, see "At the Sea Side or the Country," *The Globe*, 25 June 1903, 8. Heterosocial bathing was a pull factor that helped end vernacular bathing: John Travis, "Continuity and Change in English Sea-Bathing, 1730–1900: A Case of Swimming with the Tide," in *Recreation and the Sea*, ed. Stephen Fisher (Exeter: University of Exeter Press, 1997), 29–30.

44 Travis, "Continuity and Change in English Sea-Bathing," 29–30.

45 "Eaton's July Sale News," *The Toronto Daily Star*, 14 July 1905, 12.

46 Christine Metusela and Gordon Waitt, *Tourism and Australian Beach Cultures: Revealing Bodies* (Toronto: Channel View Publications, 2012), 111–15, 122, 140.

47 Fiske, *Understanding Popular Culture*, 11–14, 20.

48 For a comprehensive look at Toronto's waterfront and the harbour commission, see Gene Desfor and Jennefer Laidley, eds., *Reshaping Toronto's Waterfront* (Toronto: University of Toronto Press, 2011).

49 Michael Moir, "Planning for Change: Harbour Commissions, Civil Engineers, and Large-Scale Manipulation of Nature," in Desfor and Laidley, *Reshaping Toronto's Waterfront*, 30, 36–37, 45.

50 Gene Desfor, Lucian Vesalon, and Jennefer Laidley, "Establishing the Toronto Harbour Commission and Its 1912 Waterfront Development Plan," in Desfor and Laidley, *Reshaping Toronto's Waterfront*, 72–73.

51 Desfor, Vesalon, and Laidley, 68; Alan F.J. Artibise and Gilbert A. Stelter, eds., *The Usable Urban Past: Planning and Politics in the Modern Canadian City* (Toronto: Macmillan of Canada, 1979), 36; Paul Rutherford, "Tomorrow's Metropolis: The Urban Reform Movement in Canada, 1880–1920," in *The Canadian City: Essays in Urban History*, ed. Gilbert A. Stelter and Alan F.J. Artibise (Toronto, McClelland and Stewart Limited, 1977), 370–71. On Board of Trade promotion, see Gene Desfor, "Planning Urban Waterfront Industrial Districts: Toronto's Ashbridge's Bay, 1889–1910," *Urban History Review/Revue d'histoire urbaine* 17, no. 2 (1988): 85–88. For land development, see James O'Mara, *Shaping Urban Waterfronts: The Role of Toronto's Harbour Commissioners, 1911–1960, Discussion Paper No. 13* (Toronto: York University, Department of Geography, March 1976), 15.

52 John C. Weaver. "The Modern City Realized: Toronto Civic Affairs, 1880–1915," in Artibise and Stelter, *The Usable Urban Past*, 49–50. See also Gene Desfor, "Planning Urban Waterfront Industrial Districts," 79. Toronto had already set up its Board of Control with a similar logic in mind: James D. Anderson, "The Municipal Government Reform Movement in Western Canada, 1880–1920," in Artibise and Stelter, *The Usable Urban Past*, 79; Careless, *Toronto to 1918*, 190.

53 O'Mara, *Shaping Urban Waterfronts*, 15–16; Desfor, Vesalon, and Laidley, "Establishing the Toronto Harbour Commission," 58–59.

54 Roy Merrens, "Port Authorities as Urban Land Developers: The Case of the Toronto Harbour Commissioners and Their Outer Harbour Project, 1912–68," *Urban History Review* 17, no. 2 doi:10.7202/1017654ar, 92.

55 E.L. Cousins, Toronto Harbour Improvements, Cousins, 3 February 1921, 1, Research Subject Reference File: Cousins, E.L., "Toronto Harbour Improvements," 1921 folder, PTA; Tom Wickson, *Reflections*, 14; Careless, *Toronto to 1918*, 155.

56 E.L. Cousins, Toronto Harbour Improvements, Cousins, 3 February 1921, 1, Research Subject Reference File: Cousins, E.L. "Toronto Harbour Improvements," 1921 folder, PTA.

57 Jesse Edgar Middleton, *The Municipality of Toronto: A History* (Toronto: Dominion Publishing Company, 1923), 466–67; Life Saving and Police Patrol Second Annual Report, 1920, 7, 1840-L-1-1, RG 7/1 box 1, PTA.

58 Richard Baker, "Marine Unit: Lifeguards – History," http://www.mastermariners.ca/wp-content/uploads/2018/05/March-2018-Monthly-meeting.-Final-copy.pdf (accessed on 12 February 2021).

59 O'Mara, *Shaping Urban Waterfronts*, 33.

60 For development, see "The Municipal Protest," *The Globe*, 24 August 1899, 4; "The Humber Beach," *The Globe*, 2 September 1899, 13. On building a seawall: Item 143, 22 January 1906, 37, Toronto City Council Minutes, 1906, CTA. See "For Water Front Drive," *The Toronto Daily Star*, 21 May 1906, 2; and "The Sea Wall Project," *The Globe*, 24 July 1906, 12. For protection of shoreline: Report no. 11, Committee on Works, 14 June 1907, 858, City Council Appendix B, 1907, CTA; "The Western Sea Wall," *The Globe*, 9 September 1908, 3. On protecting bathing: Item 333, 27 May 1907, 162, Toronto City Council Minutes 1907, CTA. For the Guild of Civic Art: Weaver, "The Modern City," 60–61; "Report on a Comprehensive Plan for Systematic Civic Improvements in Toronto 1909, A Foreword," Toronto Guild of Civic Art Fonds 1015, SC 15 box 1, file 3, box 146634, CTA.

61 "The Whole Harbor Plan, Endorsed by Seven Cabinet Ministers, Is the Work of a Toronto Boy, E.L. Cousins," *Toronto News*, 14 November 1912, Research Subject Reference File: Waterfront Development Plan, 1912 folder, PTA. For a similar description, see *Financial Saturday Night*, 23 November 1912, Research Subject Reference File: Waterfront Development Plan, 1912 folder, PTA. The precise length of the waterfront varies in accounts: the Toronto Harbour Commission (THC)

framed it in terms of the length of the waterfront boulevard, which is listed as 12 miles:, see E.L. Cousins, Toronto Harbour Improvements, Cousins, 3 February 1921, 3, Research Subject Reference File: Cousins, E.L. "Toronto Harbour Improvements," 1921 folder, PTA.

62 Charles Mulford Robinson, *The Improvement of Towns and Cities or The Practical Basis of Civic Aesthetics* (New York: G.P. Putnam's Sons, 1901), 17.

63 John S. Pipkin, "'Chasing Rainbows' in Albany: City Beautiful, City Practical, 1900–1925," *Journal of Planning History* 7, no. 4 (2008): 328.

64 On degradation, see Desfor, Vesalon, and Laidley, "Establishing the Toronto Harbour Commission." Or to put this in Foucauldian terms, it would render the space of the waterfront knowable and manageable: see Gunn, "From Hegemony to Governmentality," 713.

65 "Putting a New Front on Toronto," *Canadian Magazine* 42 (1913–1914): 213, Research Subject Reference File: Waterfront Development Plan, 1912 Folder, PTA.

66 *Christian Science Monitor*, 1606-G-1, page 3, Research Subject Reference File: Waterfront Development Plan, 1912 folder, PTA.

67 Jason Gilliland, "Muddy Shore to Modern Port: Redimensioning the Montreal Waterfront Time-space," *Canadian Geographer/Le Géographe canadien* 48, no 4 (2004): 450.

68 See, for example, *Christian Science Monitor*, 1606-G-1, and "Putting a New Front on Toronto," *Canadian Magazine* 42 (1913–1914): 213, Research Subject Reference File: Waterfront Development Plan, 1912 folder, PTA. On the role of photography to shape meaning, see Jae Emerling, *Photography: History and Theory* (New York: Routledge, 2012), 34.

69 The Olmsted brothers' company spent a few weeks developing the plan in consultation with the harbour commission. Typically, they would been involved in the implementation but in this case it appears the Olmsteds turned the project entirely over to the harbour commission to develop. For the Olmsteds' typical approach, see Susan Klaus, "All in the Family: The Olmsted Office and the Business of Landscape Architecture," *Landscape Journal* 16, no. 1 (1997): 86.

70 *Financial Saturday Night*, 23 November 1912, Research Subject Reference File: Waterfront Development Plan, 1912 folder, PTA.

71 Charles Mulford Robinson, *Modern Civic Art or The City Made Beautiful*, 4th ed. (New York: G.P. Putnam's Sons, 1918), 61, 121.

72 "The Toronto Harbor Commissioners Waterfront Development," *The Evening Telegram*, 14 November 1912, Research Subject Reference File: Waterfront Development Plan, 1912 folder, PTA.

73 E.L. Cousins, Consulting Engineer, Toronto Harbour Improvements, 2 May 1925, 21–22, Research Subject Reference File: 1840-C-1-1 Reports E.L. Cousins. C.E. folder, PTA.

74 O'Mara, *Shaping Urban Waterfronts*, 40.

75 "The Toronto Harbor Commissioners Waterfront Development," *The Evening Telegram*, 14 November 1912, Research Subject Reference File: Waterfront Development Plan, 1912 folder, PTA. See also "The Whole Harbor Plan, Endorsed by Seven Cabinet Ministers, Is the Work of a Toronto Boy, E.L. Cousins," *The Toronto News*, 14 November 1912, Research Subject Reference File: Waterfront Development Plan, 1912 folder, PTA. On the tenacity of place, see Shields, *Places on the Margin*, 52–53.

76 "City, by Harbour Scheme, Would Add . . .," *The Telegram*, 14 November 1912, Research Subject Reference File: Waterfront Development Plan, 1912 folder, PTA. The newspapers all showed the same map, so the highlights must have been added by the harbour commission.

77 Letter to E.L. Cousins, chief engineer, Toronto Harbour Commission, from Norman D. Wilson, surveys engineer, Toronto Harbour Commission, 6 January 1915, 2, Research Subject Reference File: Sunnyside folder, PTA.

78 Ibid., 3.

79 Letter to Toronto Harbour Commissioners from Alfred Chapman, waterfront consulting architect, 29 April 1915, 1–2, RG 3/3, box 99, folder 1, Research Subject Reference File: Arthur Chapman Folder, PTA.

80 "The Toronto Harbor Commissioners Waterfront Development," *The Evening Telegram*, 14 November 1912, Research Subject Reference File: Waterfront Development Plan, 1912 folder, PTA; Lionel H. Clarke, *The Toronto Waterfront Development 1912–1920* (Toronto: Toronto Harbour Commission, [1920?]), 31.

81 Letter to Toronto Harbour Commissioners from Alfred Chapman, waterfront consulting architect, 29 April 1915, 3–4, Research Subject Reference File: Arthur Chapman folder, PTA.

82 On the rationale for an amusement park, see E.L. Cousins, consulting engineer, Toronto Harbour Improvements, 2 May 1925, 22, Research Subject Reference File: 1840-C-1-1 Reports E.L. Cousins. C.E. folder, PTA; E.L. Cousins, Report on Boulevard Diversion and Revision of Recreational Areas Sunnyside Beach, 3 October 1932, 3, Research Subject Reference File: 1840-C-1-1 Reports E.L. Cousins. C.E. folder, PTA; Address of R. Home Smith, Esq., Chairman of the Board of Harbour Commissioners, in relation to harbour development matters at a special meeting of the city council held on the 3rd of April 1923, 6, Research Subject Reference File: Robert Home Smith folder, PTA. On the financial need for an amusement park, see O'Mara, *Shaping Urban Waterfronts*, 40–41, 57.

83 "Sunnyside, Once the Most Popular Amusement Park in Toronto," *The Star*, 2 March 1956; Bruce West, "Nostalgia: A Fond Farewell, Sunnyside," *The Globe and Mail*, 2 February 1956; "Good-by to Sunnyside," *The Star*, 23 January 1956; "Only Memories to Stay as Sunnyside Crumbles," *The Star*, 2 March 1956. And for a more contrarian view: "Get Rid of the Nuisance," *The Globe and Mail*, 14 January 1955.

84 "Engines, Dredges and Divers Busy Fixing Sunnyside Stage for Summer's Joyous Play," *The Globe*, 27 April 1922, 13.

85 "Pump Will Not Stop Sunnyside Bathing," *The Globe*, 1 May 1916, 8.

86 "Warning Signs Ready for the Lake Front," *The Toronto Daily Star*, 9 August 1916, 8. Shields, *Places on the Margin*, 52–53, 63.

87 The experience is similar to what residents in the village of Iroquois experienced when the St. Lawrence River was flooded to create the St. Lawrence Seaway. See Joy Parr, "Notes for a More Sensuous History of Twentieth-Century Canada," *Canadian Historical Review* 82, no. 4 (2001); Joy Parr, *Sensing Changes: Technologies, Environments, and the Everyday, 1953–2003* (Vancouver: UBC Press, 2010), 1–20.

88 "Treacherous Beach Takes Another Life," *The Globe*, 8 August 1916, 6.

89 "Pump Will Not Stop Sunnyside Bathing," *The Globe*, 1 May 1916, 8.

90 "Warning Signs Ready for the Lake Front," *The Toronto Daily Star*, 9 August 1916, 8.

91 Ibid. "The Mayor and the Harbor Trust," *The Globe*, 15 August 1916, 4.

92 "Warning Signs ready for the Lake Front," *The Toronto Daily Star*, 9 August 1916, 8; "The Mayor and the Harbor Trust," *The Globe*, 15 August 1916, 4. Daytime highs ranged into the 30s during much of July and August: see Climate.weather.gc.ca.

93 For plans to extend the storm sewers, see E.L. Cousins, Toronto Harbour Improvements, Cousins, 3 February 1921, 9, Research Subject Reference File: Cousins, E.L. "Toronto Harbour Improvements,"

1921 folder, PTA. For drownings linked to the storm sewers, see Walter Johnson: "Boy Drowned at Sunnyside," *The Globe*, 21 June 1920, 9; Life Saving and Police Patrol Second Annual Report, 1920, 26, 1840-L-1-1, RG 7/1 box 1, PTA; "City's Lifesaving Equipment Scored by Coroner's Jury," *The Globe*, 29 June 1920, 9. For another example from 1921 see, for 22 August 1921, Life Saving and Police Patrol Third Annual Report, 1921, Extracts from the Log of the Life Saving and Police Patrol Department for the Month of August 1921, 4, 1840-L-1-1, RG 7/1 box 1, PTA; "City's Lifesaving Equipment Scored by Coroner's Jury," *The Globe*, 29 June 1920, 9.

94 Letter to E.L. Cousins, chief engineer and manager, Toronto Harbour Commission, from W.A. Littlejohn, city clerk, City of Toronto, 22 June 1920, in RG 313 box 53, folder 12, Bathing—Sunnyside Free Bathing Area 1912–1935, no. 101.S.2, vol. 1, PTA.

95 Letter to W.A. Littlejohn, city clerk, City of Toronto, from E.L. Cousins, chief engineer and manager, Toronto Harbour Commission, July 9, 1920, in RG 313 box 53, folder 12, Bathing—Sunnyside Free Bathing Area 1912–1935, no. 101.S.2, vol. 1, PTA.

96 7 May 1925, Extracts from the Log of the Life Saving and Police Patrol Department for the Month of May, page 1, Life Saving and Police Patrol Annual Report, 1925, 1840-L-1-1, RG 7/1 box 1, PTA. And for a similar example, see 26 July 1926, Extracts from the Log of the Life Saving and Police Patrol Department for the Month of July, page 11, Life Saving and Police Patrol Annual Report, 1926, 1840-L-1-1, RG 7/1 box 1, PTA.

97 Lookout Tower, Location of Life Saving Stations, Appliances, and Bathing Areas, Life Saving and Police Patrol Second Annual Report, 1920, 10, 21, 1840-L-1-1, RG 7/1 box 1, PTA.

98 Location of Life Saving Stations, Appliances, and Bathing Areas, Life Saving and Police Patrol Second Annual Report, 1920, 9, 1840-L-1-1, RG 7/1 box 1, PTA. Establishing the phone network was one of the harbour commission's first concerns. See letter to Frank Kennedy, Bell Telephone Company of Canada, from E.L. Cousins, chief engineer and manager, Toronto Harbour Commission, 11 August 1919, folder 4, general correspondence, 1914-1919, RG 7/5/3 box 1, PTA.

99 Life Saving and Police Patrol Second Annual Report, 1920, 7–10, 1840-L-1-1, RG 7/1 box 1, PTA.

100 Ibid.

101 Dean, *Governmentality*, 10–12, 30–33; Michel Foucault, *Discipline and Punish: The Birth of the Prison*, trans. Alan Sheridan (New York: Vintage Books, 1995), 202–5, 209, 211–12.

102 Foucault, *Discipline and Punish*, 215–16, 219.

103 Life Saving and Police Patrol Annual Report, 1927, 7, 1840-L-1-1, RG 7/1 box 1, PTA.

104 Life Saving and Police Patrol Second Annual Report, 1920, 15, 1840-L-1-1, RG 7/1 box 1, PTA.

105 Life Saving and Police Patrol Second Annual Report, 1920, 35, 1840-L-1-1, RG 7/1 box 1, PTA.

106 See, for example, the 1921 logbook, 30, 1840-L-1-1 RG 7 box 2, PTA.

107 7 July 1928, Extracts from the Log of the Life Saving and Police Patrol Department for the Month of July, 2–3, Life Saving and Police Patrol Annual Report, 1928, 1840-L-1-1, RG 7/1 box 1, PTA.

108 5 July 1925, Extracts from the Log of the Life Saving and Police Patrol Department for the Month of July, 1, Life Saving and Police Patrol Annual Report, 1925, 1840-L-1-1, RG 7/1 box 1, PTA.

109 Life Saving and Police Patrol Second Annual Report, 1920, 15, 1840-L-1-1, RG 7/1 box 1, PTA.

110 Life Saving and Police Patrol Third Annual Report, 1921, 2, 1840-L-1-1, RG 7/1 box 1, PTA.

111 Ibid.

112 Life Saving and Police Patrol Annual Report, 1923, 3, 1840-L-1-1, RG 7/1 Box 1, PTA.

113 See Allan Levine, *Toronto: Biography of a City* (Madeira Park, BC: Douglas and McIntyre, 2014), 130.

114 25 July 1921, Life Saving and Police Patrol Third Annual Report, 1921, Extracts from the Log of the Life Saving and Police Patrol Department for the Month of July 1921, 5, 1840-L-1-1, RG 7/1 box 1, PTA.

115 18 July 1925, Extracts from the Log of the Life Saving and Police Patrol Department for the Month of July, 6, Life Saving and Police Patrol Annual Report, 1925, 1840-L-1-1, RG 7/1 box 1, PTA. See also 29 June 1926, Extracts from the Log of the Life Saving and Police Patrol Department for the Month of June, 4–5, Life Saving and Police Patrol Annual Report, 1926, 1840-L-1-1, RG 7/1 box 1, PTA. For other examples, see 24 July 1926, Extracts from the Log of the Life Saving and Police Patrol Department for the Month of July, 9–10, Life Saving and Police Patrol Annual Report, 1926, 1840-L-1-1, RG 7/1 box 1, PTA.

116 Letter to G.T. Clark, assistant manager, Toronto Harbour Commission, from Austin P. Saunders, superintendent of the lifesaving and police patrol service, 30 March 1923, in RG 313 box 53, folder, 12 Bathing—Sunnyside Free Bathing Area 1912–1935, no. 101.S.2, vol. 1, PTA.

117 See Bylaw 12774, 29 July 1930, 805–806, Toronto City Council Appendix B, 1930, and Conference with His Worship the Mayor ..., 26th May 1932, at 10 a.m., By-Laws Bathing By-laws 1904–1935, 3/3 box 343, folder 7 (290-B-1, vol. 1), PTA. The Toronto Harbour Commissioners By-Law #20, Passed 23rd, June, 1932, Approved by Order-In-Council, P.C. 1552—13th July, 1932, By-Laws Bathing By-laws 1904–1935, RG 3/3 Box 343, Folder 7, (290-B-1, Volume 1), PTA.

118 Toronto Harbour Commissioners Waterfront, 22 February 1933, (10243) By-Laws Bathing By-laws 1904-1935, RG 3/3 box 343, folder 7, (290-B-1, vol. 1), PTA. See Toronto Harbour Commissioners Waterfront Developments: Plan illustrating bathing bylaw #20 dated June 13th 1934, 290-B-1 By-Laws Bathing By-laws 1904–1935, RG 3/3 box 343, folder 7, (290-B-1, vol. 1), PTA.

119 I have used the city's numbers, which begin in 1895, for consistency. After 1920 both the city and the harbour commission made an increasing effort to differentiate between people who were known to have drowned and people who were found dead in the water (and may or may not have died by other means). That nuance illustrates how the city and harbour commission were making an effort to take responsibility for bathers but also wanted to be clear when deaths or drowning could not have been prevented by the lifesaving service. For comparison, the median number of deaths per year was 18 prior to 1919 and 12 after 1919: Toronto City Council Minutes/Appendix for 1895 to 1935, CTA, fonds 2, series 60, items 889-903 and 2460-2470, City of Toronto Archives (CTA) and Toronto Life Saving and Police Patrol Annual Reports, 1840-L-1-1, RG 7/1 box 1, PTA.

120 Subject: Bathing Suits, letter to general manager, Toronto Harbour Commissioners, from,H. Lang, superintendent, lifesaving and police patrol services, 13 June 1934, By-Laws Bathing By-laws 1904–1935, RG 3/3 box 343, folder 7, (290-B-1, vol. 1), PTA.

121 PC 1217, Privy Council Canada, E.J. Lemaire, Clerk of the Privy Council, 13 June 1934, By-Laws Bathing By-laws 1904–1935, RG 3/3 box 343, folder 7, (290-B-1, vol. 1), PTA.

122 Letter to J.G. Langton, general manager, Toronto Harbour Commission, from A.R. Tibbits, Supervisor of Harbour Commission, Department of Marine, 28 May 1934, By-Laws Bathing By-laws 1904–1935, RG 3/3 box 343, folder 7, (290-B-1, vol. 1), PTA.

123 290-B-1, letter to Inspector Austin Mitchell from J.G. Langton, general manager, Toronto Harbour Commission, 19 June 1934, By-Laws Bathing By-laws 1904–1935, RG 3/3 box 343, folder 7, (290-B-1, vol. 1), PTA.

124 For the police response, see letter to J.G. Langton, general manager, Toronto Harbour Commission, Austin Mitchell, Inspector No. 1 Division, 20 June 1934, By-Laws Bathing By-laws 1904–1935, RG 3/3 box 343, folder 7, (290-B-1, vol. 1), PTA. For *The Star*, see "All in the Life of a Censor," *The Star*, 23 June 1934, By-Laws Bathing By-laws 1904-1935, RG 3/3 box 343, folder 7, (290-B-1, vol. 1), PTA.

125 "Bathers and the Law," *The Star*, 19 July 1935, By-Laws Bathing By-laws 1904–1935, RG 3/3 box 343, folder 7, (290-B-1, vol. 1), PTA.

126 Bathing Prosecutions, letter to J.G. Langton, general manager, Toronto Harbour Commission, from Josiah Max Bullen, McMaster Montgomery Fleury and Co., 24 July 1934, By-Laws Bathing By-laws 1904–1935, RG 3/3 box 343, folder 7, (290-B-1, vol. 1), PTA.

127 Similar battles over bathing suits played out across the Atlantic and Australia: see Barbour, *Winnipeg Beach*, 108–10; Immerso, *Coney Island*, 158; Metusela and Waitt, *Tourism and Australian Beach Cultures*, 132–35.

128 "Morality Squad Stands Pat on Taboos on Bathing Suits: Scanty Costumes on Beach Streets would mean arrest on Yonge St." *The Star*, 13 July 1935, By-Laws Bathing By-laws 1904–1935, RG 3/3 box 343, folder 7, (290-B-1, vol. 1), PTA.

129 Ibid.

130 Life Saving and Police Patrol Annual Report, 1935, 14, 1840-L-1-1, RG 7/1 box 1, PTA. On police stepping back: By-law #20 Section B, letter to E.L. Cousins, general manager, Toronto Harbour Commission, from H. Lang, superintendent, Life Saving and Police Patrol Service, 17 January 1936, contd, By-laws Bathing by-law 1936–1975, RG 3/3 box 373, folder 8, (290-B-1 vol. 1), PTA.

131 By-law #20 Section B, letter to E.L. Cousins, general manager, Toronto Harbour Commission, from H. Lang, superintendent, Life Saving and Police Patrol Service, 17 January 1936, By-laws Bathing by-law 1936–1975, RG 3/3 box 373, folder 8, (290-B-1, vol. 1 contd), PTA. On sports associations and Hall, see Memorandum for file, 17 January 1936, By-laws Bathing by-law 1936-1975, 1 contd, RG 3/3 box 373, folder 8, (290-B-1, vol.), PTA. For sports associations, see By-law #20 Section B, letter to E.L. Cousins, general manager, Toronto Harbour Commission, from H. Lang, superintendent, Life Saving and Police Patrol Service, 17 January 1936, By-laws Bathing by-law 1936–1975, RG 3/3 box 373, folder 8, (290-B-1, vol. 1 contd), PTA; Letter to A.R. Tibbits, deputy minister of marine, from E.L. Cousins, general manager, Toronto Harbour Commission, 3 March 1936, By-laws Bathing by-law 1936–1975, RG 3/3 box 373, folder 8, (290-B-1, vol. 1 contd), PTA.

132 Draft No. 22 a by-law, By-laws Bathing by-law 1936–1975, contd, RG 3/3 box 373, folder 8, (290-B-1, vol. 1), PTA.

133 Letter to the chairman and members, Toronto Harbour Commission, from E.L. Cousins, general manager, Toronto Harbour Commission, 10 March 1936, By-laws Bathing by-law 1936–1975, RG 3/3 box 373, folder 8, (290-B-1, vol. 1 contd), PTA.

134 James Woycke, *Au Naturel: The History of Nudism in Canada* (Etobicoke, ON: Federation of Canadian Naturists, 2003), 24. For a broader look at the effort to police the Sons of Freedom, see John McLaren, "The State, Child Snatching, and the Law: The Seizure and Indoctrination of Sons of Freedom Children in British Columbia, 1950–60," in *Regulating Lives: Historical Essays on the State, Society, the Individual, and the Law*, ed. Robert J. Menzies, John McLaren, and Dorothy E. Chunn, (Vancouver: UBC Press, 2002); and Veronika Makarova, "Doukhobor 'Freedom Seeker' Nudism: Exploring the Sociocultural Roots," *Culture and Religion* 14, no. 2 (2013): 131–45. See also J.C. Yerbury, "The 'Sons of Freedom' Doukhobors and the Canadian State Canadian," *Ethnic Studies/Études Ethniques au Canada* 16, no. 2 (1984): 47–70.

135 Review of the Law of Indecency and Nudity 1999, Uniform Law Conference of Canada, http://www.ulcc.ca/en/annual-meetings/365-1999-winnipeg-mb/criminal-section-documents/1841-review-of-the-law-of-indecency-and-nudity?showall=1&limitstart= (accessed 23 July 2016).

136 Bob Tarantino, *Under Arrest: Canadian Laws You Won't Believe* (Toronto: Dundurn, 2007), 92; Review of the Law of Indecency and Nudity 1999, Uniform Law Conference of Canada.

137 E. George Smith, "Doukhobor Parades Heavily Penalized: Bathers Affected?" *The Globe*, 25 July 1931, 1.

138 Review of the Law of Indecency and Nudity 1999, Uniform Law Conference of Canada.

139 House of Commons Debates, 17th Parliament, 2nd Session: Vol. 4, Page 4134, 24 July 1931.

140 Ibid., 4135.

141 Tarantino, *Under Arrest*, 93; "Decency Statute Altered in Senate," *The Globe*, 30 July 1931, 1.

142 Address of R. Home Smith, Esq., Chairman of the Board of Harbour Commissioners, in relation to harbour development matters at a special meeting of the city council held on the 3rd of April 1923, 6, Research Subject Reference File: Robert Home Smith folder, PTA. There were practical reasons for going big: the concrete bathing pavilion was cheaper to insure than a wood structure.

143 Mike Filey, *I Remember Sunnyside: The Rise and Fall of a Magical Era* (Toronto: Dundurn Group, 1996), 48.

144 "The 'Sunnyside' Development of the Toronto Harbour Commission," 3, Research Subject Reference File: Sunnyside Folder, PTA.

145 "The 'Sunnyside' Development of the Toronto Harbour Commission," 3, Research Subject Reference File: Sunnyside Folder, PTA.

146 "The 'Sunnyside' Development of the Toronto Harbour Commission," 3, Research Subject Reference File: Sunnyside Folder, PTA. For fence, see Bathing Pavilion, Sunnyside, Toronto Harbour Commissioners, Toronto 1920–1922, 200547-1, series 544, file 52 E 00673L 94, CTA.

147 Filey, *I Remember Sunnyside*, 53; "The 'Sunnyside' Development of the Toronto Harbour Commission," 3, Research Subject Reference File: Sunnyside Folder, PTA.

148 For first aid, see "The 'Sunnyside' Development of the Toronto Harbour Commission," page 3, Research Subject Reference File: Sunnyside Folder, PTA.

149 Sunnyside, children's pond from tower, date of creation, 6 August 1925, item 5924, *Globe and Mail* Fonds 1266, CTA.

150 "The Children's Pool (Sunnyside)," *The Star Weekly*, 1 August 1925.

151 Letter from Charles Hastings, medical officer of health, to Daniel Chisholm, property commissioner, 9 August 1927, RG 313 box 53, folder 12, Bathing—Sunnyside Free Bathing Area 1912–1935, no. 101.S.2, vol. 1, PTA.

152 We can think of this space as a regionally dispersed panoptic: Michel Foucault, "Questions of Geography," in *Power/Knowledge*, 72–73. On using the beach to contain behaviour, see Fiske, *Reading the Popular*, 76

153 "The "Sunnyside" Development of the Toronto Harbour Commission," 2, Research Subject Reference File: Sunnyside Folder, PTA.

154 "Bathing Beaches Are Now in Full Swing," *The Toronto Daily Star*, 14 July 1922, 14.

155 "The First Dip of the Season," Murray-Kay Company Limited, *The Globe*, 30 June 1922, 16.

156 "Bathing Beaches Are Now in Full Swing," *The Toronto Daily Star*, 14 July 1922, 14. *The Star*'s "Women's Column" argued "almost anyone can afford twenty-five cents" but it is clear the media had a distinct image of who "anyone" might be: see "From 'Swimming" Hole to Baths de luxe," *The Toronto Daily Star*, 30 June 1922, 14.

157 "Bathing Beaches Are Now in Full Swing," *The Toronto Daily Star*, 14 July 1922, 14.

158 "From 'Swimming' Hole to Baths de luxe," *The Toronto Daily Star*, 30 June 1922, 14.

159 "The Sunnyside Beaches," *The Globe*, 29 March 1922, 6.

160 "Bathing Beaches Are Now in Full Swing," *The Toronto Daily Star*, 14 July 1922, 14.

161 "From 'Swimming' Hole to Baths de luxe," *The Toronto Daily Star*, 30 June 1922, 14.

162 See, for example, "Happy Bathers Swarm the Island Beach on These Unprecedented Summer Days," *The Toronto Daily Star*, 12 August 1916, 5.

163 For an example of the camera's ability to shape rather than simply record events, see Lynne Bell, "Unsettling Acts: Photography as Decolonizing Testimony in Centennial Memory," in *The Cultural Work of Photography in Canada*, ed. Carol Payne and Andrea Kunard (Montreal: McGill-Queen's University Press, 2011), 168.

164 Sunnyside bathing station, date of creation [1924?], item 0219A, William James Family Fonds 1244, CTA.

165 For a look at the spatial constraints faced by the commission, see Toronto Harbour Commissioners: Plan Showing Location of Leases and Licenses at Sunnyside Beach, February 20, 1952, Research Subject Reference File: Sunnyside Folder, PTA.

166 "Bulletins to Tell Water's Temperature," *The Globe*, 14 July 1922, 11; Sunnyside Beach, Research Subject Reference File: Sunnyside Folder, PTA; E.L. Cousins, Toronto Harbour Improvements, Cousins, 3 February 1921, 9, Research Subject Reference File: Cousins, E.L. "Toronto Harbour Improvements," 1921 folder, PTA.

167 Letter to A.B. Horwitz, city planning engineer, City of Duluth, from general manager, Toronto Harbour Commission, dated 15 January 1935, Bathing General 1916–1958, RG 313 box 53, folder 10, no. 101.G.1, vol. 1, PTA.

168 "Bathing Beaches Are Now in Full Swing," *The Toronto Daily Star*, 14 July 1922, 14. And it was not the first time the joke had been made: "From 'Swimming' Hole to Baths de luxe," *The Toronto Daily Star*, 30 June 1922, 14.

169 "From 'Swimming" Hole to Baths de luxe," *The Toronto Daily Star*, 30 June 1922, 14.

170 "Chlorinate Beaches," *The Globe*, 5 July 1924, 18.

171 "Water at Bathing Stations May Be Chlorinated," *The Globe*, 5 July 1924, 14.

172 "Chlorination Effective Where Water Is Confined," *The Toronto Daily Star*, July 1924, 1.

173 Frank R. Shaw, "Trends in Bathing Beach and Swimming Pool Sanitation," *Canadian Public Health Journal* 23, no. 4 (1932): 154.

174 On the push for a more hygienic environment, see Katherine Ashenburg, *The Dirt on Clean: An Unsanitized History* (Toronto: A.A. Knopf Canada, 2007); and Suellen Hoy, *Chasing Dirt: The American Pursuit of Cleanliness* (New York: Oxford University Press, 1995).

175 On New York, see Andrea Renner, "A Nation That Bathes Together: New York City's Progressive Era Public Baths," *Journal of the Society of Architectural Historians* 67, no. 4 (2008), 504, 520–21. Ashenburg, *The Dirt on Clean*, 219–20; Jacqueline S. Wilkie, "Submerged Sensuality: Technology and Perceptions of Bathing," *Journal of Social History* 19, no. 4 (1986): 655.

176 In 1920, for example, the city noted that 120,000 persons used the showers at the Harrison Baths:, see Board of Control, Report no. 7, 7 April 1921, 313, Toronto City Council Appendix A, 192, CTA.

177 David Wencer, "Historicist: Swimming at the Minnies," *Torontoist*, 24 May 2014, torontoist.com/2014/05/historicist-swimming-at-the-minnies/ (accessed on 13 December 2017).

178 Report no. 10 of the Local Board of Health, 12 September 1918, pages 741–43, Toronto City Council Appendix A, 1918, TCA.

179 "Sunnyside Swimming Tank," file RG 17/3, 1–2, Research Subject Reference File: Sunnyside Folder, PTA.

180 See 1–3 August 1925, Humber Station—First Aid Cases, page 1, Life Saving and Police Patrol Annual Report, 1925, 1840-L-1-1, RG 7/1 box 1, PTA.

181 Humber Station, First Aid Cases, July, 1, Life Saving and Police Patrol Annual Report, 1926, 1840-L-1-1, RG 7/1 box 1, PTA. For example, see 1 July 1927 13 July 1927, Sunnyside Beach First Aid Cases, 1–2, Life Saving and Police Patrol Annual Report, 1927, 1840-L-1-1, RG 7/1 box 1, PTA.

182 Life Saving and Police Patrol Annual Report, 1928, 4, 1840-L-1-1, RG 7/1 box 1, PTA.

183 This was the process through the 1920s: by the end of that decade permanent stations started to be built.

184 Letter to D. Chisholm, commissioner of property, City of Toronto, from J.G. Langton, general manager, Toronto Harbour Commission, dated 21 March 1928, 2, RG 313 box 53, folder 10, no. 101.G.1, vol. 1, Bathing General 1916–1958 folder, PTA.

185 Letter to D. Chisholm, commissioner of property, City of Toronto, from J.G. Langton, general manager, Toronto Harbour Commission, dated 19 May 1928, RG 313 box 53, folder 10, no. 101.G.1, vol. 1, Bathing General 1916–1958 folder, PTA.

186 Hastings sent the letter to the harbour commission, which quickly passed it on to the city's property department, the unit responsible for free bathing: letter to Toronto Harbour Commissioner from Charles J. Hastings, medical officer of health, City of Toronto, dated 4 August 1922, in RG 313 box 53, folder 12, Bathing—Sunnyside Free Bathing Area 1912–1935, (no. 101.S.2, vol. 1), PTA.

187 Letter to J.G. Langton, general manager, Toronto Harbour Commissioners, from D. Chisholm, commissioner of property, City of Toronto, dated 9 March 1928, 1, RG 313 box 53, folder 10, (no. 101.G.1, vol. 1), Bathing General 1916—1958 folder, PTA.

188 Ibid.

189 Letter to the Commissioner of Property, City of Toronto, from J.G. Langton, general manager, Toronto Harbour Commission, 12 July 1928, in RG 313 box 53, folder 13, Bathing—Sunnyside Free Bathing Areas 1912–1935, (101.S.2, vol. 1), PTA.

190 For quote: letter to J.G. Langton, general manager, Toronto Harbour Commission, from D. Chisholm, property commissioner, City of Toronto, 22 September 1928, in RG 313 box 53, folder 13, Bathing—Sunnyside Free Bathing Areas 1912–1935, (101.S.2, vol). 1, PTA. New site: item 65, letter to J.G. Langton, general manager, Toronto Harbuor Commission, from D. Chisholm, property commissioner, City of Toronto, 10 April 1929, in RG 313 box 53, folder 13, Bathing—Sunnyside Free Bathing Areas 1912–1935, (101.S.2, vol. 1), PTA; Item 67, Minute 6666 Meeting of 18 April 1929, in RG 313 box 53, folder 13, Bathing—Sunnyside Free Bathing Areas 1912–1935, (101.S.2, vol. 1), PTA.

191 Filey, *I Remember Sunnyside*, 90.

192 "At Sunnyside Yesterday," *The Toronto Daily Star*, 14 July 1921, 3; "Summer Scenes at Sunnyside and Kew Beach," *The Globe*, 28 July 1924, 9.

193 File 5130007, fonds 70, series 330, sheet 1V, folder 32, box 158725, CTA.

194 See, for example, Bathing Children from Free Cars on Sunnyside, Alan Howard Fonds 1548, series 393, item 14341, 1 August 1917, CTA.

195 This was an effort to control moral behaviour through the built environment, a hallmark of the City Beautiful movement: William H. Wilson, *The City Beautiful Movement* (Baltimore: Johns Hopkins University Press, 1989), 73, 79–81, 85. It was also an effort to control the behaviour of a growing ethnically diverse population in North American cities and fence it into what were considered white Anglo-Saxon norms; see Emily Talen, *New Urbanism and American Planning: The Conflict of Cultures* (New York and London: Routledge Taylor and Francis Group, 2005), 113, 124. For a look at the effort to contain ethnicity in Toronto through the parks movement, see Phillip Gordon MacKintosh, "The 'Occult Relation between Man and the Vegetable': Transcendentalism, Immigrants, and Park Planning in Toronto, c. 1900," in *Rethinking The Great White North: Race, Nature, and the Historical*

Geographies of Whiteness in Canada, ed. Andrew Baldwin, Laura Cameron, and Audrey Kobayashi (Vancouver: UBC Press, 2011), 85–106. Fiske suggests how implementing a system of symbols and commodities was an attempt to define the beach experience: see Fiske, *Understanding Popular Culture*, 11, 14.

196 E.L. Cousins, Report to The Hamilton Harbour Commissioners on Waterfront Development, 15 December 1919, 8, Research Subject Reference File: Cousins, Edward L. folder, PTA.

197 For the Sunnyside Pavilion, see Toronto Harbour Commission Investigation, 1926, Sunnyside Pavilion, 15 December 1926, 12, RG 17/3, Research Subject Reference File: Sunnyside Folder, PTA. For the amusement park, see "The 'Sunnyside' Development of the Toronto Harbour Commission," page 8?, Research Subject Reference File: Alfred Chapman folder, PTA. This appears to have been a "construction" magazine and would have been printed in 1922; see letter to J.B. Jardine, Harbour Commission Building, from W.H. Hewitt, advertising manager, construction, 24 October 1922. Research Subject Reference File: Alfred Chapman Folder, PTA. E.L. Cousins, Consulting Engineer, Toronto Harbour Improvements, 2 May 1925, 8 (see also page 22 for similar comments), Research Subject Reference File: 1840-C-1-1 Reports E.L. Cousins, C.E. folder, PTA.

198 Letter to E.L. Cousins, chief engineer and manager, Toronto Harbour Commission, from R. Home Smith, chairperson, Toronto Harbour Commission, 10 September 1923, Research Subject Reference File: Sunnyside folder, PTA.

199 "Boys of East End Hold Fashion Parade," *The Globe*, 18 April 1927, 10; Mike Filey, *More Toronto Sketches "The Way We Were"* (Toronto: Dundurn Press, 1993), 80.

200 Kasson, *Amusing the Million*, 44.

201 James O'Mara, *The Toronto Harbour Commisioners' Financial Arrangements and City Waterfront Development, 1910 to* 1950, (Discussion Paper No. 30. Nov. 1984, York University, Department of Geography).

202 See in particular Mike Filey's *I Remember Sunnyside.*

203 The phrase is repeated uncritically in Toronto histories and popular writing on the beach: see, for example, Levine, *Toronto*, 150; Filey, *More Toronto Sketches*, 84; Dahn A. Batchelor, *Whistling in the Face of Robbers: The Life and Times of Dahn A. Batchelor* (Bloomington: iUniverse, 2012), 221; Fairburn, *Along the Shore*, 362.

204 Toronto Harbour Commission, Public Affairs Department, *Toronto Harbour, the Passing Years* (Toronto: Toronto Harbour Commissioners, 1985), 6.

205 Shields, *Places on the Margin*, 53.

206 Mike Filey's *I Remember Sunnyside* is the best example of this.

207 For example, Immerso, *Coney Island: The People's Playground*, 8.

208 Filey, *I Remember Sunnyside*, 56–57.

209 Latham, "Packaging Woman," 162, 165; Peiss, *Cheap Amusements*, 186.

210 Filey, *I Remember Sunnyside*, 81.

211 Walton, "Respectability Takes a Holiday," 176–93, 176.

212 Ibid.

213 Bryant Simon, *Boardwalk of Dreams: Atlantic City and the Fate of Urban America* (New York: Oxford University Press, 2004), 13, 21, 24. For the broader discussion, see Nasaw, *Going Out*, 47, 238; Eric Avila, *Popular Culture in the Age of White Flight: Fear and Fantasy in Suburban Los Angeles* (Berkeley: University of California Press, 2006), 16.

214 Gibson, *More Than an Island*, 171.

215 Royden Loewen and Gerald Friesen, *Immigrants in Prairie Cities: Ethnic Diversity in Twentieth-Century Canada* (Toronto: University of Toronto Press, 2009), 4–13.

216 Loewen and Friesen, 4.

217 Careless, *Toronto to 1918*, 202.

218 Levine, *Toronto*, 123–25.

219 Gibson, *More Than an Island*, 190; Levine, *Toronto*, 167. For examples of access, see "Drowned in Long Pond," *The Globe*, 28 June 1901, 10; and "Dangers of the Lagoons," *The Globe*, 6 July 1921, 6.

220 Levine, *Toronto*, 167–68.

221 Levine, 165–67.

222 As quoted in Filey, *I Remember Sunnyside*, 78.

223 "Sunnyside's Fame Carries to Ottawa," *The Globe*, 6 May 1925, 12.

224 Journalist Ron Csillag has pointed to the challenge of finding tangible examples of such signs, but that doesn't change the anti-semitism that drove the rumours of their existance. Csillag, "Perspectives: 'No Dogs, No Jews'—No Evidence," *The Canadian Jewish News*, 8 April 2015, https://www.cjnews.com/news/perspectives-no-dogs-no-jews-no-evidence viewed on 2 August 2019. Similar signs were reported at Winnipeg Beach, but again we do not have tangible proof of their existence: see Barbour, *Winnipeg Beach*, 73.

225 As cited in Kevin Plummer, "Boyhood, Summers, and the City," *Historicist*, 4 July 2009. https://torontoist.com/2009/07/historicist_boyhood_summers_and_the_city/ (accessed on 7 August 2019). See Harry Rasky, *The Three Harrys* (Oakville, ON: Mosaic Press, 1999

Conclusion: Bathing on the Ragged Edge

1 "Bathing in Public," *The Globe*, 10 August 1887, 5; "The Don's Victim," *The Globe*, 5 July 1902, 28.

2 Bob Tarantino, *Under Arrest: Canadian Laws You Won't Believe* (Toronto: Dundurn, 2007), 100.

3 Rob Shields, *Places on the Margin: Alternative Geographies of Modernity* (New York: Routledge, 1991).

4 T.J. Jackson Lears, *No Place of Grace: Antimodernism and the Transformation of American Culture, 1880–1920* (Chicago: University of Chicago Press, 1994); Ian McKay, *The Quest of the Folk: Antimodernism and Cultural Selection in Twentieth-Century Nova Scotia* (Montreal: McGill-Queen's University Press, 1994).

5 John Fiske, *Understanding Popular Culture* (Boston: Unwin Hyman, 1989); John Fiske, *Reading the Popular* (New York: Routledge, 2005).

Epilogue: Recrafting the Bathing Body

1 Hugh Garner recalled sprinting across the beach as a child: "They were right to call it Hog Town," *The Toronto Star*, 2 August 1975, A16. For more, see Chapter 3.

2 There was bemusement when it was discovered nude bathing was still legal in the spaces in 1929: see "12,000 City By-laws May Be Consolidated," *The Globe*, 8 January 1929, 12; "City Is Growing Up According to News from Our Town Hall," *The Globe*, 14 June, 16.

3 Sally Gibson, *More Than an Island: A History of the Toronto Island* (Toronto: Irwin, 1984), 128–30.

4 22F, Photographic Survey Corporation Ltd., 1950, Aerial photographs, TCA.

5 We see a similar absence during the mid-century in spaces such as Wreck Beach: see Carellin Brooks, *Wreck Beach* (Vancouver: New Star Books, 2007).

6 John Grube, "Queens and Flaming Virgins: Towards a Sense of Gay Community," 18 March 1986, 5, in Nude beach 1975-2006, fonds 1047, series 1822, file 402, folio 9, box 574072, CTA.

7 Sally Gibson, *More Than an Island*, 182. Winnipeg Beach served the same role for Winnipeg's gay community: see Dale Barbour, *Winnipeg Beach: Leisure and Courtship in a Resort Town, 1900–1967* (Winnipeg: University of Manitoba Press, 2011).

8 Gibson, *More Than an Island*, 195. On erosion, see Peter A. Simm, "Enhance Toronto Tourism and Recreation: Restore Clothing-Optional Status to Hanlan's Point Beach," April 1999, 5: Series 1143, item 4963, fonds 2, box 564020-folio 3, CTA.

9 Ed Jackson, "Hanlan's Point," in *Any Other Way: How Toronto Got Queer*, ed. Stephanie Chambers et al. (Toronto: Coach House Books, 2017), 130. On the 1979 court case, see "Nude Bathing May Lose at Hanlan's," *The Toronto Star*, 28 November 1979, C22. On last cottages being removed, see Simm, "Enhance Toronto Tourism," 3.

10 See Gordon Brent Ingram, "Redesigning Wreck: Beach Meets Forest as Location of Male Homoerotic Culture and Place Making in Pacific Canada," in *In a Queer Country: Gay and Lesbian Studies in the Canadian Context*, ed. Terry Goldie (Vancouver: Arsenal Pulp Press, 2001), 193–94.

11 Mary-Ann Melissa Shantz, "The Nature of the Body: A Cultural History of Nudism in Postwar Canada" (PhD diss., Carleton University, 2012), 245.

12 Samira Mohyeddin and Erica Lenti, "Reflections on Pride's Political History," *Torontoist*, 28 June 2015, http://torontoist.com/2015/06/reflections-on-prides-political-history/ (accessed on 13 September 2017).

13 No doubt there were others as well, but these three hosted gay picnics in 1973, making their character explicit: see "1973 Gay Pride Week," *The Body Politic*, July–August 1973, 7. We can add Crystal Crescent in Nova Scotia to the circuit as well: see "Getting there," *The Body Politic*, June–July 1978, 15.

14 "Islanders Say Nude Bathers Taking over Their Beach," *The Toronto Star*, 8 August 1975, A3.

15 See "Cruising Spots," *The Body Politic*, July–August 1974, 19; "Hot Spots: Toronto's Summer of '82," *The Body Politic* 85, July–August 1982, 22. On the airport, see Sylvia Stead, "Nudes Scare Families from Beach, Islanders Say," *The Globe*, 8 August 1975, 1.

16 Sylvia Stead, "Nudes Scare Families from Beach, Islanders Say," *The Globe and Mail*, 8 August 1975, 1. See, for example, this story which takes a queer space at Hanlan's as a given: "Homosexuals Find Tolerance Growing," *The Toronto Star*, 7 November 1975, B3.

17 Totally Naked in Toronto lawyer Peter A. Simm put together a package of information in 1999 to argue the merits of a nude beach at Hanlan's Point. He notes it was a Metro Toronto bylaw that was being deployed here, an updated version of Toronto's Bylaw 12774, which had been passed in 1930: see Simm, "Enhance Toronto Tourism," 14, 37. On the denouement of the charges in 1975, see "Sunbathing Legal," *The Globe and Mail*, 5 December 1975, 5; "Sunbathed Nude on Island, Five Fined," *The Toronto Star*, 13 September 1975, A8.; "Sharp Law Student Strips the Threat from Nude Bylaw," *The Toronto Star*, 4 December 1975, B1.

18 Sylvia Stead, "Nudes Scare Families from Beach, Islanders Say," *The Globe and Mail*, 8 August 1975, 1. "Sharp Law Student Strips the Threat from Nude Bylaw," *The Toronto Star*, 4 December 1975, B1.

19 For ongoing enforcement in the 1980s and 1990s, see Simm, "Enhance Toronto Tourism," 15.

20 Graeme Smith, "The New Bare Essential for Skinny-dippers . . ." *The Toronto Star*, 15 June 1999, A1. On Bylaw #20, see Draft no. 22 a by-law, By-laws Bathing by-law 1936–1975, 290-B-1, vol. 1 contd, RG 3/3 box 373, folder 8, PTA. See chapter 6 for more coverage on Bylaw #20.

21 "Michael Bettencourt, "Police Lay Off Skinny-dippers on Island," *The Toronto Star*, 16 June 1999, B5.

22 John Barber, "The Naked and the Wet," *The Globe and Mail*, 1 July 2006, https://beta.theglobeandmail.com/news/national/the-naked-and-the-wet/article730492/?ref=http://www.theglobeandmail.com&.

23 Mariana Valverde and Miomir Cirak, "Governing Bodies, Creating Gayspaces: Policing and Security Issues in 'Gay' Downtown Toronto," *British Journal of Criminology* 43 (2003): 114.

24 Nate Hendley, "Kyle Rae's Naked Ambition," *Eye Weekly*, 9 July 1998, 8.

25 Rebecca Bragg, "Here's the Skinny: Nude Beach Approved," *The Toronto Star*, 13 May 1999, B1.

26 Hanlan's Beach Naturists "Free Beach Etiquette," Nude beach 1975–2006, series 1822, file 402, box 574072, folio 9, TCA.

27 Shantz, "The Nature of the Body," 4.

28 Shantz, 5; Brian Hoffman, *Naked: A Cultural History of American Nudism* (New York: New York University Press, 2015).

29 As James Woycke demonstrates through a series of letters to a nudist magazine from men reflecting on their experiences skinny-dipping in their youth. See James Woycke, *Au Naturel: The History of Nudism in Canada* (Etobicoke, ON: Federation of Canadian Naturists, 2003), 1–17, 23. And for a similar argument in the United States, see Frances and Mason Merrill, *Nudism Comes to America* (Garden City, NY: Garden City Publishing, 1932), 5–7.

30 Merrill, *Nudism Comes to America*, 14–20, 40, 47; Shantz, *The Nature of rhe Body*, 31.

31 Woycke, *Au Naturel*, 28–29; Shantz, *The Nature of the Body*, 77–78; Fred Ilfeld Jr. and Roger Lauer, *Social Nudism in America* (New Haven, CT, College and University Press, 1964), 30.

32 Ilfeld and Lauer, *Social Nudism*, 176–230.

33 Wreck Beach faces similar challenges balancing nudity and sexuality, but it's able to do so over a broader space than Hanlan's Point: see Ingram, "Redesigning Wreck"; and Brooks, *Wreck Beach*.

34 Nate Hendley, "No Sex Please—We're Nudists," *Eye Weekly*, 9 September 1999, Nude beach 1975–2006, series 1822 file 402, box 574072, folio 9, TCA.

35 Ibid.

36 See Dave Fleming, "To Those Who Care . . ." e-mail from Toronto swims . . . HBN Message line to Torontoisland@yahoogroups.com, 27 April 2003, Nude beach 1975-2006, series 1822, file 402, box 574072, folio 9, TCA.

37 Pau Obrador Pons, "A Haptic Geography of the Beach: Naked Bodies, Vision and Touch," *Social and Cultural Geography* 8, no. 1 (2007): 132–33.

38 Ibid., 134–35.

39 Jacqueline Schoemaker Holmes has tracked the same balance at an unnamed beach in Quebec: Jacqueline Schoemaker Holmes, "Bare Bodies, Beaches, and Boundaries: Abjected Outsiders and Rearticulation at the Nude Beach," *Sexuality and Culture* 10, no. 4 (2006): 37, 40–41. See also Ingram, "Redesigning Wreck."

40 It is hard to put a finger on when bathing died out in the Don but the 1950s seem to have been the last gasp: see Charles Sauriol, "Swimming Holes in the Don," *The Cardinal*, Summer 1953, Title: The Cardinal: Nature, Conservative, Outdoors, 19511956, box 115736, folio 2, fonds 4, series 104, file 14, TCA. For the mythologizing of the Don, see Chapter 4.

41 Jennifer Bonnell, *Reclaiming the Don: An Environmental History of Toronto's Don River Valley* (Toronto: University of Toronto Press, 2014), 114. For Sauriol's relationship with the river, see Jennifer Bonnell, "An Intimate Understanding of Place: Charles Sauriol and Toronto's Don River Valley, 1927–1989,"

Canadian Historical Review 92, no. 4 (2011): 607–36. For how foundational bathing and being in the river was, see Charles Sauriol, *Trails of the Don* (Orillia, ON: Hemlock Press, 1992), 16–26, 81, 175–80; Charles Sauriol, *Remembering the Don: A Rare Record of Earlier Times Within the Don River Valley* (Scarborough, ON: Consolidated Amethyst Communications, 1981), 58, 64, 136–45.

42 Bonnell, *Reclaiming the Don*, 123–27.

43 "Turning the Corner: The Don Watershed Report Card," Don Watershed Regeneration Council and the Metropolitan Toronto and Region Conservation Authority, May 1997, 1, 3.

44 Ibid.

45 "Don River Watershed Plan: Beyond Forty Steps," Toronto and Region Conservation, 2009, v. As Bonnell notes, Metro Toronto had improved water quality by removing a number of overburdened sewage treatment plants from the river between 1956 and 1965: see Bonnell, "An Intimate Understanding of Place," 625. On the mid-century condition of the Don, see Bonnell, *Reclaiming the Don*, 122. Ontario Department of Planning and Development (ODPD), *Don Valley Conservation Report* (Toronto: ODPD, 1950), part 6, 15.

46 "Turning the Corner: The Don Watershed Report Card," Don Watershed Regeneration Council and the Metropolitan Toronto and Region Conservation Authority, May 1997, 3.

47 Ibid., 3, 4.

48 "Don River Watershed Plan: Beyond Forty Steps," Toronto and Region Conservation, 2009, (3)–22.

49 "Cultural Heritage—Report on Current Conditions," Toronto and Region Conservation, 2009. The cultural heritage report was used as background information for "Beyond Forty Steps," Toronto and Region Conservation, Don River Watershed Plan, 2009.

50 "Cultural Heritage—Report on Current Conditions," Toronto and Region Conservation, 2009.

51 "Don River Watershed Plan: Beyond Forty Steps," Toronto and Region Conservation, 2009, (3)–2.

52 Ibid., (2)–2.

53 Ibid., (3)–48–50.

54 As I have noted in Chapter 6 there is a robust Canadian historiography that looks at the canoe as an appropriated technology of colonization. See Bruce Erickson, *Canoe Nation: Nature, Race, and the Making of a Canadian Icon* (Vancouver: UBC Press, 2013); Misao Dean, *Inheriting a Canoe Paddle: The Canoe in Discourses of English-Canadian Nationalism* (Toronto: University of Toronto Press, 2013), 8–15.

55 For an entertaining look at a nineteenth-century attempt to canoe up the Don, see "The Don and the Rouge," *The Globe*, 22 June 1887, 8.

56 Margaret Bream, "Toronto's Don River Goes Wild When Flooded for Paddle the Don," *The Toronto Star*, 12 May 2012, https://www.thestar.com/news/insight/2012/05/12/torontos_don_river_goes_wild_when_flooded_for_paddle_the_don.html (accessed on 17 September 2017).

57 See http://paddlethedon.ca (accessed on 22 September 2017).

BIBLIOGRAPHY

Primary Sources

Andrews, W.D. *Swimming and Life-Saving*. Toronto: William Briggs, 1889.

Clark, C.S. *Of Toronto the Good, a Social Study: The Queen City of Canada as It Is*. Montreal: Toronto Publishing Company, 1898.

Clarke, Lionel H. *The Toronto Waterfront Development, 1912–1920*. Toronto: Toronto Harbour Commission, [1920?].

Goad, Charles E. *Atlas of the City of Toronto and Vicinity*. Chas. E. Goad: Toronto, 1880.

———. *Atlas of the City of Toronto and Suburbs*. Chas. E. Goad: Toronto, 1884.

———. *Atlas of the City of Toronto and Vicinity*. 2nd ed. Chas. E. Goad: Toronto, 1890.

———. *Atlas of the City of Toronto*.3rd ed. Chas. E. Goad: Toronto, 1910.

Helliwell, William. *The Helliwell Diaries: The Diaries of William Helliwell from 1830 to 1890*. City of Toronto Museum Services. https://www1.toronto.ca/City%20Of%20Toronto/Economic%20Development%20&%20Culture/Cultural%20Services/Museums/Toronto%20Museums/Todmorden%20Mills/Files/helliwell_diaries_1830-1890.pdf (accessed on 5 November 2017).

Martin, Ebenezer. *Treatise on the Theory of Swimming Made So Easy That It Can Be Reduced to Practice at Once*. Montreal: Lovell, 1876.

Mulvany, C. Pelham. *Toronto: Past and Present. A Handbook of the City* (originally published, Toronto: W.E. Caiger, 1884). Toronto: Ontario Reprint Press, 1970.

Mulvany, Charles Pelham, Graeme Mercer Adam, and Christopher Blackett Robinson. *History of Toronto and County of York, Vol. 1*. Toronto: C. Blackett Robinson, 1885.

Pearson, W.H. *Recollections and Records of Toronto of Old: With References to Brantford, Kingston and Other Canadian Towns*. Toronto: W. Briggs, 1914.

Robertson, John Ross. *The Diary of Mrs. John Graves Simcoe, Wife of the First Lieutenant-Governor of the Province of Upper Canada, 1792–6*. Toronto: W. Briggs, 1911.

———. *Robertson's Landmarks of Toronto: A Collection of Historical Sketches of the Old Town of York from 1792 until 1833 and of Toronto from 1834 to 1893*. Toronto: John R. Robertson, 1894.

———. *Robertson's Landmarks of Toronto: Toronto from 1834 to 1898*. Toronto: John R. Robertson, 1898.

———. *Robertson's Landmarks of Toronto: Toronto from 1834 to 1895*. Toronto: John R. Robertson, 1896.

———. *Robertson's Landmarks of Toronto: Toronto from 1834 to 1908.* Toronto: John R. Robertson, 1908.

———. *Robertson's Landmarks of Toronto: Toronto from 1834 to 1814.* Toronto: John R. Robertson, 1914.

Robinson, Charles Mulford. *The Improvement of Towns and Cities or The Practical Basis of Civic Aesthetics.* New York: G.P. Putnam's Sons, 1901.

Scadding, Henry. *Toronto of Old; Collections and Recollections Illustrative of the Early Settlement and Social Life of the Capital of Ontario.* Toronto: Adam, Stevenson, 1873.

Scadding, Henry, and John Charles Dent. *Toronto: Past and Present: Historical and Descriptive: Memorial Volume.* Toronto: Hunter, Rose, 1884.

Sheffield, T.W. *Swimming.* Toronto: Musson Book, 1909.

Taylor, Conyngham Crawford. *The Queen's Jubilee and Toronto "Called Back" from 1887 to 1847.* Toronto: William Briggs, 1887.

———. *Toronto "Called Back," from 1892 to 1847: Its Wonderful Growth and Progress.* Toronto: William Briggs Publisher, 1892.

Toronto Island Guide. Toronto: R.G. McLean, 1894.

Government Publications

The Consolidated Statutes for Upper Canada, Proclaimed and Published under the Authority of the Act 22 VICT. CAP. 30, A. D. 1859. Toronto: Stewart Derbishire and George Desbarats, 1859.

"Cultural Heritage—Report on Current Conditions." Toronto and Region Conservation, 2009.

"Don River Watershed Plan: Beyond Forty Steps." Toronto and Region Conservation, 2009.

House of Commons Debates, 17th Parliament, 2nd Session: Vol. 4, page 4134, 24 July 1931.

Ontario Department of Planning and Development (ODPD). *Don Valley Conservation Report.* Toronto: ODPD, 1950.

Report of the Commissioners Appointed to Enquiry into the Prison and Reformatory System of Ontario, 1891. Toronto: Warwick and Sons, 1891.

Review of the Law of Indecency and Nudity 1999, Uniform Law Conference of Canada. http://www.ulcc.ca/en/annual-meetings/365-1999-winnipeg-mb/criminal-section-documents/1841-review-of-the-law-of-indecency-and-nudity?showall=1&limitstart= (accessed at 1:41 p.m., 23 July 2016). 1931.

The Revised Statutes of Upper Canada to the Time of the Union, 1797–1841, Revised and Published by Authority, Vol. II, Local and Private Acts. Toronto: Robert Stanton, Printer to the Queen's Most Excellent Majesty, 1843.

Statutes of The Province of Upper Canada, Kingston: Francis M, Hill, 1831.

"Turning the Corner: The Don Watershed Report Card." The Don Watershed Regeneration Council and the Metropolitan Toronto and Region Conservation Authority, May 1997.

William Rees, The Case of Doctor William Rees, Late Physician to the Provincial Lunatic Asylum, Toronto. Quebec: Printed by Hunter, Rose and Co., 1865.

Websites

Bonnell, Jennifer and Marcel Fortin. Don Valley Historical Mapping Project. https://maps.library.utoronto.ca/dvhmp/.

Climate data: Climate Data Online. 1840–2000. Daily Data Reports, Toronto Meteorological Observatory. Environment Canada. http://climate.weather.gc.ca/historical_data/search_historic_data_e.html.

Distillery District Heritage Website. http://www.distilleryheritage.com.

Early Canadiana online. http://eco.canadiana.ca.

Gooderham and Worts: A Family Genealogy Project. http://www.gooderham-worts.ca/index.php.

Glassford, Bruce. Robert Home Smith. http://www.etobicokehistorical.com/robert-home-smith.html.

Internet Archive. https://archive.org.

Ng, Nathan. Goad's Atlas of the City of Toronto: Fire Insurance Maps of Toronto from the Victorian Era. http://goadstoronto.blogspot.ca/2012/05/1910-toronto-fire-insurance-map.html.

———. Historical Maps of Toronto. http://oldtorontomaps.blogspot.ca.

———. Fort York and Garrison Commons Maps. http://fortyorkmaps.blogspot.ca.

City of Toronto Archives

Fonds 2: City of Toronto Archives Collection: Series 1143: Reference copies of municipal reports.

__________. Series 60 City of Toronto reports collection: Annual Report of the Chief Constable

Fonds 4: Charles Sauriol Fonds: Series 104 Publications of Charles Sauriol.

________ Series 80 Photographs of the Don Valley.

Fonds 38: Toronto Police Service Fonds: Series 95 Records of coroners' inquests.

Fonds 70: Larry Becker Fonds: Series 330 Larry Becker postcards.

Fonds 200: Former City of Toronto Fonds: Series 490 Toronto Dept. of Parks and Recreation publications.

———. Series 544: City of Toronto Property Dept. architectural plans.

———. Series 724: Toronto Dept. of Parks and Recreation maps and plans.

———. Series 768: Assessment Dept.: Subseries 2: Island files.

Fonds 1015: Toronto Guild of Civic Art Fonds.

Fonds 1047: Toronto Island Archives fonds: Series 1822 Toronto Island Archives subject files.

Fonds 1244: William James Family Fonds.

Fonds 1266: Globe and Mail Fonds.

Fonds 1548: Alan Howard Fonds: Series 393 John Boyd Sr. photographs.

Fonds 2032: Toronto Planning Board Fonds: Series 727 Toronto Planning Board maps and plans.

Fonds 298: M.O. Hammond Fonds.

Toronto City Council Minutes.

Photographic Survey Corporation Ltd, 1950: Aerial photographs.

Toronto Port Authority Archive

Life Saving and Police Patrol Annual Reports: Box 1, 1840-L-1-1, RG 7/1.

Research Subject Reference File: Sunnyside Folder, Toronto Port Authority Archives.

Research Subject Reference File: Cousins, E.L. "Toronto Harbour Improvements," 1921 folder, Toronto Port Authority Archives.

Research Subject Reference File: Waterfront Development Plan, 1912 folder, Toronto Port Authority.

Research Subject Reference File: Robert Home Smith.

Research Subject Reference File: Arthur Chapman Folder.

Research Subject Reference File: 1840-C-1-1 Reports E.L. Cousins. C.E. folder.

RG 313: Box 53, folder 12, Bathing –Sunnyside Free Bathing Area 1912–35, no. 101.S.2, vol. 1, TPAA.

RG 7/5/3: Box 1, folder 4, General Correspondence, 1914–119.

RG 7 1840-L-1-1: Box 2, Life Saving and Police Patrol Log Book.

RG 3/3: Box 343, folder 71 By-Laws, Bathing By-laws 1904–35 (290-B-1, vol. 1).

RG 3/3: Box 373, folder 8 By-laws, Bathing By-laws 36–1975 (290-B-1, vol. 1).

Toronto Harbour Commission, Public Affairs Dept. *Toronto Harbour, the Passing Years*. Toronto: Toronto Harbour Commissioners, 1985.

Toronto Public Library

Baldwin Collection.

Library and Archives Canada

Peter Winkworth Collections of Canadiana

Art Gallery of Ontario

Newspapers

The Body Politic

The British Colonist

The Empire

The Evening Star (precursor of *The Toronto Daily Star*)

Financial Saturday Night

The Globe (precursor of the *Globe and Mail*)

The Telegram

The Toronto Daily Mail

The Toronto Daily Star (precursor of *The Star* and *The Toronto Star*)

The Toronto News

Secondary Sources

Adams, Mary Louise. "Almost Anything Can Happen: A Search for Sexual Discourse in the Urban Spaces of 1940s Toronto." *Canadian Journal of Sociology/Cahiers canadiens de sociologie* 19, no. 2, *Special Issue on Moral Regulation* (1994): 217–32.

———. *The Trouble with Normal: Postwar Youth and the Making of Heterosexuality*. Toronto: University of Toronto Press, 1997.

Allen, Richard. "The Social Gospel and the Reform Tradition in Canada." *Canadian Historical Review* 49, no. 4 (1968): 381–99.

An, Perry G. "Helping the Poor Emerge from 'Urban Barbarism to Civic Civilization': Public Bathhouses in America, 1890–1915." *Yale Journal of Biology and Medicine* 77 (2004): 133–41.

Anderson, James D. "The Municipal Government Reform Movement in Western Canada, 1880–1920." In *The Usable Urban Past: Planning and Politics in the Modern Canadian City*, edited by Alan F.J. Artibise and Gilbert A. Stelter, 73–111. Toronto: Macmillan of Canada, 1979.

Anderson, Richard. "The Dustbins of History: Waste Disposal in Toronto's Ravines and Valleys." In *Toronto's Water from Lake Iroquois to Lost Rivers to Low-flow Toilets*, edited by Wayne Reeves and Christina Palassio, 74–81. Toronto: Coach House Books, 2008.

Armitage, Andrew. "The Stonehookers of Lake Ontario." *Oakville Trails*, http://archive.li/qM8bE.

Armstrong, Christopher, and H.V. Nelles. *The Revenge of the Methodist Bicycle Company*. Toronto: Peter Martin Associates, 1977.

Artibise, Alan F.J., and Gilbert A. Stelter, eds. *The Usable Urban Past: Planning and Politics in the Modern Canadian City*. Toronto: Macmillan of Canada, 1979.

Ashenburg, Katherine. *The Dirt on Clean: An Unsanitized History*. Toronto: A.A. Knopf Canada, 2007.

Badger, Gerry. *The Genius of Photography: How Photography Has Changed Our Lives*. London: Quadrille Publishing, 2007.

Baigent, Elizabeth. "'God's Earth Will Be Sacred': Religion, Theology, and the Open Space Movement in Victorian England." *Rural History* 22, no. 1 (2011): 31–58.

Bailey, Beth. *From Front Porch to Back Seat*. Baltimore: Johns Hopkins University Press, 1988.

Bailey, Peter. "Breaking the Sound Barrier." In *Hearing History: A Reader*, edited by Mark M. Smith, 23–35. Athens: University of Georgia Press, 2004.

Bain, David. "John Howard's High Park 'A Square Mile or Two of Rough Ground.'" *Ontario History* 101, no. 1 (2009): 1–24.

Bakhtin, Mikhail. *Rabelais and His World*. Bloomington: Indiana University Press, 1984.

Barbour, Dale. *Winnipeg Beach: Courtship and Leisure in a Resort Town*. Winnipeg: University of Manitoba Press, 2011.

Barman, Jean. *Stanley Park's Secret: The Forgotten Families of Whoi Whoi, Kanaka Ranch and Brockton Point*. Vancouver: Harbour Publishing, 2005.

Bassnett, Sarah. *Picturing Toronto: Photography and the Making of a Modern City*. Montreal: McGill-Queen's University Press, 2016.

Batchelor, Dahn A. *Whistling in the Face of Robbers: The Life and Times of Dahn A. Batchelor*. Bloomington: iUniverse, 2012.

Beasley, Diane. "Walter Dean and Sunnyside: A Study of Waterfront Recreation in Toronto." MA thesis, University of Toronto, 1994.

Bederman, Gail. *Manliness and Civilization: A Cultural History of Gender and Race in the United States, 1880–1917*. Chicago: University of Chicago Press, 1995.

Belisle, Donica. *Retail Nation Department Stores and the Making of Modern Canada*. Vancouver: UBC Press, 2011.

Bell, David, and Gill Valentine. *Mapping Desire: Geographies of Sexualities*. New York: Routledge, 1995.

Bell, Lynne. "Unsettling Acts: Photography as Decolonizing Testimony in Centennial Memory." In *The Cultural Work of Photography in Canada*, edited by Carol Payne and Andrea Kunard, 165–81. Montreal: McGill-Queen's University Press, 2011.

Benidickson, James. *Idleness, Water, and a Canoe: Reflections on Paddling for Pleasure*. Toronto: University of Toronto Press, 1997.

Berman, Marshall. *All That Is Solid Melts into Air: The Experience of Modernity*, New York: Verso, 1982.

Boles, Derek. *Toronto's Railway Heritage*. Charleston, SC: Arcadia Publishing, 2009.

Bonnell, Jennifer. "An Intimate Understanding of Place: Charles Sauriol and Toronto's Don River Valley, 1927–1989." *Canadian Historical Review* 92, no. 4 (2011): 607–36.

———. *Reclaiming the Don: An Environmental History of Toronto's Don River Valley*. Toronto: University of Toronto Press, 2014.

Booth, Douglas. *Australian Beach Cultures: History of Sun, Sand, and Surf*. London: Routledge, 2001.

———. "Nudes in the Sand and Perverts in the Dunes." *Journal of Australian Studies* 21, no. 53 (1997): 170–82.

———. "War Off Water: The Australian Surf Life Saving Association and the Beach." *Sporting Traditions* 7, no. 2 (1991): 135–62.

Boritch, Helen, and John Hagan. "Crime and the Changing Forms of Class Control: Policing Public Order in 'Toronto the Good,' 1859–1955." *Social Forces* 66, no. 2 (1987): 307–35.

Bouchier, Nancy B., and Ken Cruikshank. "The War on the Squatters, 1920–1940: Hamilton's Boathouse Community and the Re-Creation of Recreation on Burlington Bay." *Labour/Le Travail* 51 (Spring 2003): 9–46.

Boyer, Barbaranne. *The Boardwalk Album: Memories of The Beach*. Erin, ON: Boston Mills Press, 1985.

Brace, Catherine. "Public Works in the Canadian City: The Provision of Sewers in Toronto 1870–1913." *Urban History Review/Revue d'histoire urbaine* 23, no. 2 (1995): 33–43.

Bradbury, Bettina. *Working Families: Age, Gender, and Daily Survival in Industrializing Montreal*. Toronto: Oxford University Press, 1993.

Brooks, Carellin. *Wreck Beach*. Vancouver: New Star Books, 2007.

Brown, Ken. *The Canadian Canoe Company and the Early Peterborough Canoe Factories*. Peterborough, ON: Cover to Cover, 2011.

Brown, Robert Craig. "Wiman, Erastus." *Dictionary of Canadian Biography, Volume 13*. University of Toronto/Université Laval, 2003. http://www.biographi.ca/en/bio/wiman_erastus_13E.html (accessed 11 February 2016).

Bushman, Richard L., and Claudia L Bushman. "The Early History of Cleanliness in America." *Journal of American History* 74, no. 4 (1988): 1213–38.

Butler, Judith. *Bodies That Matter: On the Discursive Limits of "Sex."* New York: Routledge, 1993.

———. *Gender Trouble: Feminism and the Subversion of Identity*. New York: Routledge, 1990.

Campbell. Robert, A. *Sit Down and Drink Your Beer: Regulating Vancouver's Beer Parlours, 1925–1954*. Toronto: University of Toronto Press, 2001.

Careless, J.M.S. *Toronto to 1918: An Illustrated History*. Toronto: James Lorimer, 1984.

Castonguay, Stephane, and Darin Kinsey. "The Nature of the Liberal Order: State Formation, Conservation, and the Government of Non-Humans in Canada." In *Liberalism and Hegemony: Debating the Canadian Liberal Revolution*, edited by Jean-François Constant and Michel Ducharme, 221–45. Toronto: University of Toronto Press, 2009.

Cavallo, Dominick. *Muscle and Morals: Organized Playgrounds and Urban Reform, 1880–1920*. Philadelphia: University of Pennsylvania Press, 1981.

Chauncey, George. *Gay New York: Gender, Urban Culture, and the Making of the Gay Male World, 1890–1940*. New York: Basic Books, 1994.

Clark, Peter, ed. *The European City and Green Space: London, Stockholm, Helsinki and St. Petersburg, 1850–2000*. Aldershot, UK: Ashgate Publishing, 2006.

Coates, Colin. "Seeing and Not Seeing: Landscape Art as a Historical Source." In *Method and Meaning in Canadian Environmental History*, edited by Alan MacEachern and Willian J. Turkel, 140–57. Toronto: Nelson Education, 2009.

Comacchio, Cynthia R. *The Dominion of Youth: Adolescence and the Making of a Modern Canada, 1920–1950*. Waterloo, ON: Wilfrid Laurier University Press, 2006.

Cook, Ramsay. *The Regenerators: Social Criticism of Late Victorian English Canada*. Toronto: University of Toronto Press, 1997.

Corbin, Alain. *The Lure of the Sea: The Discovery of the Seaside in the Western World, 1750–1840*. Translated by Jocelyn Phelps. Cambridge, UK: Polity Press, 1994.

Cranz, Galen. "Women in Urban Parks." *Signs: Journal of Women in Culture and Society* 5, no. 3. Supplement. *Women and the American City* (1980): 579–95.

Crary, Jonathan. *Techniques of the Observer: On Vision and Modernity in the Nineteenth Century*. Cambridge: MIT Press, 1992.

Cronon, William. *Nature's Metropolis: Chicago and the Great West*. New York: W.W. Norton, 1991.

———. "The Trouble with Wilderness: Or, Getting Back to the Wrong Nature." *Environmental History* 1, no. 1 (1996): 7–28.

———, ed. *Uncommon Ground: Toward Reinventing Nature*. New York: W.W. Norton, 1995.

Cross, Gary S., and John K. Walton. *The Playful Crowd: Pleasure Places in the Twentieth Century*. New York: Columbia University Press, 2005.

Crouch, David. "Places around Us: Embodied Lay Geographies in Leisure and Tourism." *Leisure Studies* 19, no. 2 (2000): 63–76.

Cruikshank, F.D., and J. Nason. *History of Weston*. Toronto: University of Toronto Press, 1983.

Curtis, Bruce. "After 'Canada': Liberalisms, Social Theory, and Historical Analysis." In *Liberalism and Hegemony: Debating the Canadian Liberal Revolution*, edited by Jean-François Constant and Michel Ducharme, 176–200. Toronto: University of Toronto Press, 2009.

Dagenais, Michèle. "The Municipal Territory: A Product of the Liberal Order?" In *Liberalism and Hegemony: Debating the Canadian Liberal Revolution*, edited by Jean-François Constant and Michel Ducharme, 201–20. Toronto: University of Toronto Press, 2009.

Daley, Caroline. "From Bush to Beach: Nudism in Australasia." *Journal of Historical Geography* 31 (2005): 149–67.

Davies, Caitlin. *Down Stream: A History and Celebration of Swimming the River Thames*. London: Aurum Press, 2015.

Davies, Stephen. "'Reckless Walking Must Be Discouraged': The Automobile Revolution and the Shaping of Modern Urban Canada to 1930." *Urban History Review* 18, no. 2 (1989): 123–38.

Dean, Misao. *Inheriting a Canoe Paddle: The Canoe in Discourses of English-Canadian Nationalism*. Toronto: University of Toronto Press, 2013.

Dean, Mitchell. *Governmentality: Power and Rule in Modern Society*. London: Sage, 1999.

de Certeau, Michel. *Practice of Everyday Life*. Translated by Steven F. Rendall. Los Angeles: University of California Press, 1988.

Dekker, Jeroen J.H. "Family on the Beach: Representations of Romantic and Bourgeois Family Values by Realistic Genre Painting of Nineteenth Century Scheveningen Beach." *Journal of Family History* 28, no. 2 (April 2003): 277–96.

Desfor, Gene. "Planning Urban Waterfront Industrial Districts: Toronto's Ashbridge's Bay, 1889–1910." *Urban History Review/Revue d'histoire urbaine* 17, no. 2 (1988): 77–91.

Desfor, Gene, Michael Goldrick, and Roy Merrens. "Redevelopment on the North American Water-frontier: The Case of Toronto." In *Revitalizing the Waterfront: International Dimensions of Dockland Redevelopment*, edited by B.S. Hoyle, D.A. Pinder, and M.S. Husain, 92–113. London: Belhaven Press, 1988.

Desfor, Gene, and Jennefer Laidley, eds. *Reshaping Toronto's Waterfront*. Toronto: University of Toronto Press, 2011.

Desfor, Gene, Lucian Vesalon, and Jennefer Laidley. "Establishing the Toronto Harbour Commission and Its 1912 Waterfront Development Plan." In *Reshaping Toronto's Waterfront*, edited by Gene Desfor and Jennefer Laidley, 49–74. Toronto: University of Toronto Press, 2011.

Driver, Felix. "Moral Geographies: Social Science and the Urban Environment in Mid-Nineteenth Century England." *Transactions of the Institute of British Geographers, New Series* 13, no. 3 (1988): 275–87.

Dubinsky, Karen. *Improper Advances: Rape and Heterosexual Conflict in Ontario, 1880–1929*. Chicago: University of Chicago Press, 1993.

Dummitt, Christopher. *The Manly Modern: Masculinity in Postwar Canada*. Vancouver: UBC Press, 2007.

Dunkin, Jessica. "Producing and Consuming Spaces of Sport and Leisure: The Encampments and Regattas of the American Canoe Association, 1880–1903." In *Moving Natures: Mobility and the Environment in Canadian History*, edited by Ben Bradley, Jay Young, and Colin M. Coates, 229–50. Calgary: University of Calgary Press, 2016.

Eisenstadt, Shmuel N. "Multiple Modernities." *Daedalus* 129, no. 1 (2000): 1–29.

Ekström, Anders. "Seeing from Above: A Particular History of the General Observer." *Nineteenth-Century Contexts* 31, no. 3 (2009): 185–207.

Elias, Norbert. *Power and Civility: The Civilizing Process: Volume 2*. Translated by Edmund Jephcott. New York: Pantheon Books, 1982.

Emerling, Jae. *Photography: History and Theory*. New York: Routledge, 2012.

Erickson, Bruce. *Canoe Nation: Nature Race and the Making of a Canadian Icon*. Vancouver: UBC Press, 2013.

Ewen, Stuart. *All Consuming Images: The Politics of Style in Contemporary Culture*. New York: Basic Books, 1988.

Eyles, Nick. "Ravines, Lagoons, Cliffs and Spits: The Ups and Downs of Lake Ontario." In *HTO: Toronto's Water from Lake Iroquois to Lost Rivers to Low-flow Toilets*, edited by Wayne Reeves and Christina Palassio, 34–42. Toronto: Coach House Books, 2008.

Fairburn, M. Jane. *Along the Shore: Rediscovering Toronto's Waterfront Heritage*. Toronto: ECW Press, 2013.

Feldberg, Gina. "Wyllie, Elizabeth Jennet." *Dictionary of Canadian Biography, vol. 13*. University of Toronto/Université Laval, 2003. http://www.biographi.ca/en/bio/wyllie_elizabeth_jennet_13E.html (accessed 14 February 2016).

Filey, Mike. *I Remember Sunnyside: The Rise and Fall of a Magical Era*. Toronto: Dundurn Group, 1996.

———. *More Toronto Sketches: The Way We Were*. Toronto: Dundurn Press, 1993.

Fiske, John. *Reading the Popular*. New York: Routledge, 2005.

———. *Understanding Popular Culture*. Boston: Unwin Hyman, 1989.

Fletcher, Ron. *The Humber: Tales of a Canadian Heritage River*. Toronto: RWF, Heritage Publications, 2006.

Foglesong, Richard E. *Planning the Capitalist City: The Colonial Era to the 1920s*. Princeton: Princeton University Press, 1986.

Foucault, Michel. "Body/Power." In *Power/Knowledge: Selected Interviews and Other Writings, 1972–1977*, edited by Colin Gordon, 55–62. New York: Pantheon Books, 1980.

———. *Discipline and Punish: The Birth of the Prison*. Translated by Alan Sheridan. New York: Vintage Books, 1995.

———. "Governmentality." In *The Foucault Effect: Studies in Governmentality*, edited by Graham Burchell, Colin Gordon, and Peter Miller, 87–104. Chicago: University of Chicago Press, 1991.

———. *The History of Sexuality: An Introduction*. New York: Vintage, 1978.

———. "Prison Talk." In *Power/Knowledge: Selected Interviews and Other Writings, 1972–1977*, edited by Colin Gordon, 37–54. New York: Pantheon Books, 1980.

———. "Questions of Geography." In *Power/Knowledge: Selected Interviews and Other Writings, 1972–1977*, edited by Colin Gordon, 63–77. New York: Pantheon Books, 1980.

———. "The Subject and Power." In *Power: Essential Works of Foucault, 1954–1984*, edited by James D. Faubion, 326–48. New York: The New Press, 2000.

———. "Truth and Power." In *Power/Knowledge: Selected Interviews and Other Writings, 1972–1977*, edited by Colin Gordon, 109–33. New York: Pantheon Books, 1980.

———. "Two Lectures." In *Power/Knowledge: Selected Interviews and Other Writings, 1972–1977*, edited by Colin Gordon, 78–105. New York: Pantheon Books, 1980.

Franks, C.E.S. "Canoeing: Towards a Landscape of the Imagination." In *Canexus: The Canoe in Canadian Culture*, edited by James Raffan and Bert Horwood, 187–202. Toronto: Betelgeuse Books, 1988.

Freeman, Victoria. "'Toronto Has No History!': Indigeneity, Settler Colonialism and Historical Memory in Canada's Largest City." PhD diss., University of Toronto, 2010.

Freestone, Robert. "Reconciling Beauty and Utility in Early City Planning: The Contribution of John Nolen." *Journal of Urban History* 37, no. 2 (2011): 256–77.

Freud, Sigmund. *Totem and Taboo: Some Points of Agreement between the Mental Lives of Savages and Neurotics*. Translated by James Strachey. London: Routledge and Kegan Paul, 1950.

———. *The Future of an Illusion*. Translated by J.A. Underwood and Shaun Whiteside. London: Penguin, 2008.

Gad, Gunter. "Location Patterns of Manufacturing: Toronto in the Early 1880s." *Urban History Review/Revue d'bis/oire urbaine* 22, no. 2 (1994): 113–38.

Garner, Hugh. *One Damn Thing After Another*. Toronto: McGraw-Hill Ryerson, 1973.

Gibson, Sally. *More Than an Island: A History of the Toronto Island*. Toronto: Irwin, 1984.

Giddens, Anthony. "Time, Space and Regionalisation." In *Social Relations and Spatial Structures*, edited by Derek Gregory and John Urry, 165–95. London: Macillan, 1985.

Gilliland, Jason. "Muddy Shore to Modern Port: Redimensioning the Montreal Waterfront Time-space." *Canadian Geographer/Le Géographe canadien* 48, no. 4 (2004): 448–72.

Goheen, Peter G. "Currents of Change in Toronto, 1850–1900." In *The Canadian City: Essays in Urban History*, edited by Gilbert A. Stelter and Alan F.J. Artibise, 54–92. Toronto: McClelland and Stewart, 1977.

Goldrick, Michael, and Roy Merrens. "Toronto: Searching for a New Environmental Planning Paradigm." In *City, Capital and Water*, edited by Patrick Malone, 219–39. London: Routledge, 1996.

Grant, Shelagh. "Symbols and Myths: Images of Canoe and North." In *Canexus: The Canoe in Canadian Culture*, edited by James Raffan and Bert Horwood, 5–25. Toronto: Betelgeuse Books, 1988.

Greenberg, Ken. "Toronto: The Urban Waterfront as a Terrain of Availability." In *City, Capital and Water*, edited by Patrick Malone, 195–218. London and New York: Routledge, 1996.

Greene, Jillinda. "The Long Lost Story of Fisherman's Island." *localmagazine.ca*. Summer 2011, vol. 2. http://localmagazine.ca/v2/wp-content/uploads/2011/07/FishermansIsland.pdf (accessed on 5 November 2017).

Greer, Allan. "The Birth of the Police in Canada." In *Colonial Leviathan: State Formation in Mid-Nineteenth-Century Canada*, edited by Allan Greer and Ian Radforth, 17–42. Toronto: University of Toronto Press, 1992.

Grimwood, Bryan S.R. "'Thinking outside the Gunnels': Considering Natures and the Moral Terrains of Recreational Canoe Travel." *Leisure/Loisir* 35, no. 1 (2011): 49–69.

Guillet, Edwin C. *Toronto: From Trading Post to Great City*. Toronto: Ontario Publishing, 1934.

Gunn, James H. *Robert Home Smith 1877–1935: A Brief Biography and Some Highlights: The Unique Life of an Early 20th Century Canadian Businessman*. New Bern, NC: 1986.

Gunn, Simon. "From Hegemony to Governmentality: Changing Conceptions of Power in Social History." *Social History* 39, no. 3 (2006): 705–20.

Guthrie, Ann. *Don Valley Legacy: A Pioneer History*. Erin, ON: Boston Mills Press, 1986.

Harris, Denise. "The Kingsway." http://www.etobicokehistorical.com/the-kingsway.html (accessed on 10 December 2015).

Harris, Richard. *Creeping Conformity: How Canada Became Suburban, 1900–1960*. Toronto: University of Toronto Press, 2004.

———. *Unplanned Suburbs: Toronto's American Tragedy, 1900 to 1950*. Baltimore: Johns Hopkins University Press, 1996.

Haun-Moss, Beverly. "Layered Hegemonies: The Origins of Recreational Canoeing Desire in the Province of Ontario." *Topia: Canadian Journal of Cultural Studies* 7 (April, 2002): 39–55.

Hayes, Derek. *Historical Atlas of Toronto*. Toronto: Douglas and McIntyre, 2008.

Heron, Craig. *Booze: A Distilled History*. Toronto: Between the Lines, 2003.

———. "Boys Will Be Boys: Working-Class Masculinities in the Age of Mass Production." *International Labor and Working-Class History* 69 (Spring 2006): 6–34.

———. "The Second Industrial Revolution in Canada, 1890–1930." In *Class, Community and the Labour Movement: Wales and Canada*, edited by Deian Hopkin and Gregory Kealey, 48–66. St. John's: Committee on Canadian Labour History, 1989.

Hewitt, Martin, ed. *Unrespectable Recreations*. Leeds: Leeds Centre for Victorian Studies, 2001.

Heyes, Esther. *Etobicoke: From Furrow to Borough*. Etobicoke: Borough of Etobicoke Civic Centre, 1974.

Hoffman, Brian. *Naked: A Cultural History of American Nudism*. New York: New York University Press, 2015.

Holmes, Jacqueline Schoemaker. "Bare Bodies, Beaches, and Boundaries: Abjected Outsiders and Rearticulation at the Nude Beach." *Sexuality and Culture* 10, no. 4 (2006): 29–53.

Horwood, Catherine. "'Girls Who Arouse Dangerous Passions': Women and Bathing, 1900–39." *Women's History Review* 9, no. 4 (2000): 653–73.

Howell, Sarah. *The Seaside*. London: Cassell and Collier Macmillan, 1974.

Hoy, Suellen. *Chasing Dirt: The American Pursuit of Cleanliness*. New York: Oxford University Press, 1995.

Ilfeld, Fred, Jr., and Roger Lauer. *Social Nudism in America*. New Haven, CT: College and University Press, 1964.

Illouz, Eva. *Consuming the Romantic Utopia: Love and the Cultural Contradictions of Capitalism*. Los Angeles: University of California Press, 1997.

Immerso, Michael. *Coney Island: The People's Playground*. Rutgers, NJ: Rutgers University Press, 2002.

Inglis, K.S. *The Australian Colonists: An Exploration of Social History, 1788–1870*. Carlton, Victoria: Melbourne University Press, 1974.

Ingram, Gordon Brent. "Redesigning Wreck: Beach Meets Forest as Location of Male Homoerotic Culture and Placemaking in Pacific Canada." In *In a Queer Country: Gay and Lesbian Studies in the Canadian Context*, edited by Terry Goldie, 188–208. Vancouver: Arsenal Pulp Press, 2001.

Jackson, Ed. "Hanlan's Point." In *Any Other Way: How Toronto Got Queer*, edited by Stephanie Chambers et al., 130. Toronto: Coach House Books, 2017.

Jackson, Paul S.B. "From Liability to Profitability: How Disease, Fear, and Medical Science Cleaned Up the Marshes of Ashbridge's Bay." In *Reshaping Toronto's Waterfront*, edited by Gene Desfor and Jennefer Laidley, 75–96. Toronto: University of Toronto Press, 2011.

James, William C. "Canoeing and Gender Roles." In *Canexus: The Canoe in Canadian Culture*, edited by James Raffan and Bert Horwood, 27–43. Toronto: Betelgeuse Books, 1988.

Jasen, Patricia. *Wild Things: Nature, Culture, and Tourism in Ontario, 1790–1914*. Toronto: University of Toronto Press, 1995.

Jennings, John, Bruce W. Hodgins, and Doreen Small, eds. *The Canoe in Canadian Cultures*. Toronto: Natural Heritage/Natural History, 1999.

Joyce, Charles Anthony. "From Left Field: Sport and Class in Toronto, 1845–1886." PhD diss., Queen's University, 1997.

———. "Sport and the Cash Nexus in Nineteenth Century Toronto." *Sport History Review* 30 (1999): 140–67.

Joyce, Patrick. *The Rule of Freedom: Liberalism and the Modern City*. New York: Verso, 2003.

Kasson, John F. *Amusing the Million: Coney Island at the Turn of the Century*. New York: Hill and Wang, 1978.

———. *Civilizing the Machine: Technology and Republican Values in America, 1776–1900*. New York: Grossman, 1976.

———. *Houdini, Tarzan, and the Perfect Man: The White Male Body and the Challenge of Modernity in America*. New York: Hill and Wang, 2001.

Kaufmann, Eric, and Oliver Zimmer. "In Search of the Authentic Nation: Landscape and National Identity in Canada and Switzerland." *Nations and Nationalism* 4, no. 4 (1998): 483–510.

Keller, Ulrich. "Photojournalism around 1900: The Institutionalization of a Mass Medium." In *Shadow and Substance: Essays on the History of Photography in Honour of Heinz K. Henisch*, edited by Kathleen Collins, 283–96. Bloomfield Hills, MI: Amorphous Institute Press, 1990.

Kelly, Colleen. *Cabbagetown in Pictures*. Toronto: Toronto Public Library Board, 1984.

Kheraj, Sean. *Inventing Stanley Park: An Environmental History*. Vancouver: UBC Press, 2013.

Kimmel, Michael. *Manhood in America: A Cultural History*, 4th ed. New York: Oxford University Press, 2018.

Klaus, Susan. "All in the Family: The Olmsted Office and the Business of Landscape Architecture." *Landscape Journal* 16, no. 1 (1997): 80–95.

Klinenberg, Eric. *Heat Wave: A Social Autopsy of Disaster in Chicago*. 2nd edition. Chicago: University of Chicago Press, 2015.

Knowles, Norman. "Denison, George Taylor." *Dictionary of Canadian Biography, vol. 15*. University of Toronto/Université Laval, 2003–. http://www.biographi.ca/en/bio/denison_george_taylor_1839_1925_15E.html (accessed 17 November 2015).

Kossuth, Robert S. "Dangerous Waters: Victorian Decorum, Swimmer Safety, and the Establishment of Public Bathing Facilities in London (Canada)." *International Journal of the History of Sport* 22, no. 5 (2005): 796–815.

Latour, Bruno. *We Have Never Been Modern*. Translated by Catherine Porter. Cambridge, MA: Harvard University Press, 1993.

Lears, T.J. Jackson. *No Place of Grace: Antimodernism and the Transformation of American Culture, 1880–1920*. Chicago: University of Chicago Press, 1994.

Lekan, Thomas M. *Imagining the Nation in Nature: Landscape Preservation and German Identity, 1885–1945*. Cambridge, MA: Harvard University Press, 2004.

Lesy, Michael. *Dreamland: America at the Dawn of the Twentieth Century*. New York: The New Press, 1997.

Levine, Allan. *Toronto: Biography of a City*. Madeira Park, BC: Douglas and McIntyre, 2014.

Loewen, Royden, and Gerald Friesen. *Immigrants in Prairie Cities: Ethnic Diversity in Twentieth-Century Canada*. Toronto: University of Toronto Press, 2009.

Löfgren, Orvar. *On Holiday: A History of Vacationing*. Los Angeles: University of California Press, 1999.

Loo, Tina and Meg Stanley. "An Environmental History of Progress: Damming the Peace and Columbia Rivers." *The Canadian Historical Review*, Volume 92, Number 3, September (2011): 399-427.

Lovbrand, Eva, and Johannes Stripple. "Governmentality." In *Critical Environmental Politics*, edited by Carl Death, 111–20. New York: Routledge, 2014.

Love, Christopher. *A Social History of Swimming in England, 1800–1918*. New York: Routledge, 2008.

MacKintosh, Phillip Gordon. "The 'Occult Relation between Man and the Vegetable': Transcendentalism, Immigrants, and Park Planning in Toronto, c. 1900." In *Rethinking the Great White North: Race, Nature, and the Historical Geographies of Whiteness in Canada*, ed. Andrew Baldwin, Laura Cameron, and Audrey Kobayashi, 85–106. Vancouver: UBC Press, 2011.

Mackintosh, P.G., and R. Anderson. "The Toronto Star Fresh Air Fund: Transcendental Rescue in a Modern City, 1900–1915." *Geographical Review* 99 (2009): 539–62.

Makarova, Veronika. "Doukhobor 'Freedom Seeker' Nudism: Exploring the Sociocultural Roots." *Culture and Religion* 14, no. 2 (2013): 131–45.

Marien, Mary Warner. *Photography: A Cultural History*. New York: Harry N. Abrahams, 2002.

Marx, Leo. *The Machine in the Garden: Technology and the Pastoral Ideal in America*. New York: Oxford University Press, 2000.

Mawani, Renisa. "Imperial Legacies (Post) Colonial Identities: Law, Space and the Making of Stanley Park, 1859–2001." *Law Text Culture* 7 (2003): 97–141.

Maynard, Steven. "Through a Lavatory Wall: Homosexual Subcultures, Police Surveillance, and the Dialectics of Discovery, Toronto, 1890–1930." *Journal of the History of Sexuality* 5, no. 2 (1994): 207–42.

McCallum, Mary Jane Logan, and Adele Perry. *Structures of Indifference: An Indigenous Life and Death in a Canadian City*. Winnipeg: University of Manitoba Press, 2018.

McCarthy, Michael P. "Politics and the Parks: Chicago Businessmen and the Recreation Movement." *Journal of the Illinois State Historical Society (1908–1984)* 65, no. 2 (1972): 158–72.

McDermott, Lisa. "Exploring Intersections of Physicality and Female-only Canoeing Experiences." *Leisure Studies* 23, no. 3 (2004): 283–301.

McDonald, Robert. "'Holy Retreat' or 'Practical Breathing Spot'?: Class Perceptions of Vancouver's Stanley Park, 1910–1913." *Canadian Historical Review* 65, no. 2 (1984): 127–53.

McFarland, E. "The Development of Supervised Playgrounds." In *Recreational Land Use: Perspectives on Its Evolution in Canada*, edited by Geoffrey Wall and John Walsh, 272–98. Ottawa: Carlton University Press, 1982.

McIlwraith, Thomas. "Digging Out and Filling In: Making Land on the Toronto Waterfront in the 1850s." *Urban History Review/Revue d'histoire urbaine* 20, no.1 (1991): 15–33.

McKay, Ian. *The Quest of the Folk: Antimodernism and Cultural Selection in Twentieth-Century Nova Scotia*. Montreal: McGill-Queen's University Press, 1994.

McLaren, John. "The State, Child Snatching, and the Law: The Seizure and Indoctrination of Sons of Freedom Children in British Columbia, 1950–60." In *Regulating Lives: Historical Essays on the State, Society, the Individual, and the Law*, edited by Robert J. Menzies, John McLaren, and Dorothy E. Chunn, 259–93. Vancouver: UBC Press, 2002.

Meikle, Jeffrey L. "Leo Marx's *The Machine in the Garden*." *Technology and Culture* 44, no. 1 (2003): 147–59.

Mellen, Frances N. "The Development of the Toronto Waterfront during the Railway Expansion Era, 1850–1912." PhD diss., University of Toronto, 1974.

Melosi, Martin V. "Humans, Cities, and Nature: How Do Cities Fit in the Material World?" *Journal of Urban History* 36, no. 1 (2010): 3–21.

Merrens, R. "Port Authorities as Urban Land Developers: The Case of the Toronto Harbour Commissioners and Their Outer Harbour Project, 1912–68." *Urban History Review* 17, no. 2 (1988): 92–105.

Merrill, Frances, and Mason Merrill. *Nudism Comes to America*. Garden City, NY: Garden City Publishing, 1932.

Metcalfe, Alan. *Working-Class Physical Recreation in Montreal, 1860–1895*. Kingston, ON: Sports Studies Research Group, Queen's University, 1978.

Metusela, Christine, and Gordon Waitt. *Tourism and Australian Beach Cultures Revealing Bodies*. Toronto: Channel View Publications, 2012.

Mohsin, Tanzina. "Greater Toronto Area Urban Heat Island: Analysis of Temperatures and Extremes." PhD diss., University of Toronto, 2009.

Moir, Michael. "Planning for Change: Harbour Commission, Civil Engineers, and Large-scale Manipulation of Nature." In *Reshaping Toronto's Waterfront*, edited by Gene Desfor and Jennifer Laidley, 23–48. Toronto: University of Toronto Press, 2011.

Moore, Peter W. "Zoning and Planning: The Toronto Experience, 1904–1970." In *The Usable Urban Past: Planning and Politics in the Modern Canadian City*, edited by Alan F.J. Artibise and Gilbert A. Stelter, 316–41. Toronto: Macmillan of Canada, 1979.

Mossman, Marjorie. "Weston." In *The Villages of Etobicoke*. Edited by the Etobicoke Historical Board, 107–108. Weston, ON: Argyle Printing, 1986.

Myers, Tamara. *Caught: Montreal's Modern Girls and the Law, 1869–1945*. Toronto: University of Toronto Press, 2006.

Nasaw, David. *Going Out: The Rise and Fall of Public Amusements*. Cambridge, MA: Harvard University Press, 1999.

Newbery, Liz. "Paddling the Nation: Canadian Becoming and Becoming Canadian in and through the Canoe." *Topia: Canadian Journal of Cultural Studies* 29 (Spring 2013): 133–61.

Noel, Jan. *Canada Dry: Temperance Crusades before Confederation*. Toronto: University of Toronto Press, 1995.

Norcliffe, Glen, Keith Bassett, and Tony Hoare. "The Emergence of Postmodernism on the Urban Waterfront: Geographical Perspectives on Changing Relationships." *Journal of Transport Geography* 4, no. 2 (1996): 123–34.

North, Michael. *Camera Works: Photography and the Twentieth-Century World*. Oxford: Oxford University Press, 2005.

Norton, Peter D. *Fighting Traffic: The Dawn of the Motor Age in the American City*. Cambridge, MA: MIT Press, 2008.

Nus, W. Van. "The Fate of City Beautiful Thought in Canada, 1893–1930." *Historical Papers* 101 (1975): 191–210.

Nye, David E. *American Technological Sublime*. Cambridge, MA: MIT Press, 1994.

Obrador Pons, Pau. "A Haptic Geography of the Beach: Naked Bodies, Vision and Touch." *Social and Cultural Geography* 8, no. 1 (2007): 123–41.

Olsen, Kevin. "Clear Waters and a Green Gas: A History of Chlorine as a Swimming Pool Sanitizer in the United States." *Bulletin for the History of Chemistry* 32, no. 2 (2007): 129–40.

O'Mara, James. "Shaping Urban Waterfronts: The Role of Toronto's Harbour Commissioners, 1911–1960." *Discussion Paper No. 13*. Toronto: York University, Department of Geography, March 1976.

Opp, James. "Re-imaging the Moral Order of Urban Space: Religion and Photography in Winnipeg, 1900–1914." *Journal of the Canadian Historical Association* 13, no. 1 (2002): 73–93.

Ormsby, William. "Rees, William." *Dictionary of Canadian Biography, vol. 10*. University of Toronto/Université Laval, 2003–. http://www.biographi.ca/en/bio/rees_william_10E.html (accessed 24 March 2015).

Osborne, Peter, and Lynne Segal. "Extracts from Gender as Performance: An Interview with Judith Butler." London, 1993. http://www.theory.org.uk/but-int1.htm (accessed on September 9 2017).

Parr, Joy. "Notes for a More Sensuous History of Twentieth Century Canada: The Timely, the Tacit and the Material Body." *Canadian Historical Review* 82, no. 4 (2001): 720–45.

———. *Sensing Changes: Technologies, Environments, and the Everyday, 1953–2003*. Vancouver: UBC Press, 2010.

Paterson, Ross. "The Development of an Interwar Suburb: Kingsway Park, Etobicoke." *Urban History Review* 13, no. 3 (1985): 225–35.

Patterson, Graeme H. *History and Communications: Harold Innis, Marshall McLuhan, the Interpretation of History*. Toronto: University of Toronto Press, 1990.

Payne, Carol, and Andrea Kunard, eds. *The Cultural Work of Photography in Canada*. Montreal: McGill-Queen's University Press, 2011.

Peiss, Kathy. *Cheap Amusements: Working Women and Leisure in Turn-of-the-Century New York*. Philadelphia: Temple University Press, 1986.

Peterson, Jon A. "The City Beautiful Movement: Forgotten Origins and Lost Meanings." *Journal of Urban History* 2, no. 4 (1976): 415–34.

Pipkin, John S. "'Chasing Rainbows' in Albany: City Beautiful, City Practical, 1900–1925." *Journal of Planning History* 7, no. 4 (2008): 327–53.

Plummer, Kevin. "Historicist: A Monument to his Dreams." *The Torontoist*, 8 May 2010. http://torontoist.com/2010/05/historicist_a_monument_to_his_dreams/.

Pollock-Ellwand, Nancy. "Rickson Outhet: Bringing the Olmsted Legacy to Canada: A Romantic View of Nature in the Metropolis and the Hinterland." *Journal of Canadian Studies/Revue d'études canadiennes* 44, no. 1 (2010): 137–83.

Radforth, Ian. *Royal Spectacle: The 1860 Visit of the Prince of Wales to Canada and the United States*. Toronto: University of Toronto Press, 2004.

Raffan, James. *Bark, Skin and Cedar: Exploring the Canoe in Canadian Experience*. Toronto: HarperCollins, 1999.

———. "Being There: Bill Mason and the Canadian Canoeing Tradition." In *The Canoe in Canadian Cultures*, edited by John Jennings, Bruce W. Hodgins, and Doreen Small, 15–27. Toronto: Natural Heritage/Natural History, 1999.

Ramsay-Brown, Jason. *Toronto's Ravines and Urban Forests: Their Natural Heritage and Local History*. Toronto: James Lorimer, 2015.

Reeves, Wayne, and Christina Palassio, eds. *HTO: Toronto's Water from Lake Iroquois to Lost Rivers to Low-flow Toilets*. Toronto: Coach House Books, 2008.

Register, Woody. *The Kid of Coney Island: Fred Thompson and the Rise of American Amusements*. New York: Oxford University Press, 2001.

Renner, Andrea. "A Nation That Bathes Together: New York City's Progressive Era Public Baths." *Journal of the Society of Architectural Historians* 67, no. 4 (2008): 504–31.

Rodgers, Daniel T. "Worlds of Reform." *OAH Magazine of History* 20, no. 5 (2006): 49–54.

Rose, Nikolas, Pat O'Malley, and Mariana Valverde. "Governmentality." *Annual Review of Law and Social Science* 2 (2006): 83–104.

Ross, Chad. *Naked Germany: Health, Race and the Nation*. Oxford, UK: Berg Publishers, 2005.

Rust-D'Eye, George H. *Cabbagetown Remembered*. Erin, ON: Boston Mills Press, 1984.

Rutherford, Paul. "Tomorrow's Metropolis: The Urban Reform Movement in Canada, 1880–1920." In *The Canadian City: Essays in Urban History*, edited by Gilbert A. Stelter and Alan F.J. Artibise, 368–92. Toronto: McClelland and Stewart , 1977.

———. *Victorian Authority: The Daily Press in Late Nineteenth-Century Canada*. Toronto: University of Toronto Press, 1982.

Rutt, Richard. "The Englishman's Swimwear." *Costume* 24, no. 1 (1990): 69–84.

Rydell, Robert W. *All the World's a Fair: Visions of Empire at American International Expositions, 1876–1916*. Chicago: University of Chicago Press, 1987.

Sanderson, Christopher, and Pierre Filion. "From Harbour Commission to Port Authority: Institutionalizing the Federal Government's Role in Waterfront Development." In *Reshaping Toronto's Waterfront*, ed. Gene Desfor and Jennefer Laidley, 224–44. Toronto: University of Toronto Press, 2011.

Sandwell, Ruth. "Missing Canadians: Reclaiming the A-Liberal Past." In *Liberalism and Hegemony: Debating the Canadian Liberal Revolution*, edited by Jean-François Constant and Michel Ducharme, 246–73. Toronto: University of Toronto Press, 2009.

Sauriol, Charles. *Remembering the Don: A Rare Record of Earlier Times within the Don River Valley*. Scarborough, ON: Consolidated Amethyst Communications, 1981.

———. *Trails of the Don*. Orillia, ON: Hemlock Press, 1992.

Saville, Julia F. "Nude Male Alfresco Swimmers: The Prehistory of a Nineteenth-century Republican Trope." *Word and Image: A Journal of Verbal/Visual Enquiry* 25, no. 1 (2009): 56–74.

———. "The Romance of Boys Bathing: Poetic Precedents and Respondents to the Paintings of Henry Scott Tuke." In *Victorian Sexual Dissidence*, edited by Richard Dellamora, 253–78. Chicago: University of Chicago Press, 1999..

Schafer, Murray. "Soundscapes and Earwitnesses." In *Hearing History: A Reader*, edited by Mark M. Smith, 3–9. Athens: University of Georgia Press, 2004.

Schivelbusch, Wolfgang. *Disenchanted Night: The Industrialization of Light in the Nineteenth Century*, translated by Angela Davies. Berkeley: University of California Press, 1988.

Schmitt, Peter J. *Back to Nature: The Arcadian Myth in Urban America*. New York: Oxford University Press, 1969, XV.

Schuyler, David. *The New Urban Landscape: The Redefinition of City Form in Nineteenth-Century America*. Baltimore: Johns Hopkins University Press, 1986.

Scobey, David. "Anatomy of the Promenade: The Politics of Bourgeois Sociability in Nineteenth-Century New York." *Social History* 17, no. 2 (1992): 203–27.

Scott, James C. *Seeing Like a State: How Certain Schemes to Improve the Human Condition Have Failed*. New Haven, CT: Yale University Press, 1999.

Seal, Graham. *Inventing Anzac: The Digger and National Mythology*. Perth: University of Queensland Press, 2004.

Shantz, Mary-Ann Melissa, "The Nature of the Body: A Cultural History of Nudism in Postwar Canada." PhD diss., Carleton University, 2012.

Shaw, Frank R. "Trends in Bathing Beach and Swimming Pool Sanitation." *Canadian Public Health Journal* 23, no. 4 (1932): 153–58.

Shields, Rob. *Places on the Margin: Alternative Geographies of Modernity*. New York: Routledge, 1991.

Simon, Bryant. *Boardwalk of Dreams: Atlantic City and the Fate of Urban America*. New York: Oxford University Press, 2004.

Sinclair, Gordon. *Will the Real Gordon Sinclair Please Stand Up*. Toronto: McClelland and Stewart, 1966.

Stevenson, Jane. "Nacktleben." In *Changing Bodies, Changing Meanings: Studies on the Human Body in Antiquity*, edited by Dominic Montserrat, 198–212. New York: Routledge, 2003.

Stilgoe, John R. *Borderland: Origins of the American Suburb, 1820–1939*. New Haven: Yale University Press, 1988.

Strange, Carolyn. *Toronto's Girl Problem: The Perils and Pleasures of the City, 1880–1930*. Toronto: University of Toronto Press, 1995.

Strange, Carolyn, and Tina Loo. *Making Good: Law and Moral Regulation in Canada, 1867–1939*. Toronto: University of Toronto Press, 1997.

Sturken, Marita, and Lisa Cartwright. *Practices of Looking: An Introduction to Visual Culture*. Oxford: Oxford University Press, 2009.

Sutton, S.B., ed. *Civilizing American Cities: A Selection of Frederick Law Olmsted's Writings on City Landscapes*. Cambridge, MA: Massachusetts Institute of Technology, 1971.

Talen, Emily. *New Urbanism and American Planning: The Conflict of Cultures*. New York and London: Routledge Taylor and Francis Group, 2005.

Tarantino, Bob. *Under Arrest: Canadian Laws You Won't Believe*. Toronto: Dundurn, 2007.

Terbenche, Danielle. "'A Soldier in the Service of His Country': Dr. William Rees, Professional Identity, and the Toronto Temporary Asylum, 1819–1874." *Histoire sociale/Social History* 43, no. 85 (2010): 97–129.

Thorpe, Jocelyn. *Temagami Tangled Wild: Race, Gender, and the Making of Canadian Nature*. Vancouver: UBC Press, 2012.

Travis, John. "Continuity and Change in English Sea-Bathing, 1730–1900: A Case of Swimming with the Tide." In *Recreation and the Sea*, edited by Stephen Fisher, 8–35. Exeter: University of Exeter Press, 1997.

———. *The Rise of the Devonshire Seaside Resorts, 1750–1900*. Exeter: University of Exeter Press, 1993.

Turner, Victor. *The Ritual Process: Structure and Anti-Structure*. New Brunswick, NJ: Aldine Transaction, 2008.

Valentine, Gill. "The Geography of Women's Fear." *Area* 21, no. 4 (1989): 385–90.

Valverde, Mariana. *The Age of Light, Soap, and Water: Moral Reform in English Canada, 1885–1925*. Toronto: University of Toronto Press, 2008.

Valverde, Mariana, and Lorna Weir. "The Struggles of the Immoral: Preliminary Remarks on Moral Regulation." *In Moral Regulation and Governance in Canada: History, Context and Critical Issues*, edited by Amanda Glasbeek, 75–84. Toronto: Canadian Scholars Press, 2006.

Valverde, Mariana, and Miomir Cirak. "Governing Bodies, Creating Gayspaces: Policing and Security Issues in 'Gay' Downtown Toronto." *British Journal of Criminology* 43 (2003): 102–21.

Walden, Keith. *Becoming Modern in Toronto: The Industrial Exhibition and the Shaping of a Late Victorian Culture*. Toronto: University of Toronto Press, 1997.

Walton, John K. "Respectability Takes a Holiday: Disreputable Behaviour at the Victorian Seaside." In *Unrespectable Recreations*, edited by Martin Hewitt, 176–93. Leeds: Leeds Centre for Victorian Studies, 2001.

Walvin, James. *Leisure and Society, 1830–1950*. London: Longman Group, 1978.

Ward, Peter. *Courtship, Love and Marriage in Nineteenth-Century English Canada*. Montreal: McGill-Queen's University Press, 1990.

Weaver, John C. "The Modern City Realized: Toronto Civic Affairs, 1880–1915." In *The Usable Urban Past: Planning and Politics in the Modern Canadian City*, edited by Alan F.J. Artibise and Gilbert A. Stelter, 39–72. Toronto: Macmillan of Canada, 1979.

———. "'Tomorrow's Metropolis' Revisited: A Critical Assessment of Urban Reform in Canada, 1890–1920." In *The Canadian City: Essays in Urban History*, edited by Gilbert A. Stelter and Alan F.J. Artibise, 393–418. Toronto: McClelland and Stewart, 1977.

Weedon, Chris. *Feminist Practice and Poststructuralist Theory*. Oxford: Basil Blackwell, 1987.

Weeks, Jeffrey. *Sex, Politics and Society: The Regulation of Sexuality since 1800*. London: Longmans, 1981.

Wencer, David. "Historicist: Swimming at the Minnies." *Torontoist*, 24 May 2014. torontoist.com/2014/05/historicist-swimming-at-the-minnies/ (accessed on 13 December 2017).

Weston Historical Society. *A Pictorial History of Weston*. Toronto: University of Toronto Press, 1981.

White, Cameron. "Picnicking, Surf-Bathing and Middle-Class Morality on the Beach in the Eastern Suburbs of Sydney, 1811–1912." *Journal of Australian Studies* 27, no. 80 (2003): 101–110.

White, Richard. "American Environmental History: The Development of a New Historical Field." *Pacific Historical Review* 54, no. 3 (1985): 297–335.

———. *The Middle Ground: Indians, Empires and Republics in the Great Lakes Region, 1650–1815*. New York: Cambridge University Press, 1991.

———. *The Organic Machine: The Remaking of the Columbia River*. New York: Hill and Wang, 1995.

Whitzman, Carolyn. *Suburb, Slum, Urban Village: Transformations in Toronto's Parkdale Neighbourhood, 1875–2002*. Vancouver: UBC Press, 2009.

Wickson, Tom. *Reflections of Toronto Harbour: 200 Years of Port Activity and Waterfront Development*. Toronto: Toronto Port Authority, 2002.

Wigley, John. *The Rise and Fall of the Victorian Sunday*. Manchester: Manchester University Press, 1980.

Wilson, William H. *The City Beautiful Movement*. Johns Hopkins University Press: Baltimore, 1989.

Wilkie, Jacqueline S. "Submerged Sensuality: Technology and Perceptions of Bathing." *Journal of Social History* 19, no. 4 (1986): 649–64.

Woycke, James. *Au Naturel: The History of Nudism in Canada*. Etobicoke, ON: Federation of Canadian Naturists, 2003.

Yerbury, J.C. "The 'Sons of Freedom' Doukhobors and the Canadian State Canadian." *Ethnic Studies/Études Ethniques au Canada* 16, no. 2 (1984): 47–70.

Young, Iris Marion. "Throwing Like a Girl: A Phenomenology of Feminine Body Comportment, Motility, and Spatiality." In *On Female Body Experience: "Throwing Like a Girl" and Other Essays*, 27–45. Oxford: Oxford University Press, 2005.

"Fisherman's Island." Beaches Living Guide, Spring/Summer 2015 http://www.beachesliving.ca/pages/index.php?act=landmark&id=172 (accessed on 5 November 2017).

ILLUSTRATION CREDITS

0.1. Map of Toronto, 1908. Plan of improvements to the City of Toronto, Toronto Guild of Civic Art, Map, 1908, Toronto Public Library (TPL)/Toronto Research Library (TRL), Baldwin Collection, T 1908/5 small.

1.1. Toronto Waterfront, Peter Street, 1844. John Gillespie and Hugh Scobie, TPL (TRL), Baldwin Collection, 974-20. 1.2. Rees's Pier, 1850. Henry William Vavasour, TPL (TRL), Baldwin Collection, 1850/5 small. 1.3. General plan for railway terminals, 1853. Hugh Scobie, TPL (TRL), Baldwin Collection, T[1853]/4Msm. 1.4. Bird's-eye view of Toronto, 1876. Designed, sketched, lithographed, and published by P.A. Gross, Toronto, Ont., Library and Archives Canada (LAC), NMC17628. 1.5. Bird's-eye view of Toronto, 1893. TPL (TRL), Baldwin Collection, 916-2-1 to 3 Cab III. 1.6. Stone distillery, 1863. *Canadian Illustrated News*, vol. 1, no. 24, 25 April 1863. Hamilton: W.A. Ferguson, 1863. Page 282. Canadiana.ca. 1.7. Gooderham and Worts Ltd., 1896. TPL (TRL), Baldwin Collection, 981-25 Cab III. 1.8. Toronto harbour postcard, 1901. City of Toronto Archives (CTA), Various postcards Series, File O340005, Fonds 70, Series 330, file 34, Sheet 2R, folder 13, Box 158719.

2.1. The Credit Valley Wharf, Toronto waterfront, 1889. University of Toronto, Toronto Insurance Maps, 1889. 2.2. The Credit Valley Wharf, Toronto waterfront, 1901. CTA, William James Family Fonds 1244, 1423. 2.3. Nairn's Wharf, 1880. CTA, Charles E. Goad, *Atlas of the City of Toronto and Vicinity* (Toronto: Chas. E. Goad, 1880), Plate 7. 2.4. Plan of the City of Toronto, sewage plan updates to 1875. *Plan of the City of Toronto* (Toronto: Maclear and Co., 1858), TPL (TRL), Baldwin Collection, Ms1921.9. 2.5. Map of Queen's Wharf Swimming Basin. CTA, Charles E. Goad, *Atlas of the City of Toronto and Vicinity* (Toronto: Chas. E. Goad, 1889), Plate 66. 2.6. View from the Northern Railway Elevator looking west, 1895. Robertson, *Landmarks of Toronto* (Toronto: J. Ross Robertson, 1896), 682. 2.7. View from Northern Railway Elevator, looking east,

1870. TPL (TRL), Baldwin Collection, B 12-20b. 2.8. Toronto, c. 1876, looking northeast from Northern Railway Elevator photograph after a drawing by G. Gascard. TPL (TRL), Baldwin Collection, E 8-170.

3.1. Plan of York harbour, 1815. Joseph Bouchette, TPL (TRL), Baldwin Collection, T1815/fold. 3.2. Toronto Island in the early nineteenth century, c. 1816. By William Armstrong, 1817, after a painting by Robert Irvine. TPL (TRL), JRR 728 Cab III. 3.3. Plan of Toronto Island based on Charles Unwin survey, TPL, Charles E. Goad, Atlas of the City of Toronto and Suburbs (Toronto: Chas E. Goad, 1884), Plate 30. 3.4. Toronto Island, 1890. CTA, Charles E. Goad, *Goad's Atlas of the City of Toronto: Fire Insurance Map* (Toronto: Chas. E. Goad, 1890), Plate 30. 3.5. The Wiman Baths, 1954. Victor Salman James, TPL (TRL), Baldwin Collection, S 1-2041A. 3.6. Wiman Baths location, 1890. CTA, Charles E. Goad, *Atlas of the City of Toronto and Vicinity: Second Edition* (Toronto: Chas. E. Goad, 1890), Plate 30. 3.7. Turner's Baths, Hanlan's Point west, c. 1909; 3.8. Fence along Long Pond, 1907; 3.9. Long Pond Bridge, 1907; and 3.10. Hanlan's Point on a Sunday, 1911. CTA, William James Family Fonds 1244, Items 6001, 229, 190A, and 6012.

4.1. The middle Don and 4.2. The Don River and land ownership in the valley, 1878. *Illustrated Historical Atlas of the County of York and the Township of West Gwillimbury & Town of Bradford in the county of Simcoe, Ont.* (Toronto: Miles and Co., 1878). McGill University, Rare Books Division, elf G1148 Y6M5 1878. 4.3. Castle Frank, 1796. Picture after a drawing by Elizabeth Simcoe, 1880, TPL (TRL), Baldwin Collection, X 18-33. 4.4. River Don Straightening Plan, 1886. CTA, Fonds 200, series 725, file 12. 4.5. "Dunnett's Swimming Hole," West Don River, c. 1900. William Wallace Judd, TPL (TRL), Baldwin Collection, 978-13-11 small. 4.6. Winchester Street Bridge over Don River, as reconstructed, 1909. Photo taken in connection with Bloor Street Viaduct construction. CTA, Fonds 200, series 372, subseries 41, 544. 4.7. Boys swimming in the Don River at "Bare Ass Beach" in Riverdale, 1923. James & Son Picture, 1923. *Toronto Star* Photograph Archive, TPL. 4.8. Don Valley, scene at paper mill dam, 9 July 1915. CTA, Alan Howard Fonds 1548, John Boyd Sr. photographs Series 393, 13427. 4.9. "Old swimmin' hole," between 1920 and 1934. CTA, M.O. Hammond Fonds 298, File 22, Folio 22. 4.10. "Police officer and (naked) boys on road," pre-1940. CTA, Alan Howard Fonds 1548, John Boyd Sr. photographs Series 393, 0024. 4.11. Cycling beside the Don River, between Don Mills Road and Leaside, c. 1912. CTA, William James family Fonds 1244, 8156. 4.12. Skinny-dipping in the Don River, c. 1909. CTA, William James family Fonds 1244, 1797. 4.13. "Little of everything," *Toronto Daily Star*, 8 July 1909.

5.1. Humber River, Weston, 1871. William Arthur Johnson, TPL (TRL), Baldwin Collection, 969-1-13. 5.2. The aquatic promenade, Humber River, [1908?] and 5.3. Boat livery and restaurant, Humber River, 1910. CTA, William James family

Fonds 1244, Items 183A and 2523. 5.4. Views of a sedate Humber River, 1900–43. CTA, Fonds 70, Series 330, File 49, File 490008, Folder 28, Sheet 2V, Box 158719. 5.5. William Gamble Mill, Humber River, 1905. Attributed to George Edward Alexander Robinson, TPL (TRL), Baldwin Collection, 987-4-41. 5.6. "Humber River Project Means Civic Beauty," 1911. *Toronto Daily Star*, 19 May 1911, page 18. 5.7. The Humber Valley Surveys, c. 1910–1940. CTA, Fonds 200, Series 724, File 1, Subdivision plans, Box 200760, Folio 1. 5.8. Humber Boulevard, October 1913. CTA, Fonds 200, Series 372, Subseries 53, 83. 5.9. Humber Boulevard Tea Garden Rooms, 6 October 1917. CTA, Alan Howard Fonds 1548, John Boyd Sr. photographs Series 393, 14545. 5.10. Bathers and cars in Humber River, 1922 and 5.11. Bathers at Humber River dam near the Old Mill, c. 1912. CTA, William James family Fonds 1244, Items 1237 and 9159.

6.1. The Sunnyside Bathing Pavilion in 2021. Photo courtesy of Ryan Masters. 6.2. "Bathers at Sunnyside Beach," 1911 and 6.3. "Bathers at Sunnyside Beach," [1909?] CTA, William James family Fonds 1244, Item 194. 6.4. "Bathers at Sunnyside Beach," [1909?] CTA, William James family Fonds 1244, Item 194A. 6.5. "Bathers at Sunnyside," c. 1910–12. CTA, William James family Fonds 1244, 220A. 6.6. Kew Beach bathing pavilion, 17 July 1915. CTA, James Salmon Collection Fonds 1231, 0539. 6.7. "The Robert Simpson Company Limited," *The Globe*, Wednesday, 17 July 1907, page 3. 6.8. "The Robert Simpson Company Limited: A Summer Sale at Simpson's," *The Globe*, Saturday, 4 June 1910, page 3. 6.9. The Toronto Harbour Commission Waterfront Plan, 1912. Toronto Harbour Commissioners: Engineering Department, University of Toronto Map and Data Library, G3524.T621 G45 9 1912. 6.10. Sunnyside, 1926. TRL (TPL), Baldwin Collection, 942-1-65. 6.11. Making land for the boulevard, c. 1920. CTA, William James family Fonds 1244, 1117. 6.12. Lookout Tower, 1920. Ports Toronto Archives (PTA), Life Saving and Police Patrol Second Annual Report, 1920, page 21, 1840-L-1-1, RG 7/1 Box 1. 6.13. Sunnyside Bathing Pavilion crowded with bathers, 1924. CTA, William James family Fonds 1244, 219A. 6.14. Sunnyside, children's bathing beach, 1925. CTA, Globe and Mail Fonds 1266, 5486. 6.15. Sunnyside Bathing Tank, 1925. Toronto parks, Sunnyside, Airmaps Limited, 1925, TPL, X 64-316. 6.16. The free bathing station at Sunnyside, 14 July 1924. "Bathing cars, at Sunnyside," Alfred Pearson. CTA, Toronto Transit Commission Fonds 16, Series 71, 3272G. 6.17. "Sunnyside, crowd in amusement area, looking west," 1 July 1924. CTA, Globe and Mail Fonds 1266, 3062.

INDEX

C

D

N

O

P

T